GUERNSEY'S COAST

The definitive celebration of our island's coastline
as chronicled in the major Guernsey Press series

GUERNSEY'S COAST

The definitive celebration of our island's coastline
as chronicled in the major Guernsey Press series

ROB BATISTE

Published by Guernsey Books

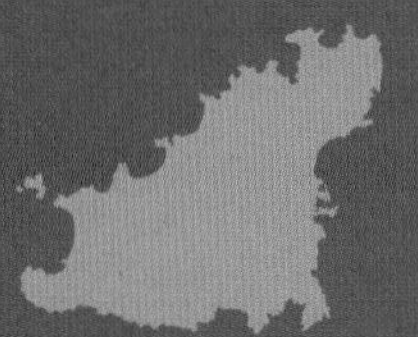

CONTENTS

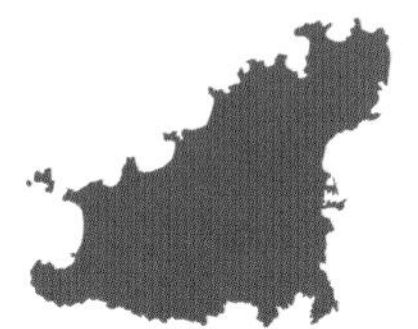

PUBLISHER'S FOREWORD

IT WAS more than three years ago but I remember it like it was yesterday because Rob Batiste was quite simply buzzing and his enthusiasm was infectious. The Guernsey Press sports editor was eager to write about something else other than just sport and had offered to put pen to paper for a new feature in the newspaper about the island's coastline.

Rob had taken his tape recorder to Cobo and met up with Herbie Nichols (my mum's next door neighbour coincidentally) and the 'Coboite' had provided Rob with one of the most enjoyable afternoons at work he could remember as they strolled around the bay.

Perhaps Rob won't forgive me for putting this down in print but I remember him saying, "Darren, this is brilliant, Herbie's story is amazing", before asking me if I wanted to listen to the tape.

I didn't listen to the tape, I waited for the feature to appear in print and I was captivated.

Perhaps even Rob could not have imagined what would follow. Yes, Cobo had Herbie but Rob soon realised that every bay had 'Herbies' of their own and set about meeting as many of them as he could. Rob wanted to hear their story too and share it with islanders.

As a reader of the Guernsey Press I looked forward to seeing the Coast features appear as they regularly did over the next four years.

More than three years later it was my turn. I could not stop buzzing when Rob asked me if I would like to help him publish Coast as a book.

I hope and trust that Rob is pleased with the result. It is certainly going to take pride of place on my bookshelf when I am not thumbing through the pages.

Darren Duquemin
Publisher

AUTHOR'S FOREWORD

MOST of us islanders are guilty of taking our beautiful island for granted.

I did for 49 of my first 53 years.

Not anymore I don't and these past four years have been one glorious learning curve as to what, exactly, Guernsey is all about – the history, the people that made it great, made it affluent, made their money, livelihoods and reputations.

Our coast is something truly special and the joy of it is that it forever changes with the seasons, the tides, light and day and the work of nature.

I consider myself very lucky to be a Guernseyman. Sure we have too much traffic, we might not appreciate some modern developments, but it always remains Guernsey and the late 19th century photographic work of Guerin and Singleton may show a very different island to what we know and love. It highlights that things have not changed so much to diminish the beauty of this 25 square miles and, as far as this book is concerned, near to 40 miles of coastline.

My story of Guernsey's coast starts and finishes where I started and would hope to finish – Cobo. It's more than a stunning sunset, it is a beach that would not be out of place anywhere in the world.

I first saw it as a circa 1960 toddler from a sandy viewpoint underneath a blue granite seawall that was less than 200 yards from my bedroom in, then a quiet, Le Feugre.

From the cottage bedroom I shared with my brother Andy I could not see the sea, but you could invariably smell it.

When I was ill I would be wheeled by mum down through the tiny La Ruette or Pierre Samson lane that joins Bouverie Road and the coastal junction that leads onto the coast road under the pine covered hillock that is Le Guet, then south towards Albecq where Dr Heard's surgery housed surely the waiting room with the best view in the world.

Cobo – the bay – has changed little in half-a-century.

Sand levels alter from time to time, the old wooden groynes have long gone as have the wooden sea breaks at the foot of the southern slipway under Le Guet. But the pink granite rocks never change and if you ever need reminding as to where you are, the Rockmount pub is forever there to remind you.

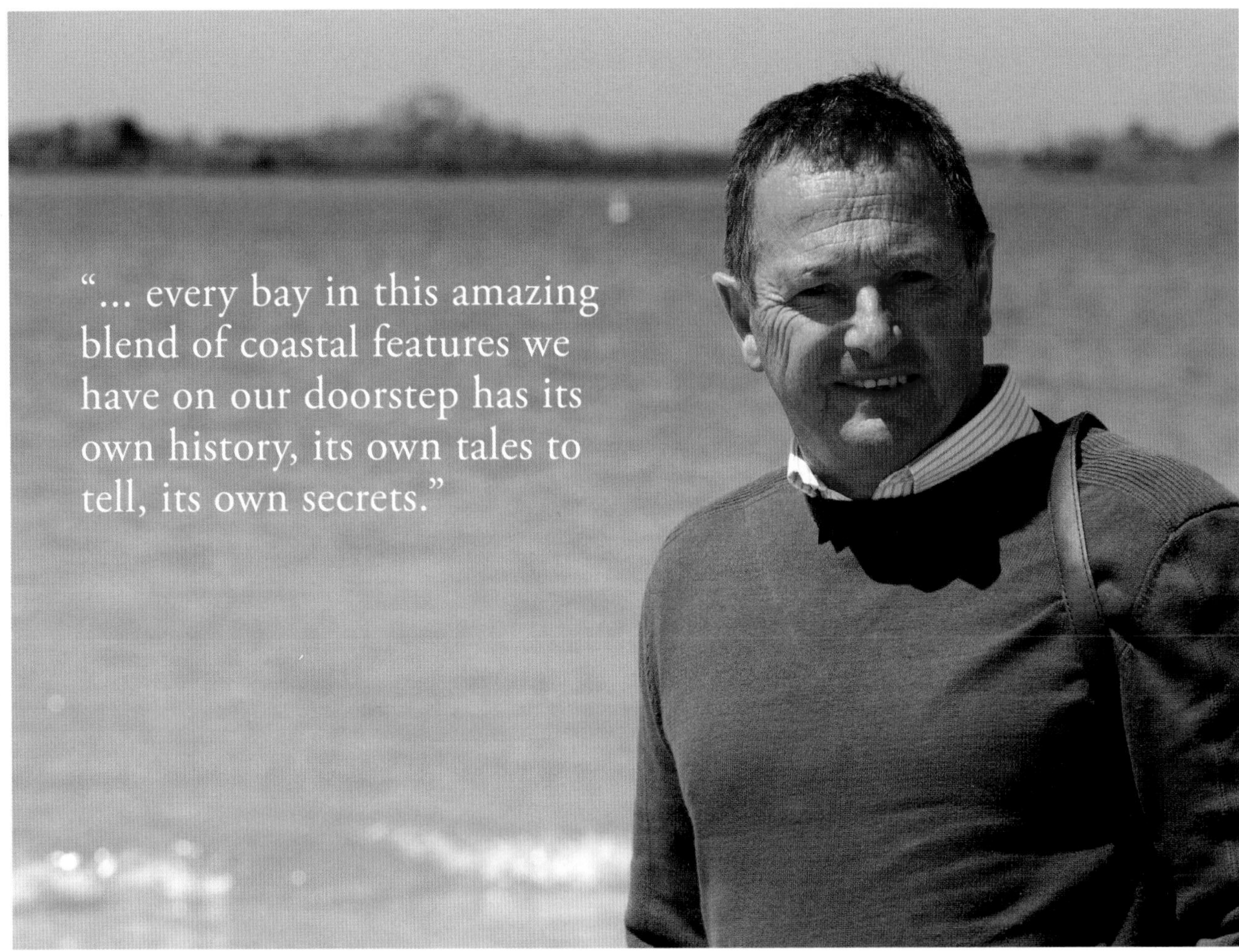
"... every bay in this amazing blend of coastal features we have on our doorstep has its own history, its own tales to tell, its own secrets."

It is beautiful even when the gales throw up the mountainous seas that crash over the wall, threatening destruction, delivering the saltiest of roars as water smashes into granite.

Cobo has more than most bays. It has the stunning views which alter with virtually every moment of every day as the wind, clouds, tides and seasonal light plays its unending game. Cobo has a village, a church, a mission hall, a post office, supermarket, hotel, wonderfully successful cricket team and a pub any ambitious publican would give their right arm for.

This is where my coast story starts and finishes, but every bay in this amazing blend of coastal features we have on our doorstep has its own history, its own tales to tell, its own secrets.

In the 31 chapters squeezed either side of the start-finish point I hope to give every person who loves this island and is proud of it as I am, a warm feeling of local pride and possession as they soak up not just the startling views and scenes provided by the brilliant Andrew Le Poidevin and the team of Guernsey Press photographers past and present, while at the same time introducing them to a wealth of people that know it best and make our coastline a treasure trove of information.

Guernsey's coastal story does not end here, but this very largely tells the story so far.

Rob Batiste
Author

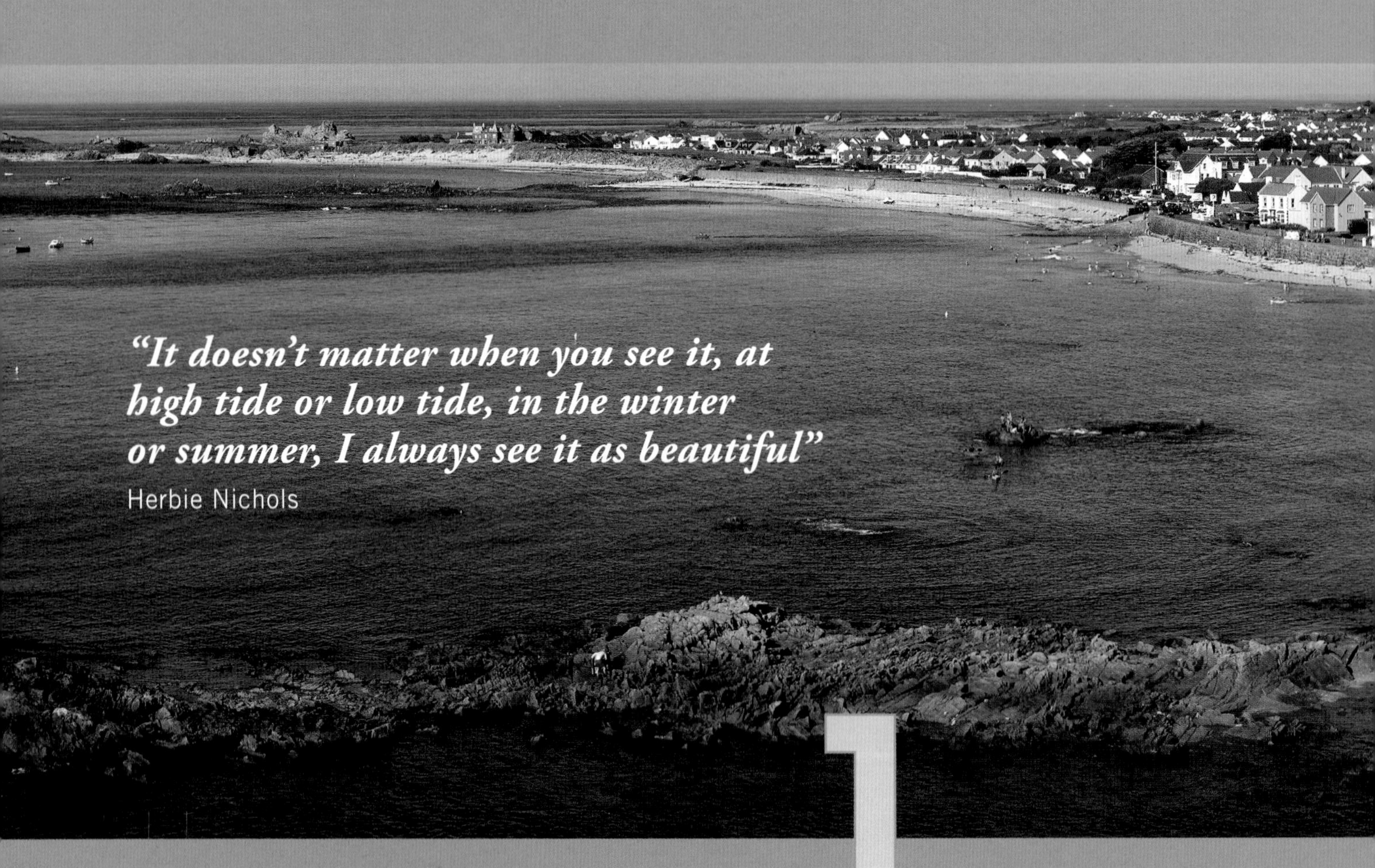

"It doesn't matter when you see it, at high tide or low tide, in the winter or summer, I always see it as beautiful"

Herbie Nichols

CHAPTER 1

COBO

Both wild and stunningly beautiful, Cobo Bay offers so many visual variations that every day of every year is different down this way. Locally, there is no more popular place to visit and it is where our COAST story starts.

MAN OF THE SEA

HERBERT NICHOLS looks down at Cobo from our viewpoint at Le Guet watchtower and is unequivocal in his opinion.

'It doesn't matter when you see it, at high or low tide, winter or summer, I always see it as beautiful.'

He's right, too.

In high summer it can provide the king of all sunsets. In winter: vicious, dark, foreboding waves that crash over the sea wall. It's always different.

Herbie, 78, knows Cobo, its beautiful bay, rocks and seas, better than anyone.

For virtually his entire life he has lived within a stone's throw of the beach, the last half-century and more halfway along Bouverie Road where he and wife Pat built their little home – Manilla Cottage.

For 40 years he fished out of the bay and ashore he has seen generations of villagers come and go.

There are not many of his old friends left.

Little that happens in or affects Cobo escapes this genial character.

The first question I put to him is simple enough: Where does Cobo start and where does it finish?

His view may not be the official one, if there is such a thing, but is not met with disapproval when we meet up with an even older 'Coboite' at the conclusion of our meeting, 94-year-old Will Le Tocq.

'It starts,' says Herbie, 'at Albecq Bay and finishes at the Saline,' pointing down across the bay to the small kink in the road that separates Cobo and Grandes Rocques.

'It certainly goes back to the Ozanne tower [up through the lanes halfway to Saumarez Park] and as far as the bridge [approaching Les Genats, not at St Sampson's].

Opposite
Herbert Nichols on the Cobo slipway
Below
Cobo takes another battering from the sea

A STORMY NIGHT

HIS memories of Cobo life and its activities are endlessly fascinating to someone himself born just 150 yards from the Cobo sea wall, the very one that crashed into the bay on one distinctly rough April night in 1962.

The incident is as good a place to start with Herbie.

The Guernsey Evening Press and Star's headline of Friday 6 April was straight to the point: 'Gale wrecks Cobo Road.'

A 100ft gap was torn out of the sea wall as winds reached 66mph, wrote the unnamed correspondent.

There was talk of 40ft waves, but what was not open to conjecture was the sea water in residents' downstairs rooms.

'It could have been much worse,' said Herbie. 'They were very lucky that it happened when the tide was cutting. It was the day after the highest tide.

'We always maintained that it was like an explosion.

'In fact, Laurie Duquemin from the Post Office reckoned it was a mine that had been washed up and hit the wall which caused it.

'The houses round there shook with the explosion.'

The official line and, probably the correct one, was altogether different.

'They [the authorities] maintain it was due to the hydraulic action of two waves, one a big curler which hit the wall and the trapped air which was hit by a second one.'

Every islander will have seen either at firsthand or pictures of huge seas crashing over the beach wall and into the grounds of the Rockmount, Cobo and former Les Pieux hotels.

But Herbie reckons that Cobo has never felt the full force of the elements.

'We've always been lucky that the [strongest] wind has never clicked with the [very highest] tide. If that ever did happen, it could cause a lot of damage.'

Half-a-century ago the wall would have been protected by a series of wooden 'breaks' or groynes.

The last of them disappeared in the early 1960s and most of them had gone when the beach suffered the first major wall slip in 1962.

Indeed, the day after the slip an article appeared in the GEP that posed the question: 'Was it down to the virtual absence of the wooden breakwaters which once withstood the full force of the sea?'

A full set of groynes was never to reappear in the bay, the final ones being removed from near the foot of the slipway under the Guet around that time.

All pictures and overleaf
The 1962 storm wreaked havoc on the Cobo seafront

ROCKMOUNT
HOTEL

CATCH OF THE BAY

FOR nearly 40 years Herbie Nichols fished out of the Long Port Bay.

These days only Steve Fallaize does so full-time and as he nears his 80th birthday, 'Mr Cobo' can only look back with fond memories of his days catching shellfish for a living.

'When I was fishing, there were between four and six of us full-time.

'We used to fish up to seven miles out and the boats were not equipped like they are today.

'We first used to go out with one which had a petrol engine. It was not very powerful.'

There was no shortage of fish, though. Catches were invariably very good and Cobo was, he says, particularly yielding of mackerel, pollack and bass.

'The line fishing was good and the long-lining was good with mainly skate. That was in early spring and the fall.

'But there's not the skate like there used to be.

'There was an abundance of crayfish and when I started, the worry was selling enough fish for your wages. We just couldn't get rid of all of it. We used to ship smallish quantities to Jersey on the mailboat.'

For many years, he ran a weekend stall in the Fish Market.

'Money-wise we didn't do that well but we had the best years for quantity of fish.'

After leaving school in January 1944 and initially working for The Star newspaper, where his first wage was 10 Reichsmarks (£1), he stayed in printing until the 1950s by which time he was back living at Cobo, had bought a little boat and 'started messing about on the beach'.

Before too long he was fishing out of Cobo in the summer months, St Peter Port in the winter. Eventually he took up the stall in the market.

'On Fridays and Saturdays the market was heaving.'

Today, the shellfish are not to be found at Cobo in anywhere near the same quantity of half-a-century ago.

'There's still quite a bit of lobster but hardly any big spider crabs or chancres.'

Left
Bringing the fruits of the sea to the table. Herbie and Pat Nichols in their fishmongers shop with Betty Morshead

FLYING THE FLAG

IN SHORT, it is the big rock with the flag on.

And Herbie Nichols has climbed [more often than most] upon the outcrop of red Guernsey granite that stands proud and beautiful under the richest of west-coast sunsets.

He reveals it is a mile from flag to shore and, to my amazement, there was a time not so long ago that on the very lowest of spring tides you could walk to it without getting your best shoes wet.

Yes – walk to the rock, as long as you knew the way, says Herbie.

'There is a little peak [of rock] that when it comes out of the water, you know you can walk across. The braye was dry.'

Herbie has visited the rock at least 50 times.

'I would think it's that many, mainly to change the flag.

'It's a fantastic view. You can see Lihou and right around [to the west].'

For those who have never been there or slept on it as Andy Le Tissier and Mark Trenchard did for charity in November 2001, it stands high out of the often raging seas.

'It is probably about 50ft high and there's a sheer drop of about 40ft on the north side.'

But the former fisherman's days of climbing the rock are, by his admission, up.

'I climbed up last year but I don't think I'll be going up any more. I'll go with them but probably stay in the boat.'

Meanwhile, Andy and Matt do not rule out a Grosse Rocque Challenge Two.

By camping for 50 hours on the uncomfortable and draughty rock, they raised a little over £5,000 for the Help a Guernsey Child charity.

Opposite
Herbie Nichols and Bernie Martel ready the flag to be raised on Grosse Rocque
Below
Sunset heaven

VIEW FROM LE GUET

COBO village has changed beyond recognition in the past 50 years but is still unmistakably Cobo to Herbie.

Born in Farnborough where his soldier father and Guernsey mother were living in married quarters, he came to the island in 1932 aged two.

His first home was in the row of small cottages at Cobo which nowadays face the entrance to CheckersXpress.

For the last half-century and more, he and his wife have lived in Bouverie Road, no more than 200 metres from the sea.

Off the reception area at the Cobo Bay Hotel is a print of the Guet end of Cobo with not a tree in sight on the hill overlooking the bay and the coastal road runs next to the sea wall, which has not been the case since the Occupation.

Herbie remembers the scene looking down from the Le Guet. 'When we were kids there was a lovely grassy slope down from the magazine and people used to just spend their days there looking at people go by. They'd come from Town to do so.'

On the grassy common that separates the beach and the road, corrugated-iron holiday huts pandered to the summer living of the well-to-do from St Peter Port businesses.

There was also a granite cottage where

today drivers will slip in to gaze over the bay scene in front of them.

Then came the Germans.

They built a railway that ran on the Guet side of the coast road.

'The railway ran from Town to L'Eree transporting rock and cement to build the bunkers.'

At Cobo the railway cut through what is now playing fields at La Mare de Carteret and ran along Bouverie Road before joining up with the coast at Le Guet.

'In those days the Wayside Hotel was a German hospital and had a big red cross painted on top.'

Herbie recalls planting pine trees at Le Guet in 1937.

'In those days there were no trees. It was all gorse.

'We used to come and play up here. It was all paths between the gorse.'

The northern end of Cobo was unrecognisable from today.

Those who nowadays use La Mare de Carteret for recreational purposes might be shocked to learn that until the very early '60s a 20-25ft-wide river cut a swathe through it right up to the bridge that crosses Route de Carteret.

Owned by Lord de Saumarez to the east side of the river was a beautifully kept path that linked the coast and the bridge and enabled a pony and trap to transfer the gentry.

That path, says Herbie, was in place until the Germans arrived on the scene.

The whole area was transformed with the installation of the main drain from the Vale Pond to Long Port around 50 years ago.

The river, with its bullrushes and swans, disappeared and in a relatively short time the area was made into playing fields and half-a-mile inland the two Mare de Carteret schools were built.

Above
German soldiers patrol beneath Le Guet prior to the fortifications being built

Left
The view from Le Guet in the early part of the 20th century

FOURTH BARON'S LEGACY

ONLY islanders approaching their 80th birthday have ever seen Le Guet without its pine dressing.

Herbie Nichols is among them, having grown up when not one sat on the steep slopes underneath the watchtower.

It remains a wonderful area to grow up in and certainly was in 1937 when Herbie was among a group of Castel schoolchildren who planted pines at Le Guet.

'It was all gorse then – no trees', he recalled.

But that was not entirely true.

Approximately a decade earlier, under the instruction of the fourth Baron de Saumarez who some years earlier had returned from Japan to save the family's estate, some were planted.

Rare Japanese conifers were also planted on the steep slopes above Cobo from the mid 20s and, sad to say, 80 years on, the forest is worryingly thinning.

The nature of the pine – mainly Monterey at Le Guet – is that the roots spread wide but not deep.

Many of those early trees have grown and fallen as the area regularly catches the full force of the south-westerly gales.

The watch-house itself dates back to Napoleonic times with the high vantage point first used as a promontory with warning beacon 100 years earlier in the late 16th century.

It may even have been there when the Armada came up the channel in 1588.

Even now, one can see surprisingly far and wide.

You have to know where you are looking, but Victoria Tower – all magnificent pink Cobo granite – can be seen in the distance.

Part of Herm can also still be seen. But before the trees arrived, the watchhouse offered views of virtually the whole island and certainly all the beacons. Sark and Vazon could be seen clearly.

From the end of the Napoleonic era to the 20th century, written accounts of Le Guet were few and far between, but it came into its own with the outbreak of the Great War when its lofty position was ideal for spotting passing submarines.

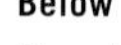

Below
The old coast road at Cobo in the late 19th century. Le Guet is bereft of trees

Its importance increased during the Occupation years. An air raid siren was fitted and its first worrying blast came that fateful day when big, black transport planes approached carrying the vanguard of the invading forces.

The alarm stopped but the 'all-clear' signal never sounded.

The Germans soon transformed the watchtower into a dangerous cocktail of machine-gun and cannon fire.

For much of the Occupation the beach was out of bounds to locals and Herbie recalls how the Germans would test their armoury and shooting skills with long-range machine-gunning of a tall, slim rock poking out of the sea at Albecq.

'It's only half the size it used to be because they shot at it so much,' he said.

Le Guet's other outstanding feature is the 100ft rectangular slab of pink granite that sits below the watchtower. It survives thanks to the intervention of Lord de Saumarez, the fourth baron who, not satisfied with owning a large slice of Castel, extended his estate in 1871 to take it in.

Look carefully and you can find the remains of five quarries which have provided the red and pink Cobo granite for Victoria Tower, Grandes Rocques Hotel, the slaughterhouse and St Matthew's Church.

The main quarry housing 'the chimney' is the biggest and most obvious, but Lord de Saumarez admired the spur sufficiently to rule that it would never be smashed for stone during his ownership.

Quite how many tons of eye-catching granite are housed within the huge slab is anyone's guess, but we are all indebted to de Saumarez's decision and the intervention of the relation who, when James St Vincent (1843-1937) was a successful and rich diplomat in Japan, wrote to him about the financially struggling third baron's decision to sell the entire estate.

The fourth certainly got his money's worth from his new property addition, its various quarries providing quality stone for his many building operations.

Douzaine permission to wall the entire Guet estate had been granted in 1732 to Pierre Dorey, one of probably two owners of the area.

Dorey, whose home still exists today on the south side of the forest, wrote to request permission for the wall.

It was given under one condition – he would have to build a road through the forest to make the job of those who carted vraic from the beach that much shorter and easier.

Above
'The Chimney'
Saumarez's favourite slice of Cobo granite

Below
A scene outside Chick's Hotel at the foot of La Banquette

Although you would not know it, the remains of the 'vraic road' are present, well hidden by many inches of pine needles and damaged by time and uncaring users.

Dorey's desire to keep islanders off Le Guet of the mid 1700s primarily lay in the vast stretches of gorse that covered the mound – it was a popular fuel for the ovens of Guernsey kitchens.

Baron de Saumarez's 1871 purchase of Le Guet was not total: one small area was kept free for the public and excluded from the enclosure was another prominent granite rock at the top of Albecq Hill called Le Rocher au Veau or, in English, Calf Rock.

It is still there today, tucked away in a private garden of a modern bungalow built by Tony and Margaret Nussbaumer who, with the ownership of the Cobo Bay Hotel and tenancy of the Rockmount, have played their own significant roles in the modern history of the area.

But back in the late 19th century on this triangle of land the education authorities took pity on those children who had to walk a long way from the Vazon end of Cobo to Castel School and built an infants' school which survived until the Germans opted to demolish it.

That was not the only significant building in the area to be flattened by Hitler's men. The Cobo Institute, since rebuilt, went along with the first Cobo Hotel at the foot of La Banquette Hill that meets the coast road.

On the passing of the fourth Baron de Saumarez in 1937, the Guet and the entire estate switched hands for probably the final time.

Having bought the land from his cash-strapped father 68 years earlier, the fourth baron had performed heroics in not only transforming the park and gardens surrounding the manor just a mile or so to the east, but also ensuring the coastal landmark is resplendent in the early part of the 21st century.

Having lived to the ripe old age of 94, the estate was sold to the States of Guernsey in 1938 for the sum of £25,000.

VILLAGE CRICKET

FIFTY years ago in May a small group of Cobo locals met in the back bar of the Rockmount Hotel to form what has gone on to become one of the most successful cricket clubs in the Channel Islands.

The formation of Cobo in 1957 gave the village a sporting focus and as the area developed, so did the team.

Within 10 years of taking their place in the Guernsey Cricket League, Cobo had lifted the island's Division One championship and it has been almost non-stop success since.

The inaugural minutes show the club was initially known as Rockmount Cricket Club, but within a year the name changed to Cobo.

Most of the players lived in the village or at least drank in it.

Brian Le Prevost, the current chairman, was too young to play in the first sides but well remembers the characters of those early years.

'It was very much a crowd of local Cobo lads who got together to play friendlies.

We played the likes of the New Brighton pub in Fountain Street and visiting campers.'

The novices used any patch of grass to play.

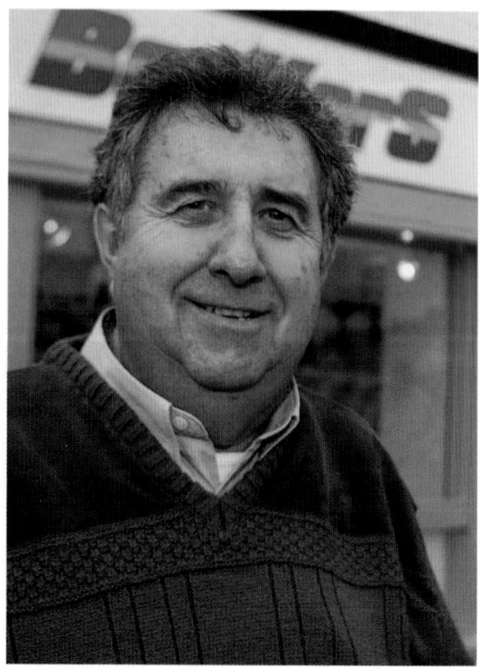

This page
Brian Le Prevost: Cobo boy and stalwart of the village cricket club

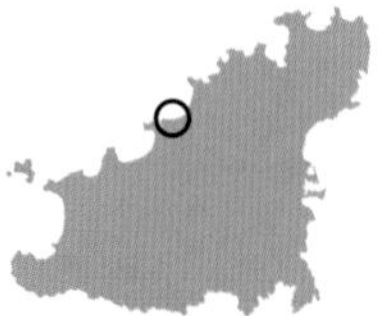

One was the area in front of what is now a pumping station above La Mare playing fields and another the former hockey pitch at Saumarez Park.

'We played on anything that was available,' Brian recalled.

The club was approaching its 40th birthday when it opted to branch out and challenge other village sides – in the UK.

In 1990, Cobo was accepted into the National Village Cup having met most of the competition criteria: that the team emanated from a village of fewer than 2,500 people and was totally surrounded by green fields.

The story made the sports pages of the Mail on Sunday under the headline, 'Plane sailing to Lord's?'.

The picture showed the 'Beach Boys' sitting on rocks opposite the Cobo Bay Hotel.

The club retains strong local connections.

The first-team captain is Stuart Le Prevost, born within a boundary throw of the bar that has been the focus of the club for half-a-century.

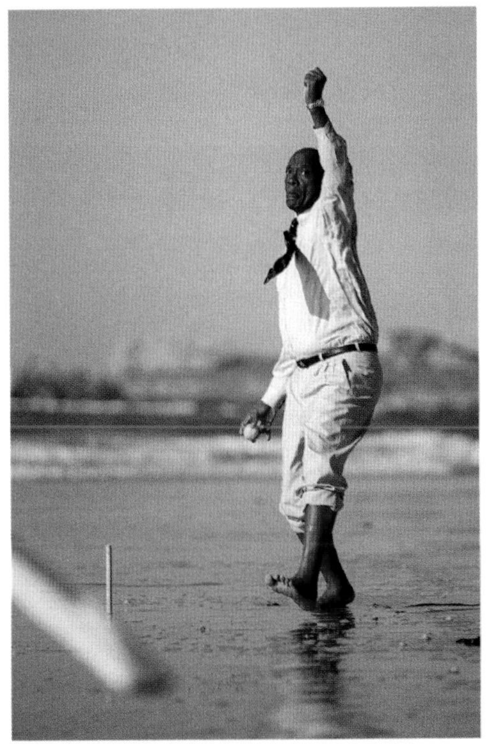

Hotelier David Nussbaumer is president, as was his father in the 1970s. The club is proud of its traditions and its character. As long as it stays close to its roots, it should remain successful, said Mr Le Prevost.

'When [for a few years in the 1970s] we spread too far in terms of recruiting players, we started to lose our local identity.

'But while the strand of the local families – the Batistes, Mechems, Nussbaumers and Le Prevosts – were in it, it has always been successful.'

Above
Cobo Cricket Club's 1961 promotion-winning team a few of which were at the club's 50th anniversary at the Cobo Bay Hotel in 2008

Left
The legendary West Indies fast bowler Wes Hall swaps the sands of his native Barbados for Cobo on a visit

“Beneath the road, on a spring tide, it was not uncommon for mullet to swim up the stream and into La Mare, as would salmon and eels”

Roy Mechem

CHAPTER 2

LONG PORT

Many people assume it is simply part of Cobo, but it has a little known identity of its own with its small fishing fraternity and a reef which gets you up close and almost personal with the magnificent Grosse Rocque.

LONG TIME NO SEE · A LONG TIME BACK
MARITIME VICTIMS · SIR FABIAN TO MOOR AT LONG PORT

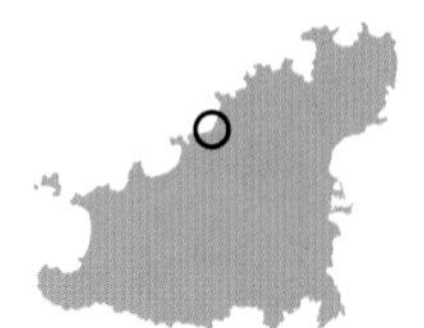

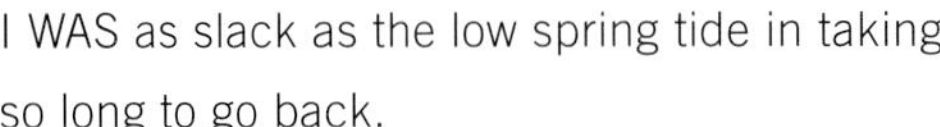

LONG TIME NO SEE

I WAS as slack as the low spring tide in taking so long to go back.

Racing over rocks, much of them covered in seaweed, is one thing when you're 10, but 40 years later, when the knees are all but shot to pieces, it is another ball game.

But the spring picture and unexpected situation was just too good to resist.

It was Easter Monday afternoon, the sun was shining and it was the last big spring tide for a month. Who's to say the big ball in the sky that makes for pretty pics will be out when the spring lows next return and, anyway, that would be too late for deadline.

Long Rock – the apt name given to the rocks that stretch out the best part of a mile to the Grosse Rocque – won't have changed in 40 years but as I headed down, first over beach that was still exposed only 45 minutes before low water, it was with a touch of nervousness.

After all, I had managed to fall off a sea wall at L'Eree recently through no other reason than sheer inability to pick up my feet properly. That time the (landside) fall into sand was only 2ft; to do so out at the end of the reef might be regrettable and involve a red-faced call to the emergency services.

Another concern was not knowing how long I'd have out there, my intention being to go as far as I could to the 'big one' with the flag on without getting my feet wet.

As a kid, I had a mate to raise any unexpected alarm. This time I had my mobile, should the legs not do their job properly.

A few minutes earlier, the nice lady at the Guet tearoom had said she'd wave, but I very much doubt she would have noticed as I reached the first of Long Port's 'Twin Peaks'. I have no evidence that these sharp, rocky elevations have names, but if you want one, how about 'Gull's Relief' for the rise nearest the beach?

It's not, to be honest, much of a peak but it offered the opportunity to get the idiot-proof digital camera out and see what I could shoot looking back across Cobo from a position beyond the most westerly-moored fishing boats.

The view is spectacular, but I hadn't got the best one, that belonging to the trio of kayakers who beneath my perch, just 50m. away, were exploring the pink rocks. No problem for them going the extra yards I needed to, to reach my destination.

Ten metres below Gull's Relief is a clear divide in the reef, which I mentally noted that I had better not be west of an hour later. Make that half-an-hour, just in case my knowledge of rising spring tides is not what it should be.

Climbing out of the gulley, the reef switches from part-weed cover to almost total coverage for the next 100m.

Fortunately, the weed has dried out nicely and in the best tradition of Sir Ranulph Fiennes, it's onwards towards the bigger peak, which cannot be more than quarter-of-a-mile from the Grosse Rocque.

Beneath the peak is a very large pond, where I imagine the cabous must be cod-like, but it's so deep it would be foolhardy to venture into it.

The second peak seems to have avoided the attention of seagulls, possibly because the most comfortable sanitary point for them is only a short distance away underneath a flagpole and the elevated view is no doubt better.

Full zoom gives a better indication of the scale of bird deposits, but without a boat to get there, I was not going to sample the smell at close quarters.

Sadly, my own point of no return was but yards away.

Looking down from the peak it was clear

Opposite
Le Guet provides the backdrop to Cobo and neighbouring Long Port

that emulating old Guernseymen in walking to the Grosse Rocque was impossible. In fact, it's hard to imagine it being possible, given that there must be 50m. of water between the main reef and the rocks which lead up to the one which is given a new flag every Liberation Day.

It looked deeper than ankle-high and I was not brave enough to try. But Herbie Nichols, the bay's most famous and knowledgeable fisherman, insists that he has walked this walk all the way and you can blame it on global warming for not being able to do so in the early 21st century.

'It used to dry out,' said soon-to-be octogenarian Herbie. 'If you'd have known the way you were going, you could have still waded out up to your waist.

'I've been ormering to the Grosse Rocque loads of times. Right beneath the Grosse Rocque was very good for ormers, but there doesn't seem to be a lot left.'

Long Rock is also good for fishing and was a spot well utilised by once ace angler Brian Robson.

Back in 1982, he smashed the island shore-caught bass record with a monster 15lb 9oz catch from the part of the reef which he calls La Cauchaonesse. The spot is only accessible at low tide, just past the moorings, and while the sand eels were a feature of Long Port, the bass were never far away.

'There used to be a lot of bass on that reef but there's no sand eels any more,' said Brian, recalling the not-too-distant days when the eels would be prevalent on the shingle area of the beach, mainly in April and May.

As a former competitive angler, Brian has no problem with divulging the whereabouts of his favourite spot.

Below
Grosse Rocque
Right
The village at Cobo as seen from the Long Rock reef
Far right
The high point of Long Rock standing proud

'It was just before you got cut off by the tide. You could only ever fish there for about two-and-a-half hours.'

The name La Cauchaonesse stems from the old Guernsey French word of cauchaon (bootie or bed-sock). Herbie explained the sock connection further.

'When the tide is at the bottom of the slipway, it's time to leave, but you've got two gullies to cross and either you have to wade and get wet or take your shoes and socks off.'

A LONG TIME BACK

'LONG where?' 'Long Port,' you tell people.

'Ah, you mean Cobo,' comes the reply.

But I don't. Long Port is the beach that stretches out towards Grosse Rocque.

And both it and the Mare de Carteret area that lies immediately to the east have changed more than you might imagine over the past century.

Today it seems quite unremarkable.

On the upper beach there is a decent stretch of sand right up to the break in the road where the little slip divides what everyone knows as Cobo from La Saline, which everyone refers to as Grandes Rocques.

The beach is no good for swimming and the signs are pinned to the pink granite wall to remind you of the dangerous currents that lie in wait, but as a place to sunbathe it is perfectly fine and sheltered from north-easterlies.

Back in the 60s I recall a small grassy area, the equivalent size of a six-yard area on a football pitch, perhaps even smaller, on which local lads used to erect a tent and camp overnight.

But pre-war, before the effects of erosion and bigger tides made their dramatic mark on the beach, the patch was more the size of a field and was used to graze cattle.

Herbert Nichols, long-time resident of Cobo, former fisherman and harbourmaster, recalls the greenery of Long Port.

Born in 1930, he was not surprised to see the grassy stretch in the photograph used here to show the proximity of the 1937 Briseis wreck to Grosse Rocque.

'In those days if you were on the beach wall, you could just step onto the grass.

'It went roughly to the first set of steps from Cobo.'

It was a favourite haunt for young locals like Herbie.

'In the centre there was a hollow and we'd lay there as kids and if it was blowing hard you

Both pictures
The Long Rock contains many gullies and deep pools

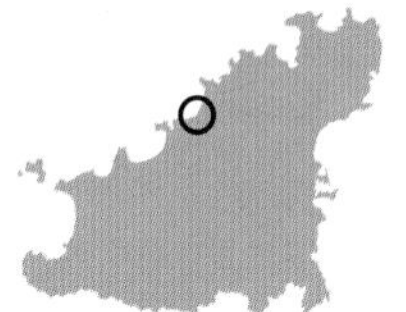

didn't feel the wind. You were out of the way.'

Another old Cobo-ite, Roy Mechem, was brought up across the road in the quaint little cottage tucked away in the north-west corner of the playing fields.

His parents, Jim and Harriet, grazed their prize-winning goats on the grassy patch over the wall.

Cattle were also tethered there.

But as Roy revealed, the Long Port field was not in the slightest a natural phenomenon.

'Years ago the sea wall broke there and they filled it up with ground and rock.

'I heard [the wall collapse] happened at the weekend and they brought the ground by horse and cart from the Carteret quarry [next to Cobo Motor Works].

'People didn't work Sundays then but they worked all weekend to fill up the hole,' Jim recollected.

'The grass grew on it and it was a nice spot to go and sit. But over the year the big spring tides washed it away.'

Another feature of early 20th century Long Port beach was referred to as 'Le Nocq'.

Long before the Water Board introduced the freshwater drainage scheme which today takes water out into the bay, there was a less elaborate system of pipes that went from the 'Mare' to the beach through the road, and was covered by large wooden beams so horses and carts or early motor cars could cross it.

Beneath the road, on a spring tide, it was not uncommon for mullet to swim up the stream and into La Mare, as would salmon and eels.

At the 'Mare' itself, Lord de Saumarez's waterways system, which ran virtually from La Mare de Carteret bridge to the coastline through today's playing fields, featured a fairly wide river that was bordered by reeds and enjoyed by a colony of swans.

They were still using it until the river was drained and filled in 1967.

MARITIME VICTIMS

COBO and Long Port people have viewed many a wreck over the centuries. An extended line drawn through the centre of the reefs that flank the bay and the outer reaches of water beyond Grosse Rocque account for eight known and named victims of the sea.

Some date back to the days of sailing power, the most recent the tragic Prosperity on La Conchee reef off Perelle, and before that La Salle, which shocked us on the bus as we headed for Castel School on a wintry morning in the mid-60s.

Before that, in 1937, the vessel Briseis struck Les Grunes some way north of Long Port and, holed, was then pushed by the tide to its sinking point off Grosse Rocque.

An amateur photograph shown here appears to feature the Briseis to the left of the Grosse Rocque.

Below
Grosse Rocque as close as you will get on foot
Right
A 1937 view of the Briseis wreck off Long Port

SIR FABIAN TO MOOR AT LONG PORT

LONG PORT has a celebrated new mooring holder. Some time in the coming weeks Lt-Governor Sir Fabian Malbon is planning to move his boat onto a mooring there.

Sir Fabian's will be one of 30 moorings allocated by local harbourmaster Lionel Girard on the Long Port side of Cobo this summer.

And while the stretch of water on the north side of the Cobo slipway is no longer the home of any full-time fishermen, the harbourmaster insists it remains as popular as ever for part-timers like him.

Lionel has been fishing out of the bay for 30 years.

Among his fellow 'LPs' have been his brother Mick, the hero of the 1969 Muratti final, and until ill-health sidelined him, Ricky Mills, one of Guernsey cricket's greats.

'I've dived and potted all my [adult] life and it's a lovely area to work from.

'They are nice people to work with and it's ideal in the summer. Easy to get up and down.'

Coastal catches these days in no way match the grand ones of generations past, but there is still enough yield to keep people like Lionel interested and the weekly summer crab draw at the Rockmount back bar alive.

For sailors, using Long Port is a six-month exercise from the first day of April.

The bay is shallow, the bottom clear of rocks and the passage west a clear one for little fishing boats.

'It's straight in and straight out and there's nothing much to bother you,' said the harbourmaster, whose nautical patch stretches south at Vazon and extends to Grandes Rocques.

It's his job to allocate all the moorings and as far as Long Port is concerned, there is little room for more.

'I've had up to 36 but that would be the limit.'

'From the wall onwards I look after all that. I also take the boys out to [raise] the flag [on Grosse Rocque].'

Right
Swans on the old La Mare de Carteret waterway
Opposite
Cobo and Long Port Harbour Master Lionel Girard

"When we came back [after the Occupation] it was indescribable. The place was wrecked by the Germans who had ripped up skirting boards for firewood"

Claude Way

CHAPTER 3

GRANDES ROCQUES

The beach and rocks stretching out west never seem to change, but elsewhere at traditionally popular Grandes Rocques much has changed over the past century and more.

A GRAND TYPE OF BAY · LEFT TO DIE · EVER-CHANGING SANDS
A NICE LITTLE EARNER · THE WAY HOME

A GRAND TYPE OF BAY

YOU could call it the beach with the wrong name. We all know it as Grandes Rocques when, in fact, its official title is Saline Bay.

Regardless, for a succession of generations the stretch of sand between Cobo and Port Soif remains hugely popular with both locals and tourists.

The beach itself has altered little. There have been uglier periods when a mass of small stone has stretched for most of the way across to make the less hardy of us feel even less attracted to swimming in a sea chillier than most bays in the west, due to it falling away more sharply.

All the significant changes have occurred at the top where, sadly and in the name of environmental protection, most of the dunes have been replaced by blue-granite armouring.

But 40 years ago, in the halcyon days when Herbie Saunders operated a deckchair and woopie-float business, the bay oozed charm and man-made sunspots beneath the dunes.

As our 1969 picture shows, families or small groups would shut themselves away from the rest of the beach, cocooned by the pink granite stone, which is a feature of the area.

No doubt, much of that stone emanated from the only pink-granite slipway the island possessed, remnants of which can still be seen from time to time when the natural shifting of the sand fully exposes it.

Like so many things, the German occupying forces brought about the slip's downfall.

Before the war, there was a natural route for local fishermen over the dunes and onto the beach via the long slipway (at least 50 metres), but the Jerries' aversion to locals on the beach led to them closing it off.

Today the dunes are at their highest where once the likes of Nicholas Ogier would drag their dinghies down into the water.

Just when the slip was put in place is unclear, but States archivist Darryl Ogier has his own theory, having failed to unearth the usual States legislation for the building of one.

His educated guess is that it was built some time after 1900 when Lord de Saumarez took ownership of the old Grandes Rocques Hotel, added a storey and gave it a more gothic look.

As the obviously wealthy de Saumarez felt the need for his own golf course and a purpose-built school for his asthmatic son, it would have made sense to build his own landing stage with stone from the many quarries he owned.

Through the Guernsey Militia years the bay also doubled as a shooting range.

Old maps clearly illustrate the shorter ranges – 100 to 300 yards – on the headland dividing

the hotel and the elevated battery with its coquelin [winkle] sitting proudly atop.

For longer target practice, the militia men fired from vantage points all the way back to Cobo, more than 1,000 yards away.

The derivative name of Grande Rocque refers to the mass of magnificent ruggedly pink granite on which sits the battery, a strongpoint established in the early 19th century as part of a comprehensive scheme for insular defence, mounted in response to the threat of attack from the French.

More than 100 years later, the Germans gave the headland an uglier, cemented look with a swarm of bunkers.

Of further archaeological importance were the remains of a medieval fishing settlement, which were uncovered on the headland in an excavation in 1985, seven years after the spectacular grounding of the oilrig Orion.

Given the bay's natural features that stretch out towards the Grosse Rocque, it is no wonder the kayaks have replaced the leaky and cumbersome floats of Herbie Saunders.

Ant Ford-Parker, co-owner of kayaking group Outdoor Guernsey, rates the bay on two fronts.

'It's great for kayak fishing. In fact, most kayak fishing is done in that bay,' he said.

Bass, pollack and wrasse are most commonly caught, while for those experienced kayakers who prefer more adventure, the rocks and gullies offer satisfaction.

'For people with a bit of skill, it's very exciting.'

Above
Grandes Rocques has been popular with beach-goers for generations

LEFT TO DIE

THE two-way mirror that assists drivers as they exit Grandes Rocques Road marks the point where 67 years ago Nicholas Ogier met a cruel and mysterious death.

Unsurprisingly, the story still pains Joyce Domaille, his daughter, today.

Her father, who fought in the First World War and lost an eye and suffered wounds to his chest and side in action, had stayed in the family home at Linda Cottage when the island became occupied by the Germans.

With most of his family evacuated, the 50-year-old grower and part-time fisherman was living alone and taking his meals at his mother's house in the old cottage which now makes the corner at Grandes Rocques opposite the butchers' shop.

But on a dark Sunday evening early in January 1941, he met his death in disturbing circumstances, dying from exposure and heart failure trapped in a ditch beneath the then granite Grandes Rocques Hotel perimeter wall.

Trapped, he screamed for help long into the evening but under curfew restrictions nobody helped.

At the inquest, neighbours admitted to hearing something but were too scared to go out.

Mr D. Le Page heard noises 'like shouting, from nine in the evening until midnight'.

Nicholas was left to die and was found by his son 'wedged in a gully' nearly two full days later.

His surviving daughter remains unsure of the exact truth to her father's death, but has built up her own picture of the night he perished.

'I believe he went to my gran's for his supper on the corner about 6pm and then went across to the Grandes Rocques Hotel,' she said.

'He decided to cross the field and the silly chap probably decided to jump over the wall.

'From what I can make out, he fell, became jammed and died of exposure.'

It was probably his wish for a Sunday evening tipple that led to the tragic accident.

At the inquest, Inspector W. Sculpher said he had been told that Nicholas Ogier had been seen rattling at the hotel window at about 7.30pm.

But, oddly, the inspector reported that the man who supposedly saw him at the window was not known.

'Knowing my dad he probably thought he could go over [to the hotel] for a drink, but I don't know.'

Summing up the inquest, the coroner said no evidence had been given to prove how the Grandes Rocques man died.

'He may have crossed the field and fallen accidentally, he may have dropped in.'

An open verdict was recorded.

Joyce says it took her a long while to believe her father had died and on the family's return after the war she refused to accept the fact until walking around the whole area in search of him.

'All of this [the old days] has good and bad memories, but the saddest for me was that I never saw my dad again.'

Below
Nicholas Ogier before his tragic death

EVER-CHANGING SANDS

ALAS, you'll no longer find too many real 'Guerns' and natives of Grandes Rocques.

But among them are Fred Domaille, 81, and wife Joyce, 77, an Ogier dating back to the time when Grandes Rocques Road – which runs from the Wayside Cheer junction and the filter which separates the Galaad and Carteret roads, virtually parallel with the beach – was full of Ogiers.

The two are a grand old couple from an era when their road was aligned by carrot fields one side and greenhouse after greenhouse on the other.

Dotted among the mass of glass was the old Guernsey cottage, Beaulieu, where Joyce was born and grew up before moving 100 yards east to the border of the Port Soif football ground and the charmingly attractive Linda Cottage.

She estimates that she and near neighbour Rex Le Sauvage are the only survivors of the pre-war years when the neighbourhood pub was the Grandes Rocques Hotel, men were men and loved a 'spree' (binge) and virtually the whole road was, in some way, an Ogier.

Of all matters Grandes Rocques, arguably the least change has been with the bay itself.

'The changes have been subtle,' said Fred.

'The dunes used to sweep down to the beach and there were not the big rocks that there are now,' he continued, with reference to the rock-armouring that has taken up half the length of the beach and kindly provided a home for all the local rats that think nothing of a night feed from the scraps left on the beach.

Like most west-coast beaches, Grandes Rocques experiences regular changes in sand levels.

'Sometimes there are pebbles across the beach and at other times they are covered by sand,' says the former Navy man.

And while Cambodia had Killing Fields, Grandes Rocques had the Carrot Fields.

'As a boy in the 60s, I vividly recall the carrot

Below and opposite
Grandes Rocques Battery many years apart

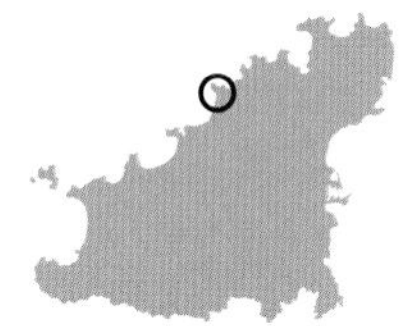

patches that lined the beach side of Grandes Rocques Road.'

The sandy nature of the entire area made the land ideally suited to growing carrots and no doubt the tamarisks, which provide a natural seashore windbreak, were put there for a purpose.

Apparently, the Lenfesteys were the main carrot growers of the area, but sadly nobody has bothered to keep up the tradition for many years.

'It's too much like hard work, and you can buy them cheaper from Israel,' said Fred.

Other services in the immediate post-war years arrived in quaint old ways.

'Our milkman was Will Bougourd who used to bring our milk with a can and a measuring jug, fetched off his little hand cart,' recalled Joyce.

Then there was the barber, long before Keith Le Page began operating his modern successful hairdressing business. But it was from the same building, recalled the Domailles.

'First it was Mr Falla and then, I think, a Mr de la Mare, who used to come down from the Bridge on certain days.'

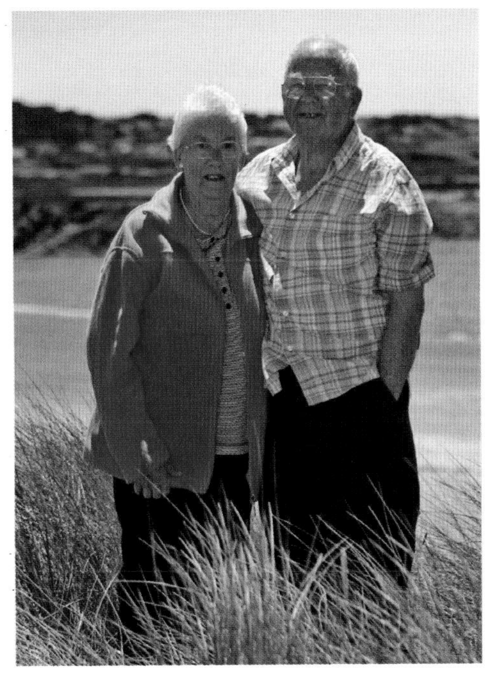

Left
Fred and Joyce Domaille have spent a lifetime at Grandes Rocques

A NICE LITTLE EARNER

VISITING Grandes Rocques beach in the 1960s offered so much more than it does these days.

The dunes offered countless areas of natural protection for beachgoers, you could buy a tea basket from the kiosk and if you could not get a deck chair or windbreak from there, then there was always little Herbie Sanders, who would hobble about hiring out chairs and woopie-floats that provided the adventurous with dangerous opportunities to explore the deep bay between the two lines of rocks which lead out to the Grosse Rocque.

Herbie was quite a character, one still fondly remembered by the Domailles.

To a young Joyce Ogier, the beach was his and she let her children know it.

'I'd say [to them]: "If you don't wash you can't go on Herbie's beach",' she said. 'It seemed he was always there in the summer. He was as good as gold.'

The floats were, one seems to recall, a little on the heavy side, likely to provide you with a splinter in the foot and you were lucky to stay afloat, such was the amount of water they would take on board.

Hop-along-Herbie, despite his physical handicap and the need to keep his takings satchel dry, was very adept himself.

'He used to go out pedalling himself but he'd go stood up,' says Fred.

'He would have his moneybag on the side of him. It was a surprise he didn't fall in.'

It must have been a nice little earner because he walked to and from his home in the Ramee every day to do it. And when he did catch a bus, it's said he would get off a stop early to avoid paying a little more as it was a fare stage at the one closest to his house.

It enabled him, too, to treat himself to a cruise, which had a profound effect on his life.

His spell on the Love Boat won him the affections of a far younger, attractive lady more suited to hula-hooping and garlands of flowers around her neck than living in the Ramee.

But, nevertheless, the lady from the South Pacific – probably Tonga – saw enough in Herbie to come back with him to the Ramee and spend his money.

Joyce is clear in what happened.

'They married and she led him a merry dance. There was a lot of a to-do.'

Fred said: 'My dad told him he was a bloody old fool.'

Local author George Torode briefly featured Herbie in one of his books on local life.

George is unsure whether the Anglo-Pacific Oceanic alliance ever got as far as the tying-the-knot stage, but agrees that she saw poor old Herbie coming.

'She spent most evenings drinking with the men down at the Rockmount while he was at home.'

Sadly, his Pacific lady was nowhere to be seen when, in 1995, aged 86 and suffering from dementia with no immediate family recorded in the official death notice, the man originally from the Rhonda Valley, south Wales, passed away in Summerland Nursing Home.

Herbie was one of just many colourful characters associated with the area over the ever-distant decades.

Fred will talk amusingly about old 'Fif' Mahy the fisherman, 'Charger' Le Sauvage and, most funny of all, a chap called 'Jubilee Up'.

And why Jubilee Up?

'Because he was always jumping.

He never stood still – he was like a puppet,' said Fred. 'I can close my eyes and still see him coming down the Grandes Rocques road.'

Jubilee was from an era when 'sprees' were a common thing among the hard-working men.

One such man who liked a spree was Joyce's uncle Alfred, or Growbox, as he was known.

Left
Colourful character
Herbie Sanders
Overleaf
'Grande Rocque' Hotel
circa 1880

When a sozzled Growbox had obviously had enough at the Grandes Rocques, he would be lifted aboard his trap and his pony [Tommy] would quietly take him home, the full length of Grandes Rocques road away.

One of the best Grandes Rocques tales is of the drink-drive fugitive who anchored his boat in the bay, rowed ashore and walked the short distance to the Rockmount for a few beers with his old mates.

Alas, the constabulary got to know he was at the Rockie and duly arrived to make an arrest.

At this point, the accused convinced the officers that he would have to collect his dog aboard his boat.

The fools fell for it.

With the officers in tow and aboard his dinghy, the man rowed out to his fishing boat.

Whether it was sheer impulse or a crafty plan, on reaching his boat the fugitive jumped aboard, kicked the dinghy away and in a flash had the engine going, ripped the anchorage away and headed off to the UK, where he still lives today.

GRA

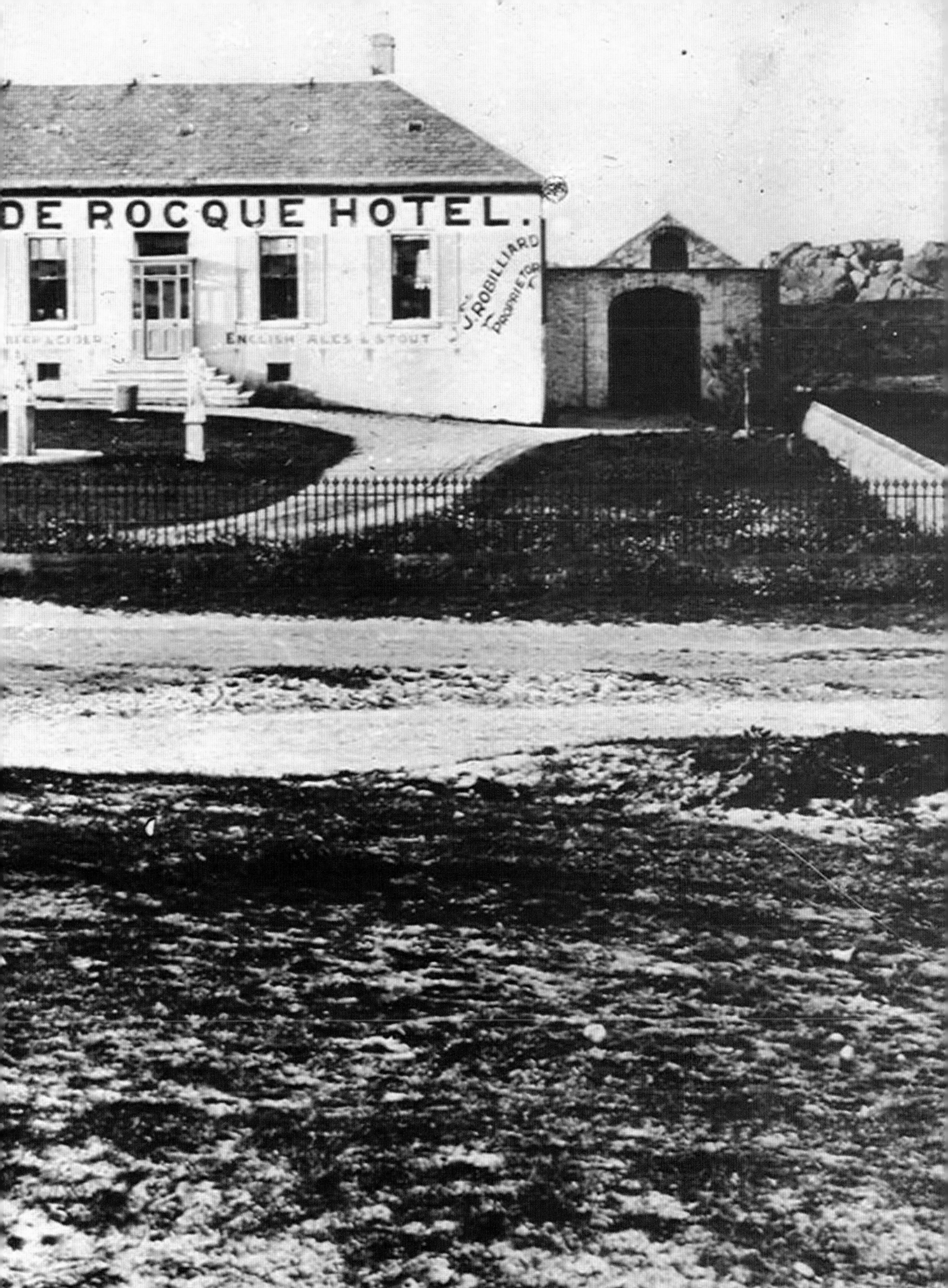
DE ROCQUE HOTEL.
J. ROBILLIARD
PROPRIETOR
ENGLISH ALES & STOUT

THE WAY HOME

THE Germans all but wrecked it, that great Sea Lord de Saumarez transformed it into a school for his ailing son and plans for the 1951 Festival of Britain were drawn up there.

The former Grandes Rocques Hotel has certainly seen some sights.

On its pink granite perch, the building has lorded it over the area dividing La Saline and Port Soif for more than 200 years.

For 50 of those years it was run by the Way family and for decades there was hardly a more popular 'mein host' than the man never seen in public without his bow tie, Claude Way.

It is 20 years since he shut the door on one of 20th century Guernsey's finest hotels – the Grandes Rocques – but get him on the subject and he will happily take you back to golden years for an area which you can't help thinking has left behind its great fun and charm.

While a stone's throw away islanders in their hundreds would pile into the Wayside Cheer for cabaret shows in the summer or great-value mass dinners in the winter, Claude Way established a hotel business of the highest reputation working alongside his wife, May.

Within its noted ballroom, badly damaged by a severe storm in late 1987, the Ways staged functions for just about everything worth celebrating and they mostly kept coming back, year in, year out.

It was Christmas 1937 when Alan Way and his family of five moved in.

Claude still recalls as a boy being sent to raise the red flag on the coquelin on top of Grandes Rocques Battery by way of warning that the Militia were to start their shooting practice.

Apart from five years in the Occupation, Claude remained there until 1988.

His father, a former steward at the Royal Guernsey, ran the hotel with his French-born wife Marie-Louise, either side of a period when he was forced out by the Germans, who had not taken it well when early in the Occupation one of their officers was struck by Claude's father.

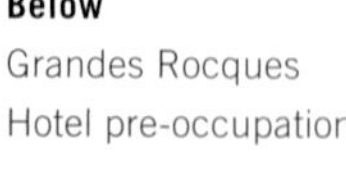

Below
Grandes Rocques
Hotel pre-occupation

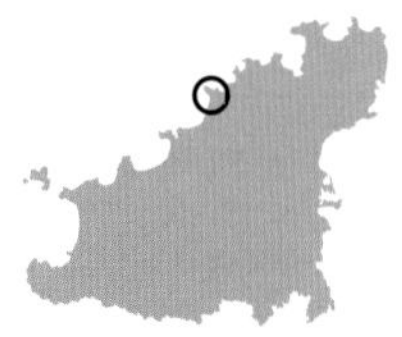

Far left
Claude Way
Left
Pub regular 'Fif' Mahy
Overleaf
The Grandes Rocques Hotel's Foil and Pistol public bar

'My father wouldn't let a German go upstairs with a woman. "I'm not a brothel keeper," he said.'

Alan Way's punishment was six days in prison.

But with the Germans fancying the hotel for themselves, the Ways were forced out until after the war.

Firstly, Mr Way was given a temporary public house licence for Rockpond, a detached house halfway between Grandes Rocques and Cobo.

And when that ran its course he was given another temporary licence for a bar at the Mare de Carteret house, the big pink-granite property which overlooks La Mare de Carteret playing fields.

The evacuated Claude recalled the hotel as a mess when he returned after the war.

'When we came back it was indescribable. The place was wrecked by the Germans [around 30 were housed there] who had ripped up skirting boards for firewood.'

But when Home Secretary Herbert Morrison decided to holiday here in 1947, it was at the Grandes Rocques he stayed.

Indeed, Claude's father recalled Morrison's basic drawings of the planned festival of Britain, etched in ballpoint pen on the back of a discarded cigarette packet at the hotel.

Either side of the war the hotel ran a popular public bar – the Foil and Pistol.

With a no-women rule, the bar was a haven for the local fishermen and growers, as well as other west-coasters.

Claude chuckles as he recalls the old characters – men such as 'Fif' Mahy.

'I've got a great respect for them. They were all hard-working, nice people and we never had any trouble in the bar.'

As Guernsey life changed, the Foil and Pistol trade gradually declined and, in 1980, the pub was shut.

On 17 March 1988, the Ways locked up and moved out, leaving a grand old building that in the intervening years seems to have lost its once proud place in the community.

"It's like riding nature's rollercoaster, but better because there is a risk factor. It's not in a controlled, safe environment"

Greg Rutsch

CHAPTER 4

PORT SOIF

Great sands, great views and great seas. Port Soif is a watery playground with its glorious pink stone and craggy rocks offering a variety of recreational possibilities to those drawn there.

ISLAND PLAYGROUND · SAND AND STORMS
SWELL BEACH · DUNE BUGS

ISLAND PLAYGROUND

WERE Port Soif's upper beach never to be relieved of the water that covers all that nasty, foot-scraping rock – yes I'm a bit of a wuss – then it would be the perfect beach.

Number one in Guernsey.

But one thing we have yet to work out is a way of stopping the tide. Twice a day for ever more, the plug will be pulled and out it will go to reveal the stone and the rock pools for the little ones.

But even so, it remains a beach of so many possibilities.

It offers good swimming at high and low tide – shame about the middle section – sand which allows everything from sunbathing in the soft stuff to playing cricket and football on the harder surface, one of the island's best beach kiosks and, if you get bored with just lounging about, exciting fishing possibilities and even more thrilling deep-water jumping.

Generations of island youths have sampled the blood-pumping thrill of throwing themselves off those pink peaks which separate the Port Soif and Grandes Rocques headlands.

And it is not just one set of rocks that has a habit of inducing panic among mothers when they find out what their little Johnnies have sloped off with their mates to do. No, mums, your boy has only been throwing himself off 20-30ft rocks, feet first. So don't worry.

And by the way, your husband knows all about it, as he did it 25 years ago and told your lad where best to go.

I'd long forgotten my own dare-devilment at Port Soif until family friends came over this August and the four boys nipped off for a bit of off-beach fun.

A few of the adults followed from a distance and, if the truth were told, probably wished we were young enough and still had the head for heights that Greg (16), Seb (11 or 12), Harry (16) and Ellis (16) all from the Forest of Dean area, clearly possessed.

They loved it and kept going back for more,

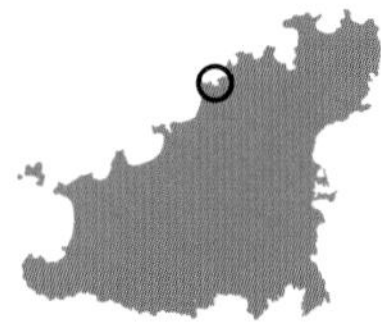

mixing with some of the local boys and girls out on the glittering pink granite outcrop. Greg said: 'It's like riding nature's rollercoaster, but better because there is a risk factor. It's not in a controlled, safe environment.

'But you can also just chill out with your mates for a while and take the jump and get the adrenaline rush. It makes you feel carefree when you are in mid-air – it feels like nothing else matters. It's just living in that moment.'

But if jumping, or 'tombstoning', is not your cup of tea and dangling a rod into the deep blue water below is, then Port Soif's grand rocks offer a quieter sort of playtime.

It's safe, although the 'island' referred to in Len Le Page's everything-you-need-to-know fishing publication highlights that it can be cut off for a short while. But sand can be reached with a shortish cast and the big rocks offer great shelter from the south-westerlies.

Finally, if you are the type who needs a bit more blood pumping through your veins but don't have a head for heights, then there are two more sporting options open to you – and only one necessitates getting wet.

You can hop over to Portinfer for a spot of bodyboarding in the sometimes monstrously high seas that crash in there.

Or slip on the trainers and shorts and pop off on a coastal run on perfect paths with brilliant views to the north and with a loop around the Portinfer shooting range.

Above
Catching a wave at Portinfer
Opposite
Jumping for joy from the rocks at Port Soif

SAND AND STORMS

THERE cannot be many, if any, sizeable chunks of Guernsey land that have undergone more changes than central Port Soif.

We are talking the area tucked inside the coast road which, over the past 40 years, has been developed as a versatile sports ground by the Rovers Athletic Club who hold the area on a 99-year lease.

Over a century it has served the island better than meets the eye, first as a golf course, secondly as the venue for Guernsey's biggest public event – the North Show – and then as a vital source for sand to sustain the boom in post-war island housing, and now as a burgeoning sports centre.

These days it is an emerald visual delight, breaking up the sprawl of housing that has developed around it over the past 40 years. And to that end, we all should be indebted to Rovers Athletic Club for establishing and forever improving a wide range of sporting facilities down there. Rovers has achieved much in 40 years on site.

First, the expanse was merely a football field serviced by a corrugated asbestos hut.

In recent times cricket has come along, and with money from the island's link with the International Cricket Council, not only has a grass square been laid, it has been surrounded by an outfield in impeccable condition, thanks to a superb irrigation system.

Archery, too, is playing its part in this most western of the island's sporting centres, but the history of the 'estate' might have gone horribly wrong but for the intervention and, later, understanding and support of local builders' merchant J. and D. Norman.

Sixty years ago, had J. F. [Jack] Norman not dug his heels in and kicked up a fuss against the Housing Authority, a major States housing estate would stand in place of today's wide expanse of greenery and recreational delight.

Billets d'Etat of 1949 and 1950 demonstrate just how close this lovely north-western tip of the island came to being a coastal Bouet.

The building firm E. J. Duquemin and Co. Ltd had been looking to utilise the area's vast (for Guernsey) sand resources back in the late 1930s when it was still well kept.

In those days it was utilised as a nine-hole golf course for the sleepy Grandes Rocques Golf Club and, each early September, as a venue for the annual two-day North Show and Battle of Flowers.

Duquemin bought five fields totalling 42 vergees as it sought to provide sand for the building of the new St Saviour's Reservoir.

Well, that was the plan until Adolf Hitler started to get ideas above his station.

The E. J. Duquemin & Co minute book of 1938 shows that 'due to international trouble' the secretary had suggested the matter of entering an agreement on supplying the reservoir be left until after the North Show lease ran out in 1940.

A year later the Germans arrived, the land formed part of the Todt's route for a west-coast railway and Duquemin's business plan never took off.

But a decade later the firm, keen to cash in, offered the fields, advertised as low-grade agricultural land, as a building site.

The States Housing Authority as good as bit their hand off and after the States Engineer had completed his report, the authority announced plans to buy the land and build 58 houses, with a further 18 to come once the area over which sand had been excavated had been filled and raised.

The States offered just £2,500 for three of the fields, totalling 31 vergees, but as they dithered about taking the whole site, the Normans stepped in and bought the land for £7,000.

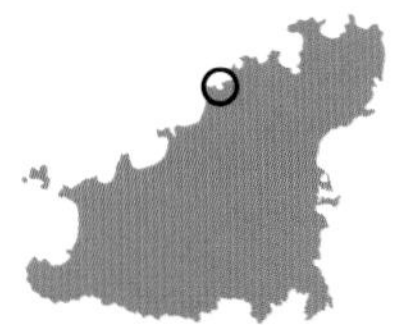

States Housing was not at all happy and, determined to get the land for cheap housing, went back to the States with a view to bulldozing the Normans aside and effecting compulsory purchase.

Within a year of announcing the plans to buy the land, a compensation figure of £8,625 was agreed by arbitrators – only, incredibly, for Housing to make an astonishing about-turn.

One month it was wanting the land for much-needed housing, the next it had come to the conclusion that it had, after all, sufficient building sites available to meet requirements for some time.

J. and D. Norman was suddenly left alone and over the next 12 years, up until 1962, fully used the area for extracting sand vital to the development of Guernsey.

Angered by Housing's plans for compulsory purchase and only half the story being told to the public, Jack Norman wrote to the Guernsey Press to put forward the facts as he saw it and took Housing president P. de Putron to task for his claim that the need for sand was not paramount.

'Everyone in the building trade knows that the need for sand for building purposes is not only paramount, but very acute in view of the prevailing shortage.'

He added: 'If the States take this one, which is one of the last remaining sources of sand, where are they going to get it from?'

Six decades on, Geoff Norman, son of the late J. F. Norman and now chairman of NP Holdings and chairman/MD of J. and D. Norman Ltd, said it was important not only for

Above
The wider Port Soif area with the sports ground and bay at its heart

the success of his family's business but for the island that the States backtracked when it did.

'All sand extracted on the island in those days was dune sand and it was required for building purposes.

'There was enough here to meet the needs for most of the island.'

Jim Mechem, now 82, worked the area for many years for the Normans and recalled the extent and nature of the site which, not many years earlier, had seen Battle of Flowers floats exhibits light it up.

Mr Mechem said that the whole area of the current sports fields was dug out to a level of around 10ft.

'It wasn't bad sand, although it held quite a lot of water. It was very fine and it used to sell well. The whole area down to the bungalow was stripped out.'

And when the sand had gone it was replaced by hardcore which included concrete from Les Beaucamps military huts.

Ultimately it was topped off with soil from the airport site.

Nowadays, the only remnants of sand excavation are to the south-west of the sports fields and within the National Trust area.

'Where the reeds are was the last area of excavation,' said Geoff Norman.

Excavating Port Soif had dated back to the 19th century, although slightly to the north of the modern sports ground.

The 1900 Ordnance Survey maps show three granite quarries and one large sand pit in use on the common land which stretches from Port Soif headland several hundred yards towards Portinfer.

Of those quarries the largest is still partially visible at the northern end of the car park near the kiosk.

To see exactly where the other two were dug it is best to look down from the air, and aerial photography shows exactly where the granite pits were eked out.

Nowadays all that is left of the old sand pit is a grassy mound with sandy tracks rising to its not-so-high summit.

Children still use it as a natural playground but in the summer of 1974, Rovers footballers prepared for their first season in the Priaulx League with lung-busting hill-runs on its slopes.

North Show's arrived at Port Soif in 1926 and continued until the outbreak of war.

The Northern Agricultural and Horticultural Society took on the venue as a replacement for the Cycling Grounds and it proved adequate enough that the organisers did not revert to the initial plan of alternating the show between Castel, Vale and St Sampson's.

Col. D. C. Le Pelley, the society president in 1926, informed a show luncheon that year of its original plans to take it around the northern parishes, but after two in Castel to start with, they had stuck with the 'Track' for four years.

Whether the move to Port Soif for the seventh annual show was part of the society's plans to give each parish a slice of the action or as a result of expulsion from the Track is unknown, but it worked out well.

The 1927 Guernsey Press description of the first day scenes were: 'Port Soif resembled a huge encampment with no fewer than 20 marquees filled with luscious exhibits of fruit, vegetables and flowers, and three marquees devoted to fur and feather fancies.'

But after 13 shows within a stone's throw of the beach, war came to spell the end of an era.

The 1939 show did not go ahead as the country stood on the verge of war with Germany and after the Occupation Saumarez Park, now under States ownership and no longer the private property of Lord de Saumarez, became the show's new and, it would seem, permanent home.

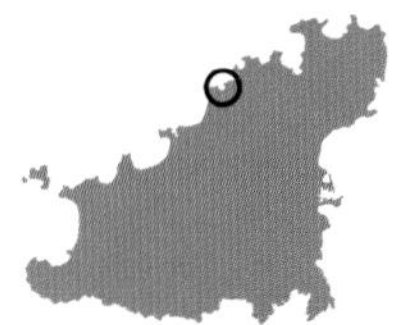

SWELL BEACH

WITH the tide up, Port Soif transforms into a beach of real beauty. And when the sea laps the soft, sloping sands of a summer's day it appears a perfectly safe environment for children to splash about in.

But when the tide is right out and the water line falls somewhere between the massive rocks which post the bay's entrance, it is best to keep a close eye on the youngsters as, not far away, the tides can run dangerously fast.

Couple that threat with big breakers and Port Soif suddenly becomes one of our more dangerous beaches.

But it is not only children in danger and on a lovely August afternoon in 1969 tragedy struck the bay, as a 22-year-old local man was swept away by a combination of massive breakers and the tide.

Michael Firth had gone swimming with his girlfriend when, at around 3.30 in the afternoon he was carried out to sea in the heavy surf.

The young woman just escaped drowning, clinging onto rocks.

A big St John Ambulance operation failed to track down the missing swimmer, but as hundreds of curious holidaymakers and islanders watched the search, St John staff officer Ron Herve also needed rescuing.

Caught in the giant swell, he broke an arm and suffered shock.

Later, Area Commissioner Reg Blanchford told the Press of the unusually dangerous conditions and of 'freak waves' that were as high as any seen in the area.

Left
The North Show and Battle of Flowers Port Soif-style
Above
Port Soif: a visual delight

DUNE BUGS

PRAISE where praise is due. Take a bow, Environment Department. Many a time it has clocked strong criticism for not dealing with this, that or the other in relation to island beaches, or taking a particular stance on an issue.

For example, what to do about the erosion at the eastern end of L'Ancresse has been a recent big issue.

But when it comes to the restoration of Port Soif's dunes, theirs has been a 10-out-of-10 performance.

A quarter-of-a-century ago the then Board of Administration identified the big problem of the bay's natural dunes being destroyed by a combination of wind erosion and the public.

This page
Digging to save the dunes in 1980s
Opposite
The saving of the dunes has been a success story for the Environment Department

By the end of 1986, the mobile dunes had moved to within five metres of the road and other parts were being damaged by people who would walk straight through them and onto the beach.

It was then that work sanctioned by the BoA under the direction of the States Engineer began and, nearly a quarter of a century later, the top of this beautiful shallow, horseshoe-shaped bay is gloriously restored.

Back in 1986, the first part of the plan was to stabilise the beach. In came the diggers and the boulders.

With the boulders in place, the dunes were allowed to grow back over with the aid of grass which is especially evolved for dune habitat.

Port Soif is Guernsey's last remaining mobile sand dune and the Environment Department works to actively manage it through monitoring the fencing which helps to stabilise it, ensuring that vegetation is kept in good order and occasionally removing excess quantities of windblown sand which encroach on the footpath.

The result is an attractive backdrop to the bay that provides an effective coastal defence to the road behind.

Year by year the mobile sand dune has gradually accreted through onshore winds driving sand up the beach.

During storms the sediment is drawn down the bay, but the sand is not permanently lost by tidal or wave action due to the sheltering effects of the headlands.

Consequently the beach and the mobile sand dune behind it can always rebuild after the storm has passed.

By the mid-1990s fencing was erected across the top of the beach to stop the practice of people simply hopping up and over the dunes.

The coastal pathway that runs along the top of the dune was then planted with Marram grass and gorse.

Marram is tough and is most suited to sandy coastal areas, where it does a valuable job in trapping the windblown sand and stabilising dunes through its extensive network of roots.

The dune provides a varied habitat for thousands of invertebrates, where the bare pat-

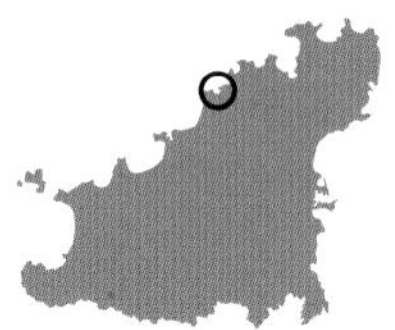

ches of sand provide warmth and the tussocks of Marram and other plants provide shelter.

I'm reliably told that one of the most distinctive is the striped snail Helix pisana, which attaches itself to plants high above the surface of the dune.

I will take their word on that one, as snail-searching is not my favoured pursuit on a visit to Port Soif, but what I can see with my own eyes is just how well the upper beach has recovered and that it looks resplendently healthy.

The management of the sand dune behind Port Soif has long included encouraging pedestrians to keep to the footpath.

Taking short cuts or jumping down the dunes onto the beach can create loose areas as the vegetation's roots, which stabilise the dune, become damaged.

When a large bare patch of sand on the dune occurs this can 'blow out' during a storm, causing a large hole to develop.

Environment says that such blowouts are sometimes difficult to repair as vegetation can be slow to establish.

So people, the answer is don't.

Stick to the paths.

Left
The dunes' vegetation provides a magnet for snails

"It would have been a bit dodgy coming in there under sail as there is quite a lot of reef on the outside"
Barry Paint

CHAPTER 5

PORTINFER
PECQUERIES & PULIAS HARBOUR

These days it is best known as a playground for pranksters, but in times past Pulias and Pecqueries had a part to play in the local fishing industry. Andrew Le Poidevin's title shot recreates the old harbour as it might have looked.

A PURPOSE FOR PULIAS

PULIAS Pond. Tucked away, as it is, between Pecqueries and Port Grat, can anyone tell me its purpose, one good reason for its existence?

It's there for a much better reason than simply to act as a display point for pranksters to leave garden gnomes or traffic signs and irritate the people who have to wade into the middle of the 'stinky pond' to the flat rock to retrieve them.

But as inconsequential an area of coast as it undoubtedly is in the early years of the 21st century, Pulias did have a history of usefulness.

Very little about it is recorded, but close inspection of the 1787 Duke of Richmond map of Guernsey reveals there once was a Pulias Harbour.

It has long been gone but the map is clear evidence that prior to the placement of a shingle bank to keep the seas at bay from this little sanctuary for birds and stolen gnomes, local fishermen of the north-west coast had another area in which to moor their sail-propelled fishing boats.

The 1787 map indicates a spur of some sort which, no doubt, would have kept the craft sheltered from the worst of the south-westerlies, and although you will find no one alive to recall such a harbour, the old tales remain, to add credence to the story of a purpose for Pulias.

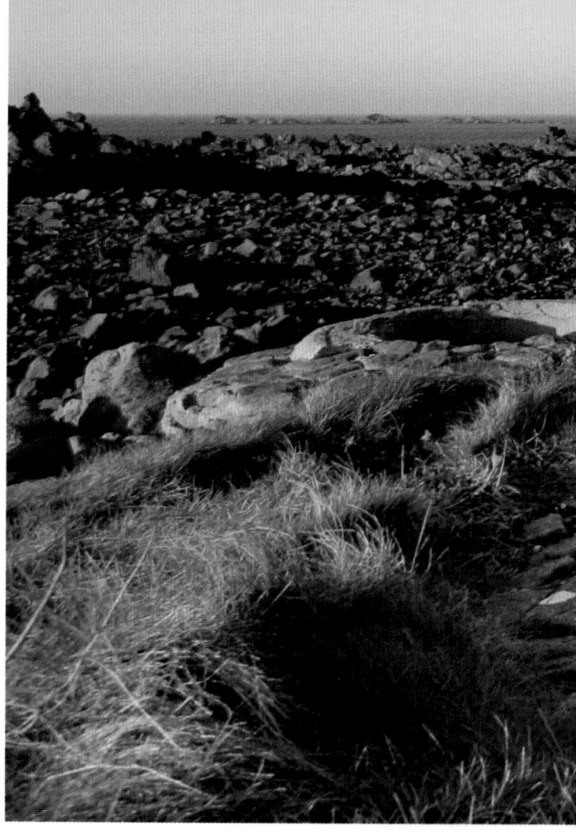

Those tales refer to the flat rock in the middle of Pulias Pond as Lunch Rock, a place where the wives of local fishermen would leave lunch for their husbands, who would sail up the channel and without having to come ashore, reach across and collect their grub.

The mere fact that a harbour had disappeared off the Guernsey maps by the end of the 19th century tends to suggest it was not a very handy place to have one.

That is borne out by Barry Paint, who, before taking a seat in the States, had acquired more knowledge of local waters and its approaches than arguably any living person.

'I'd never heard of it as a port,' admitted the former pilot.

'It would have been a bit dodgy coming in there under sail as there is quite a lot of reef on the outside.

'There are several channels in there but weaving your way in the rocks under sail would not have been easy and there is quite a strong current there too.'

Nearby Port Grat is, Barry says, far better suited to mooring fishing boats and provides easy access to the seas.

The wall on the south side of Pulias indeed

Above
German gun emplacements overlooking Pecqueries Bay

Opposite
Pulias prank: Father Christmas turns up in all sorts of places

looks every inch a piece of coastal wall, although there is no record of when it was built.

What is on record, though, is a lovely old tale that appears in a scrapbook of historian J. P. Warren's 'Study in the History of Guernsey', held in the Priaulx Library.

Under the headline 'The alarm of Pulias,' it tells the story of three unruly young Guernseymen – they had them then, too – who threw the island into a state of panic, and supposedly caused the death of some with flaky hearts, with their drunken frolics on the night of Sunday 4 March 1781.

It was an unsettling period in which to be a Guernseyman.

As an island, we feared a French invasion.

But that night these three young Militiamen over-indulged and on the way home up the coast from a muster of Militia forces, reached a lonely house near the marsh of Pulias at the foot of Noirmont Hill, on which a watch was kept and there was a warning beacon ready to be fired.

The story goes that the practical jokers knocked on the door of the cottage and made themselves out to be members of a 10,000-strong French invasion force.

The only people at home were a blind old man and his wife, who subsequently raised the alarm.

She told her story to the men at Noirmont, who lit the beacon, and the signal spread like wildfire along the coast.

It was enough for the garrison troops to be called onto parade.

The Militia, minus the three drunks, also turned out and the hunt began for the enemy.

Quite where you would hide 10,000 French soldiers with muskets in the Guernsey of 200 years ago takes some imagination.

And it wasn't long after daylight that the powers realised they had been well and truly had.

An official enquiry was set up into this breach of security and although fingers of suspicion were pointed at an unnamed trio, no individuals were brought to book. Not immediately, anyway.

Three Militiamen did make a sudden departure from the island, though.

Elisha Dobree mentions names in her book, 'Livres des Crimes', but no more than that Mr Falla and his friends, who returned to the island years after, were heavily fined.

PULIAS TRAGEDY

THE 'Grand Saut Rocher' reef lurks half-a-mile from the entrance to the old Pulias harbour and on a wicked night in November 1848, claimed the lives of eight mariners.

The tale of the doomed Sea Witch bears an uncanny resemblance to the Prosperity tragedy 126 years later in that it involved a cargo of wood and the crew had been so close to safety.

It was between 4 and 5 in the morning when the 199-ton brig, on its way from Sierra Leone to London, went aground close to Pulias.

The master and seven crew perished.

Three survived.

Masses of African oak bobbed about in the angry sea the following day as hundreds of islanders arrived at this under-developed and inhospitable piece of coastline to see the wreck with their own eyes.

The Star newspaper captured the mood in words so typical of the time, when using 100 when 10 would have sufficed was the order of the day:

'The capacious bay itself is an awful but sublime object of contemplation. Thickly strewn with gigantic granite rocks of every diversity of form, it proclaims, in its rugged features, inevitable destruction to any vessel that may have the misfortune to be driven within its limits.

'On this wild scene was behold most prominently the fore part of the wreck, firmly fixed in the rocks, surrounded with a confused mass of spars, rigging, timbers etc., twisted and crushed into every imaginable form.'

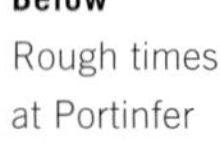

Below
Rough times at Portinfer

SCOT ON THE ROCKS

Many of the beams of the African oak were spread over the rocks and such was the close proximity to the shore that it took little effort to discover the eight drowned seamen, who were taken to nearby Grandes Rocques barracks.

In the coming days, they were taken the two miles north to Vale Church cemetery, where their bodies lie in one tomb.

The wreck of the Sea Witch resulted in more calls for a lighthouse at Pleinmont.

In a letter to The Star, 'A Sailor's Friend' argued that it was high time we had one.

'The chief objection [is] that it would be so frequently mistaken for the Scilly light as to lead to a far greater loss of life and property than at present. This is too absurd to argue about.'

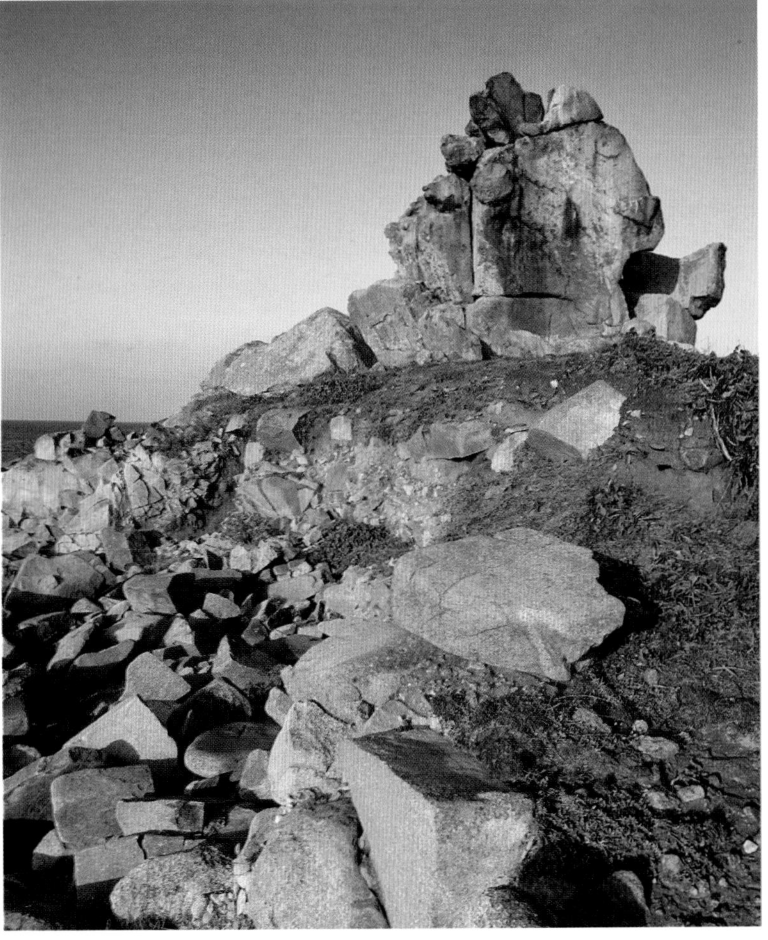

Above
Kellys Rock, named after Scot 'Walking Kelly' whose real name was Hubert Haig

PULIAS pond stands no more than a couple hundred metres east of Cliff Rock, the tall grey granite clutch of stone that will catch the eye as you swing past the old La Passee housing estate and approach the coast road at Les Pecqueries.

Cliff Rock is also known as Kelly's Rock in testament to the strange behaviour of the erstwhile local Scot, known by most in the early years of the 20th century as 'Walking Kelly'.

Real name Hubert Haig, he always dressed in a kilt and took it upon himself to walk 20 to 30 miles every day.

One of his stopping-off points was Les Pecqueries, where it was the norm for him to take himself off to the headland and break stones, hence the unofficial naming of the rock as Kelly's Rock.

SURFING AT THE GATES OF HELL

ON A spring tide and with a gale blowing from Les Hanois, Portinfer proves how fierce and unrelenting the forces of nature can be – and it's the perfect place to take a 6ft short board.

I just wish the caller had been right.

We were talking Portinfer and what its history might be when the man on the other end of the phone said: 'Do you know, Portinfer translates to "the Gates of Hell"?'

Sounded good to me.

After all, how many times have we sat in the warmth of our buffeted cars in the top car park, overlooking a raging sea thumping into the headland which divides Port Soif from Portinfer, and seen a foaming, watery hell climbing towards us, only to stop a few dozen yards away?

That's Portinfer at its most spectacular, with a spring tide and gale blowing down from Les Hanois. Under a blue sky or the blackest of storm clouds, it is an impressive sight and one of those natural reminders of the phenomenal power of the sea.

But Portinfer does not mean anything akin to 'the Gates of Hell', as good a description as that may be.

Dive not into the bulging seas in this rock-strewn bay but into the century-plus old book, 'Ancient Names of the Bays Etc.' – riveting title – and the official definition of Portinfer is as ordinary as the bay at low tide, when its beautiful white sand is exposed, as well as dozens of large granite boulders awaiting the errant surfer or bodyboarder.

Portinfer means anything from harbour to port, or carrying place.

Where hell came into it, I don't know, although it is a hellish thought to be aboard any form of craft being driven through the relatively narrow entrance of this bay in the midst of a westerly gale.

All in all, Portinfer is not much of a bay, other than for those who like the thrill of balancing atop a 6ft short surfboard or simply watching those monstrous winter waves crashing in from the Atlantic.

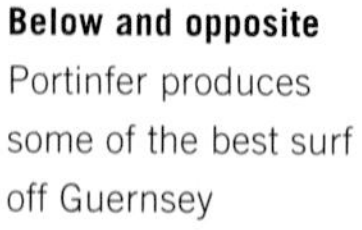

Below and opposite
Portinfer produces some of the best surf off Guernsey

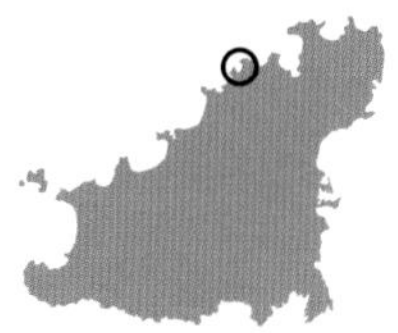

In common with Les Pecqueries around the corner, low- and mid-tide is not such a pretty sight, although at the waterline on a biggish low there is the potential for some fun body-boarding and swimming.

It has been many a year since yours truly has experienced such things, but in about the same youthful period, Portinfer did yield another unexpected delight near the end of the long reef you look across at from the top of Port Soif.

Venture down there on a summer's day and you will find two 'wells', ideal for diving or a spot of bombshelling into clear blue waters.

I'm told by the bloke who came up with the 'Gates of Hell' suggestion that the two wells have Guernsey-French titles – Le Grand Pisce and Le Petit Pisce – but you will have to take his word on that.

To find the 'pisces' requires much clambering over rocks close to 300m from the shingle-strewn top of the beach, with its wall of blue pebbles threatening to break over the coastal path.

One man who thrives on the bay's big waves is ace surfer Jonny Wallbridge.

He describes Guernsey waves as weak and soft, so relishes the rare chance to challenge himself on the bay's biggest rollers.

Portinfer, he says, 'packs more of a punch' than anywhere else locally.

'As far as Guernsey goes, Portinfer is the most consistent spot and provides the biggest waves,' he said recently, after what he described as the worst winter for surfing he has known.

'I haven't surfed for seven weeks,' he groaned.

'I will surf Portinfer more than anywhere.'

And he scoffs at the suggestion that those boulders you see at low tide are any threat to his safety.

'The bigger it is, the further out it breaks, so the rocks are not a problem.

'You can get some big sessions down there, usually winter or autumn time when you get a big swell tracking across from America.'

FIRST MENTION OF THE 'I' WORD

THERE will be some who hold the opinion that those who filled in the quarries at Portinfer to facilitate a shooting range should have kept right on going until the whole of Pecqueries Bay had been filled with rubbish to road level.

Indeed, the arguments as to the usefulness of Les Pecqueries and its potential as a landfill area raged for quite a time in the early months of 1983.

And study the ongoing saga through the front pages of the Guernsey Press that spring, and for the first time the 'I' word crops up.

We're talking INCINERATOR.

Yes, it is just 27 years since the option to burn our rubbish was seriously aired as part of the debate as to whether Pecqueries Bay should be filled with our rubbish. Among the options for the reclaimed land, never the prettiest, was a golf course.

As time has proved, if there are two things guaranteed to get Guerns in a frenzy, they are the mention of additional golf courses and incinerators.

There will be petitions, there will be marches – and so it was back in 1983 when it leaked out that the Board of Administration was secretly planning to place a 300ft stone breakwater across the entrance of one of Guernsey's least loved, least utilised bays and cover the rock pools beneath millions of tons of garbage and soil.

The BoA project did not have a chance, although it is said (not proved) to have had an ally in the Vale douzaine.

Les Pecqueries lies partly in Vale, partly in St Sampson's, and while the latter remained against the BoA plans, another of those political leaks at which Guernsey is so adept revealed that by a vote of nine to five, the Vale douzeniers were in favour of filling in a bay that may seem fairly useless to the unbiased and untrained eye, but was a supposedly important breeding ground for spawning fish.

Eric Walters, the people's deputy of all people's deputies, was having none of it, even though it was not on his patch.

He complained to the BoA 'in the strongest possible terms'.

It was his belief that not only did the board want a refuse tip and land reclamation scheme, it also planned to install a baling plant at Portinfer.

Naturally (and who could blame them?) the neighbours were also up in arms at the thought of losing their sea views and quickly set up Les Pecqueries Bay Residents' Association in a bid to fight off the planners in suits.

Among the enraged locals was a Dr Ferguson, who brought out a nice piece of medical terminology to describe the situation: 'We hope to arrest the development of this cancer before it reaches an incurable stage'.

To be fair, it had barely been diagnosed before the whole idea was cured by the power of the people, particularly those with friends in high places, namely the ever-persuasive Conseiller Roger Berry and La Societe Guernesiaise.

The conseiller, who was at the height of his political powers, slammed the idea.

He was putting his cards down in favour of filling in Belle Greve Bay.

Now, that would have been a fight to the political death.

The outed BoA did not say too much, other than reveal that should Les Pecqueries be filled, it would be very useful in staving off the day of a need for an incinerator.

A spokesman for the department was hardly emulating Nostradamus in adding: 'We're not facing a crisis but we certainly cannot afford to be complacent'.

Meanwhile, the petition grew as long as the

Opposite
Campaigners meet with Conseiller John Dorey in 1983 at the height of the row over the Pecqueries

line of lorries queuing up to dump rubbish at the close-to-capacity Bordeaux quarry.

Before long, 3,000 signatures had been gathered and it was clear that the BoA was on dodgy ground with its plan.

Twenty-seven years on, it has been long forgotten, but the waste issue rages on.

All the available quarries have been filled, Longue Hougue too. Belle Greve is an even bigger no-no and nobody can make up their mind about the big 'I'.

Were they right to leave Les Pecqueries alone?

It has to be said it is not much of a bay, with very little sand, and is hardly ideal for swimming.

But would it have made a good golf course?

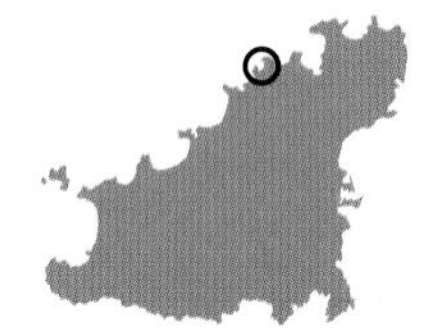

SIGHTS SETTING

FRANCIS QUIN, deputy of charm, has shot at Commonwealth Games and World Championship level and has taken his shotgun to clay target centres around the globe.

But in terms of setting, none compares with Portinfer, where the Guernsey Clay Target Club has had its home for the past 40 years.

'On a quiet day, you will see nothing better,' said Quin, still a crack shot, who recalls the club's arrival on the headland where previously a large quarry existed.

'On a high tide and on a still day you can see the [biodegradable] targets perfectly of the two international ranges.

'On a low tide, the fishermen's orange [pot] bobbers can sometimes catch the eye of the shooter,' he added.

The light conditions are superb and the club would not want to be anywhere else.

The range has slowly developed since the days when the Board of Administration agreed to the sport being accommodated on the site of the former Les Pecqueries Quarry.

The States agreed to it in 1968 and within a couple of years, the club was up and running there, Colin 'Doc' Best having managed to find sufficient topsoil to cover the required area.

For a while, a BMX track existed alongside, but that soon died a death and without a penny from government, the Clay Target Club has turned the area into a top-class range, where shooting is confined to Sunday mornings.

Francis can recall only one day when a major shoot was blown off-course.

'Going back to the 70s and the Channel Islands English Skeet Championships, it was blowing so hard that the clays wouldn't come out of the hut,' he said.

The shooters quickly realised it was a useless situation and abandoned the range for the warmth of the Rockmount.

Opposite
Francis Quin on the Portinfer shooting range

"In some cases I don't think people realise that the beach [Picquerel] is actually there, as you don't see it from the road"

Lara Bourgaize

CHAPTER 6

GRAND HAVRE
LES AMARREURS & LADIES BAY

Once the western entrance to the Braye which divided mainland Guernsey and the separated Vale, Grand Havre embraces seven beaches: Rousse, Le Picquerel, Les Amarreurs, Ladies Bay, Chouet, Tiger Bay and Grand Havre.

PARADISE FOUND

USELESS facts – they are everywhere but to prove that even the most inconsequential is worth recording, here is one associated with Le Picquerel.

Tap in the name on Google and among the more immediate offerings is a gem that tells us that it is a village in Guernsey and that it is 2.9 miles (4.7km) north of St Peter Port and 29 miles (47km) north west of St Helier.

Well, there you go.

I prefer to think of Le Picquerel as one of the seven corners of Grand Havre which, within

its total environs between the twin heads of Chouet and Rousse, boasts seven beaches: Tiger Bay (real name Champ Rouget), Chouet, Ladies' Bay, Les Amarreurs, Grand Havre itself, Le Picquerel and Rousse.

So much choice, so much natural beauty.

Back in the 19th century a small shipyard existed at Les Amarreurs, but sadly you won't find any traces of it.

A century ago Grand Havre also had a regatta to rival that of any staged locally.

Its shape and vantage points made for ideal viewing of the small sailing craft competing against one another on the water.

But despite a short revival 30 years ago, (the last one was staged in the early 80s) the regatta is now a thing of the distant past and would never return to its glory days simply because of the introduction of the motor to replace sail.

After all, there are a very limited number of things you can do to amuse on the water when you bring size and horse power into the equation, as opposed to basic seaman's skills.

Its two havens – Les Amarreurs and Rousse – were built shortly after the reclamation of the Braye, which makes the two of them about 200 years old.

With the reclamation, 'La Bouche du Valle' was shut once and for all, and with it the tidal movements of hundreds of centuries altered, as water no longer flowed from west to east and vice versa.

But since the bouche was silenced it is a fair bet that very little has changed about this under-used collection of bays under the one grand title.

That, in itself, is a shade puzzling as everything is there, certainly at half tide upwards.

At low tide it is a beachcomber and naturalist's paradise, but they are small in number and when you reflect on the general absence of crowds it is probably a good thing for Grand Havre and only adds to its charm.

Sundown over Les Amarreurs can be a staggeringly beautiful scene that nowhere in Guernsey can beat.

Opposite
The view from Rousse Tower

THE ESTATE WITH ITS OWN, GLORIOUS BEACH...

HOUSING estates tend not to be known for their exciting visual situation.

Well, not Guernsey ones anyway – with the wonderful exception that is Le Picquerel.

For that we can probably thank a man of the cloth and the Germans.

Before the war Le Picquerel's sandy mix of common land and scrub featured a nice tearoom and two little cottages.

But come the Occupation all three were flattened and, with the war over, consideration was given to what do with this western part of wider Grand Havre.

The Rev. Parkinson, who owned the land, agreed to sell to the States and in 1949 the go ahead was given to build some much-needed homes for workers and their young families.

In total, 16 were built and were standing by 1950.

Structurally, they are little changed in 60 years, but one thing they will always have is a wonderful view of one of the island's finest bays and the sound of the sea washing the shore at only a proverbial stone's throw away.

No. 9 Le Picquerel is no more than 70 metres away from the beach and, if you hadn't noticed already, this officially unnamed stretch possesses some of the finest sand on our western shores.

For 60 years now, children of the Picquerel have had nature on their doorsteps.

This is one place where nobody can claim to be bored.

If it's not the softest of sand and a safe stretch of water to swim in that attracts you, then you can always try shore fishing or go cockling on the lowest waters.

Then, of course, there is a common for the youngsters to kick a football around on.

Lara Bourgaize and her five children have been brought up on this salty funland of natural riches.

First it was daughters Emma, then Christina, Kelly and now – certainly making the most of the place – twins Troy and Blake.

The identical 10-year-olds live on the beach when they are not at school at Hautes Capelles or tucked up in bed.

Below
The beach at Le Picquerel
Opposite
The housing estate at Le Picquerel

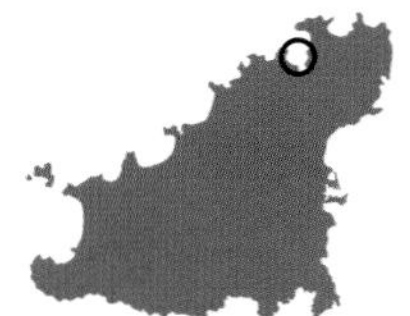

And mother Lara, who has lived on the estate for the past 13 years, believes the headland offers just about everything to keep her youngest two occupied, living the most healthy of existences.

'The boys are fishing mad,' she said.

'They stand in the water and walk backwards up the beach as the tide comes up.

'It's great for baiting too. They had a bass only last week.'

It was mid and very much flaming June when we spoke in Lara's front room about the benefits of living so close to the sea.

She said that the views towards Les Amarreurs and the Vale Church can be so startlingly attractive that she has to drag herself out of bed sometimes.

'To my two if I say "come on, we have to go out", they say they don't want to, simply because there's so much for them to do here.'

Troy and Blake bring home a variety of fish, most notably mullet, bass and bream. But Lara prefers to contribute by bringing home cockles when the tide drops and leaves the Rousse fleet of fishing boats high and dry. 'Jason, my partner, gets them out [of their shells] alive and fries them up with garlic and herbs.'

Perhaps pre-war, when a kiosk stood on this same headland, islanders were more inclined to use the Picquerel section of Grand Havre.

But with the tea and ice-cream supply long gone and no toilet facilities closer than the Vale Church corner of Grand Havre and at Rousse, perhaps we have the reason why this superb stretch of sand is so wastefully unused.

Above
Le Picquerel residents Lara Bourgaize (left) and Linda Ridley
Opposite
The Bourgaize twins Troy and Blake fishing on 'their own beach'
Overleaf
Le Picquerel children making the most of their natural playground

You can drive past after a summer's day and it is either totally empty or frequented by only a few locals.

'It's got more popular in the last couple of years,' reckoned Lara, while neighbour and good friend Linda Ridley, who has lived on the estate for 17 years, suggested: 'People seem to think it is our beach.'

Given their proximity to one another I guess that is a sound suggestion.

'You used to be able to go down there and there would just be people from the estate – it was so quiet,' said Linda.

'I think you get more from the Peninsula using it than other locals,' added Lara. 'It is so lovely. So white.'

And what you see is what you get.

This is not one of those beaches that harbours hidden dangers such as underlying and unseen currents.

'The tide comes in very quick from when it is low, but even then it doesn't get very deep until you get towards the top of the beach,' said Lara.

'It's a beach that is just about ideal for children, as long as they are supervised.'

But Lara is happy enough for this stretch of sand over which the North Legioners gaze out across the wider bay, to remain unofficially for locals only.

'In some cases I don't think people realise that the beach is actually there, as you don't see it from the road.

'There is also the toilets situation to keep them away.'

No other estate offers as much to this young mother.

'I wouldn't want to move to another one,' she says.

'And nor would her boys who, when asked how often they go fishing, reply in unison, "every day".

About 50 or so under-18s live in the houses, divided into two lines of eight in a V-shape fanning out from the Houmet end.

But not too many of the boys go fishing, which leaves only more for Troy and Blake to catch.

And as long as they are living at home on the Picquerel, it will be easy enough for them to do.

PowerMatch

Ted Baker

GUERNSEY'S OWN LITTLE OYSTER BAY

OYSTER farming has been a feature of Grand Havre for decades.

But after Richard Falla ended more than 20 years of often back-breaking work by handing over to Len Collenette, it is now Chris Le Pelley who is working the bay's beds in conjunction with the Jersey Oyster Co.

There are three specific areas of shellfish farming in wider Grand Havre: one close to Chouet tearoom and the other two near Rousse pier.

Just around the headland at Port Grat is a fourth.

Chris grows the oysters from seed to a good size, at which point they are harvested and exported to Jersey.

Having previously operated his Rocquaine Shellfish Ltd business from that bay, he opted to move up the coast to the more sandy, more accessible and, most importantly, protected Grand Havre beds. Before he left the Rocquaine operation a major storm wiped out 80% of his stock, but he feels Grand Havre offers him more peace of mind and the chance of making money from growing oysters from seed to a point where they are moved on to either Jersey or France.

'We have been running the three sites for two years and we only grow seed.

'We bought the seed in from Europe and/or locally, but now we just deal locally after the disease problems in Europe,' said Chris.

'We grow the seed for about a year until it reaches a certain size and export it.

'We sell on to other sea farms who grow them to maturity.

'It has been successful.'

It's not one of those jobs that needs daily attendance.

'It requires below a two-metre tide to work it. We usually operate when they get down to a 1.6m tide.'

Although irregular work, it can be tough.

'You have got to turn the seed regularly. It's not a daily job but every eight weeks during the growing season we go down and turn the bags.

'We try to get the seed down for April/May time and it has a huge burst in springtime and again at the end of the year, when the water is still warm. We look to export February, March, April, May.'

As harvesting and laying new seed can be quite labour-intensive, Chris calls upon the Jersey side of the operation to help out in those periods.

Left
Sunset over Grand Havre
Opposite
Playtime on the pier at Les Amarreurs

THE BAY OF THE BIG HARBOUR

THE bay of the big harbour eh?

Where are the cranes and the ships? Well, there might have been, you know. Step back in time a mere 330 years and this bay of bays was being eyed seriously as a harbour for the Royal Navy of King Charles II, one of parallel importance to that in St Peter Port.

Deep in the Island Archives is a Royal Survey of Guernsey made by Col. George Legge, the man charged with creating a map of the then two islands of Guernsey.

In 1680 Clos du Valle was still separated from the other nine parishes by the Braye du Valle channel, the western end of which was at Grand Havre.

Various island authorities were consulted by Legge as to the suitability of a navy base at this western end of the channel, but the majority were against such an idea.

While some thought that at high water it suited nicely, with its broad extent of water, on the downside its approaches were hazardous, the general depth too shallow and this harbour would dry out at low tide.

Most of all, though, it was not considered large enough for a naval harbour where large sailing vessels required space to manoeuvre.

So, after a great degree of head scratching and consideration, Legge suggested the place be 'spoiled' so the dastardly French could not make use of it if they chose to invade.

What exactly Legge meant by spoiled is unclear, but anyway, the authorities of the time were having none of it.

The Grand Harbour was for preserving, nothing was done and it retained the look we enjoy centuries later.

Instead, the Martello towers either side of the mouth of the greater Grand Havre, to the west at Rousse and the east at Chouet, were to assume even more importance in keeping guard against prospective invaders – well, the French.

As the esteemed Guernsey historian Victor Coysh once noted in his appreciation of the bay: 'To observe Grand Havre at high water and when the tide is low is to behold two entirely different scenes'.

While that can be said about many west coast bays, the vastness of this one makes it even more startling at opposite ends of the tidal range.

At high tide dozens of small fishing boats ride their moorings.

And at low water you can walk from Rousse Pier to its brother pier at Les Amarreurs.

In its time Grand Havre has been the scene of the odd ship's downfall.

Back in 1859, the barque Offspring went aground. But the wreck that really caught the eye was the steamer Ravensdale which, 80 years ago this November, steamed virtually all the way into the Houmet Tavern.

Now that must have been quite a sight, although not half as much of an attraction as it would be today with a packed room of diners chomping away in the conservatory out front.

It was a Sunday evening and the bells were ringing out from the Vale Church when the Ravensdale, carrying a cargo of basic slag bound for St Helier, somehow managed to miss the entrance to the Little Russel and headed up the now closed-off Braye and right into Rousse.

Its progress was stopped by the Platiere Rock, just off Rousse Pier.

The local fishermen jumped into their boats and raced to her assistance, but the Ravensdale – which had set out from Keady in Lincolnshire – was able to reach the beach under her own steam and came to rest on a sandy bottom opposite the Houmet.

John Le Tocq rushed to Mr E. Mahy's residence at the Garenne to implore him to

phone for a lifeboat, all this happening while the congregation of the parish church were enduring evensong, distracted by the thought of what might happen to those poor men on the loose steamer just across the bay.

They need not have worried and any prayers were answered by a full complement of seamen being rescued.

By the time the lifeboat arrived everyone had been saved.

It turned out that the Ravensdale's lack of direction owed everything to a fault in its compass.

It brought much excitement to many islanders, who rushed there on a Sunday evening and were lured to see the odd sight of this hunk of metal sitting between Rousse and Picquerel for many days to come. Within a fortnight the ship had been unloaded and its cargo transferred from the stores of local coal merchant William Bird on South Side into another ship, before transferring to its original destination.

By now Guernsey Railway Co. Ltd had bought the Ravensdale, so badly pierced by the Platiere rocks that it would have to be abandoned.

The price: £15,000.

The enterprising Guernsey Railways plugged the holes by cementing over the cracks and ultimately it was switched to St Sampson's.

Above
The Collier Ravensdale aground in front of the Houmet

WHY THE BIG HARBOUR IS HOME

PAUL PENNINGTON'S wife jokes that only one thing keeps them from moving to Dorset and their beloved holiday destination, Weymouth.

And that, she says, is Grand Havre.

'Big Paul', a professional fisherman by day and a part-time one in the summer months, has loved this bay since his days as a kid and is kind enough to give me a leisurely scoot around wider Grand Havre at high tide on the most fantastic mid-June late afternoon imaginable.

The tide is springing, the kids of Les Amarreurs have no need to dive off the end of their pier as it is always swishing around their shins, and the kayakers are out in force.

'It's still one of the finest bays, this one,' he says as he stands at the tiller of his open 16ft old Guernsey fishing boat Sitra.

'I've never been bored down here, whether it is cockling or swimming,' he adds with a sweep of self-nostalgia born out of childhood memories.

Sitra does not have as many neighbours as she once would have had, but while the total number of boats moored at the Rousse side of 'GH' has reduced in these modern times of fashionable marinas, it remains busy enough and could easily be mistaken for the most beautiful of small Brittany ports.

It is more than a quarter-of-century since GH staged the last of its annual regattas.

They were not quite the salty spectaculars of its grandest period in the 1920s and 30s, but fun all the same.

Paul misses them and the associated land fun, such as tug-of-war between those in rival parts of this bay of many areas.

Fishing-wise, it still stands the test of time,' says the man who has moored here for 30 years. Not the oldest-serving by any means, but experienced enough.

'It still has pretty good fishing if you know where to go,' he adds. 'The mackerel are a bit scarce this year but they might still come on.'

And you don't have to go out of the bay to catch good fish.

'Even on the outer moorings we go fishing in the autumn and get a lot of bass and bream.'

Up until 200 years ago or so, the ships came sailing into Grand Havre and would have picked their way up the channel that divided mainland Guernsey and the Vale.

Now we are restricted to a high tide tour of the bays within a bay.

Les Amarreurs is the most inviting, unless your interest lies in windsurfing or kiteboarding across Ladies' Bay into Chouet.

As bays go, Les Amarreurs is some way short in the quality sand stakes as opposed to Le Picquerel across the bay, but the old stone pier has entertained youngsters for generations.

This particular afternoon they have rushed to the pier from school, and up close aboard Sitra it is easy to see why.

The sea is flat, clear blue and lapping the last 10 metres of the pier.

Perfect, in fact.

Below
A deserted beach at Le Picquerel
Opposite
Local fisherman Paul Pennington

"Chouet in those days was very special to me and I have very fond memories of the place. Unfortunately, today it has changed beyond comprehension and has lost a tremendous amount of its character"

René Mouraille

CHAPTER 7

CHOUET

No place smells quite like this part of the island coastline, but it was not always so and it was the perfect home to the fictonal Guernsey character Ebenezer Le Page.

CHEWY CHANGES · STRANGER THAN FICTION
CHOUET'S COWBOY CLUB · FROOME WITH A VIEW

CHEWY CHANGES

IT'S a 'mineral-resource safeguarding area' to the planners.

To you and me, just plain old Chouet with the pronunciation emphasis on the chewy. Not 'shoo-eh', simply 'chewy'.

As an area, we know it mainly as a place to dump household waste. In recent times there's been a nasty smell in the air and on several Sundays throughout the year there's banger racing on the beach.

But, as the Royal Haskoning report into the island's coastal defences is pleased to announce, Chouet is much more than a mineral-resource safeguarding area – does that mean emergency quarrying reserve? – and somewhere to put our rubbish and race around noisily in old cars.

Chouet is steeped in history – and, to be more precise, for the best part of a couple of centuries, quarrying – and is home to an array of fortifications dating back to the Napoleonic wars of the late 18th century and the German Occupation.

Like many island spots, it has probably lost a lot of its charm and character. Certainly one-time Chouet resident Rene Mouraille thinks so.

On a rare return to the island last year, he visited the property that replaced the little house, not much bigger than a hut, that he grew up in with his grandparents, Bill and Ellen Domaille. Called Tiger Bay, the building has been replaced by a modern bungalow. Rene recalled living on the headland just after the Occupation until leaving the island in 1957.

Among his recollections are the building linked to the Ebenezer Le Page story.

'My cousin, James Youlton [Guernsey lifeboats], lived there for a while and I seem to recall it was a white cottage that overlooked

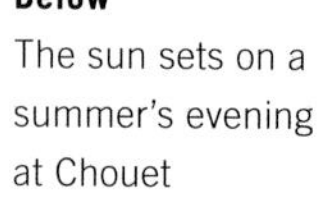

Below
The sun sets on a summer's evening at Chouet

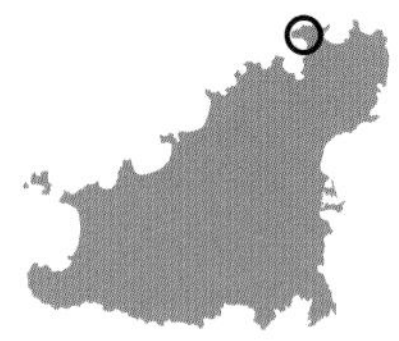

Ladies' Bay,' he said.

'There were two stone quarries a little further toward the Martello tower and between them ran a German tunnel which had a side chamber running off at a right angle. The tunnel must have been at least 200m long.'

He said there was also a German bunker at the top, which had steps running down to it.

'I remember the door was rather odd, being square-shaped, and halfway up the wall it had a metal door still attached. I think it was a signal station but can't be sure,' he said.

'Tiger Bay was actually lived in by my grandparents, but they couldn't have been very comfortable as it looks so small. It was situated in an old granite quarry.

'I don't know much about the house that was located on the site of the [destroyed] German tower, but I suppose it must have had quite a nice view.'

Rene said that the granite quarries were remarkable and there was a great deal of wildlife and yellow gorse.

'Chouet in those days was very special to me and I have very fond memories of the place.

Unfortunately, today it has changed beyond comprehension and has lost a tremendous amount of its character. I was very sad to learn of the loss of the German tower. It should never have been destroyed,' he said.

'Sometimes at night you could hear strange noises out at sea. It sounded like a naval battle perhaps 30 or 40 miles away. I have only heard it twice and the old man [Bill] called it "les cannons des noises", which was some phenomenon far out under the ocean.

'With hindsight, it may well be associated with tectonic-plate differential, but it was eerie to lie in bed listening to it.'

Half a century on, Chouet headland retains fantastic views across Grand Havre and out to sea. It's also popular with joggers, dog walkers, model plane enthusiasts and, half hidden away in the bottom of a shallow gravel quarry, pistol shooters.

But, for sure, more has gone than remains.

Above
Erosion is a problem for this section of coastline
Overleaf
The hole at Mont Cuet

STRANGER THAN FICTION

EBENEZER LE PAGE never existed, of course, but read G. B. Edwards' masterpiece and there are times when you can simply shut your eyes and smell the Chouet sea air.

Strictly speaking, Le Moulin – old Ebenezer's lifetime home – never existed either, but study a copy of Ebenezer Le Page's Guernsey map (to be found in many a local bookshop) and there is no mistaking where it was mythically situated.

Author Edwards probably had in mind the now-demolished granite cottage within the small copse of pines adjacent to the 'Torrey Canyon quarry' when he chose 'Ebby' a home.

It was situated just 50 yards from the sea and no more than 100 from the little bay known on the old maps as Champ Rouget, but otherwise as Tiger Bay to informed locals.

The book never exactly pinpoints Ebenezer's home, but the reader is left in no doubt that it is at Chouet, close to the common and within yards of the sea.

Another pointer to the exact position of Le Moulin is when in the most vicious of winter gales he half expects Mont Cuet to come tumbling down on top of him.

The old cottage was flattened many years ago and there are no obvious remnants, although there is a 20m stretch of granite wall, possibly a boundary one to the north. And it is probably just as well it is no longer there and indeed that Ebenezer is long gone, because he would not have been a happy chappy.

In truth, he seldom was. As he became old and cars replaced horse-drawn carts as a mode of travel, he hated them and avoided riding in one until the very last days of his mythical life.

So it hardly takes a genius to imagine that this fiercely proud, stubborn and most

CHOUET BAY, GUERNSEY

grumpy of old Guernseymen would have been driven to distraction by the steady stream of vehicles heading for the green tip and the recycling bins, not to mention the lumbering, rubbish-laden lorries which also go north up the Mont Cuet Road, bound for the dump.

Nor would he have been happy to live under a model aeroplane launching pad and would surely have caused a stink about the stink of the island's biggest tip across the road.

On the plus side – and somehow I don't imagine it would have been much of a plus for him – he could have toddled along the small, dusty path to the nearby tea rooms for a cuppa or sat at the barbecue table in front of his house, looking down at the pretty anchorage of a dozen or more fishing boats.

Chouet headland will not have altered in shape in 100 years, but take away the cars and lorries and it was still pulling many islanders towards it at the end of the 19th century.

The 1901 census proves it, with reference to several families living there.

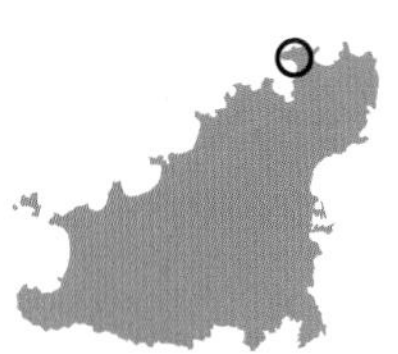

Nowadays, there is just one house situated on the Chouet headland, but a century ago, when Ebenezer was still a very young man living with his parents there, he would have been close neighbours to a family of five living in Martello tower number 10.

Looking at the surviving tower, which stands proudly looking out south-westwards towards Grand Havre, it is almost unbelievable to think that, in 1901, 73-year-old Isaac Goddard lived in it with his wife, Jane, 65, their daughter, Elizabeth, 46, and her two children, Francis de Francise and Ellen de Francise.

The de Francise name is both unusual for Guernsey and rare, but could there be a Spanish link?

George Domaille, veteran of the entire L'Ancresse area and whose boyhood goes back to the early 1930s, was passed down the story of a Spaniard being washed up on the rocks at Chouet and, rather than return home, he opted to stay and live in the tower.

It was said that his name was Francisco and that he married a local woman and had at least two children, one of whom became a schoolmistress. Could Elizabeth, who originally hailed from Alderney, have married Francisco and by the 1901 census had he done a runner – or simply died?

What the Goddards lacked in comfort they made up for with idyllic summer views.

The picture across the bay towards Grand Havre and Rousse is surely unchanged in 1,000 years, let alone 100. By day in 1901, the area was relatively busy with quarrymen going about their business at any of the 14 quarries shown in the Chouet/Mont Cuet area on period maps.

Virtually all of them have now been filled, but one of those remaining has been known as Torrey Canyon oil quarry for the past 40 years. Ebenezer would not have been happy about that, either. Once Mont Cuet is filled and the large, green hougues of the distant past return and are once again safe to explore and utilise, the headland we know as Chouet, but shown as Mont Crevel on the 1787 map by the Duke of Richmond, will be restored to its natural best.

But that is many, many years away yet.

Above left
Chouet circa 1950 including the probable cottage home of G.B. Edwards' famous Guernsey character

Below
The road where Ebenezer lived

Overleaf
The German tower which once overlooked Chouet

DANGER
PLEASE
KEEPOUT

CHOUET'S COWBOY CLUB

FOR as long as there has been a little isle called Guernsey – or previously Guernesey, Sarnia or Lisia – there has probably been a lovely, quiet, sandy stretch of white beach at Chouet.

And, until the quarry blasters came along a couple of centuries ago, the only sounds to be heard were the waves, the wind and the seabirds.

Then, in 1970, the old bangers arrived a dozen times a year to shatter the solitude of a beach which for nearly 40 years now has been the spiritual home of the Guernsey Autocross Club.

And while the noise-abatement people probably don't appreciate the skill and fun had by all those banger racers either side of the supposedly hot-spot summer months when it is out of bounds to them, Chouet is obviously as suited as anywhere locally to this form of motorsport.

Apart from the roar of engines, which, it's said, can sometimes be heard in Herm, they don't do anyone any harm and the beach recovers in no time at all.

John Bichard, secretary of the GAC and the 'voice of autocross', said they couldn't get a better venue anywhere else and it has long been 'an accepted part of island life'.

But why are they a perfect match?

'It's a clear beach with good access. You've got the slip going straight onto the beach. The main thing is access.'

But it's more than the positioning of a slipway, surely?

In terms of sand, it is 'perfect', John acknowledges.

'It's not too soft, because running road tyres on it you don't need patches of soft sand. It's not a wet beach either. It has no streams moving across it, or big puddles.'

And while Vazon may allow for a bigger

circuit, Chouet is perfect for the club which started out in the sludge of St Sampson's Harbour and saw its hopes of a race track at Pleinmont rejected and then settled on the beach under the jurisdiction of the Vale parish, to which the club has to answer.

'Vazon gets wet, but this one doesn't because it is sloped,' says our resident expert, who has been involved with the club from the early 1970s.

Its hard surface also allows for a quick, natural recovery.

Racing goes ahead on a dozen or so Sundays a year and, John says, providing the sea goes right up the beach afterwards, it will be back to normal in two days.

'The sand is quite hard and you don't churn up big holes.'

The parish's accommodation of motor sport has allowed the club to develop out of all recognition from its early days.

Membership in 2007 rose to 140, of which

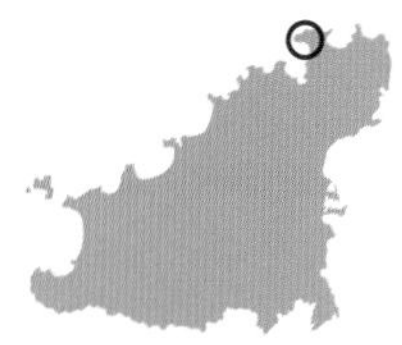

50 to 55 drive regularly. In the early days, drivers battled it out for the grand slam and man-of-the-day trophies. Now there are 45 at stake over the calendar year.

But there again, the sport has become altogether more serious than the initial days, when destruction appeared every bit as important as racing.

'It's definitely more serious now. They weren't so bothered about keeping the cars in those days.'

John explained the process that allows the sport to continue.

'We have to go to the Vale constables for permission and through an advocate it goes to the Royal Court, because we are applying for change of use of the beach.'

In theory, he says, the club could use the beach on any Sunday outside June, July and August, but does not wish to be greedy.

'We've stuck to 14. We race from September to May every two weeks. No application has ever been rejected.'

And with the course a good deal shorter than the one set up for sand racing at Vazon – by approximately a third – autocross can operate from half-tide down.

'Generally, we can get onto the beach three hours before low tide and start racing.'

With every passing year the club gets ever ingrained in the public psyche, which must be encouraging given that there is a degree of rebelliousness about the organisation.

John refers to it as 'a cowboy club'.

'We are a stand-alone club. Not affiliated to anyone.'

But like all the best cowboys, these guys – and girls – are serious.

They might not chew on cheroots and stare menacingly from under wide-brimmed hats, but the Chouet banger-racers have plenty of horsepower and, it seems, staying power.

Above left
Autocross stalwart
John Bichard
Below
Bangers are mashed
on the Chouet sands

FROOME WITH A VIEW

YOU need to be a fairly hardy soul to go bird-watching at the island's marine wildlife observatory at Chouet.

If the stiff northeasterly doesn't get you, the smell from Mont Cuet a few yards away just might.

It was six years ago that Roger Berry, then president of the Board of Administration, officially opened an observatory paid for by the RSPB and built by Vic Froome and Tony Grange.

Ronez provided all the materials free of charge and suddenly Guernsey's birdwatchers and those with a keen interest in general marine life had a solid roof over their heads, as opposed to crouching among big rocks across the little stony bay once known as Les Landelles on the way to Creve Coeur.

There is no better place locally to observe the annual autumn peak sea-watching period, but you might be advised to bring your own clothes peg to clip onto your nose.

The strong north-westerlies push gannets, kittiwakes, Arctic skuas, bonxies, manx and sooty shearwaters our way as they battle their way along the English Channel towards the Bay of Biscay.

And studying them from the relative shelter of the small, concrete hideaway facing north is a reward Vic and many others take advantage of.

Talking to me about birds goes over my head in much the same way as the thousands of gulls that plague the area. But I do know a gull when I see one and there are a fair few down this way, their natural waste staining the rocks white either side of the observation point.

'Guernsey is artificially feeding 4,000 gulls a day and another 2,000 with our sewage outfall,' said Vic, as a large proportion of them circled over the smelly dump or awaited their turn while plonked on a rock close to the sea, just a few metres away.

The observatory's walls tell the uneducated – like me – just what might be seen from the viewpoint.

'We try to get people to realise it's not all about birds,' he added.

But as fish tend to stay below the surface, in the main it is birds, including storm petrels, otherwise known as St Peter birds because they look as if they are walking on water as they venture out at dusk from their breeding colonies.

Above left
Cormorants enjoy a rest off Creve Coeur
Above right
Gulls flock to Le Grand Camp Bay
Right
Marine life observer Vic Froome

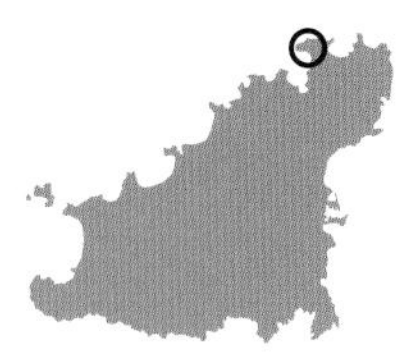

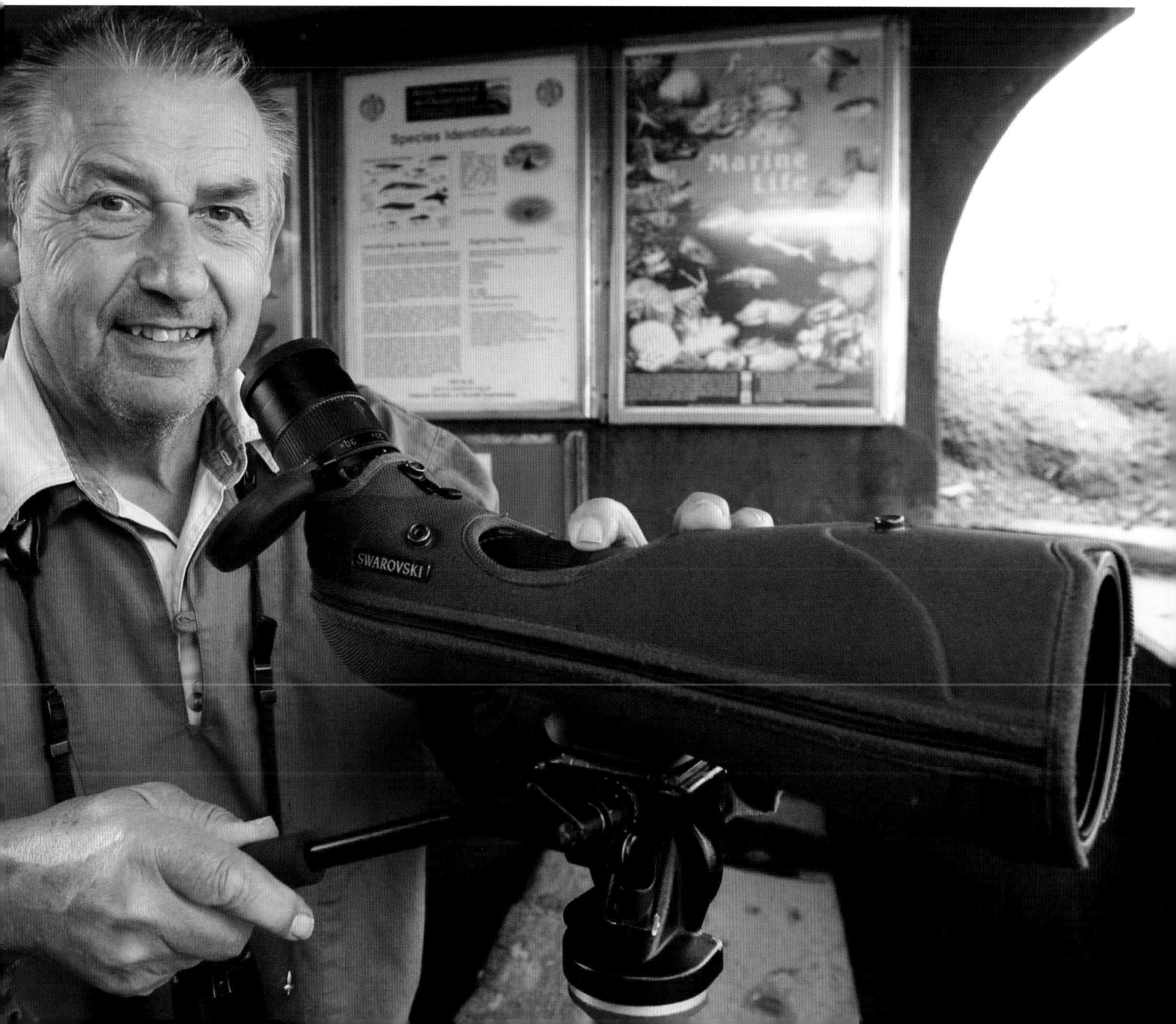

"There are quite a few anglers who will come out here [to Big Bill] and the Bailiwick record bass was caught here"

Jason Brown

CHAPTER 8

PEMBROKE
& LA JAONNEUSE

The western end of wider L'Ancresse takes in rugged Creve Coeur, little La Jaonneuse, a headland with two forts and a section of Guernsey's most popular stretch of beaches.

NORTHERN ROCK · FADING STAR
LONG LOST CAUSE · BAY WATCH

NORTHERN ROCK

IT IS all there to see and yet you don't see it.

On the face of it, the half-mile between Creve Coeur headland and the slipway at Pembroke is one of our coastline's quieter and uncelebrated spots, but talk to the 'knowledge' and you quickly discover there is more to the place than you ever would have imagined.

The 'knowledge' is George Domaille, stalwart of the L'Ancresse Common Council, and over a very wet autumnal hour in his company trudging the headland, beach and rocks, it proves remarkably revealing.

Sure, I knew all about the Star Fort, the now well-disguised earthwork fortification on the Pembroke headland, but La Chaise au Pretre was news to me, as was the rock which may well have provided Victor Hugo with the inspiration to finish off Gilliatt, the hero of the classic Toilers of the Sea.

Then there are those mysterious boulders with similarly-sized holes that lie on the upper reaches of the Pembroke beach which, until the Germans came along, ran either side of a large shingle bank as a natural break in between the original sea walls.

It's all such a shame that this unheralded stretch, which includes the delights of La Jaonneuse beach, is blighted by the stench that so often blows off the nearby Mont Cuet dump.

But back to the start with that chair of the priest, the Anglophile name for the megalithic La Chaise au Pretre, which sits at the foot of La Hougue au Pretre close to the path that swings around the Creve Coeur headland from Chouet into greater L'Ancresse.

The legend of La Chaise au Pretre is that a holy prior from the old Priory of St Michel du Valle had contact with the Devil on this windswept spot looking north-west.

Having vanquished the Devil, the prior was so pooped that he sank back exhausted into a conveniently shaped armchair of grey granite.

I'm sorry, but I'm not having it myself.

To fight and beat off the Devil is one thing, but to suddenly find at your disposal such a remarkably shaped seat of stone is just too much to believe.

Nevertheless, it is an impressively set-out clutch of stones and you can see where those

Below
La Jaonneuse

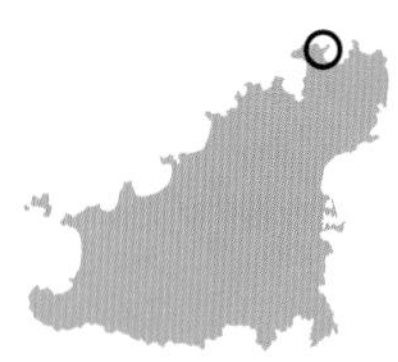

who made up all this folklore nonsense got the idea from.

The prior's seat is, says our resident expert, often misidentified and the publication Megalithic Guernsey is among those that looked at the wrong set of rocks.

Fewer than 50 metres away from the real Chaise au Pretre is another intriguingly shaped rock, which the young George Domaille delighted in fooling about on with his mates back in the early 1930s.

For some unknown reason the rock took a hit from the Germans, but George knows it well enough and is sufficiently clued-up to Gilliatt's story in Toilers of the Sea that he is confident that Hugo may well have had this rocky outcrop in mind when he described the place Gilliatt chose to end his life by drowning.

His theory that the strangely named Gild-Hol-'Ur seat was situated at Creve Coeur stems from the fact that it fits the description in the book. 'It's the only one I know that was a proper seat,' he said.

'It was rounded all the way around the back and about 2ft 6in. deep. It was a seat that 10- to 15-year-olds could sit in quite comfortably. Quite why somebody should use an explosive charge and blow it up I don't know.'

I have an open mind myself on this theory, but I have firm negative thoughts as to George's next move, which was to pick up a handful of samphire and begin to eat it.

A rare enough plant, related to parsley and fennel, it is supposedly in season during spring, rather than summer.

Aficionados swear by the superior flavour, but again I'm not so sure and the clump from which George seeks a mid-afternoon bite is on the way out quickly. A week later, when I return to have another look through glasses that are not drowning in heavy rain, the samphire is as good as gone for another year.

George had also shown me the salty pleasure of another natural rocky delight in the form of sea beet, an ancestor of common vegetables such as beetroot, sugar beet and Swiss chard.

Wikipedia will tell you its leaves have a pleasant texture and taste when served raw or cooked, but I prefer to see them healthily spouting in between the stones at Creve Coeur than on any plate of mine.

Above left
Gilliatt's viewpoint?
Below
La Chaise au Pretre

FADING STAR

Top
Fort Pembroke
Above
UK archaeologist
Rene Mouraille
Opposite
Fort Pembroke on
Chouet headland

HERE'S a good local pub quiz question for you: which Guernsey headland has two forts? No need to look at any upside-down writing at the foot of the page, because I will tell you.

A small percentage of the Guernsey population will know the answer, but at the same time they may not know which is Fort Pembroke and which is the Star Fort.

That may sound a nonsense, but there is reason to doubt the real history of the old 'Platon' and its forts, one stone-built, the other of the earthwork variety and these days largely camouflaged by undergrowth.

Rose Henry – expert on all things L'Ancresse and the author of the History of L'Ancresse Common – believes the earthy Star Fort to be nearly 200 years old and the result of the early 19th-century conviction of the then Lt-Governor, Sir John Doyle, that Napoleon was likely to attempt to invade the Channel Islands.

She has documentary evidence to make her point, it coming in the form of the 'Actes des Etats' of 1815, when a request was made by Doyle for the States to recompense the owners of the land on which the fort encroached.

In that official States document, the fort was referred to as Fort L'Etoile, Fort en Etoile and Fortress de L'Etoile and the total area of the land utilised amounted to six vergees and 22 and three-quarter vergees.

The respected Guernsey historian James Marr, echoed Rose's views. In his book Bailiwick Bastions, he reckoned that it was likely to have been constructed so the Militia could practise and was never a long-standing operation.

He points out that James Cochrane's island map of 1832 makes no reference to the Star Fort and because of that he concludes that its transient career had already come to an end, within two decades of it being constructed.

Meanwhile, Eric Grimsley, who penned a book on the Martello towers of the Channel Islands, accepts that it was odd to build an earthwork fort so late as 1815 but it probably happened and for no other good reason than it was a useful exercise to occupy the time of unoccupied soldiers.

'There is no good reason for having it there,' he concedes.

But UK archaeologist and Guernsey raised Rene Mouraille is not entirely convinced of the documentary evidence and would not be surprised – indeed expects – that over the course of time the two forts have been muddled somewhere.

He is confident that the earthwork star-shaped fort is post-medieval and not the early 19th-century creation suggested by others.

With regard to the documentary evidence in Rose's book, Rene has thought long and hard as to its relevance and draws his own conclusion.

'I think what this statement is referring to is land being purchased at the former Fort L' Etoile, which may have been refortified at this time as a temporary fortress of six vergees, which is around three acres, while Fort Pembroke was under construction.

'The 22 vergees [around eight acres] more than likely refers to land needed to build Fort Pembroke which is a little closer to the sea

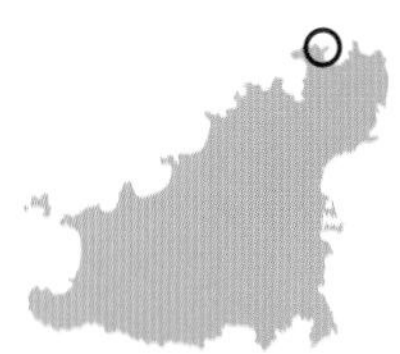

edge. I think Fort de L'Ancresse and Fort L'Etoile are one and the same... ie Star Fort at L'Ancresse.'

Rene has been fascinated about the earthwork fort from his childhood days living in the area. 'I first came across it in 1965 while over here on holiday,' he said.

'I found an old Victorian map in Bill Domaille's Nissen hut at the back of our house at the Chouet. I noticed there were two forts marked next to each other at Pembroke. I knew the stone fort well, having visited it many times, so thought I'd have a closer look. 'I remember standing on a mound surveying the area for any signs of ruins or foundations – it was then that I realised that what I was standing on was in fact a civil war earthwork.'

Rene, whose day job is as a ranger for Newark and Sherwood District Council and who looks after Newark Castle, is intrigued and impressed by the Guernsey earthwork.

'Where I live we have the finest surviving earthworks of this period in the UK, and I knew exactly what I was looking at. I remember being very excited at the time at having found it but didn't report it to the authorities as I thought it was known about.

'The creation of star forts was a direct result of the introduction of black powder in use with French forces in Italy during the mid 15th century.

'Unlike their stone predecessors such as castles, earthen star forts stood up far better to enemy cannon fire having flatter and far lower profiles. Being made of earth and timber, they were cheaper and quicker to construct.'

He says one of the earliest examples of such defence works was at the second siege of Padua in 1509, when a monk and engineer, Fra. Giocondo, was entrusted with the city's defence.

Having torn down the old stone walls of the city, he built a large ditch and earthworks around Padua on which French cannon fire made little impression, resulting in the withdrawal of the French Army. '

This type of star fortification developed into sophisticated designs enclosing entire cities,' said Rene.

'Engineers such as Leonardo da Vinci were employed to design the defences of Florence. In the mid 1500s these designs spread all over Europe, with Italian engineers heavily in demand.

'Later, in the 17th century, such engineers as Menno van Coehoorn and Sebastian Vauban took these designs to their limits.'

As to why the Guernsey Star Fort at Pembroke is so important, he said:

'It is perhaps the only surviving fort of its kind in Guernsey and perhaps in all the Channel Islands.

'It would have been Parliamentarian and constructed to defend against Royalist landings at Pembroke Bay. I would suspect there may be others awaiting discovery.

'This fort deserves better presentation and is a worthy and interesting monument.'

Rene is willing to concede he may be wrong in his view that the earthwork is post-mediaeval, but does not think he is, on the grounds that the Pembroke example is more akin to post-mediaeval Civil War ones and that, had this type of fort been built in 1815, it would have been a largely obsolete type of defence, owing to the introduction of mortars during the 18th century.

He also questions why there was the need for two forts side by side at the same location. It does seem very odd.

'If this fort was built at this time, then it must have been in 1815, not 1816, as Napoleon had escaped from Elba in February 1815 but had met his fate at Waterloo on 18 June of the same year.

'This fort could well have been constructed very quickly as a result of the renewed French threat.

'But I still find this puzzling, as the Star Fort has every indication of being Civil War design rather than later. However, we must not assume anything at present, and it is possible that it may have been built as a temporary fortification prior to the building of the stone Fort Pembroke.'

He goes as far as saying that if the stone fort predates 1780-90 or even around these dates then it is more than likely that the Star Fort is of English Civil War times rather than later.

'I do know that 16 forts and 58 coastal batteries were built in the late Napoleonic period and perhaps around 1805, Fort Pembroke may have been part of this construction programme.

'The only way we may be able to verify this would be through archaeology and to put exploratory trenches in to look for dating evidence.'

Above
The old Star Fort's earthen slopes
Opposite
The fort interior

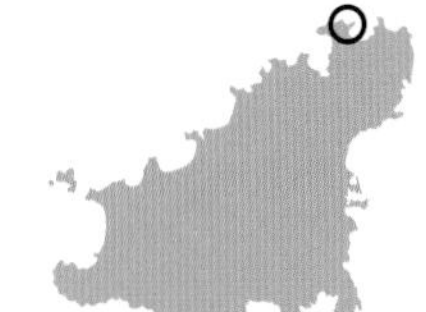

LONG LOST CAUSE

REGARDLESS of the true story of the earthwork fort at Pembroke, it has long been a lost cause in terms of upkeep.

Most people would simply not know it is there, its prongs heavily disguised by bracken and long, wild grass.

Aerially, it can be picked out easily enough and the likes of the L'Ancresse Common Council president George Domaille would ideally like to see it well maintained.

There was, he said, a time when it was looked after to maximise its looks but that drew in youngsters who, probably blissfully unaware of its historical significance, would use it for testing their off-road biking capabilities.

While Rene is keen not to be seen to be criticising others' work on the history of the site, he wonders whether the earthwork site could be what was originally known as Fort de L'Ancresse and an obsolete and forgotten civil war site ignored on some maps, as it had been buried in undergrowth and simply forgotten.

Until such time that detailed archaeology and dating evidence is conducted, we will never know for sure.

'If this old fortification was indeed reworked during the early 19th century, it may leave us with a problem archaeologically.

If the ditch was re-cut at this time, they may well have destroyed any dating evidence within the layers of the ditch. Let's hope that is not the case,' he said.

'Once Fort Pembroke had been built, the old star fort would have been abandoned and by the time the area was surveyed for mapping it may well have been overgrown and hidden from the eyes of the surveyors, who may well have been English, having little knowledge of the history of the area.'

For now, though, the counter views put a nice, mysterious slant to the whole story and, as Rene suggested: 'You could say it's the riddle of the lost fort in the dunes.'

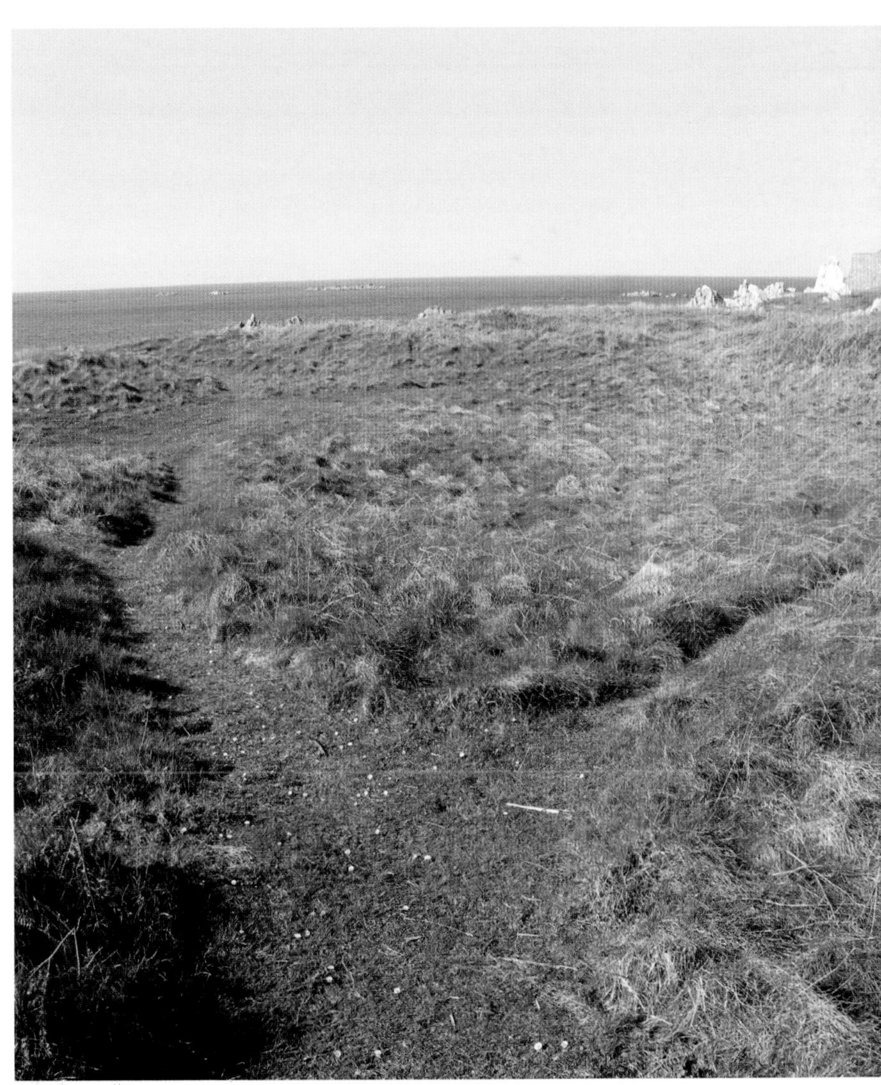

BAY WATCH

LA JAONNEUSE bay. Beautiful at mid to high tide, but bring your nose-clips.

Generations past saw it not only as a horse-shoeshaped, soft, sandy alternative to the nearby flat and harder expanses at Pembroke and L'Ancresse, but it had additional advantages, in that few Guernsey beaches threw up more vraic for collection by horse and cart.

That is the reason for a blue granite slipway, which has impressively remained unharmed by the elements and which splits the beach neatly in two.

Were it not for the smell drifting over the hougue, it would still be a belter of a beach for those simply wanting a place to lay quietly in soft, white sand, but the stink is rarely not in the air and you won't find any ice cream vans loitering, only dozens of birds in Guernsey's answer to the Leaning Tower of Pisa – Martello Tower No. 9 – just a few yards away.

La Jaonneuse had little history of note until it exploded into the public eye in the Occupation.

A large sea mine drifted into the bay and halfway up the beach it exploded, not only stunning the pigeons on top of Tower 9 but leaving a crater, 50 to 60 feet across, in the beach.

The site of the explosion is, I'm told, still partially visible from time to time.

Like other bays, La Jaonneuse is affected by a more wholly natural sand movement: the tide. On a wet, glum early-November afternoon the sand had been driven high up into the rock armouring and virtually covered a large section of the slipway.

Come another day and near the top of that slipway it is a struggle to see over it from one side of the beach to the other.

The 1787 Duke of Richmond map of the headland refers to it as Le Platon, but to most of us it is a grassy plateau which has, at its outer reaches, some traditional Guernsey fishing spots, places such as Moorings Rock, Big Bill, The Slipper and Conger Rock.

Two of them explain themselves but nobody, not even the 'knowledge' – George Domaille –

Below
La Jaonneuse under a vraic attack

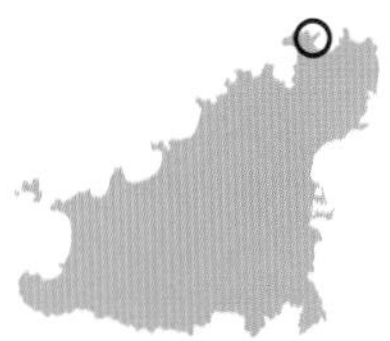

seems to know why Big Bill and the Slipper are named as such.

If the latter is shaped thus then it has not caught the eye of the island's most knowledgeable angler, Len Le Page.

The headland provides four marks for his updated book on Guernsey angling – Big Bill, The Slipper, Moorings and The Battery, which looks across L'Ancresse.

Big Bill and The Slipper are not always accessible. Bill is accessible only from half tide down to halfway up and while you can stay on it safely enough on neap tides or small springs, it is best to give it a miss on big springs, suggests Len, who suggested we ask an altogether more younger and nimble top-flight angler to give Coast the low-down on the merits of Big Bill.

That person is Jason Brown and earlier this week, when the tides suited a visit across the waterfilled gulley that cuts off Big Bill from the rest of the headland for anything up to six hours, he gave the mark a go.

Jason recalled first going to the mark with his brother as an eight-year-old and how his sibling teased him that they were about to get cut off.

Into adulthood and caught with the bug of shore fishing, he has often deliberately got himself isolated on the rock, which looks out towards Alderney and Les Casquets.

That he does not use it as often as he might is down to the time restrictions and that he is a married father of two young girls.

'It's not so much a hassle to get out here but if you want to stay for the [most favourable] high tide you are going to be here for a long time. It's a spot for those who want to be here for the day.' Yet it is seldom short of takers. 'There are quite a few anglers who will

Above
George Domaille and his dog Tinker
Overleaf
'The Leaning Tower of La Jaonneuse'

Above and right
Jason Brown goes fishing at 'Big Bill'

come out here and the Bailiwick record bass was caught here,' he said. 'It has a nice clean bottom, which makes it fishing-friendly. There is also plenty of tide movement and fish like to move along with the tide.'

The variety of fish caught off Big Bill is extensive.

'There is bass, black bream, red mullet, grey mullet, sole, plaice, mackerel, garfish, pollack – virtually everything, depending on the time of the year. Anything [fishy] wanting to come into the bay will mooch around here. It's also popular with the commercial fishermen, who will be putting their nets down as soon as they are allowed from early autumn time.'

Big Bill, of course, has also provided generations of youths with a summertime launching pad into the blue depths below.

The Slipper gets surrounded for up to two hours on either side of high springs, but is safe enough. Back at the headland base, if you study hard enough and are prepared to delve into the undergrowth, you can find remnants of the old sea wall which – until the Germans put in their own heavily-concreted version – swung around until the point, where it met the large shingle bank and which would have covered much of the car park and the bus turning point.

George recalls it well, not least for the pond that sometimes filled behind it and in which he and his pre-war mates splashed about.

That was before Tower No. 8 – which sat where the German bunker makes the corner – was brought down to free up the invaders' line of fire.

A few yards away over the wall, if you look hard enough, is the remains of the original sea wall. There is precious little of it left, but you begin to appreciate its shape and nature when you discover the many large, smoothed boulders between the line of the old wall and the sand.

The clue lies in the same manmade holes that were created by its makers to lift them into position.

Once looking out over Pembroke were the tearooms that previously had been a venue for badminton pre-war.

But in 1963, the tearooms became a fully-fledged hotel known as La Jaonneuse Restaurant and Hotel, run by a Mr and Mrs Phillips and which had accommodation for 21 in 11 rooms.

Since then, the site has undergone extensive renovations and is now home to attractive self-catering apartments.

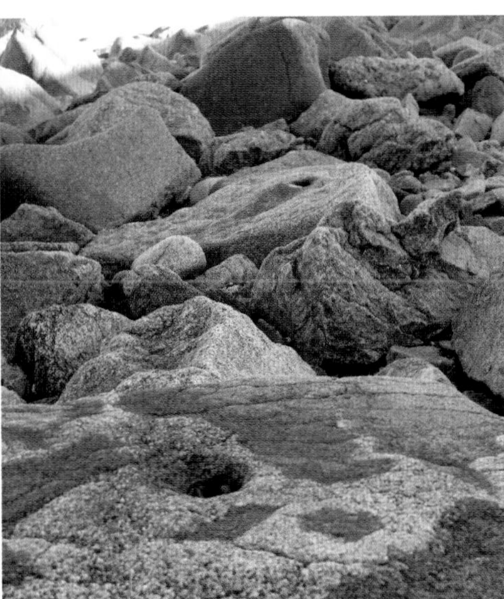

Left
Part of the old Pembroke seawall

"It wouldn't be a common if you started planting trees, it would be a park"
George Domaille

CHAPTER 9

L'ANCRESSE
& LA FONTENELLE

With its common, splendid golf course and wide expanse of beach all seems well for L'Ancresse. But all the while the sea threatens to immerse much of it and erosion is an ongoing issue for many who care and have responsibility for the area.

COMMON GOVERNOR

GOVERNOR is the highest title you will come across in Guernsey history and long ago it was watered down to Lieutenant-Gov.

We don't do kings.

But if there were a King of L'Ancresse there is no doubt who would be on the the throne and we could add another George to the list of monarchs.

George Domaille has not one drop of royal blood but he is the king of L'Ancresse, as was his uncle Jack previously.

George, now 80, and a council member since 1974, has reigned for 22 years and he shows no sign of standing down.

When it comes to the wider L'Ancresse area nothing gets past old George's gaze. He is as stubborn as they come and protects his kingdom with all he's got, which is a vast knowledge of what can and cannot be done, its history and a fierce passion to preserve it for further generations.

His army is his compatriots on the L'Ancresse Commons Council and he has a little canine bodyguard in the shape of Tinker, a quaint Fox Terrier.

It is commonly assumed George's enemy is the golfer whom as a group he has battled against for many a year, not through any great dislike of the sport and the fact that it is parked on his common, but that they are always wanting to make subtle and not so subtle changes.

So while, behind the scenes, golf looks to re-shape its links course to improve safety, they do so in the knowledge what they want may well not be want George wants, or will allow. The referee is the States of Guernsey's Culture and Leisure department.

He assures this former hacker of long irons, that he has no problem with golf at L'Ancresse and, indeed, respects it for what it has brought to the common, which is sound management

Below
George Domaille on his patch with Tinker

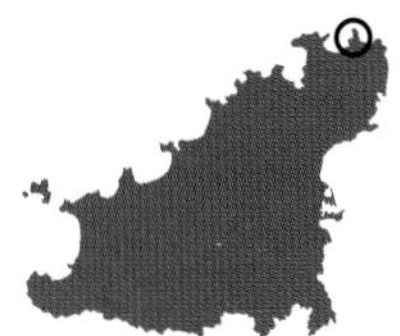

and constant manicure.

'I am not against the golfers but like the dog-walkers and the horse riders, there are some who think they have a god-given right. They haven't.

'The common is for other people as well.

'There are only 1,300 golfers at L'Ancresse and there are 60,000 islanders to use the common if they want.

'Golf is a good use of the common and it is well used. It takes up about half of the common.'

For the record the common amounts to 300 acres or 741 vergees.

George may well be considered a grump to golfers, but when you take a tour of his domain with him he is remarkably informative. His passion for his Guernsey hits you with the force of a Ping driver struck by one of his enemy.

So what exactly he is in charge of?

Well, the Commons Council was formed in 1898.

It operates on a small budget from the States with which it has to manage how to manage the forever invasive gorse which, history tells us, in a dry summer is a major fire hazard.

The council is responsible for the various car parks, it keeps an eye on drainage and generally maintains a large area which is controlled by nature more than ever a single man.

George knows it inside out.

He knows too that the golfer is also his friend.

It is a blessing that they are there to preserve the common and keep it so prim and proper, where people can soak up its natural beauty, albeit under the threat of being clonked on the head by a Titleist.

Golf has, after all, been at L'Ancresse before there was a commons council.

The course has seen several re-designs, although none perhaps as important as the one around the corner.

Above
Twin Towers at L'Ancresse

When it was redesigned at the turn of the last century the keeping clear of dense gorse was taken into consideration, as were the Martello Towers such as those which sit on and close to the 15th and 16th fairways respectively.

There were the cattle too, to avoid, but these days the herd is virtually non-existent, at a recent count [mid September 2010] a bare six.

Ten years into a new century he sees his major problems as fighting the gorse. 'There is still too much of it and we are looking to keep it in check.'

Back in the days of Miss Melbourne's goat herd, as many as 120 cows parked on it, and the sheep of course, the gorse as well as grass was managed more easily.

He loves and surely don't we all, the open space that the common offers so close to arguably the island's finest stretch of sand.

And that is why George rejects the idea of planting trees on it as suggested to his council recently.

'It wouldn't be a common if you started planting trees, it would be a park.

'It feels open as it is.'

I am sure many a high-handicap golfer hopes the open-ness remains.

SAVING L'ANCRESSE

BELIEVE some experts and Guernsey's major golf course – one that has served the island so well for 120 years – will have some very large water hazards in years to come.

So vast will the watery hazards be that golf course designers may be called into give L'Ancresse links a Sarnian interpretation to the magnificent 17th at Sawgrass in Florida.

The warning signs are there let it be said.

Since the Royal Haskoning report into the state of the L'Ancresse sea wall which protects the 15th and 16th fairways from the open sea, there has been much alarm from informed locals as to what we might see on our common in years to come.

And, the bad news for golfers, is that the birdies and eagles they go after on a daily basis will one day be replaced by mullet, bass and the odd spider crab.

Rosemary Henry, Vale parish douzenier and vice-president of the Vale Commons Council, is a harbinger of doom when it comes to the fate of the common she loves and wants to preserve for generations to come.

The Common is in her blood, her father Tom having sat in the role of president of the council which like to direct the common users on what they can and cannot do, how the area is maintained and what should be done to ensure it is around for many hundreds of years yet.

But, as Rose and many an expert will tell you, if that wall goes then we can all kiss goodbye to the common we see now.

There have been some clever computer graphics to prove the point.

This is how Rose sees it:

'According to the Royal Haskoning report of 2007 the wall is nearing the end of its useful life.

'Remedial work has been carried out on those sections displaying excessive wear and possible safety hazards, but there does not appear to be any long term management plan to safeguard L'Ancresse Common from the not so distant predicted erosion.'

And that is very bad news for the golfers as Marcus Hamon, head greenkeeper on the links, will tell you.

He has been battling all year to recover the usually magnificent undulating 15th fairway from the sea water flooding from last winter.

Large parts of the 15th fairway and parts of the 16th resembled ponds as the gale-propelled high seas burst through the gap in the sea wall at L'Ancresse and ran down natural paths into the low-lying fairways.

The result has been a year-long battle to get anything worthwhile to grow in these normally immaculate areas which the golfers have become accustomed to,

'This has been the worst year for me since I came down 22 years ago,' said Marcus.

'They have had flooding before, but this year we cannot get anything to germinate because the salt content is so high.'

Rose can appreciate the problems facing Marcus and his crew.

'The Haskoning Report states that there are many sections of the wall that are in need of repair now [2007], especially in the centre of the bay where damage and movement in the concrete requires emergency work.

'Without further investment the central wall is likely to fail in the very near future.'

News that makes Marcus very nervous.

'I have been told,' he said recently, 'that sea water is actually coming under the wall and if that is the case the whole 15th fairway could be contaminated.'

Letting the wall go and allow nature take its course is a scenario golfers, greenkeepers and Rose, dread.

'The report says that removing the wall

Opposite
Rosemary Henry's family have been part and parcel of the L'Ancresse story

[which has been suggested] could have an adverse effect on the environment, erosion of the low-lying hinterland of the common could occur as could losing part of the golf course and threaten the structural integrity of the pre-Martello towers and to the loss of potential archaeological interest.'

The few pros and many coins have been aired in the Guernsey Press ever since Haskoning's views were made public. Rose has made her own studies and conclusion.

'Removing all or part of the sea wall will undoubtedly create a softer coastline but at what cost?

'Today's generation are the guardians of the island's heritage and L'Ancresse Common, stretching from the Vale Church to Fort Doyle.

'It's all a designated area of special environmental and archaeological importance, let alone Guernsey's largest playground.'

Naturally, she is not content to follow the 'do nothing' scenario which crops up in Haskoning's summary.

'In other words, let the sea have it and the flood extents map shows large areas of the common under water with Fort Le Marchant cut off and part of the Fort Doyle area submerged.

'At the very least an attempt to save the

historical part of the islands coastline should be made, but under the current financial constraints this probably nothing more than a pipe-dream!'

Being the man of the shop floor as it were, Marcus the greenkeeper, does not want to get ahead of himself in quite the same way as Rose, but is nevertheless nervous for the future.

'If that wall goes the speed of erosion will increase.'

That's bad news for the 15th and 16th holes, in particular.

An elevated station above many of the closing holes at L'Ancresse normally shows a 15th in all its majesty of tightly mowed mounds and hollows offering a variety of shades of green under a summer sun.

But in 2010 many of those hollows have looked sick, the grass having been burnt off by being submerged by the sea for an extended period.

Below
L'Ancresse sea wall receives another hammering

'We have put water on it, verti-drained and reseeded. But nothing has worked this year,' says Marcus, who kicks at the ugly weed in one of the ailing hollows.

'It is slowly coming back but it is taking time.'

His worry is that before it recovers it could be submerged again by winter storms.

'It has been heartbreaking to see. We've done everything we can but I have never seen so much "GUR" [ground under repair] in one area of the course.'

The clever-dicks might say that if you put a golf course next to the sea what do you expect.

The Royal Jersey links course at Grouville has been known to be snowed under by sand blown off the adjacent beach, and occasionally milder sandstorms have affected the second hole at L'Ancresse which runs parallel with Ladies' Bay.

'High tide on the second with a westerly means the second cops it with salt spray and when that happens we just put water on it and flush it out.'

Above and left
Rosemary Henry hopes that her beloved Common never looks like this

But flushing is not the remedy across the way on the 15th where they have moved to reduce further salty damage by installing a pump in the well of one of the bigger hollows and the capability is now there to pump flood water underground into the ditch hazard close to the 16th green and then out onto the beach through the outfall pipe.

It's a partial solution but not the answer.

The future is uncertain for our common.

WHAT LURKS BENEATH

NEVER has so much ragworm bait been dug in one go as the day the cable came ashore at L'Ancresse Bay in September 1972.

Len Le Page, for 30 years angling correspondent of the Guernsey Press, but in his day job a 'top knob' at the Guernsey Telecoms, joked as much when he attended one of the pre cable laying meetings all those years ago.

In the presence of British Telecoms representatives and the Guernsey and Jersey telephones bosses overseeing a multi-million pound project, Len chips in with the question: 'Who is going to get all the bait?'

'They looked at me puzzled, but thankfully my boss [Alec Forty] knew what I meant.'

Len was in charge of 'external plant; when in 1972 the UK to Guernsey No.5 analogue cable was brought into L'Ancresse.

'Previously the cable had come in at Fort Doyle,' says Len who goes on to relate how that cable from Dartmouth was laid in the late 1930s, the German forces turned them off during the Occupation and they were brought alive again after the war.

But by the seventies it was clear that new cables were required and the hunt was on to find the most suitable place to bring them in.

'After surveys, L'Ancresse came out as the best of the bunch,' said Len.

Other north-west beaches were looked at but none suited like L'Ancresse.

'There is a clear path in at L'Ancresse and the advantage was that the cables could come up the beach and go straight into town.'

Len said that preparations for the laying of the new cables was a three to four-year job.

And by late summer 1972 the big event happened.

The 700-ton Dutch cable ship, Directeur Generaal Bast, checked the whereabout of the

Below
The laying of telephone cables at L'Ancresse in 1972

market buoys up the bay and nosed her way to within 400 yards of the beach.

The 'DGB' as she was affectionately know to Len and colleagues, had been chosen for the task because of her shallow draught and within her bowels was two-and-a-half-miles of cabling.

Two caterpillar tractors were used to pull the cable ashore where a trench and junction point awaited.

The cables were buried by JCB to the low water mark on the spring tide while, for the 1972 job, the sea end of the cable was left in six fathoms of water off L'Ancresse to await them being joined to the main section of 88-mile cable that would come out at Bournemouth.

By 1988 a new cable was required to meet modern demands and in April that year UK to the CI No. 7 was brought ashore, only this time its UK link would be Dartmouth and not Bournemouth.

The Guernsey end of the new link was then claimed to be the longest optic fibre cable in the world, if only for a very short period.

Since then the cabling into L'Ancresse has been improved with the addition of two more to supplement No.7.

In March 2006 the Hugoworth Cable & Wireless owned optic fibre was laid and two years later Wave brought their own in.

Out to sea the practice is now to bury the cables which are many in their number.

'If you look at a map of the Channel seabed there is a right mish-mash of cables,' said Len.

'There are lots of cables between France and the UK of course.

'In the early days they were not buried and that is why they incurred a lot of trawler or anchor damage.

'In more modern times they are buried, ploughed in with the object of being a metre deep.'

Above
The 'DGB' at anchor in L'Ancresse

All very modern, all very complex and a far cry from the days when the island telecommunications cable in to Telegraph Bay was seemingly left for dead and one day the old wire stuck reared its ugly head into the beach.

'The cable to Sark was laid in the early part of the 20th century and taken out of service when Sark became served by a radio link.

'The chief engineer went down to Telegraph Bay one day and found the cable broken and sticking out at low water.

'They put a "tapper" [portable phone] on it, turned the handle to ring the station and the answer was a softly spoken "hello".

'It was the lady at the Sark Exchange.'

A short while later the Telegraph Bay link to Sark was removed once and for all.

SPLIT OVER TACKLING EROSION

TO ROCK-ARMOUR or not to rock-armour? That is the question. Well, it is for those who have a deep fondness for the eroding coastline at La Fontenelle Bay and nobody, or body of persons, is more concerned for its future than L'Ancresse Commons Council. Last year it got itself into a planning row over its unlawful rock-armouring of part of the bay. And the bad news for the council was that La Societe Guernesiaise was not on its side.

'Rock-armouring produces an unnatural look to the shore and adds to the over-development of the island,' said La Societe's marine biology and entomology secretary Charles David.

At the time Mr David said: 'There is no need to protect this piece of common. The erosion here has been going on for years.'

The Societe man went further, saying that depositing the large boulders on the beach damaged sensitive habitats on the common, including heathland and seasonally wet areas with interesting flora, including some very rare plants.

The Societe line is that rock armouring often exacerbates the problem of coastal erosion.

'This is because the artificial slope of the armouring reflects waves at high tide, leading to more scour on the beach and lowering of beach levels.

'If the armouring has no foundations, that will lead to the rocks slumping down the beach, reducing their effectiveness.'

But how much is the armouring destroying the valuable and rare soft-cliff habitat, as La Societe claims?

Its stance has left council members bewildered and questioning why rock-armouring is so good and a proven effective barrier for other northwest bays, but not in this quiet backwater.

Rosemary Henry, one such council member, said recently: 'The path I used to walk my dogs on has gone into the sea.'

She wonders just how much more of it will disappear – and how quickly.

Time is undoubtedly of the essence and many islanders will have great sympathy with the council for its efforts to save a section of well used coastline and, ultimately, a whole headland.

'Safeguarding the coast is to everyone's benefit,' said council president George Domaille last year.

And why would anyone argue with that?

Right
The heavily-pebbled La Fontenelle Bay
Opposite
The bay is suffering from severe erosion

FLIGHT OF FANCY

MANY an airport around the world has its runway jutting out to sea. Funchal, in Madeira, Hong Kong and Kansai, in Japan, are just three that spring to mind.

Guernsey could have added to the list if, as proposed by the Guernsey Society of Charted Architects in 1967, it had torn up the concrete and returned La Villiaze to prime agricultural land and built a 7,000ft runway jutting eastwards from La Fontenelle Bay near L'Ancresse.

The society was very serious too, paying little attention to the dogdragging fraternity who have always liked nothing better than to park their wagons at Fort Doyle and jaunt off towards Fort Le Marchant with a multitude of Fidos.

It would have spelled the end of plans for Beaucette Marina and also my pleasant little jogs along the well kept paths adjacent to the rugged, badly eroded Fontenelle Bay, not to mention screwing up the Guernsey Rifle Club's activities at Fort Le Marchant.

It would also have spelled the end for one of the island's favourite fishing spots at Fort Doyle and the nearby 'Lace'.

But on the plus side, a northern airport would no doubt have saved the day for the pistol shooters, whose unwanted sounds would not have upset the neighbours because their pinging ammo would have been drowned out by the roar of jet engines.

The airport would also have ended those erosion worries for George Domaille and his team on L'Ancresse Common's Council.

The planners saw little problem with access and noise pollution would have been checked by the prevailing wind and the alignment of the runway to ensure all flights would approach from the sea.

Returning La Villiaze to the cows, all 230 acres of it, would also have spelled an end to all that awful screeching of jet engines and quieter, lazy sunny afternoons and evenings for all those on the approach paths in leafy St Martin's and St Peter's.

The other benefits were seen as increased safety – only the lives of those on the plane would be in danger – road transit to and from the resited airport would be slicker and, as the north is proven to be sunnier, there would be fewer delays.

When unveiled at the Chamber of Commerce's quarterly bash in November 1967, members were drinking to the idea.

Below
La Fontenelle Bay
Opposite
An artist's impression of the proposed airport

'Exciting' . . . 'imaginative' . . . 'the thinking of the future' were the sort of comments emanating from the meeting, but none of them was spoken by the then president of IDC, Deputy Tom Ogier.

He was, it was reported, not going to be pressurised by attending a meeting at which the media would be present and which would be seen as a dress rehearsal for a forthcoming States debate on the subject.

Dave Prigent, within not much more than a decade to be the editor of the Guernsey Press, added his weight to the argument for moving the airport.

'I cannot understand the minority hysterical outburst against such a sensible proposal,' he said of the project in a 'virtually unused bay'.

On the face of it, Mr Prigent and the project's supporters had valid views and La Fontenelle would have made an ideal site for an airport.

But it was a case of right place, wrong time. The time for such ideas belonged to the 1930s, before the island had ploughed so much money into resurfacing half the Forest from grazing land to concrete.

An airport at L'Ancresse had been seriously considered at the time of the great airport debate in 1936, but it seems not out Fontenelle Bay way.

Interestingly, L'Ancresse would have been the cheapest option then.

Figures at the time reckoned the preparation of the three shortlisted sites were £51,550 [L'Eree], £23,979 [L'Ancresse] and £38,553 (La Villiaze].

The last mentioned won the day, which will forever please those who prefer to exercise their hounds, or themselves, in the oasis of natural peace which La Fontenelle offers.

It may be suffering from erosion, but it is a little piece of treasured wild country – and we don't have much of that.

ABOUT A BAY

LA FONTENELLE is situated between Fort Le Plomb and Fort Doyle and must be one of the most sheltered around Guernsey because of its location and the outlying rocks and reefs.

The bay is marked as a small vessel anchorage, but this would be only for yachts and small craft. Most of the seabed is low rock around the edges but there is a good strip of sand in the centre. Its main features are the Plomb Rock, on the tip of the peninsula, which is used as a navigation mark when approaching the Little Russel from the north-east.

There are two forts, Martello tower No. 4 and the one near Fort Doyle. On the outer part of the bay is the Demi de Fontenelle, which can be a dangerous rock at high water because it cannot easily be seen. The prefix, demi, in any rock's name means that it is visible only after half-tide down or before halftide up.

GIVE THE PLATTE A WIDE BERTH

LOOKING out from Fort Doyle, it is hard to believe that there is 2.1km of sea separating you from the lighthouse directly ahead. But you would not want to go there anyway.

The Platte Fougere, all 82ft of it, is not a place to be anywhere close to if you are aboard a boat.

Surrounded by sharp-edged rocks with all the effectiveness of a killer shark, the Platte may look idyllic on a still, spring tide, but it hides a thousand dangers.

And before a warning light was installed 98 years ago, many a ship and its crew had foundered in the area.

The lighthouse marks the northwestern approaches to the Little Russel.

It is intended to keep shipping away from the many dangerous rocks and reefs in the northeasterly corner of Guernsey – the Grandes Brayes, the Petites Brayes, the Rocque Vielle, Les Fourquies, the Bouettes de Brayes, the Petite Canupe, the Grande Canupe and the Grune La Fosse.

There are many others but the list would be too long to mention them all. The lighthouse is fitted with a Racon, which is a device that returns a radar impulse from a vessel to correctly identify its position on a screen.

The light is visible for 16 miles, flashing white and red every 10 seconds.

It is also sectored white and red, the red sector at 85 degrees through west to 155 degrees.

It was at one time powered by an electric cable from Fort Doyle, but when a break was found in it not so long ago, it was decided to power the light with a generator to save the cost of laying a new cable.

Below
On the rocks: motorcruiser Power Game II got too close to the Platte Fougere

"Sometimes the problem was that they didn't blast properly and lots of rock would come over. But to me it's the only place in the world to be"

Ron Bougourd

CHAPTER 10

MIELLETTE BAY
& NOIRMONT

Tucked away around the corner from Beaucette Marina at one end and Bordeaux at the other, narrow and quiet lanes lead to a small bay and its majestic little offshore islets of Omptolle and Houmet Paradis.

IDYLLIC MIELLETTE · OVERLOOKED BEAUTY
MOVING WITH THE TIMES · OCTOPUSES TO OCCUPATION

IDYLLIC MIELLETTE BAY

EVERY DAY, thousands of cars take the main road from L'Ancresse to Bordeaux, swing around the sharp bend at the end of La Rochelle and Grande Rue roads and never consider branching off through the lanes and heading down to this special place of glorious views: the Little Russel, the little offshore islets of these parts and Herm and the Humps beyond.

In the middle of a summer's night the oyster-catchers can strike up an irritating chorus for the insomniacs in the area. And when a north-easterly blows in from Siberia in the depths of winter, it can be a draughty place.

But these are minor blots on an otherwise perfect landscape at this north-eastern part of Guernsey.

It's not a place designed for cars.

You can, of course, wind your way around the area in the comfort of your car but, so narrow are these lanes, that you fancy that if it were not for the needs of homeowners, a good case could be made for making them pedestrian and bicycle-only.

Right
Low tide off Omptolle
Far right
Fishermen take a short cut inside Houmet Paradis

GU138
GU138

OVERLOOKED BEAUTY

RON BOUGOURD, now 82, has been lucky enough to live at Noirmont for the vast majority of his life. And one look from the top-floor of his house – Noirmont Villa – across the Little Russel towards France, is conclusive evidence as to why the retired grower refuses to move away.

'It's a view to die for,' he says. And having also sampled that breathtaking view up the full-length of the Little Russel and beyond to Alderney and France to the north, and down to Jersey beyond Sark in the south, I am not about to disagree.

Straight ahead across the Russel is the Humps north of Herm. The view evokes the thought that, had the house stood in 1917, then shipwrecked sailor Harry Manning would not have starved to death. Someone at Noirmont would have seen his desperate attempts to attract attention.

On the day I visit, the sky is blue enough and visibility so good that I'm sure you could spot a modern day Robinson Crusoe raising the alarm from the Humps.

Ron's house is built from stone from his own front garden. But beside the quarries below, Noirmont and little La Miellette on the way to

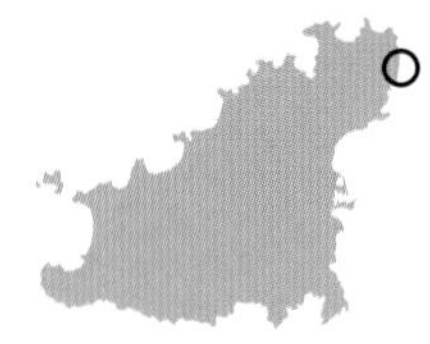

Beaucette (or 'Byocette' as some older Guerns refer to it), was fairly deserted: an empty peninsula once the quarrymen went home after another long day.

When Ron was a child, the house he has lived in for 30 years was one of just two in the area. It was the only one on top of the hill.

In front of Noirmont Villa was an old Napoleonic battery, now long gone, a victim of the decision to knock the two quarries into one in the mid-50s.

On top of Noirmont an iron gate on the corner suggests something once there that no longer exists. Ron fills in the mystery as to why there appears to be a gateway to nothing.

Until well after the war, the quarries – Noirmont and La Miellette – were separated by a narrow strip of rock that allowed a young Ron and his youthful friends to take the short route to the beach for a spot of ormering.

It helped to have a head for heights as the locals picked their way down to the peninsula, but such delights disappeared at the tail-end of the Falla's reign of working the quarries.

Alf Bougourd, also now into his 80s and still living nearby on the road to Noirmont, was working in the quarry at the time when the two monstrous holes became one.

He described the path to the beach as a 'rough track', but when Falla's chose to replace the crane with a system of loading boxes by tractor, the quarry was opened and a roadway created into it and down to the bottom.

Instead of loading the two-ton wooden boxes by hand – the quarrymen would collect nine pence a ton – and watch it hauled by the steam-powered crane to the top.

Tractors loaded straight into the noisy Pearce Arrow lorries, surplus American army trucks from the First World War.

Both Ron and Alf refer to the westerly section of the Noirmont quarry, now used by Guernsey Sea Farms for cultivating oysters, as 'The Flower Garden' – named after the beautiful pink stock flowers that covered the upper reaches of the cliff face.

Sadly, they are no longer evident and many of the quarries that the resident octogenarians grew up among have also gone.

The 1900 ordinance survey map shows the extent of quarrying in the area.

Where today lies a large well-kept expanse of field above the southern leafy lane route into La Miellette, was a large quarry which ultimately ended its days as a tip.

Another stone's throw north is another sizeable hole backing onto a private property alongside the northerly descent into La Miellette.

Across the narrow lane is a further water-filled private quarry used by the Guernsey Freshwater Angling Society and from which, it is said, the carps are as long as your leg.

Opposite
A view from Noirmont
Above left
Omptolle's bird sanctuary
Left
Noirmont erodes

I've heard it said that there is a 37-pounder lurking down there, it's been caught three times and is awaiting to be snagged a fourth.

Incidentally, the nearby La Lande quarry – another half-mile at most westwards – is the water-filled hole which yielded the island freshwater carp record of 38lb 30oz.

The area has long been the peace haven of the north but half-a-century ago living with the associated noise of quarrying – blasting and haulage – was something the 'Noirmontiers' became used to.

'We didn't really notice it because of the quarries all around us,' Ron recollected.

'Sometimes the problem was that they didn't blast properly and lots of rock would come over. But to me it's the only place in the world to be.'

A large part of that natural joy is the little La Miellette beach itself.

The sand may stretch not much further than 50 metres, but under the right conditions it is an unheralded beauty.

'Moll [Ron's late-wife] and I used to use it a lot,' he said. 'Mothers came along with their prams and babies.'

But, with the advent of the car, the beach is left relatively unused by the public, not that the residents probably mind.

The splendour of the east-coast vista rates with anything elsewhere locally, but it has seen dark days too.

In a flashback to his youth and fun days with good friend the late Roy Le Prevost, he recalls looking north from the Noirmont headland at a fellow Channel Island being bombed to – what he thought – would be smithereens.

'HMS Rodney was bombarding Alderney and all we could see was flames and smoke.

'We said poor little Alderney thinking it would never survive. But we were wrong, the smoke finally cleared and there it was still there.

Opposite
Bygone years of Noirmont and La Miellette
Overleaf
Idyllic La Miellette Bay and its islets

MOVING WITH THE TIMES

RESIDENT Ron Bougourd, who knows the north-east better than most, said it has changed greatly over the decades. 'The whole coastline from Beaucette to the granite point has eroded.'

He recalled the coastal track that linked Miellette to Beaucette quarry, but now sits beneath an elevated beach of pebbles pushed up by the tides to swamp the old roadway.

Across the way at Noirmont and near the entrance to Guernsey Sea Farms, there are even more worrying signs of erosion.

By the year, the dusty approaches to the quarry slip into the sea – at least five metres of coastline in 40 years – despite in recent times the placement of rock armouring by the quarry owners.

Meanwhile, the old pathway to the Noirmont headland has slipped away and it is no longer possible for children to comfortably walk around it on their way to Miellette beach.

Across the way at Houmet Paradis, the beautiful island is also forever shrinking, said Ron who has looked down on it from his home for half-a-century.

'Houmet Paradis was twice the size it is now and had two large fields with stone hedges. It's gone back a lot.'

Charles David, the marine biology secretary of the La Societe Guernesiaise, is another big fan of the area.

'It's certainly important for wading birds,' he said, while pointing to the presence of an oystercatcher dipping its feet in the shallows between Miellette beach and Omptolle.

Joining Miellette and Omptolle is a natural spit, or 'tombolo'. A tombolo, Italian from the Latin tumulus, meaning mound, (also sometimes known as Old Norse Eyrr – gravel beach) refers to a landform where an island is attached to the mainland by a narrow piece of land such as a spit or bar.

Right
Man with an amazing view: Ron Bougourd looks out from his Noirmont home
Far right
La Miellette's stony upper beach at high tide

Once attached, the island is then known as a tied island. They usually form because the island causes wave refraction. This deposits sand and shingle moved by long shore drift in each direction around the island where the waves meet.

'It's probably natural,' said Charles. 'I don't think it is artificial, unlike the one at [nearby] Houmet Paradis which is probably more artificial.'

The Societe man loves the area for many things, not least the beauty of the spring and summertime flora.

The wealth of yellow sea radish attracts a

particular kind of big black bee, while Yellow Bird's Foot is particularly pretty and unusual.

He is old enough to recall the cart track which joined La Miellette to Beaucette long before it became a marina, and where the eroded land meets the shingle beach closest to Miellette, he points out the clear evidence of the quarry spoil which formed the track.

As for the shingle bank he highlights how it differs from others down the coast, in that it consists of very flat stones.

There is a lot of non-local rock in the shingle and flints that probably emanate from a bed of chalk off the north coast of the island.

OCTOPUSES TO OCCUPATION

BACK IN 1950, mates Peter Bean, Edgar Bean, Edward Le Noury and Stan Martin had no computer wizardry to entertain themselves with. And anyway, in the summer where else would you want to be other than the beach?

For this quartet, summer meant spending hours messing about on the quiet, idyllic Miellette Bay at low tide hunting for what the island hasn't seen on its shores for half-a-century – octopus.

Not the tentacled giants of the deep but ugly little things. Most of the catch were small and medium, nevertheless many measured up to 2 or even 3ft-long.

That early July with the spring tide opening up the full delights of this quiet north-east beach, the boys took their hooks and went hunting among the seaweed and stones.

The rocks they couldn't turn over would be ripe for a good poke with a hook and the Guernsey Press was more than ready to splash the boys over its front page when one day they caught 160.

Every octopus caught was one less for our local fishermen to worry about as, apparently, the octopi – described as 'unpleasant creatures' by the newspaper at the time – had a nasty habit of playing havoc with crabs and lobsters in the men's pots and nets.

The lads always believed they were doing the fishermen a big favour and nearly 60 years on, Peter Bean still does.

As he and Stan reminisced about their octopus-hunting days, Peter pointed towards the causeway to Omptolle as their access to the hunting grounds.

'They were everywhere,' said Stan, recalling a period when the local youngsters had lived on the Miellette. It was during the long school holidays and it was usually on a Saturday that they would go in search. Peter, now 72, remembered: 'You could tell where they were because of the empty crab shells.'

But, by the early-60s, octopus hunting had died out.

The winter of 1962 was especially cold.

Speaking in the sun-trap garden of Miellette residents, John and Gill Creber, Peter said: 'Somebody once told me that that cold winter had wiped them all out.'

Right and far right
Octopus hunters then and now: (from left) Edward Le Noury, Edgar Bean, Peter Bean and Stan Martin. Edgar was unavailable for the reunion shot

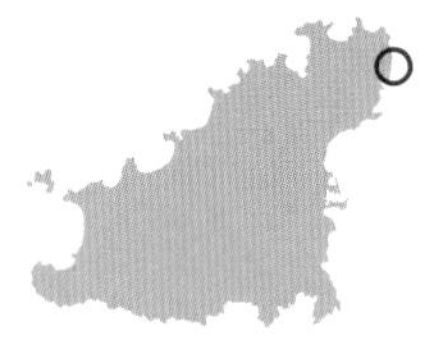

Islanders' Miellette memories also feature German mines, and an explosion during the Occupation that killed local man Harry Hamon just a few metres away from John and Gill Creber's house.

Here was a Guernseyman who loved the beach and ormers so much that he learned the precise whereabouts of the mines in order to pick his way through them to the beach.

But when the Germans noticed a worn pathway through them it is thought the mines were moved and the unmarried middle-aged man paid with his life.

The story is confirmed by Harry's nephew, Charlie Meagher, who was with him just a few strides back that fateful day in February 1945.

'We were heading for the beach and chatting away. There was a sign up with 'Achtung Minen' and a skull and crossbones.

'We'd been through there a number of times before,' recalled Charlie, who still lives close by.

'There was Uncle Harry, myself and uncle Ren [short for Renee].

'I remember Harry said "We'll put the nipper in the middle [Charlie, nudging 16 at the time], but we hadn't taken five strides and the whole thing went bang".'

Most probably, Charlie recalled, it was Harry's pet spaniel Lion that tripped the mine.

Immediately it was obvious Harry, who moments earlier had been whistling the popular tune of the time, 'Painting the clouds with sunshine', had been badly hurt.

Old Dr Fox was called and Harry, who had previously received a commendation for rescuing a dog from nearby Paradis Quarry, was rushed to the emergency hospital, which we now know as the Castel.

He had head and leg injuries and, after surgery, to amputate the leg, he died the next day.

The Hamon family had not appreciated the Press headline 'When Fools Rush In' but, in truth, it had not been a clever thing do to. 'The path was getting worn with our little feet going to the ormering tide,' said Charlie, who strongly suspects the mines were moved as a result.

"The tiny isles, such as Houmet Paradis, are part of our lives. I remember a man who used to sleep overnight there, just for the joy of it"
Yvonne Ozanne

CHAPTER 11

BORDEAUX

The island's finest natural harbour outside the two main ports, Bordeaux can yield many a tale from the past while always offering often stupendous views for those who both live there, visit and pass.

UNDERRATED JOY

Above
The old, curved Bordeaux slipway at low tide

I HAVE long thought that a coastal car park is a sound measure of the beauty of the view in front of it.

Nobody keeps figures as to the number of cars that, over the course of the year, are parked on our coastal promontories, but I would hazard a guess if someone did, that the two at Bordeaux and one a harbour-mouth away at La Banque Imbert, under the shadow of Vale Castle, are busier than most.

The views northward and out across the Russel towards Herm and Jethou, with Brecqhou and Sark plugging the gap, are staggeringly beautiful.

Here you get the full and spectacular visual benefit of living in the largest mass of the Bailiwick of Guernsey.

In front of your very eyes lies the sight of islands which, under a Guernsey sun, are the collective match for any around the world.

Turn your gaze left up the channel and towards Beaucette, north of the pebbled Petils Bay, and the islands become islets and the charm is no less appealing.

The combined glories of Houmet Paradis, Omptolle and Benest, with Platte Fougere and the SW Platte and Corbette beacons momentarily splitting the fastmoving tide, make any stroll northward from Bordeaux an underrated joy.

They were sufficiently impressive to capture the imagination of Victor Hugo, whose Toilers of the Sea is the story of lonely man living opposite Houmet Paradis.

Like all good things it has to end somewhere. And, in terms of unbroken coastal walking, that end comes just before Beaucette with the tiny but quaint little bay of Miellette.

At high tide there is but a narrow slice of sand to the left of the pebble bank, but on a quiet summer's afternoon or evening with the tide well down, Miellette opens to a lovely, fairly secluded, sandy bay.

Just don't go too far because, as the signs all along this part of the coast constantly remind visitors, it is a dangerous tidal stretch.

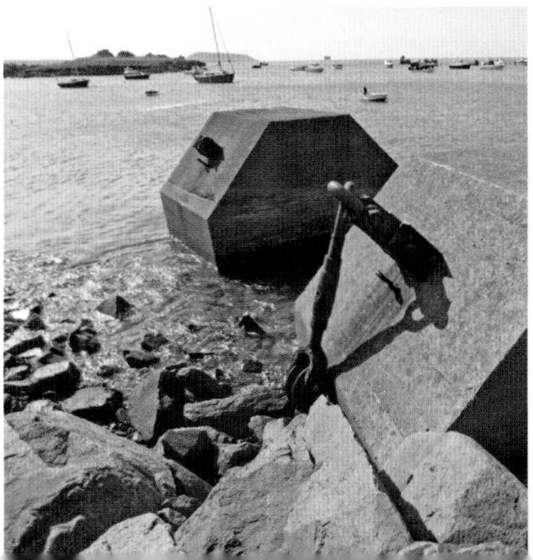

Above
Bordeaux at low tide with Houmet Paradis in the background

Left
Vast concrete blocks are a reminder of Guernsey's quarrying days

SPRING HIGH, SPRING LOW

WHATEVER the state of the tide, Bordeaux is a harbour picture unrivalled in Guernsey.

So little has changed over the centuries, the most recent alteration being the sloping pier, which appeared on the scene in 1906.

The purpose of its slope was primarily to enable the landing of explosives for the nearby quarry, one of the island's biggest and deepest, until the quest for granite ended in the mid 60s. It was gradually filled and now stands as a scruffy hougue reminiscent perhaps of the one which originally sat there overlooking the area.

A modern reminder of those quarrying days are two massive concrete holdfasts which dominate the drop into the top of the bay.

They were laid in 1959 when a new Blondin cableway was installed in response to the enlarging of the operation.

As quarrying ran its course, the holdfasts remained and should do so for as long as they enable visitors to look at them and scratch their heads in bewilderment.

They may be lumps of concrete but they are part of a proud story of Guernsey past.

Ashore at Bordeaux, little changes.

Shortly after the Second World War, a concrete-block shed appeared to serve the boat owners and moorings committee, the earlier fishermen's sheds on the Le Poincon rock which juts out near the jetty having been removed by the Germans during the Occupation.

As somewhere to live, Bordeaux offers some of the best views from a small group of properties that run parallel with the sea wall.

Below
Safe and picturesque harbour
Opposite
Bordeaux Haven is claimed to be the oldest house in Guernsey

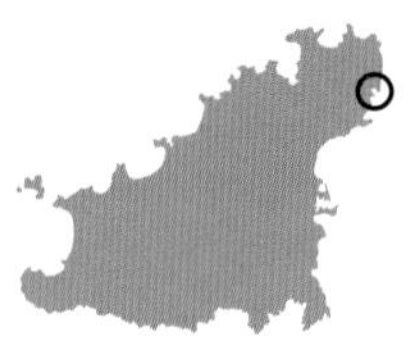

THE all-white Bordeaux Haven, which is occupied by Gordon and Marjorie Brown on one side, Delma and Keith Laker, their daughter and son-in-law, on the other, is built against an outcrop of rock and is thought to be the oldest complete house in Guernsey, dating back to 1300.

The Lakers have lived there for many years, having purchased the house from the island's former Magistrate, Francis Coningsby.

Keith said that while the morning sunrises are spectacular, his favourite view of the bay is during summer evenings.

'In the evening light the backdrop of Herm with its beaches lit up by the sun is very beautiful,' he said. 'That takes some beating.

'Also, late in the day, on a high tide in the summer, with the children jumping off the wall and the boats coming in and out.'

Others would argue that the early summer morns are the time to be at Bordeaux and this long-term resident sees much beauty in that moving picture.

'This time of the year the sun comes up over Shell Beach, but it will move progressively south over the summer. It's a stunning position,' concludes a grateful Keith, who often wonders what living there meant to the many who have occupied the haven over 700 years.

Completing this stretch of coastline is the Banque Imbert, once referred to as Beauquin Bay.

There are undoubtedly more impressive stretches of sand on our coastline, but it fulfils the purpose of lazing on and staring into a panorama of islands, Brehon Tower and all the sea traffic this busy stretch of east-coast water offers the observer.

It's no wonder that the entrepreneurs want to build a cafe restaurant close by to take advantage of this visual wonder – and it's a shame the powers-that-be won't allow it.

A PARADISE IN PARADOX

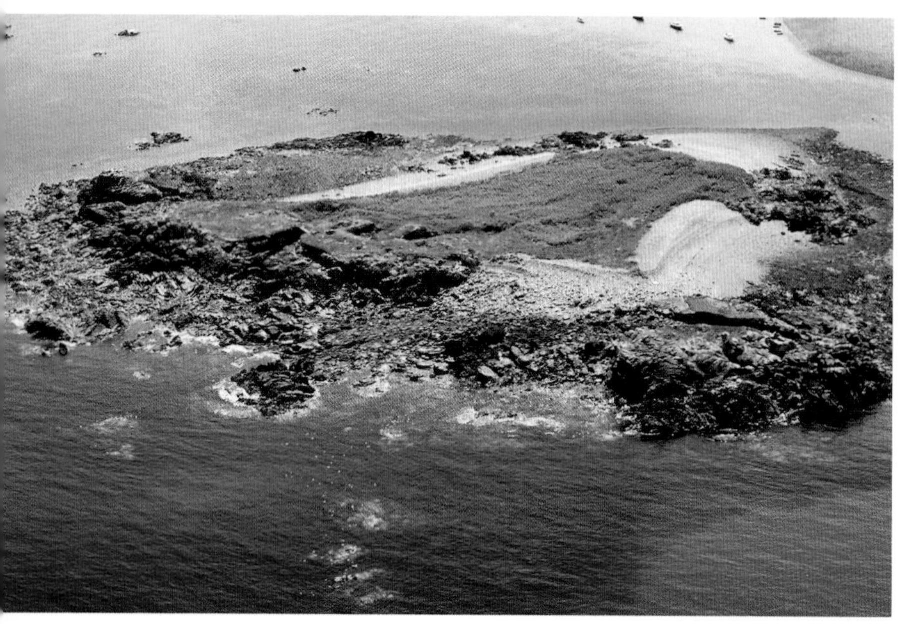

Above and overleaf
Paradise on Paradis
Opposite
Omptolle and Petit Omptolle with Herm in the distance

NOT A LOT has changed in this north-east area of the island over the past half-century, the most significant being the opening of Beaucette Marina, around the corner from Miellette, in 1969.

The other side of Miellette is Hougue Noirmont, which for more than 30 years has been the home of Guernsey Sea Farms.

The Hougue Noirmont quarry, all three-and-a-half acres of it, was cleared for use in late 1972.

The fresh water was drained and the coastal area was cleared of rubbish and weeds.

It was refilled with saltwater and the specialist hatchery and nursery for shellfish, including oysters, was born.

Not much more than a stone's long throw away from Hougue Noirmont is Houmet Paradis, accessible by foot during low spring tides.

Given its name, I find the four-acre islet once quarried by Mowlem something of a paradox.

When separated by the tide, it is a vital element in an idyllic picture.

Visit it and, apart from the solitude of it, Paradis is a disappointment to someone with no great appreciation of flora, fauna or bird life. It smells and is not a place to picnic.

That said, it's comforting to know it's there, untainted by the modern world. It's a nature reserve and should always remain so.

Presumably, it was for that very reason four years ago Paradis was bought by an anonymous Guernsey-based consortium of businessmen for £125,000 and its custodian, the National Trust of Guernsey, breathed easily again.

The freehold of the island had attracted unprecedented interest for an auction, with more than 300 enquiries worldwide.

The Martel Maides sale was even previewed by the Daily Telegraph. Potential owners enquired as to the possibility of jetties, dwellings, opening a casino and even a mini castle.

To the relief of every islander, the island with zero rateable value remained in the safe hands of the trust.

The late Roland Ogier, then president of the trust, was ecstatic.

'We will do the best we can to look after it and it is the intention to encourage people to understand and appreciate a wild area like this.

'It's a lot more than a rock out to sea and it is an important part of our heritage.'

Yvonne Ozanne, author of Love Apple Island – A Life on the Islands of Guernsey, was equally happy with the auction result.

As she wrote at the time: 'The tiny isles, such as Houmet Paradis, are part of our lives. I remember a man who used to sleep overnight there, just for the joy of it.

'In the morning he woke to a clear dawn, gently lighting the islands, with the sound of the sea and the seabirds in his ears. The ferns and bracken smell like aniseed and pine, paradise indeed.'

I'm not sure I would agree about the smell,

Yvonne. My nasal experience reminds me that it was once used for fish-curing.

Never mind, it is a special place.

Bird lover Nigel Jee also slept easier following the auction.

'The islets around Bordeaux are so vital,' he said.

Paradis provides undisturbed roosting places for seabirds and waders and is a breeding site for terns, oystercatchers and gulls, as well as being richer in flora than any other of Guernsey's tidal islands, including Lihou.

Omptolle has a larger colony of common terns, while Houmet Benest, closest to Bordeaux harbour, is rich in flora.

South of Paradis and connecting with Bordeaux is the little stretch of pebble known as Petils Bay.

Offshore, you will see a couple of dozen pleasure or small fishing boats moored, while on spring high tides the spot is handy for fishing from the vantage points provided by the rock armouring.

Houmet Benest

Just 200 yards from the shore at Bordeaux, its triangular shape measures 80 by 50 yards. In the 18th century, a gun battery was built there to protect the harbour from the French. But nowadays it cannot be seen for brambles and loose rocks. Used by the Germans during the Occupation, the islet was believed to be the smallest British possession armed by the enemy.

Hommetol or Omptolle

Accessible over a natural causeway and just a stone's throw away is Petit Hommetol. The larger of the two is covered in turf and flowers and on its western side lies a shallow cave and a natural arch.

Houmet Paradis

Originally named Houmet l'Eperquerie due to the mediaeval practice of gutting fish and leaving them split open on perches or perques.The German forces occupied it and traces of the electricity cable which they installed can still be seen on the beach opposite the Vale shore.

HAPPY DAYS

BORDEAUX'S most knowledgeable old Guern, Cedric 'Sid' Hockey, recalls the fishing boats of 50 years ago and petrol-pinching from the Germans during the Occupation.

ONE five-letter word from the mouth of Cedric 'Sid' Hockey and I'm charmed.

'Birdo', he says, speaking of the Bordeaux area he's known since birth. 'It's as I knew it as a nipper. There's one thing that doesn't change in this island and it's the rocks.' Sid is an old Guern and certainly fits the tag as 'Birdo's' oldest and most knowledgeable one.

Coming up to 74, he was brought up around the place – and loves it. It's a family thing.

His father and brothers were Birdo-ites and, blow me, his old dad even used it to escape the island in the Occupation.

Fred Hockey – accompanied by, among others, sons Fred, George and Harold – fled from under the Germans' gaze and made the trip to the English south coast.

No doubt Sid would have wanted to have joined them but, being a good deal younger, he had already been evacuated to the north of England.

'Dad pinched the petrol from the Germans at the White Rock,' recalls the last surviving of seven Hockey boys. There were five girls, too.

Sid recalls all the old post-war fishermen who used Birdo as their base.

'I was brought up with all the old full-time fishermen. They're all gone now, though.

'There was Dan Domaille, Bert Le Noury, Fred Noyon and Eddie Le Noury. There was also Barlow Corbet.

'They were all good old sticks. They all made their own willow pots. All were hard men, salt of the earth.'

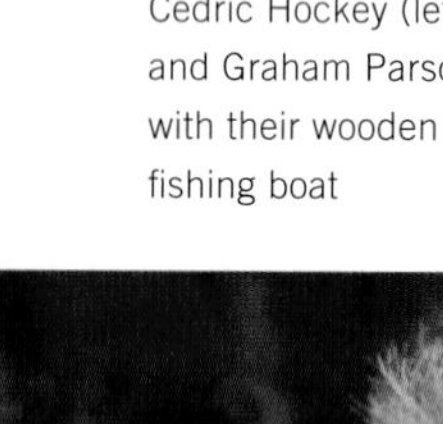

Below
Bordeaux stalwarts Cedric Hockey (left) and Graham Parsons with their wooden fishing boat

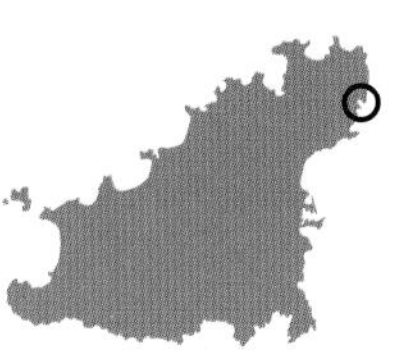

Half a century on, the bay is as busy as ever, except that the craft are no longer fishing boats. All but four are fibreglass and Sid's 17-footer Guernsey open fishing boat is one of those four wooden ones.

He's proud of The Mischief, which is a throwback to the days and another generation. Sid resumes recalling the names of old Birdo harbour users.

'Gerald Ozanne, Altie Torode, Jim Davison and Bill Le Tissier, who had the oldest boat I knew. It was called The Rover.'

Apart from three years as a full-time fisherman, Sid has fished only as a hobby but loves his recollections of 'the happy days'. Among the stories is the flotilla of Birdo boats heading off to Herm.

'Me and Bert [his brother] would leave on the half tide and row there. Then we'd get a rope back.'

Above
Painters seem oblivious to a stranded boat on the half-tide rock
Left
The Moorings Committee building

But it was his dad who taught him, as it were, the ropes.

'I used to go with my father before his boat had an engine. I'd row him. We used to go up the Brayes and around the Platte [Fougere] and go for whiting.

'You knew your rocks when you were rowing.'

The Mischief is his fifth boat and Sid's had a mooring at Birdo since the age of 10.

'It's a natural harbour. Not a made-up one like most of them,' he said.

'It's only a south-east wind when it's dangerous. It's a sheltered harbour. We're all right with an easterly, it's only the south-east.'

Accessing it is little problem, either, although it has been known for boats to hit Tommy rock in the entrance, one being Piablo five years ago.

Sadly, fishing has gone the same way of the traditional wooden boats. 'In them days there were three times the number of fish.' Nowadays, he satisfies himself with just four pots. 'Enough for a feed.' But it's Birdo that he loves. 'I've always been pleased to be brought up down Birdo. I haven't seen no change at all.'

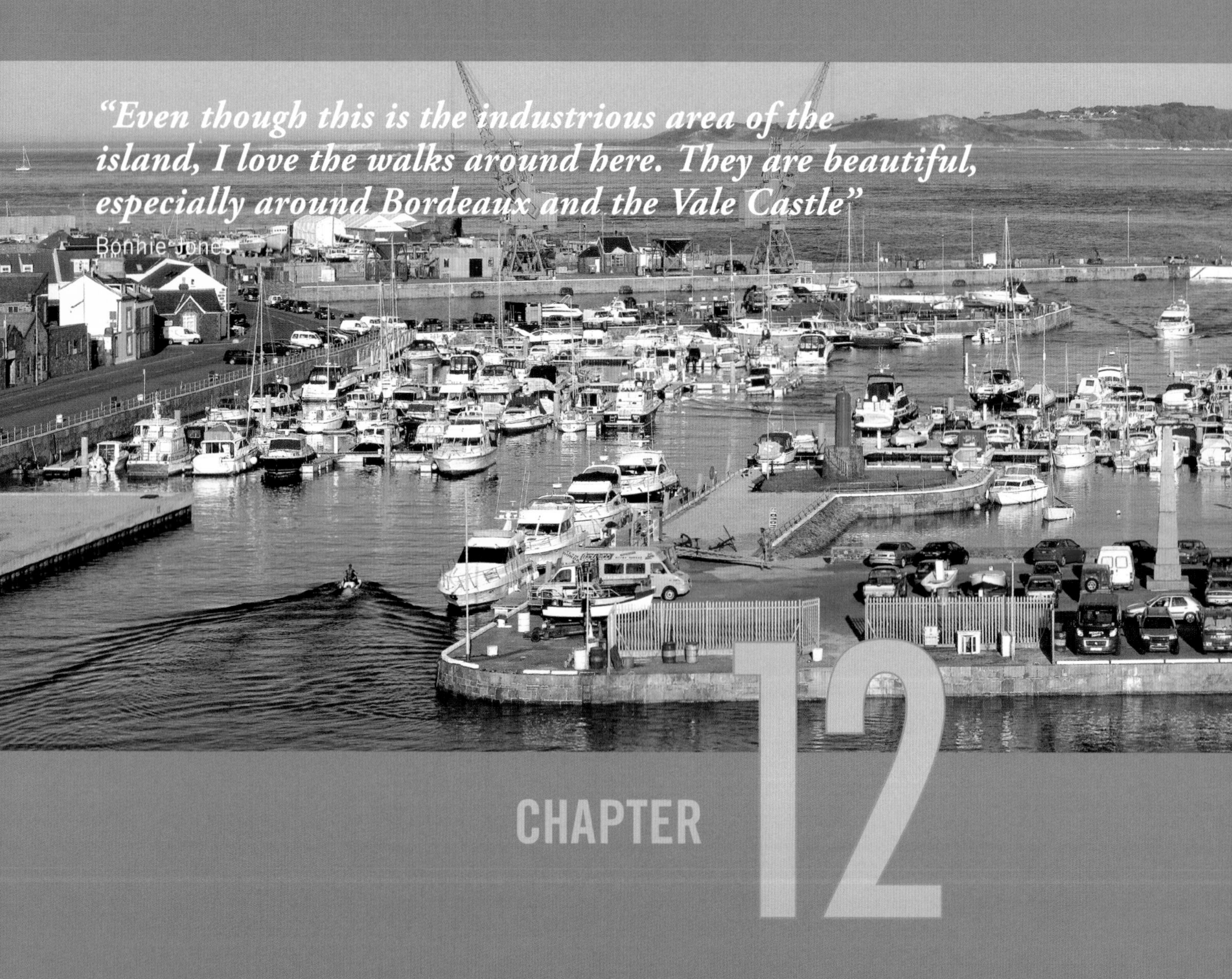

"Even though this is the industrious area of the island, I love the walks around here. They are beautiful, especially around Bordeaux and the Vale Castle"

Bonnie Jones

CHAPTER 12

ST SAMPSON'S
NORTH & SOUTH SIDES

With its North Side and South Side, Guernsey's second port and its joining Bridge has been the centre of some of the island's major industries, most notably stone and oyster production.

NORTHERN STAR · SEPARATED BY A CENTURY
TO THE RESCUE · KEEPING WITH TRADITION · HARBOUR LIFE
MY KIND OF TOWN · WHAT BECAME OF THE PUB PARROT?
CHANGING TIDES · LEADER OF THE PACK · ROUGH WATERS

NORTHERN STAR

DAVE JONES is not the sort for pussyfooting around a subject. Nor, I suggest, is Delma Whales, resident of Les Monmains off the North Side and long-term neighbour of the States minister.

Get the two of them on the subject of St Sampson's – harbour or town – and there is not much need for prompting. Pick them up on the health of the area and whether it is, as BBC Guernsey suggested recently, dying, then the pair have some forthright views.

'All we will soon have is takeaways and hairdressers,' says Deputy Jones. 'It [St Sampson's] has died because it hasn't the same community spirit,' adds Mrs Whales, who has lived there virtually all of her 78 years, the last 54 of them with husband, former CI darts champion Art under the shadow of what was Mowlem's stoneyards.

The Joneses, Dave and wife Bonnie, live a very short distance away in Pilots Lodge, a converted former cafe overlooking Abraham's Bosom.

They first lived on North Side 31 years ago and, after a spell in St Andrew's, returned to Pilots Lodge in 1994 and ran their little harbour cafe until closing it in 1999.

Opposite
Moored up on the North Side
Below
Community spirit: 'North Siders' Deputy Dave Jones with wife Bonnie (left) and neighbour Delma Wales

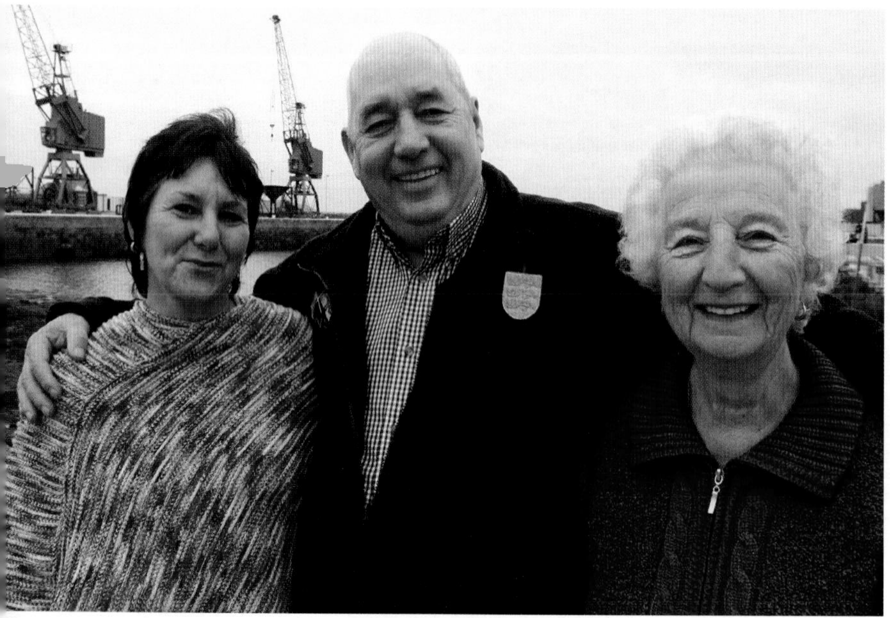

Moan as he surely will about what he sees as the harbour's demise, Dave is still passionately in love with his rooms with a splendid view. He admires what St Sampson's stands for, although it is not the quiet and idyllic spot it once was.

'At night the place went dead. It didn't have the Kevs we have now. Now it's become a racetrack at night. But we've enjoyed living here.

'It's the heart of the industrial north of the island and a large part of what the island has achieved has been built on the backs of people living in this area,' he said.

Bonnie says she feels 'very lucky and blessed' to have so much at her disposal just

minutes away from her house.

She works in a local shop, which is less than 10 minutes' walk away from their home, and, therefore, has no need to worry about morning traffic or parking problems.

'It is lovely in the mornings to walk alongside the marina, which, I have to say, I was opposed to at first.

'You have to accept the marina is here to stay now and you cannot turn the clock back.

'The one thing that does spoil it, though, is the litter that has been deliberately left behind from the night before. Chip papers, polystyrene, empty cans and sometimes broken glass. I cannot understand how anybody, even the careless and ignorant, can just walk away and leave their rubbish behind.

'Surely they must know that somebody has to come behind them and clean up their mess. It is certainly not left by anybody who loves and respects their island home.

'I think States Works do a wonderful job, not only on the Bridge but on the island as a whole.

'I have seen at first hand the mess they face in the early hours of the morning. It is disgusting and shameful and it must be heartbreaking for these men, who start their day picking and cleaning up this rubbish only to have to repeat it all over again the following day.'

Bonnie says that she does not go into Town if she can help it.

'I prefer to support the shops on the Bridge as much as possible, although it is a bit worrying that we seem to be losing a lot of retail shops.

'Even though this is the industrious area of the island, I love the walks around here. They are beautiful, especially around Bordeaux and the Vale Castle. Sometimes I cycle through the lanes. That's why I love living on North Side.'

Delma has an encyclopaedic knowledge of the area.

Apart from the war years, she has always lived in the Monmains, while her husband was born and raised in nearby Trafalgar Road.

She is eager to show me a picture of the staff of nearby Huelins on the day the North Side timber firm closed.

'I could name every one of those staff,' she boasts, and that is some boast considering there are in the region of 100 men and women in the shot.

'You got to know the faces,' she recalls of a bygone era when St Sampson's was a far busier, bustling place than today.

'When we were kids [30s and 40s] it was a dirty, filthy, dusty area. But it was a wonderful place to live. 'You don't get the bustle of the harbour you had.'

She tells many a charming tale of local characters, one of them being the 'Duncombe man' who would stand in the coal baskets as they were swung from ship to shore.

'We could watch him for hours.'

Unsurprisingly, she is not keen on the new

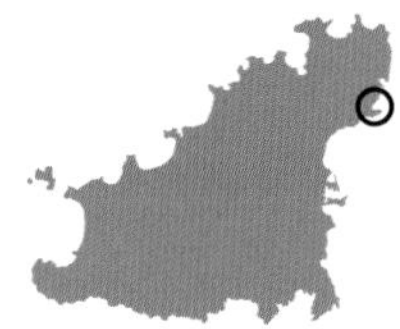

marina with its twinkling, white cruisers and powerboats.

'They cut this harbour's throat when they put in the marina,' she says. The Housing minister agrees.

'Twelve old Guernsey boys gave up their boats because they couldn't afford the mooring charges, he says.

'It was poor, but a closely-knit area up to the late 1960s,' adds Delma.

'There were little grocery shops like Moriarty's and the cafe on the corner of the Hure Mare and the Trafalgar. Miss Lower had the tiny shop that was the office of the weighbridge by the gates of the now coal yard and there was also Mrs Brache's little shop in Longree Road.'

She can still recall the dirtiness of the air of those distant days, much of it caused by Griffith's Yard. 'White dust used to spew out around the neighbourhood and at times the street resembled a huge snowfall.'

Deputy Jones, meanwhile, is more concerned with the future, being deeply suspicious of the motives of English planners.

The Leale's Yard topic crops up in discussion and he taps me on the wrist to command my attention while he lists all the harbourfront properties that were once shops and are now cafes or takeaways.

He says the Leale's Yard development could, done properly, be a boon to the area.

Done badly and out of character and it could foul up further an area already paying the penalty for an island dependent on the car.

Above
The Bridge shops with Leale's Yard behind

SEPARATED BY A CENTURY

THE North Side of 100 years ago was a dusty, grey place where hard graft and back-breaking days for a relative pittance were the order.

It was a story of stone, coal, horses, stables and ships.

But there was money to be made in them Guernseymen, as south-coast stonemason John Mowlem was quick to recognise.

The quarryman's son from Swanage made a fortune out of our granite and for the best part of a whole century was a major player in the island's economic story, employing hundreds of men and boys to eke the stone from what are water-filled storage supplies dotted around the Vale and St Sampson's parishes.

The panoramic pictures on these pages tell their own story. Taken 107 years apart from the same spot at Vale Castle looking west, only a handful of landmarks link the two, most notably the blue granite steam crusher tower in the former Mowlem stoneyards.

Where today stands the Ronez yards, the Total oil tanks and a myriad small businesses was the Mowlem site linking the cracking yards and some of the many quarries the firm dug deep into.

There is no better and more detailed account of life under Mowlem than the story told by the island's renowned historian, the late Victor Coysh.

As a former Mowlem employee, albeit briefly before a career in journalism, he wrote a substantial piece for the Guernsey Society describing life under the stone merchant and founder of the famous civil engineering firm.

Employed at Mowlem's North Side offices, under the shadow of the Vale Castle and next to the yards of William Griffiths & Co, Fry's and J. and A. Falla, Coysh paints a vivid picture of the horse stables, engineering stores, crushing mills and cracking yards, all adjacent to the harbour from which the stone was exported and not far from the quarries.

Two of these quarries were at Les Rocques Barrees, inland from Bordeaux Harbour and connected with the crushing plant by means of an elevated roadway, part of which passed over a public thoroughfare near La Hure Mare. Part of it can still be seen today, 78 years after Mowlem ended his Guernsey operation.

This bridge still exists, as does what Coysh called the 'highway'. Sadly, much of the once railed embankment to the north is overgrown and is easily mistaken for hedging, while the stretch to the south under the castle where today's Ronez yards exist has long disappeared.

Mowlem's largest quarries were at La Grosse Hougue in St Sampson's and Jamblin and Juas in the Vale, all of which are now water-filled. But stone was also excavated for the firm at

Right
Separated by a century: North Side at the height of its stone trade days and (below) now as an industrial complex

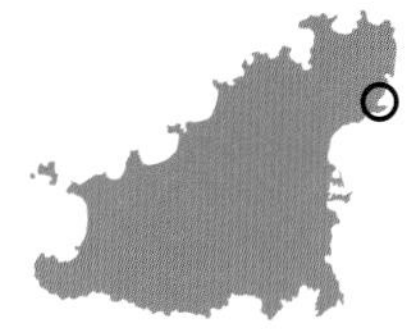

Beaucette and even on the islet of Houmet Paradis, north of Bordeaux.

Mountains of granite were hauled by the company's horse-drawn box carts from quarries to crushers and Coysh writes of 'the pleasant sound of these ponderous vehicles lingers in my memory still. They were painted in a very pale yellow shade (known as 'stone' colour, appropriately), with black metalwork. Their shires were splendid animals, their gleaming harness enhancing their good looks'.

Most of the horses were stabled on the North Side, but a few were kept at Baubigny, near the Mowlem owned quarry, also now waterfilled.

Mowlem quarried Guernsey for virtually a century. With our stone he renewed the paving of Blackfriars Bridge with granite setts, as well as repaving London Bridge, the Strand and the Thames Embankment.

At the height of the stone industry, as many as 30 ships at a time, most of them under sail, packed into St Sampson's to be loaded with stone. Some were Mowlem-owned and one was named after the man himself.

The schooner was built at St Sampson's in 1841 and when she was lost five years later, another 'John Mowlem' was launched.

Generally, these ships brought coal and timber to the island and returned to England with stone.

It was in the 1880s that the first great steam-driven crushing plant was built by Mowlem on the North Side and the fine boiler house chimney close by was constructed in 1890.

It still stands proud today, engraved with J. M. & Co., an inscription that can be found at entrances to all the man's quarries.

Resembling Victoria Tower in design, the

Right and bottom right
Visual reminders of the Mowlem quarry business

crushing plant still graces the harbour scene, together with the adjacent water tower and boiler house.

But by 1930 the mills has been silenced and the horses were idle.

Mowlem's gave up its Guernsey enterprise and before long the local side of it was acquired by the Falla brothers.

These days any number of small companies operate from the area, while tucked away underground, the tunnels which once saw horse-drawn carts transport the stone to and from the crushers are left dark and silent.

Mowlem's Sarnian links are detailed in a six-year diary of the man's business life in the mid 19th century.

It highlights just how hands on the Swanage man was in ensuring that the operation succeeded.

One notably interesting entry referred to Monday 18 May 1846 when he was clearly desperate for stone to fulfil his Blackfriars Bridge deal.

'Hired a horse and gig on a chaise and drove to St Sampson's with young Burley.

'Saw Le Maitre [his local foreman] and numbered about 24 vessels in the harbour.

'As it was blowing very hard south by east and the rain heavy, I did not proceed to the quarry as I intended but sent for all the men to meet me after work at St Sampson's. I drove back to Mr Burley's to dinner and at six o'clock I was again at St Sampson's.

There I saw a great number of the men and addressed them thus: "Men! I have served you many times and oft. I have crossed the channel in gales of wind to meet you and pay your demands. I have never deceived you and I pay your demands. I have never deceived you neither have I ever asked you one favour. I am now going to ask you to make a few thin cubes for Blackfriars Bridge. I cannot control you but I ask this as a favour – one hundred tons will be enough, it is not much more than a ton for each man and I shall like them in a fortnight."

'When this order is completed, I shall, if I live, take up the list and carefully look through the names and see who are my friends.

'This was a hard hit to those who did not intend to serve me. On this I left them with a kind goodnight.'

TO THE RESCUE

FRENCH Accents she is now and French accents no doubt were prevalent in the same North Side building when, for just 20 years, the island's lifeboat operated from St Sampson's.

The period was from 1861 to 1881 and, in truth, was not the most glorious two decades for the RNLI in Guernsey.

While it might have had fine boats to row to stricken people's rescue, it seldom did, certainly in the case of the one most associated with Guernsey's second harbour.

The shed at North Side was built in July 1861 for £134.

It housed the then lifeboat, Rescue, which was replaced in 1875 by John Lockett.

The decision to site the station at St Sampson's as opposed to St Peter Port was made by Captain Ward, the visiting RNLI inspector of lifeboats.

He selected the site which was gifted by the harbour committee and Rescue was moved from Mr Stonelake's yard on South Side to the new boat house which was subsequently occupied by its replacement, Louise Hall.

The house required enlarging to accommodate John Lockett, but by 1877 and at the suggestion of the local RNLI committee, the lifeboat was temporarily moved to a new station at Les Landes.

The arguments against Les Landes' remoteness were countered by the fact that it was the most easterly point of the island and was nearer to the entrance to the Little Russel.

Additionally, the boat could be launched regardless of the direction of the wind – not the case at St Sampson's – and a large number of fishermen lived close by and were happy to man it. Farmers, too, would kindly loan horses to assist in launching.

But there were further complications.

When J. Bougourd stepped down as coxswain, the only two crew members qualified to replace him were, in one case, shut away in the madhouse and the other, wait for it, was subject to insanity.

Ultimately in this period of RNLI indecision, Les Landes was deemed impractical and it was decided to take the lifeboat to Town.

John Lockett returned to St Sampson's for an unspecified period while the new home was prepared, but in 1881 and forever since, St Peter Port took over.

Incredibly, the 10-oared 32ft-long John Lockett proved largely a waste of time.

As recorded in J. M. David's Wrecks of the Bailiwick of Guernsey, 25 sea disasters were recorded during its time on station and only on one occasion did she turn out. And then it was not launched.

Above
The St Sampson's lifeboat John Lockett was introduced in 1875

KEEPING WITH TRADITION

GARY BLANCHFORD is a self-proclaimed traditionalist.

To him, St Sampson's Harbour signifies one of the last areas of the island which has a visible link to the 19th century.

For that reason he set up his own website, 'Save St Sampson's Harbour', when in July 2000 the States pressed ahead and approved in principle the construction of a new 350-berth marina at a cost of no more than £1.75m.

In addition, he collected 4,000 signatures in a campaign to save the site from the developers.

But he failed and in March 2003 the States ignored the public opposition and agreed to go ahead with the development. Within a few months, St Sampson's Harbour was emptied of vessels and moorings and two years later the first boats slipped alongside the new pontoons.

That was early summer 2005, but the website remains and must surely be the only one devoted to a single area of Guernsey.

Below
The new marina at St Sampson's initially drew much criticism

Why?

'I've always had an interest in St Sampson's. I've always been a boating man and had my boat moored there for 30 years.'

The retired policeman confesses to being a historian and has a special interest in the shipyards and ships of the Nelson era.

'I like tradition. I am a traditionalist. St Sampson's I saw as probably one of the last areas of Guernsey that was still as it was in the 1800s in terms of how the harbour was and how the boats were moored.'

But he is big enough to see why people, like me, were happy to see it transformed into a modern marina with the vast collection of expensive, twinklingly white, modern cruisers.

He agrees that the inner harbour was dirty but knows where the blame for that lies. '

The Board of Admin let it go. It hadn't been cleaned for more than 50 years. It had deteriorated and deteriorated. It should have been dredged because it had 18 inches to two feet of sludge in the bottom of it.'

He insists he does not have anything against marinas per se.

'I have nothing against them and St Sampson's looks very nice. I wasn't against a marina, but St Sampson's as a marina.'

He may have lost the battle but the war against further destruction of the old harbour continues.

'If something happens, I will go along, take photographs and put it on the front page of the site.'

Two of the more recent Blanchford gripes which resulted in positive action being taken were the temporary removal of the granite setts on the slipway at Abraham's Bosom and the dangerous nature of the ground where today's South Side bus stop sits.

No sooner had the setts which formed the top half of the slipway been removed pending

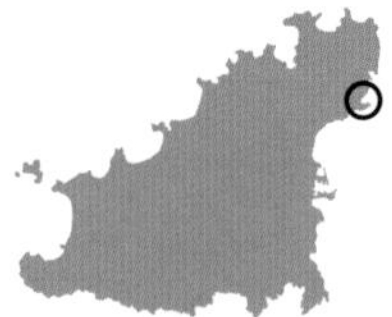

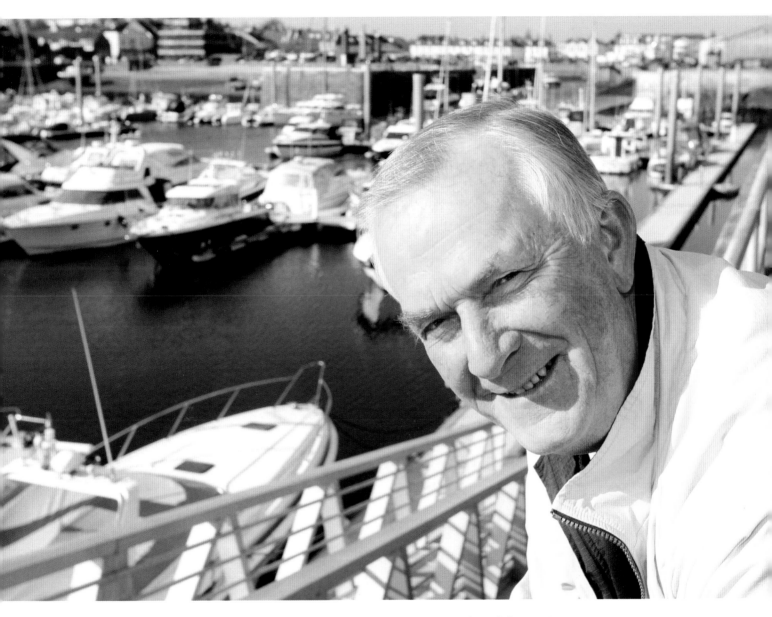

replacement by tarmac than he had a photograph on the site and official replies to his letter of complaint to Roger Berry, then president of the BoA.

Blanchford won the day and the cobbles returned, albeit incorrectly laid. But one stretch of blue granite cobbles did get away, much to the chagrin of Gary and fellow St Sampson's lover Deputy Dave Jones, who were distressed to see the cobbled road around the former Griffith's Yard stripped out and replaced by tarmac.

Then there is the question of the mystery disappearance of the granite water troughs and fountain that were trademarks of the North Side until the mid 60s.

'It was still there in the 60s when I went on patrol on my bike.'

St Sampson's is still special to Blanchford.

'The marina is irrelevant and not unattractive. I don't think St Sampson's Harbour has changed too badly. But I think they always should try and keep the facade of it close to what it is today.'

Above
Boat owner Gary Blanchford

HARBOUR LIFE

ST SAMPSON'S Harbour. It's ever-changing, yet it never changes.

Like a living room, the shape remains constant, just the decor is forever being updated.

The latest adornment was the pleasure-boat marina in the inner harbour. To the neutral islander, it would appear to be an improvement on its dirty, tidal predecessor, but for many of the local mariners it was another retrograde step in the evolution of a harbour, which started out as a creek with sandy bays on both south and north sides until the filling of the Braye du Valle in the very early 1800s.

Throughout the 19th century, piers came and were extended as St Sampson's moved to cope with the demand of a stone industry every bit as dependent on the island workforce as

Below
The Marine and General boatyard with the power station behind

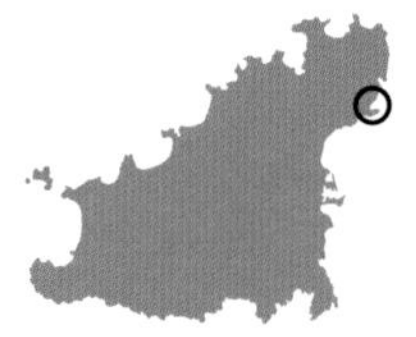

the growing explosion of the mid 20th century and now, into the 21st, finance.

For the past hundred years or more, the harbour itself has scarcely altered. The main quays are the same, the Crocq is untouched and it's only the shapes and sizes of the boats that have altered, along with the ever-changing industries down its flanks, which we all know as North Side and South Side.

Is it a better or worse place than 100 or 200 years ago?

It's impossible to answer an impossible question. The exhausted, dust-ridden stone workers of the early 19th century would be amazed by its transformation, but would not most of us wish to dip into an era of no cars, no pressure and no rat race?

After scouring dozens of old pictures of St Sampson's and having lived within a good stone's throw of the Bridge for a quarter-of-a-century, one concludes there is nothing too much wrong with it other than the horrendous traffic that clogs up the Bridge six days a week.

The harbour serves Guernsey well and remains spectacularly beautiful at high tide on a sunlit summer's day. Could it be better?

Back in the late 1980s, Board of Administration president Roger Berry had his own ideas of making St Sampson's a bigger, better and safer place with an emphasis on the BIG.

While today we worry whether Long Port will ever get its hands on Belle Greve, in 1988 the threat came from the BoA and its plans to build a £30m. outer harbour, which stretched grotesquely deep into the Little Russel.

The idea was that it would provide welcome deep-water berths for bulk fuel tankers and subsequently rid St Sampson's parishioners of their sleepless nights worrying over whether they were about to be blown sky-high. Well that was the theory, but did anyone living in the area seriously lose sleep over whether a gas tank or oil tanker would explode and take out the neighbourhood?

I think not.

According to the BoA, though, the benefits of such a scheme would be not simply life and property preservation.

St Sampson's would have additional moorings for both local and visiting 'yachties', part of the inner harbour would have been filled to provide a second bridge on the Bridge and the traffic difficulties would immediately be solved.

Not only that, but Marine & General, the island's one remaining shipyard, would be shipped out to Longue Hougue and the freed-up industrial space would provide valuable room for even more cars.

For easing of traffic flows, I happen to think the area could benefit from a second bridge of some sort across the Crocq to join South to North Side, but how would that affect Marine & General?

This parishioner is simply relieved that the Board of Admin's plans for a massive harbour seem to have died along with many of the industries that had brought the docks to life over the past 200 years.

For a start, one of the most beautiful of island viewpoints, the car park beneath Vale Castle, would have lost its idyllic outlook forever. The extent of the planned outer arms was such that the view across the Little Russel towards the southern end of Herm and Jethou would have been obliterated. As for the tidal issues surrounding the scheme, it is reported that the massive pier extensions would have caused untold damage elsewhere.

No, the creek-that-was has undergone enough change over 200 years. The 1806 Sir John Doyle project to fill in the Braye for good should do us nicely for a few more years yet.

MY KIND OF TOWN

CHERISH the old ways, appreciate the new.

It's not a bad ethos to have in a world that changes ever faster, albeit a touch more slowly in Guernsey and particularly in St Sampson's.

Peter Stewart, 59, is such a man.

Born in Bradford of evacuated parents, he was brought to Guernsey and to within a stone's throw of St Sampson's Harbour aged two.

His heart has been there ever since.

It's highly doubtful if there is any living man more 'anorakish' about the area than Peter, the boat-spotter, the harbour boy who came to appreciate that change is not always bad. He's old enough to remember the horses and carts of Peter Le Feuvre in New Road, Fred Harper, the haulier, the thriving Manuelle's quarry, the busy stoneyards, the regular coal shipments and the weighbridges in daily use, not to mention the old harbour characters.

Spending three hours in Peter's company, walking the north and south sides, it's relatively easy to shut your eyes and imagine a bygone life of charm, dust, dirt and ships, ships, ships.

Make no mistake: today's St Sampson's Harbour is a quiet place, compared with what once existed. Even before Peter came along, ship movements were not what they once had been, in the days of quarrying and stone exports.

Peter's childhood memories stem from the oddest of bases, certainly the most odd-shaped house preceding the threepenny house in the leafy Castel lanes and the amazingly stylistic snail-shaped modern building at Le Bigard on the south coast cliffs.

The reward for his mother, Joan, of working as caretaker of St Sampson's Parish Church, was the keys to the bizarre church house – still standing – just inside the gates of the J.W. Mowlem & Cooperation.

Mrs Stewart lived there until Christmas and it is with obvious pride that her son shows off the quirky building in which he grew up, at the very heart of the town. His town. Just down from his bedroom window, less than 10 metres away, stands the once-busy blacksmith's building, another throwback to an era when horses were integral to life.

His childhood tales would make every bored local teenager wish they, too, had the same opportunity for exploration and free-spirited, harmless fun, in a time when the words 'health' and 'safety' were more associated with whether you still had a cold and if that dog with a foaming mouth really did not bite, as its owner claimed.

Peter, as he will tell you, got up to all sorts and had only one severe ticking off from the legendary PC Trotter. Perhaps his favourite story relates to the towering stacks of stone,

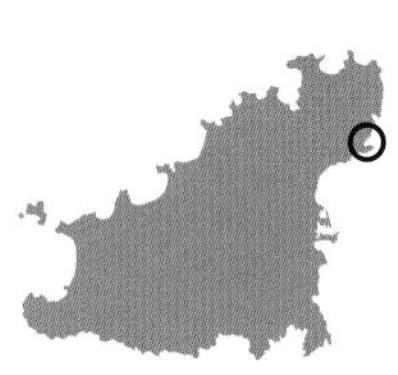

Left
'St Sampsonite'
Peter Stewart

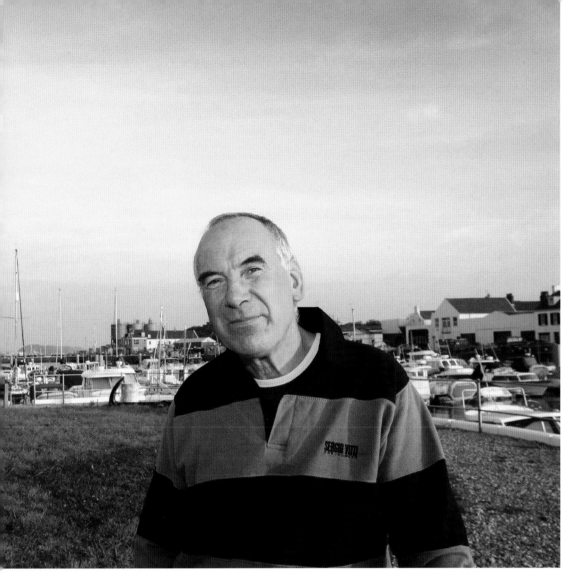

which would often dominate Manuelle's stone yard on South Side.

At its peak, the company was St Sampson's answer to Kitzbuhel.'We'd find sheets of corrugated iron, turn an end up and fire ourselves down the piles,' said Peter.

And if that was not thrilling enough, the local boys might have chosen to cajole one another into descending more than 200ft, down vertical ladders, into the base of Manuelle's quarry.

Then there was the time Peter and his mates were playing around the area which today houses the Fuel Supplies storage tanks.

'We came across some anti-aircraft shells in an old corroded case.We broke the case open and half-a-dozen of us walked to a nearby telephone box where we phoned the police and told them we had found some bombs.'

'Where are they?' said the officer on the safe end. 'In the telephone box with us,' came the reply.

'He went mad,' laughs Peter, who reports the canisters were later safely destroyed.

But Peter was a good boy and did his bit for the Stewart family in terms of bringing home valuable fuel for the winter fires.

At a time when Bird's, Nicolle's and Jory's all had coal sheds on South Side, it was habitual for kids and some housewives to wait for the lorries to spill coal from their overloaded sides.

'Once the lorries came off the South Side weighbridge, they had to do a U-turn in the road. Like everybody wanting something for nothing, women and kids would hang around with their buckets and shovels to collect the spills. Some of the drivers would deliberately give it extra stick to ensure coal would fall off. We virtually bought no coal in our house because I used to go over to North Side as well.'

Above
Craning for a better view of the sunrise

There it was anthracite (for the growing industry) and not house coal which was brought ashore. But that did not stop Peter who, when everybody had gone home, would jump into the hoppers and sweep up the leftovers.

'I had a large wooden box on a pair of wheels and I've been known to fill my cart up so much that I couldn't push it. My father, when he'd finished his day's work at Manuelle's, would have to come and help me push it back.'

Coal was not the only scraps the young Peter got his hands on. They extended to the wheat and maize unloaded by dockers for a company called J. H. Miller.

'I used to pick up any sweepings in a sack and would weigh it on my mother's kitchen scales. My main buyer was Mr Mauger, who kept fowls. I charged tuppence a pound, but one day he said to me if I'd allowed for the coal mixed in with it and the chippings off the quay...'

Another profitable exercise for Peter and his mates would come the way of beer bottle deposits.

At a time when a returned VB or Pony pint bottle was worth one old penny, it was the norm to collect the empties thrown into the harbour off the ships. One way of spending the profits was at Mr Harvey's North Side chippie. Trannie's on South Side was popular, too, but was a posher establishment, Peter recalls.

'This was my playground and I have always been fascinated by it,' said the man who in his hobby as a boat-spotter still spends many of his spare hours studying the commercial shipping movements.

'It was always so busy with ships and there was the toing and froing of the lorries.' Take away the manic traffic and it's altogether quieter now, he insists.

'In the late fifties there would be 50 to 60 ship movements a month. Today, it's gone really quiet and it could be a dozen or less. We've also now just seen the end of the coal era.'

And before coal went, St Sampson's said goodbye to the import of timber and bagged cement.

'I think what was the old St Sampson's Harbour has been spoiled – things removed, things built. Containerisation has, in its way, killed off the harbour.

'But it's still got a lot of charm as a commercial harbour.'

In recent times, it has become noted more for its switch to a modern marina. Not everybody was happy with the changes and Peter holds his hands up and admits he helped collect signatories to Gary Blanchford's anti-marina petition. But, now it's in place, he can see the benefits.

'I didn't like the idea but now it's been cleaned up, it looks a lot better. It was underused really.'

One project too far, though, was the Board of Administration's plan to build the deep-water berths and with it, move all cargo shipping closer to Brehon Tower than the Mariners.

'I didn't see it as really necessary. They have built enough ugly things already.'

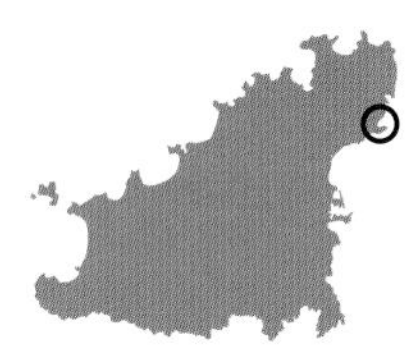

WHAT BECAME OF THE PUB PARROT?

MICHAEL PALIN argued till he was blue in the face that his caged parrot was dead. Deceased. No more.

Pushing up the daisies and so on. It was one of the classic comedy sketches of all time.

Now, should the Monty Python star arrive at North Side to enquire after the health of St Sampson's infamous parrot, he would have no need of convincing, because it most certainly is dead and has been for a long, long time.

Nobody is quite sure how long ago the Trafalgar Inn parrot had shuffled off this mortal coil, but probably half-a-century or more.

Few islanders recall the North Side squawker, but one who does is Delma Whales, 78.

She was just a young girl when Mr and Mrs Jim McCord ran the North Side pub, a cricket ball throw away from the harbour in Trafalgar Road.

'Poll', as she called it, without recalling whether that was the bird's proper name or not, was an entertainment in its own right, regardless of how many pints the hard-drinking punters downed.

It was renowned for its bad mouth: hardly surprising that a bird so naturally clever in terms of picking up the lingo should learn a few choice words.

Delma was too young to go into the pub, but would dart along the road from her Monmains home in the late 1930s to see it receive its weekly wash on the pavement outside the pub. 'Ooh, you bugger,' the parrot would say as Mr McCord soaked him.

'He used to hang it outside and stand it on the ledge,' she recalls.

'My god he could swear. 'We used to ask, "Does your mother do the washing?", and he would say, "How the hell do I know?". '

We called it Poll, as you would as kids.'

But the 200-year-old-plus pub has a whole lot more history to it than simply a dead and mischievous trained parrot.

There are tales of privateering and an underground network of tunnels leading to the corner of Trafalgar Road and the junction with La Hure Mare and, more intriguingly, under what is now Quayside and into the harbour. Jim Langlois, whose company, John Ogier Ltd, has had ownership of the pub – also formerly known as The Star – since as far back as the 19th century, confirms the legend.

John Ogier, whose name the company takes, was his grandmother's uncle.

Jim has heard the stories and, while unable to verify them, does know for a fact that Ogier owned the whole row of houses along Trafalgar Road, including the curved building known as Trafalgar House on the corner.

'The pub was reputed to have a tunnel under Quayside and into the harbour, but I don't really know where the entrance is,' he said.

The tales of tunnels make sense, he adds.

'John Ogier was a ship owner and lived in the house on the corner and in the basement is where he kept all his ship supplies.

'I can remember when he renovated it there was a big balance weight in there.'

He, too, has vague memories of the pub parrot.

'They used to put it on the pavement on a card table.'

Sadly, nobody remains who can shed light on the lifespan of the inn's famous bird, remembered and revered to this day on the hoarding outside the pub's entrance.

Whether the real Poll looked as healthy as the one in this particular picture is open to doubt.

Parrots might be one of the longest living birds with a capacity to earn a Queen's telegram, but any sitting on the bar inside a smoky working men's pub is likely to be falling off its perch before too long.

Above
The famous Trafalgar Inn parrot

CHANGING TIDES

THE tale goes that the grass on reclaimed land, where the sea once flowed between mainland Guernsey and Le Clos du Valle, has a salty tang.

As I have yet to suss a way of communicating with the local bovine community, I will take the suggestion very seriously while passing on actually trying it for myself.

But it makes sense. Just 201 years ago, where today you will find main link roads such as Route Militaire and Braye Road, hundreds of homes and two major industrial estates, was sea.

It may not have been deep and blue, but it was sea nevertheless and at high tide there was but one way to cross between mainland Gvarnsey (period spelling) and the Clos du Valle: The Bridge. But it wasn't called that at the time. Pre 1805, it was Le Grand Pont, or Pont du Diable (the devil's bridge).

Nowadays there may be a growing number of hooded little devils spoiling the image of Guernsey's second harbour, but the devilish connection stemmed from the unscheduled arrival in Guernsey of Robert the First, Duke of Normandy, in 1032.

While many modern-day Roberts are otherwise known as Robs, Bobs, Robbies or Bobbies, Duke Robert had the rather unkind sobriquet of Robert the Devil.

Local tradition has it that the devil built a causeway to gain access to Vale Castle and that the devil might have been the Duke of Normandy whose fleet and large army ran aground here 975 years ago.

If Robert's engineers built the Bridge, it was no more than a crude effort and nothing like the line of boulders with gaps through which the sea could pass, topped with wooden planks, which was put in place in the early 13th Century. Nearly six hundred years later, it would seem not much had changed.

Right
The way it might be: Guernsey as it would look were it not for the reclamation of the Braye du Valle 200 years ago

But then, fortunately, along came Sir John Doyle, lt-Governor of Guernsey from 1803 to 1816.

With France and England once again at each other's throats, a nervous Sir John believed a French invasion to be imminent and the virtually undefended Clos du Valle an easy target.

But while he eyed a reclamation of the Braye, the Trotts, Fallas and Torodes of the time wanted to deepen and widen it to enable better access for stone-laden ships from the northern-parish quarries.

Sir John got his way and by 1814 the island was shown on maps as one solid mass.

Nearly 300 acres were reclaimed and in truth it was a relatively painless and simple exercise.

In 1806, tenders went out for the construction of dams at both ends of the Braye and within two years, it was complete.

At the Grand Havre end Thomas Henry built an embankment out of large boulders and a brick wall to keep the sea out, with a gravel bank piled against the wall. In time, it had to be further strengthened by unwanted quarry stone.

At the Bridge, a stone wall was built parallel with the bridge, then filled with clay.

Sluices were incorporated at both ends of the Braye to allow surface water to escape.

The French for sluice is 'nocq' and, of course, St Sampson's retains its own Nocq Road to this day.

How long it took to drain the area is unclear but in 1811 Sir John sold the reclaimed land to six local landowners for the sum of £5,000.

By 1928 the land had been subdivided to 160 proprietors.

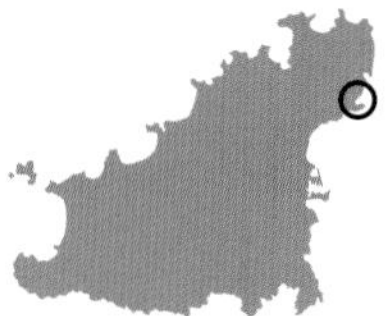

Were there losers in all this?

Is modern-day Guernsey worse off for the decision?

Long term, did Sir John do us a disservice?

Just imagine what lives we might have if Guernsey were still divided and the two parts connected only at the eastern and western ends of the Braye.

Well, if something similar were to be proposed in the 21st century, there would surely be a resounding 'no' from property owners unwilling to give up their front-garden access to the nautical playground.

Think Poole's estuary and you perhaps get an idea of what might have been had the Braye remained.

Back in the early 1800s, the saltpan owners were compensated for their loss of income.

But compensation to owners and the cost of the Crown-owned Braye totalled just £3,250.

Sir John had got his wish and made a profit. The six original purchasers of the reclaimed land were Pierre Yves Bardel, Henry Giffard, Daniel Mollet, Pierre Mollet, Isaac Carre and Jean Allez.

FACTFILE

BEFORE the reclamation of the Braye, there were just four crossing points between the mainland and Clos du Valle, other than those in place at the Vale Church and St Sampson's.

They were at Point Allaire, a short way east of the Vale Church, Pont Colliche between the Bailloterie and the salters on the other side, the tertre, where today stands Lowlands, and an unnamed causeway, which ran from near Oatlands to L'Islet.

Below
St Sampson's in all its magnificence

LEADER OF THE PACK

THE long list of shipwrecks outside St Sampson's Harbour tells its own story.

Mess with the fast-flowing stretch of tidal water flowing down the east coast at your peril. Just ask the owner of the 65ft luxury yacht, Never Say Never, which went aground on Black Rock last month and ever since has been sitting in Marine & General's repair yard.

But it's 55 years since the last major accident involving commercial shipping – the Fermain – and that has much to do with two things: the power of modern coasters and the skills of the port's pilots.

In the early 21st century, St Sampson's shipping benefits from three experts in one of the oldest professions in the business.

The skilled piloting trio are Captain Tich Harvey, Barry Paint and Roddie Ray and between them it is their job to safely guide the variety of tankers and supply ships into and out of the island's most northern harbour. They work in pairs, four days on, two days off.

Of the three, Capt. Harvey has a special association with the area, as it was where he grew up, having lived in Roland Road as a boy. Indeed, he even recalls the Fermain grounding, which occurred while he was doing a stint in the local chippie.

He went to sea at 14 and it's been his job ever since.

The captain is a modest man.

'There's no magic. It's just down to experience,' he says of his job – and in that field, few have as much knowledge of Channel Island waters.

'I joined Commodore in 1958 and then went into the navy and did 12 years there. I joined Condor in 1972 and then Commodore in 1973.'

He has been a master since the hot summer of 76. In his time he sailed several of Commodore's freight ships and a few of the Condor hydrofoils.

'But I preferred the container ships,' he says. He has been one of the island's six pilots since 1989.

Three of them work mainly at St Peter Port and the other three at St Sampson's, but you won't find a stronger tide around Guernsey than the one that rips along this stretch of coast down the Little Russel.

It can run at up to five knots and when you are at the wheel of a cargo ship, that does provide a certain stimulation of the thought process.

'Your first problem is getting out of that tide and when you have done that, the next one is stopping the ship,' he says.

'You've got a full blown river going north, which means you have to crab your way into the harbour.

'As you come out of the tide, you have a situation that the front of the ship is out of the tide but the back of it is still in it. The next thing is to stop it in the slack water outside the harbour so you don't dig a hole in the harbour bed.'

For entering the harbour, a howling south-easterly is bad news, but the captain says it is rare to abort a planned entry. He can recall only one personal instance of not being able to berth a ship in 18 years.

'There might have been two or three between us.'

For every visiting ship, it is the job of the pilot to join it either to the north or, more regularly, from the south. Invariably the pilot takes full control of the approach and takes the wheel upon getting on board.

'Although the captain is always responsible for his ship, we generally take the helm and get it in. You get the odd one or two characters who would rather be on the wheel themselves

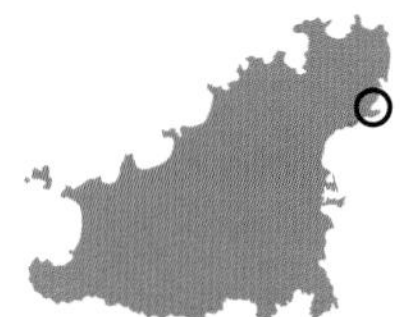

and you would then give them the orders, but 99% of captains are happy for you to take it.'

Occasionally you get a suspicious one and Capt. Harvey recalls boarding one tanker in the northern approaches when the captain was not so sure the Guernseyman was right.

'His GPS was telling him that he was travelling forward at 1.5 knots, which he assumed was forward when, in fact, due to the tide, it was backwards at 1.5 knots. It's vital to get the bloke's trust in the first few minutes.'

When the ship is coming from the north, the pilot prefers to board south of Roustel, but a stranger to St Sampson's might request the pilot to come aboard close to the Platte Fougere.

For the more popular southerly approach, the pilot normally boards when the ship is in the lee of the island between St Martin's Point and Lower Heads.

In his time, Capt. Harvey, who took over duties from Ted Noyon, has held a pilot licence for Weymouth, St Helier, Alderney and Sark but it's his native harbour that is most special to him.

'To me it's still a special place. It's attractive and has got a special charm.'

Above
Harbour pilots Captains Tich Harvey, Barry Paint and Roddy Ray

ROUGH WATERS

THE stretch of coast between Fort Doyle and Mont Crevelt has always been something of a graveyard for ships, although the building of the Platte Fougere lighthouse in 1909 seriously reduced the number of maritime disasters in that area.

Still, even nowadays it can be an awkward place, because as well as the rocks which abound, strong tides race down this narrow reach of the Little Russel.

In the days of sail and when navigational aids did not exist, the loss of vessels must have been enormous.

A glance at Ray Dafter's book Guernsey Wrecks highlights the extent of the perilous approaches to St Sampson's.

Arguably the reef's most famous victim was the Dorey collier Fermain, which struck a reef just north of the Black Rock at the mouth of St Sampson's Harbour on 30 December 1952.

Legend has it that the crew were so keen to reach harbour and the pubs before closing two days before new year that they shut down the fires that powered the steamer a trifle too early, particularly considering the gale force winds and flood tide that evening.

It had not the power to avoid the reef and it became stuck there for weeks.

Ten days later, it was confirmed that Guernsey Contractors Ltd, through its principal, Jack Norman, and Messrs. John Upham Ltd, had bought the wreck lock, stock and barrel.

No time was lost in recovering the 1,300 tons of Welsh coal targeted for local glass-houses and two weeks after it had become the island's newest attraction, Messrs. Norman, Upham and Peter L. Dorey boarded the ship for the first examination.

The next day construction began on a ship-to-shore causeway and the plan was hatched that once the roadway was complete, Upham's men would open the portside of the vessel like a can of beans and out would flow the coal.

A stream of lorries piled rubble onto the beach near the stoneyard and every passing hour saw the 1,000-yard gap between road and ship getting smaller.

It took a week to complete the causeway. Three weeks after the accident, 30 men and more than a dozen lorries and an excavator were used to level the beach and construct the causeway.

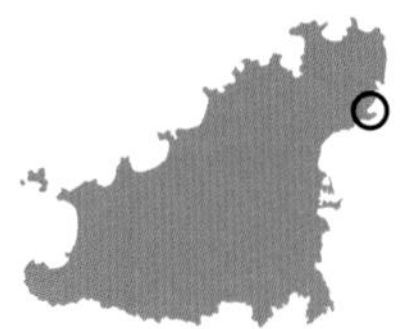

The first load of anthracite was offloaded on Monday 19 January 1953.

Before the Fermain, many others had come a cropper in the vicinity.

In the early 20th century the Tops'l schooner, Bessie, came to grief in Bordeaux Harbour.

In his Le Guernesiais notes of 1953, an anonymous contributor to the Guernsey Evening Press wrote: 'I have seen her figure-head salved from the wreck and now adorning a building near North Side, Vale.'

More than 50 years later, attempts to find the property with the Bessie figurehead have proved fruitless.

The barquentine, Dunsinane, was stranded on 13 August 1904 very near to the spot once occupied by the Fermain.

The vessel was built in Dundee in 1874 and was locally owned. Her master was Captain P. Mahy and in 'unaccountable fashion she drifted on to the Black Rock on leaving St Sampson's Harbour and became a complete wreck'.

Some years later, the Weymouth packet, Ibex, struck the Platte Fougere reef and founded. She lay on the bottom for six months before being raised.

Her hulk was towed into St Sampson's and ultimately she was completely repaired and went on to perform yeoman service for years to come.

It was probably due to her sinking that the lighthouse was erected: she was the last straw. Before then, the Platte Fougere rock had been marked only by a buoy. This was better than nothing, but in foggy conditions and at night, it was invisible.

In 1921, the small steamer, Clarrie, sank off Bordeaux having just sailed from St Sampson's laden with stone.

In an effort to raise her, the Hethery Brae herself sank following an explosion.

On 30 October 1935, the collier, Lancashire, was in considerable danger off Bordeaux. In the height of a storm, her engines broke down and she was forced to anchor perilously near the Houmet Paradis islet. The lifeboat, Queen Victoria, stood by and later towed the steamer to St Peter Port.

In March 1938, the Dutch freighter, Tommeliten, went aground almost on Bordeaux slipway. This time fog was to blame. She was refloated without serious injury.

Left
The collier Fermain got stranded off Black Rock on 30 December 1952

Overleaf
14 years earlier SS Tommeliten ran aground close by at Bordeaux

*"Today it is dilapidated and neglected.
All around lie the unlovely signs of industry
and the Martello looks wisely out to sea"*

Victor Coysh

CHAPTER 13

LONGUE HOUGUE
TO SPUR POINT

As St Sampson's eases towards its major port rival, the coastal territory turns a tad ugly. It was not always so, though, and the view across the Russel offers something special to those who live along this stretch running parallel with Bulwer Avenue.

TURNING UGLY · SINKING FEELING · AT THE COALFACE
KEEPING THE ISLAND GOING · VICTIMS OF A MODERN WORLD
LIVING ON THE EDGE · QUARRY COLLAPSE

WHERE GUERNSEY TURNS UGLY

Above
South Side at high tide

WHEN I set out on this Guernsey coastal odyssey, I did not expect to use the 'u' word.

All Guernsey is beautiful, I thought.

Even the walk around stinky Mont Cuet offers beautiful views of an often raging sea.

Well, I was wrong.

The half-mile stretching from South Quay, St Sampson's, to Spur Point is as ugly as Guernsey gets and it's all in the name of power and – dare we say it in an island in which our government never makes mistakes? – mis-management.

The Longue Hougue reclamation site had to happen somewhere, it's just a shame it is slowly developing like an ulcer on the gateway to Guernsey.

And the bad news?

It is likely to get a whole lot worse before it gets better.

At some stage of the inert waste infill project it seems inevitable the much-touted incinerator will be plonked there to dominate the easterly view of irritated islanders living on the rising slopes away from St Sampson's.

People like me.

It was a point made to me by Scott Ogier before the 2003 election.

The man vowed to fight it and I vowed to vote for him.

Four years later it was interesting to hear Deputy Ogier's view on the Longue Hougue development.

'The pace of change can be slow and four years on most people would have hoped we would be further on with our solid waste strategy,' he said.

'Longue Hougue still stands ready for whatever solution we implement. Were it not for our change of direction, we could have had a 100ft-high incinerator standing there burning our waste, recyclable or otherwise. I see that possibility becoming more and more remote as mainstream society adjusts to the challenges which climate change throws up for us.'

The deputy firmly believes that the islanders'

response to the issue will reap benefits in the end.

'Four years on, who still believes we should be throwing plastic, paper, cardboard, aluminium and other metals into bonfires?

'It is my firm view that whatever goes onto Longue Hougue in the next few years will not be as visually intrusive as that which was planned in 2004 and will be considerably more environmentally acceptable. Society and its expectations have quite simply moved on.'

Still, everything about the area is x-rated, not to be publicised and, as soon as possible, hidden.

Even Mont Crevelt, a fortification dating back to 1779, is non grata and unexplorable, while its rival across the harbour, Vale Castle, is treated with every respect by those with the job of preserving and making the most of our island history.

To the immediate south of Mont Crevelt is more unedifying coastline which the Board of Administration was not so long ago considering as a potential third harbour.

Back in the late 1980s the board examined three possible designs for a harbour at Spur Point, ranging in price from £13m. to 16.5m.

Instead, it decided to concentrate on expanding St Sampson's Harbour.

'The Spur Point idea would have given three ports within two miles of each other,' said a BoA spokesman.

Also, crucially, 'it would be a financial liability and would also be visually and environmentally unacceptable'.

Thankfully, we escaped that near miss but one senses there may be more potential visual crises ahead.

After all, we are not a million miles away from possible Billsonland and we all know what the words Belle, Greve and reclamation do to islanders' blood pressure.

IN BRIEF

THE Longue Hougue Reclamation Site covers an area of more than 12 hectares and is enclosed by a rubble-mound breakwater one kilometre in length.

The total tonnage of stone in the breakwater, ranging in size from 5kgs to four tonnes, is in excess of 555,000.

Three quarries in the Cherbourg area provided the stone.

They were at L'Ouest, Brix and Montebourg and supplied over 400,000 tonnes of material.

Stone was stockpiled at a disused quay in the port of Cherbourg and shipped to Guernsey using two flatbottomed barges, each carrying approximately 4,200 tonnes at a time.

Although production of stone at the quarries began in October 1990, shipments did not start until late January 1991.

The 130,000 tonnes of material stockpiled on the quay thereby avoided any delays to shipment other than weather restrictions.

The existing outer marina moorings at Longue Hougue were opened in 2002 and were expected to last 15 years, but the area is filling with inert waste more quickly than expected.

It is expected that only 100 will be available by the end of 2008 and that there will be just 30 left by 2012.

Below
Longue Hougue Reclamation

SINKING FEELING

GUERNSEY'S biggest ships were built on South Side.

Sad, then, that so early into the 21st century and just 150 years on from the height of the local industry, not one single shipbuilder remains.

'It's a shame that we've seen the last of the shipbuilding yards in the Channel Islands,' said Marine & General's technical director Andy Way, whose company's repair yard is the last link with the golden age of shipbuilders which surrounded the harbour in the mid-19th century.

In a then thriving shipbuilding market which stretched from the South Esplanade along Les Banques to St Sampson's, South Side housed the most yards and, in Ogier's, certainly the biggest.

He may not have been the most prolific – de la Mare at La Piette built nearly three times as many – but Ogier's built the biggest and the finest, most notably the Golden Spur at 200ft long and weighing 656 tons.

A map of the harbour, dated between 1812 and 1894, shows the yards of Ogier, Stonelake, Thom, Lidstone and Rankilor to the south.

Sauvarin and the Domaille/Brache yard stood at the north.

Ogier's yard, situated today where Wine & Beer Importers stands, operated until 1924, its final years dedicated to repairing and modifications rather than building.

Ogier, it is reported, tried hard to keep up with modernisation in the ship industry, but he built just one steamer, named Commerce.

But by then it was simply not viable for little old Guernsey to follow the move into iron-hulled ships and so after building six brigs, four brigantines, three schooners, one ketch, four cutters, two gaffs and a steamer, Ogier closed its doors for the last time.

The practice for launching at St Sampson's

Right and overleaf
Marine & General is at the heart of harbour life at St Sampson's

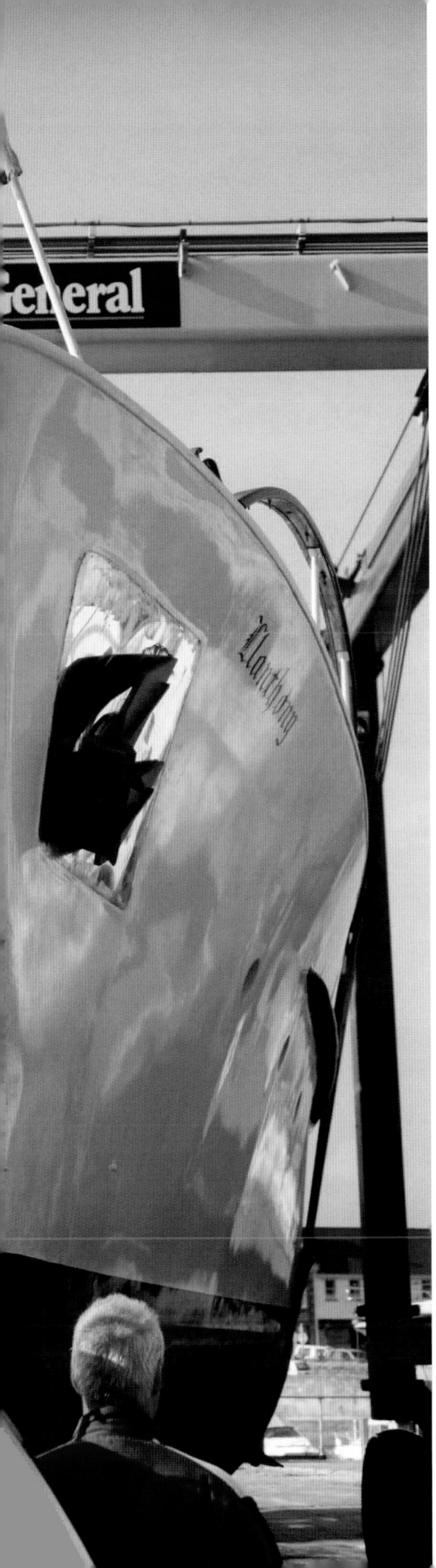

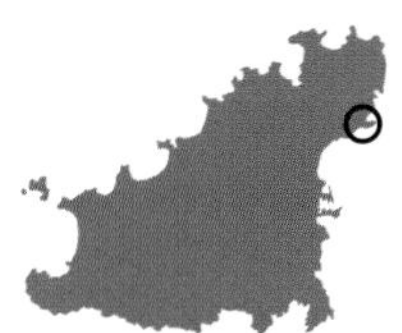

was made more interesting with the arrival of trams in the late 19th century.

E. W. Sharp's book The Shipbuilders of Guernsey reports that 'the ways were cleared off [the road] so as to enable the 8.30 tram to run'.

It's also clear that the custom of the period was to leave the coping stones of the quay loose opposite a berth to allow the laying of the ways.

Marine & General's top man expects 'ways' meant greasy boards, but what is certain is that St Sampson's has seemingly launched its last locally-based ship.

The company has built many a boat in its time, but nothing to compare in size with Ogier's handiwork.

'From the early 1980s we built Trident, Trident 4, Condor Kestrel and Trident 5 and rebuilt Trident 6 after Commodore sliced it into two,' said Andy.

Like Ogier's nearly a century ago, the company has faced up to the necessity to change and seems to be doing so successfully.

'The majority of our business was commercial shipwork and particularly the Condor fleet, and we did a lot of work for the quarrying industry.

'But the marine side of the business died due to the demise of commercial shipping and so we decided to introduce a 70-ton boat lift.

'Up to two years ago we serviced all the locally operated boats, but the last big one to come up [the slip] was Condor 9.'

And with it came the end of an era.

With a lift now operational the concentration is on repairs to smaller private boats.

'It's a shame the last repair yard has disappeared,' said Andy.

'Because the cradle is not operating we are limited to the leisure boat market.'

CONDOR
CONDOR

CONDOR
CONDOR 7

AT THE COALFACE

THE Sunday afternoon island car tour has long been part of Guernsey life.

But one place vehicles stayed well away from when cars began to take over our roads was South Side, St Sampson's.

And why didn't they come?

Four letters – D-I-R-T.

The coalyards of South Side were not for sightseers, as Jurat David Jory recalled when quizzed on the background to the family business – coal merchant A. E. Jory.

'In those days [the 1950s] people didn't have cars, but if they did they wouldn't have come down here.'

And this popular pillar of local society would know that all too well, having left Elizabeth College and jumped into the family business to succeed his grandfather.

'My father [a civil servant] had ink on his hands and I had coal dust in my ears,' he joked.

It is 30 years since the Jory business departed South Side with the writing well and truly on the wall for the local house coal industry.

Not one yard remains but at its height 200,000 tons a year was imported into the island via St Sampson's and the whole of South Side, from the weighbridge at the entrance of Church Road to the southern jetty jutting out into the harbour mouth, was lined with coal merchants.

'It was nothing to come down here on a Monday morning to see two colliers on North Side and two on South Side,' said the man whose business arrived in the area at the start of the 1950s.

Bird's was the first big coal importer of the area, its big sheds adjacent to the northern end of Bulwer Avenue seen on area maps dating back to 1873.

By the time A. E. Jory arrived on the scene, Nicholls had replaced Bird's at the northern end, while between there and Walter Bird, where today Wine and Beer Importers stands, was the Jory business and the coal yard owned by the ship owners Onesimus Dorey.

'My little store,' as Mr Jory refers to it, stood in what now is part of the barriered no-go area to the sea side of the blast walls.

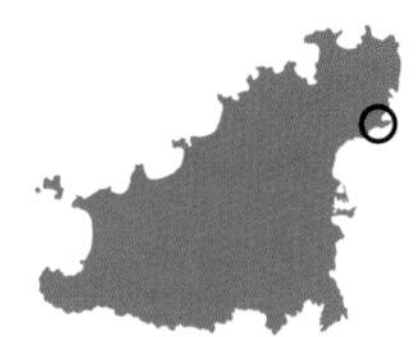

Walter Bird had strong connections with the most successful football club in the island, then and now: Northerners AC.

Rival merchant Mr Jory recalled: 'He had his lorries swept out and cleaned up by his drivers so he could take the supporters to the football and cheer on the team.'

The South Side merchants dealt purely with house coal, while across the harbour on North Side, E. J. Henry brought in the anthracite for the growing industry.

They were dirty old days and many men could have auditioned for the Black and White Minstrel Show.

'When they were discharging the anthracite and there was a southerly blowing my mother would have coal dust all over her house and she lived by the Vale Mill.'

Left
Dirty work at coal merchant A.E. Jory

KEEPING THE ISLAND GOING

FORGET la-di-da St Peter Port harbour.

St Sampson's is the man's man's harbour. The hub of the island.

Captain 'Tich' Harvey, one of the three pilots who guide today's fuel ships in and out of the port, has no doubt about the real importance of the one-time northern creek.

Without it, he says, Guernsey would come to a standstill.

'It's where all the fuel comes into the island and without fuel the island would come to a grinding halt.'

St Sampson's was built primarily to export.

But as it heads towards its 200th birthday as a port integral to the commercial success of the island, it is fuel imports that make it and the island tick.

Oil, gas, coal, sand and cement.

Without its regular visitors – import coasters – Guernsey would just not function.

Fuel Supplies has been importing since 1955.

The Shell-owned company might not have as large a share of the fuel market as Total, which nowadays acts on behalf of Esso and also enjoys the lucrative States fuel contracts, but in terms of sailings into the island is its rival's equal.

Total deliveries come ashore on the north quay using flexible loading arms which pump the fuel via pipes straight into its tanks across the road at North Side.

Shell operates on South Side, with two loading arms bringing the various types of fuel ashore under the main road off the Bridge and into its Bulwer Avenue storage tanks.

Both companies get their fuel from Rotterdam and use two Fisher/Everards coasters, the Alacrity, Allurity and Agility, for which Allied Coasters acts as the local agent.

Both coasters are soon to be replaced by new Russian purpose-built coastal tankers of the maximum length for this harbour, 80m.

For Shell, it's a minimum five-hour operation to unload a cargo of fuel – that after an initial 90-minute period of onboard procedures which include testing the fuel.

Mark Poole, operations manager for Fuel Supplies, is one of three supervisors for the company, which has deliveries virtually every other week.

There were 19 in 2006 and on the day visited, the company was dealing with its 16th of 2007.

That night's delivery included avgas, jet fuel and premium unleaded motor spirit.

The jet fuel, kerosene, is to feed the airport, the avgas is needed to operate the likes of Trislander planes and other small private aircraft and the unleaded motor spirit goes into our cars' fuel tanks.

The amount of fuel cargo fluctuates and is somewhat dependent on the tides.

'Because it's coming on the back end of the tide – we work on 8m. tides upwards – this one has a reduced cargo,' said Mr Poole.

'Normally we will try to schedule the boat for the middle of the tide. That gives us about a week's window.'

As Alacrity was guided through the pierheads by local pilot Barry Paint just after 10 at night, the tide was an 8.1.

In terms of manpower the onshore operation is not vast.

Present on the quay were dockmaster Mike Gaudion, Fuel Supplies' duty supervisor Peter Blake and two operators.

Allied Coasters also had a presence at the docking and while the motor spirits were offloaded a States harbour watchman with special constable clout was present.

It is not a place to take chances and at some point Health and Safety is and involved, more often than not in the shape of John Colley.

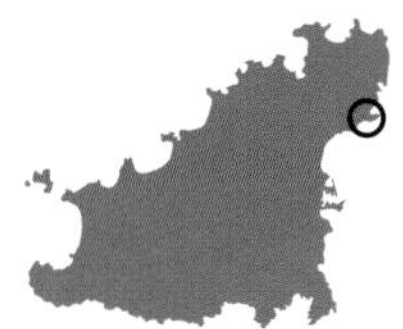

Left
Fuel ship Alacrity creeps into St Sampson's under dark

The operations manager described unloading as a 'normally straightforward' operation.

Three pipelines were used for this particular load. The motor spirit comes up one line and the jet fuel up another.

'When we get aviation fuel in, we first do a flush to make sure everything [in the pipes] has been gone.

As it's a different colour [very blue] we can tell what's what,' said the ops man.

'We're the only ones who supply aviation fuel so we have to be spot on with regard to quality' The avgas supply will keep the company going for a couple of months, but the jet fuel will last only about three weeks.

The motor spirit is about a month's worth.

Within six hours of Alacrity tying up alongside, the tanks are empty.

But it will be another five days before the fuel is ready for public consumption.

'It will be another day before samples can be taken and sent away [to Jersey] for testing.

'Tonight's jet will not be on line until Friday, all being well.'

Alacrity had docked within an hour of Ronez's cement boat leaving the island.

The Ronez boat generally makes a dozen visits per year, bringing in cement dust, which is fired into storage silos on shore.

Guernsey Gas Ltd has regular sailings too, a variety of ships arriving at St Sampson's on 20 occasions in 2006 – and then there are boats for sand, aggregate and coal.

The boats and their cargos

All regular visitors to St Sampson's Harbour in 2007

- Agility, Allurity and Alacrity (fuel)
- Sigas Lotta, Sigas Lydia, Sigas Laura and Sigas Linda (gas)
- Mungo (building sand)
- Jaynee W (heavy oil)
- Ronez (pulverised flue ash or cement)
- Nina 1 (house coal)
- Ardent and Lark (sand or limestone aggregate)

There were 118 import dockings in the first eight months of 2007.

VICTIMS OF A MODERN WORLD

SOUTH SIDE is one long, sad tale of what once was.

The trams, the cranes, the coal sheds, the stoneyards, the weighbridge, the regatta.

All gone, left to be fondly remembered in black and white or sepia photography.

The trams were first to go.

They ran between Town and North Side from the latter part of the 19th century to the early years of the 20th.

Over the years the neighbourhood waved goodbye to the noise and dust of coal and stone and the once mighty annual North Regatta was finally laid to rest about the turn of the millennium.

The last weighbridge at the entrance to Church Road was closed in August 1983, leaving what weighing there was to be done at the harbour to the one remaining States-operated one on the North Side.

After decades of use – it had opened in 1922 – the old machinery had worn out and parts could no longer be obtained.

By the end of the decade the row of South Side diesel-electric cranes had been dismantled and sold for scrap.

The writing had been on the wall for the 'old greys' when one dropped the Condor Kestrel.

The Board of Administration called for a detailed survey of the island's harbour cranes and the result was that seven were immediately shut down.

It left South Side with no working cranes.

After 40 years of almost daily haulage they disappeared.

But there was still the regatta, at the time the biggest and best the island had.

Inaugurated around 1950, by the early 1970s it was a five-day affair which provided fun for all, in and out of the water.

In the 1970s the local business community was backing the event to the extent producing

Right
Old time St Sampson's has included regattas, trams and, briefly, banger racing

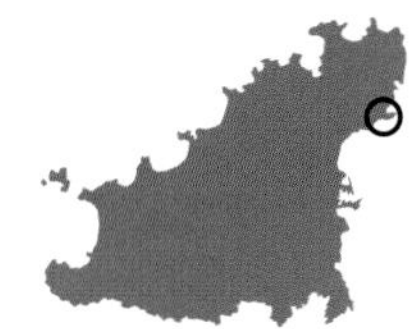

daily regatta week advertisement features in the Evening Press & Star.

On the sea, the programme included races from powerboats to dinghies.

When the tide went out in this period the mucky, gluey harbour bed was used for the precursor to autocross – Guernsey's then youngest and zaniest sport, N-Autocross.

On the shore, you could catch fancy-dress competitions, angling showdowns, clay pigeon shooting at Mont Crevelt, tug-of-war on the Crocq and bands on an erected stage.

Nowadays, you need to be parachuted to get into Mont Crevelt, the Crocq is a car park and the regatta a distant memory, a victim of the harbour's changing face and marina.

LIVING ON THE EDGE

NOBODY should be the slightest bit surprised that if you dig a hole virtually the depth of a southcoast cliff, something or somebody might fall off the edge.

Thirty-eight years ago a large landslip carried dozens of graves from neighbouring St Sampson's Church cemetery into the 250ft deep Longue Hougue quarry, which ultimately led to the closure of it as a long-standing supply of granite.

Gravestones disappeared, never to be seen again, and worried neighbours fretted as to whether they should stay living on the edge.

Nobody was killed and nobody has been since, despite further smaller slides.

But back in 1919 one poor old dear did die – as she tended her pet rabbits in her back garden, close to the western edge of the island's then biggest hole, worked by A. and F. Manuelle.

The dreadful day was 22 August 1919 and while it was desperately sad, there was something Monty Python-esque about the story that appeared in the Guernsey Evening Press and Star.

Mrs W. Martin was seen by a neighbour feeding her bunnies when, said the neighbour, 'she threw up her arms, screeched and disappeared'.

With the octogenarian went two gardens and the wash-houses of two former cottages in Church Road.

It took two years to recover Mrs Martin's remains from the foot of the quarry but, freakishly, the rabbits survived the experience and were discovered alive and well amid the rubble.

Church Road inhabitants Steve and Tracie Queripel have lived within 20 yards of the quarry's western edge for 20 years and had never heard the tale of poor Mrs Martin.

'We knew about the graves that went in but we didn't know about the woman,' said the Queripels, who have brought up three children in their home overlooking the quarry.

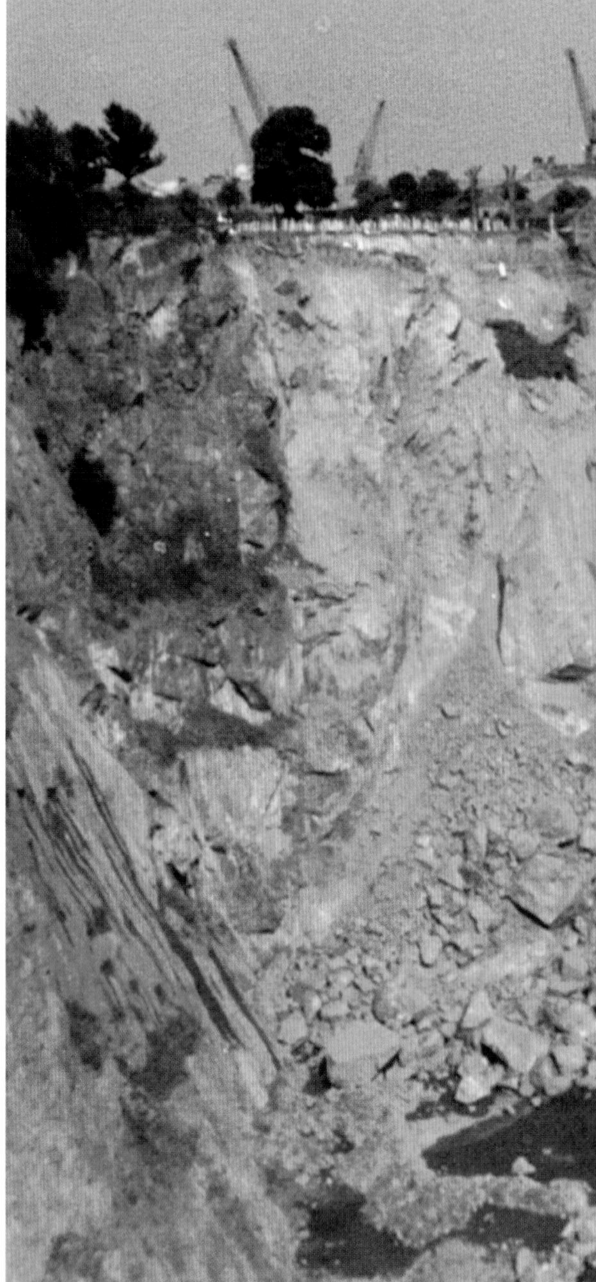

Above
Landslide at Longue Hougue in 1969

It has never freaked them out in the way it did others, but they do admit to having the occasional fearful thought of a disaster.

'Sometimes, you do wonder,' said Steve, whose great-great grandfather once worked in the quarry, of which he has a splendid view from his upper floor loo.

When they bought their terraced house in 1983 they considered it good business, although when they went to court to sign the deeds, the advocate pointed out to them that the States Water Board would take no respon-

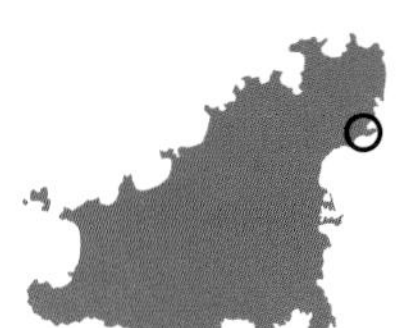

sibility should their house or part of their property disappear.

'I would prefer to live in a farmhouse in St Peter's,' jokes Steve, 'but you bought what you could at the time. We wanted a place to park our car and boat in the garden.'

Before committing to the purchase, the Queripels took the advice of a builder friend and Steve's grandfather.

'I spoke to my grandfather about it and he said the landslip was further up.

'A survey we had done by a local builder also said it would be fine.' And it has been.

Many others were not so sure, obviously.

In the period 1971 to 1979, five of the eight houses remaining in Church Road changed hands three times and one property four times.

There was even serious consideration given to compulsory purchase – this after the Water Board's offer to buy the quarry and land on which the houses stood was turned down.

One building that did disappear was the old rectory.

But for a quarter of a century, and as it filled to become the biggest single water storage in the island (bigger than the St Saviour's reservoir), all has been quiet on the Longue Hougue quarry front.

Even the friendly ghost of an old woman in the Queripels' household is rarely felt.

And, as Steve said with tongue firmly in cheek, living on the edge has one benefit: 'You are guaranteed that nobody is going to build behind you.'

FACTFILE

- Friday 29 August 1969: part of St Sampson's churchyard was sealed off after a massive landslip on the north-east face of Manuelle's quarry at Longue Hougue. Dozens of graves slid to the bottom of the 250ft quarry which had been mined by A. and F. Manuelle for 80 years.
- The slip involved more than a 100-yard length of quarry face.
- In addition to the graves, an engine house for the blondin overhead bucket system plummeted to the quarry floor. Long fissures, four inches wide in places, appeared in the churchyard path.
- Longue Hougue quarry landslips continued until around 1980.
- On becoming a water reserve, the quarry surpassed St Saviour's Reservoir as the biggest single storage facility for fresh water, with a capacity of 308 million gallons compared with the reservoir's 240 million.

SEEING THE QUARRY COLLAPSE FIRST-HAND

Above
Former quarryman Fred Brown who captured the pictures (right) on the day of the big slip

THE day the quarry collapsed had far-reaching consequences for staff at Manuelle's.

For men like Fred Brown, the day marked the end for them at this long-standing local quarry firm.

Fred, now 87, was operating the blondin [lifting mechanism] that fateful day and guessed something serious was amiss the previous evening.

'I happened to see by the blondin house a crack, a very fine one.

'I said jokingly to my mate, "it's going to slip".

The following morning it had got a bit wider and all the men were stopped from working, they stayed up top.

'You could hear the cracking of the stone moving. I went to the other side of the quarry and watched it go.

'That was it. The end of the job. I went to Ronez afterwards.'

As for the blondin that Fred had operated, it remains underwater in the quarry to this day.

'When there is a drought you can see the remains of it towards O'Toole's yard way.'

Fred holds fond memories of the quarry, next to which he still lives in one of the terraced houses he had occupied for much of the time after joining Manuelle's having left the army.

He and his wife Marion have lived in the same house overlooking it since 1954, 30 yards or so away from the remains of that in which the fated Mrs Martin lost her life in 1919.

The late Peter Allez, who lived across the road from him, had first told him of the tragedy.

'He said that the rocks that fell on her were

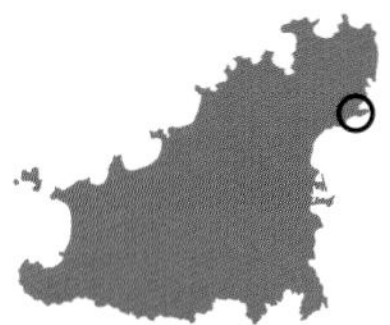

in the shape of the cross.'

Living so close to the quarry has never concerned him.

'It never worried me because behind me is solid rock,' said the man who operated the blondin and the 1,001ft-long lifting line across the breadth of the quarry for 20 years.

They were, he says, hard and dirty days for the quarrymen.

'We worked eight to five and Saturdays were more or less maintenance days.'

'One time when they were cutting by hand there were 10 cutters either side of the swamp hole and four loaders loading the [lifting] box by hand.

'Then on top of them there were the workers sieving out the dust.

There were about 31 [of us] then and when it was manhandled with a digger, it went down to 19.

'Between five and five-and-a-half- tons of stone a day we used to pull out of the quarry.'

"I've seen my sister swimming in water so full of sewage that she was brushing away the stuff with her arms"

George Staples

CHAPTER 14

BELLE GREVE

There are those who would fill it in for a golf course, or enclose it and introduce lagoons with modern waterfront properties for the 21st Century. But to most it is simply a great bay with an uninterrupted view of 'our' islands.

BAY FOR ALL SEASONS · EXPLOSIVE HISTORY
DANGER UNDER THE SEA · STEAMED UP, BLOWN UP

A BAY FOR ALL SEASONS

IT'S intriguing to imagine what was going through the head of whoever it was, whenever it was, when he christened the slice of eastern seaboard between the Salerie and Richmond Corner Belle Greve, meaning beautiful beach.

After all, apart from the view eastward across the Little Russel to Herm and Sark, what exactly makes this most controversial stretch of our coastline worthy of the title?

It's not impossible, of course, that centuries ago this giant of Guernsey bays – only Rocquaine and Vazon rival it for size – enjoyed long strips of golden sands.

But you somehow doubt it.

Considered ugly by many, there are those who would happily fill it in – cover up all that horrible black granite.

For 30 years it has been viewed as the prime candidate for land reclamation and long before Charles Billson saw the potential of it as our 'Little Venice', Roger Berry's Board of Administration was mulling over a 100-year scheme to reclaim it with non-noxious material.

That was 1988 and its roots were in the 1980 recommendation of consulting engineers Lewis and Duvivier, which also included the original concept of the North Beach Marina.

It was seen as ideal for commercial warehouse and factory development.

By the late 1980s the board had concluded that any reclamation would be best left as 'the open heathland type which does not provide any obstruction to the view'.

My cynical side tells me that heathland would have ultimately given way to commerce and that the factories would have gone up. Thankfully, it appears that nothing of the sort will happen.

Now the attention reverts to Belle Greve's prime problem – sewage.

It's fashionable to believe that our handling of it is of primary importance, but virtually four full decades after the current outfall scheme was completed, what has changed to demand a quick fix?

At high tide Belle Greve undergoes a vast change of character, all those dark outcrops covered and temporarily forgotten.

When the plug is pulled, the rocks return to view in the same way as happens at Cobo

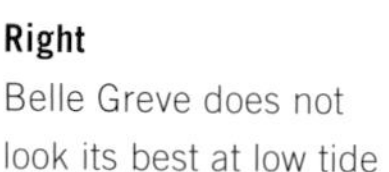

Right
Belle Greve does not look its best at low tide

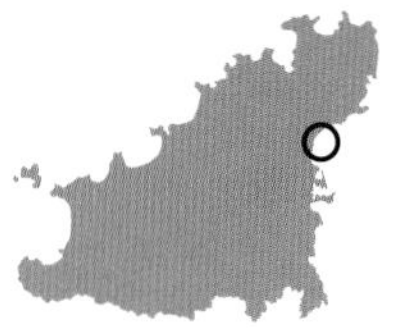

and Rocquaine. The only difference is that out west, they are pink and glint in the sun.

But as a stretch of water between Salerie and Pike's corners, the bay offers so much, not least that staggeringly beautiful view of Herm, Jethou and Sark.

Were that ever taken away, Guernsey would be a whole lot less appealing.

On terra firma, the same stretch of coast has seen more changes than most in modern times.

It's strange to think that landmark businesses such as Fruit Export and Bougourd Bros stood proudly until relatively recently, but anyone under the school-leavers' age will probably recall neither, just years of extensive construction which has left us with the Admiral Park complex.

Even that gets the tongues wagging.

While some, like me, see an attractive, modern piece of architecture, there are, no doubt and certainly among the older generations, hundreds of islanders who wish they had never set eyes on such incongruous buildings.

I suspect it will remain our most hotly debated piece of coastline for decades to come.

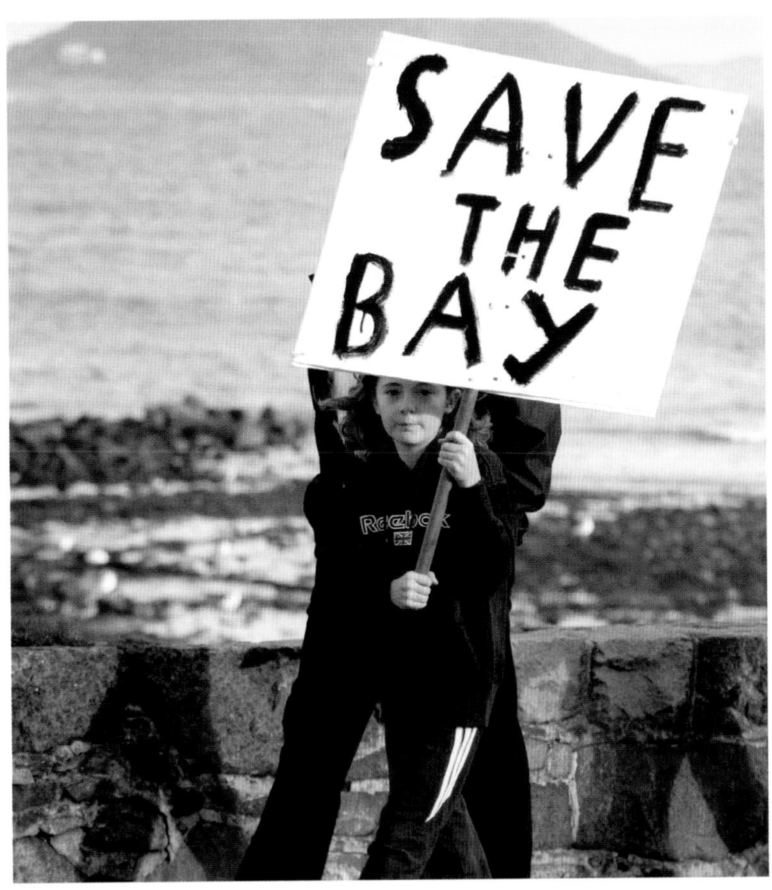

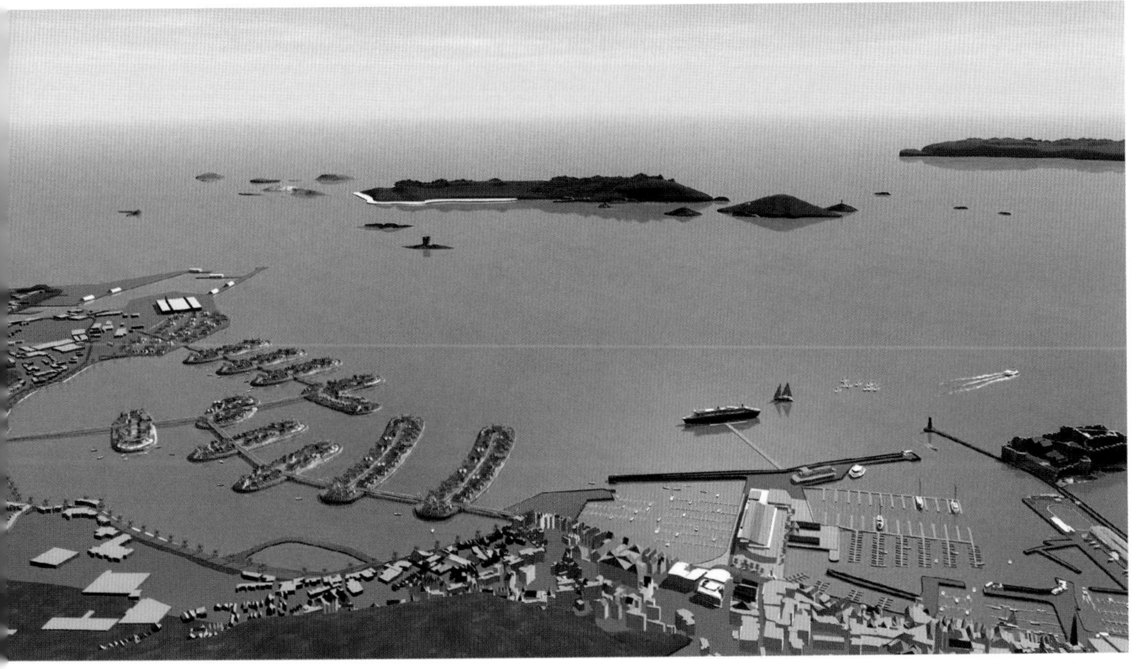

Above and left
For change or not?

EXPLOSIVE HISTORY

BORN in a castle. Now, few islanders can make that boast.

But it's one that octogenarian George Staples, a man arguably more steeped in knowledge of 20th-century Belle Greve Bay than anyone, can put his hand on his heart and say is true.

Back in 1925, George was one of three Staples children (there were eight in total), born in the Ivy Castle, otherwise known as Chateau des Marais.

He laughs at the fact before we turn to one of the subjects most dear to him: Belle Greve, a stretch of coast he knows like the back of his big old stonemason's hands.

No sooner was he out of nappies than George was experiencing the natural delights of the controversial, oft-targeted bay.

Whether it be fishing, swimming, baiting, or simply fooling about on it, Belle Greve was a versatile playground for this burly man who, approaching his 84th birthday, still has a boat in the Pool in St Peter Port harbour and regularly scours the Bailiwick marks for the fish he loves to eat four times a week.

For 60 years he has lived, with wife Joan, within a stone's throw of the bay, in the house he built behind the Absolute End in Bouillon Lane.

His passion for the area is as strong as his grip and, not unnaturally, he was among the marchers who, a couple of years back, strode along the front to protest against Charles Billson's plans to turn the bay into a so-called 'Little Venice' off the Little Russel.

Now, that's a subject to get him going, but to suggest he is against change would be a mistake.

For a start, he has his own perfect vision of the Belle Greve he won't see in his lifetime.

That involves a road that stretches from St Sampson's to Town... 'so the bay can be flooded and allow an ormer farm'.

He seriously doubts if such a project will ever happen but the idea of a pond with minimal tide, which would cover much of the bay's unattractive black granite, is not one he baulks at.

On the question of sewage, he firsts tells

Right
The remains of the concrete pool built by the Germans
Opposite
Belle Greve 'old boy' George Staples

CHAPS
JEANSWEAR

a story from his childhood and addresses it seriously. Pointing across the bay from our Salerie vantage point towards the refurbished Commerce House at Les Banques, he says:

'As young kids me and my sister Anne used to swim on the beach there. I've seen her swimming in water so full of sewage she was brushing away the stuff with her arms in the water.'

That was the early 1930s when, he says, there was more sand on Les Banques than there is today and certainly more sewage.

'We have to advance with the times and if, according to European law, we are seen to be infringing rights then we will have to do something about it.

'It should be the island's number one priority. That and waste disposal should be put above everything else, including health and building new schools.'

He does not like the incongruous Admiral Park but does admire the renovation of Commerce House, which, he recalls, was close to the 'old circus field'.

The field, he says, ran all the way back into the Bouet, a short distance from the brick chimneys which he estimates stood twice as high as those which tower over St Sampson's these days.

Much of his childhood was spent in the company of fellow Amherstian and sporting legend, Les Collins.

'Les and I used every bait patch on this beach. We dug from here by the [QEII] Marina to St Sampson's.'

And during the Occupation, the two daredevils would risk incurring the wrath of the Germans through illegal visits to the beach, which included lobbing rocks at the Teller mines.

'There were 50 of more of these big crosses [at Les Banques] with a Teller mine on them. We'd heave rocks at them but they never went off. I think you would have to ram them with a ship.

Above
Ripe for reclamation? Some think so, some not

'You weren't allowed on the beach, but kids are kids, aren't they?'

Relating such stories gives him obvious joy.

Another favourite of his is how the Germans' saltwater pool, the remnants of which can still be seen near the Longstore, failed so miserably.

'When the Germans built an electricity station in the Bouet, they also constructed a big pool to hold water when the tide went out, I suppose so they could cool the water in the electric station.'

The pool, he says, was certainly substantial, the four- to five-feet high concrete walls sticking out 100 yards or so into the bay and at least that distance across.

But no sooner was it built than the tide dropped and such was the pressure on the poorly constructed walls, with insufficient foundations, that the pool emptied itself and the

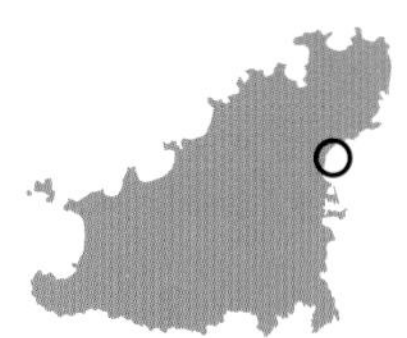

structure collapsed, taking all the sand with it.

Even today, large slabs of concrete from those pool walls still lounge about fairly close to the sea wall and the remains of the filter is there, built into it.

Before entering the army, a teenaged George sought to earn a living from the bay through making salt.

'I was about 15 or 16 and I'd come down to the bay two or three times a day to get sea water and pedal it back to the Coutanchez.'

The image of a youngster transporting water on a bike takes some imagining, but George explained just how he did it.

'It was like a pair of perambulator wheels with a little truck on top of them and a crook handle which attached just under saddle of the bike.

'Bear in mind the tyres were the sort of hosepipe type because you didn't have pneumatic ones in those days.'

Didn't he spill a lot?

'One used to have a plank of wood floating in it and hessian over the top to minimise it [the slop].'

He described the container as a 6ft hip bath, about 15in high and 6ft long:

'The sort you used to have your bath in, in front of the fire.'

Each load was enough to fill three cast-iron copper dome-shaped bowls, which would take eight-to-10 hours to boil down – all in the quest for 4lbs of salt.

'We used to make salt for a living as there was no other way to make money in those days.'

The Longstore sea wall has always been a popular fishing spot and George again chuckles while recalling the time – and he was now living in Bouillon Lane – he caught two huge bass off it.

Children had alerted him to the fact that there was a shoal of big fish over the wall.

His lack of bait was solved by Percy Bougourd's offer of the guts from a freshly-caught mackerel and no sooner had his line hit the water than George was reeling in a 10-and-a-half pounder, to be followed minutes later by a 10-and-a-quarter pounder.

His recollections stretch far enough back to recall sea breaking over the tram as he travelled towards St Sampson's.

'It used to be beach where Jack Norman's yard [Norman Piette] was.'

Spur Point is an area he would happily see developed, but other than that and his dream road, he hopes future generations will leave Belle Greve well alone.

'It's nature as it is meant to be.

'People may say it's ugly at low tide, but I don't think it's ugly at all.

'It's got its compensatory factors and what better vista could you have than to look out across to the islands.'

DANGER UNDER THE SEA

NEVER mind the smell. People have been badly hurt doing their part to relieve the island of its sewage via the Little Russel.

Ridding Guernsey of its 'ones and twos' using outfall pipes into Belle Greve can be dated back to about 200 years ago, but it was the major sewage scheme of 1968 to 1971 which nearly cost lives.

In 1971, four men were injured in a mystery rock-face explosion 60ft under the seabed, as the scheme to lay an extended outfall approached its conclusion.

Police and ambulances rushed to the scene to hear a survivor inform rescuers that three colleagues were lying injured near the drill face, 3,650ft out to sea.

Two doctors were sent down the shaft and within an hour the injured men were brought to the surface, requiring hospital treatment.

All four of the injured worked for the contractors Marples Ridgway, who, at the time, were at a loss to explain the explosion other than to surmise that the drill might have struck an unexploded detonator or a fragment of gelignite left in a fissure.

The £500,000 project had started in June 1968 and seen two previous accidents before this most serious one.

In January 1970, a worker collapsed from gas poisoning and work was suspended, and in a separate incident a man suffered a serious leg injury in a blow-back at the drill face.

Below
Work starts on the outfall pipe near the Red Lion in the 1960s

STEAMED UP, BLOWN UP

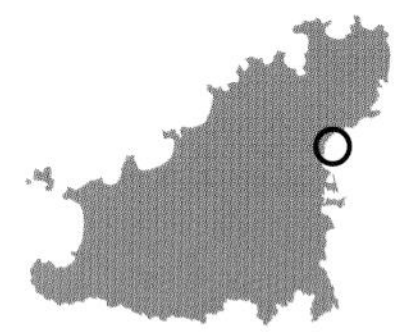

Above
Hougue a la Perre was once used for executions

BAILIFF'S CROSS is generally considered the site for the island's executions, medieval moons ago.

But they were carried out elsewhere and in more salty surroundings, too.

Four hundred years ago, if you were soaking up the scenery with a coastal walk along Belle Greve, rather than perusing the latest super-sized liner anchored off Town as you might today, the 16th-century alternative was to stop and see a good old hanging.

Two areas of the Belle Greve stretch were used for executions: one on the shore below where once stood Martello tower No. 1 at Hougue a la Perre, and the second half-a-mile northwards on Kemp Rock, situated off the beach opposite the Halfway.

The rock got its name from a soldier who was sentenced to death for murder.

But while imprisoned and before he felt the hangman's noose, he successfully carried out a DIY execution.

Even then he was made to suffer.

His corpse is said to have been chained to the rock which later carried his name.

Exactly when all this happened is open to question, but while it would seem to be true, other suggestions have been given for the christening of this unspectacular piece of black granite.

As it is so close to Camp Code Lane, the rock has also been referred to as 'Campy', which lends itself to the suggestion that it might have been called Camp Rock in the first place.

Martello one saw its final days in the latter years of the 19th century.

A print dated to 1830 shows the tower sitting atop a large hougue close to a low cliff in the region where today our oversized buses kip down for the night.

At the time, the low hill at what might also be called Tram Shed Corner was much wider than it is today.

Those passing along the shore therefore had to climb the slope, cross the summit and descend the other side.

Plainly, it was no good for running a coastline tram service and in 1896 the States granted permission to level the hill and tower one was blown up, leaving a gap where the road runs to this day.

First Tower Lane, an adjacent road, is a reminder of the edifice, which was survived for 62 years by its nearest fellow Napoleonic granite pepperpot-shaped fort.

Tower No. 2 stood near the top of Track Lane but in 1958 made way for a block of States flats, thereby proving the theory that the island government has always been capable of destroying its heritage.

Steam trams had first appeared between Town and St Sampson's in 1879, huffing and puffing their way over the Hougue a la Perre which had, slightly to its south, one of a few shipyards working off Belle Greve.

In 1839 James Sebire was granted permission to build vessels in a field where today the refurbished Commerce House sits.

Whether it is the same field which, in the early part of the 20th century, lent itself to the visits of big circus acts is quite possible.

For sure the Circus Field that very elderly islanders will recall and the incumbent of which is referred to as Sloans Circus in the wonderful Ebenezer Le Page, was either next to Sebire's former yard or within a stone's throw of it.

Not uncommonly, Sebire's vessels were launched on rollers and, as Eric W. Sharp once recalled in his review of island shipbuilding, it was nothing for a launching across Les Banques and into the sea to take an entire day.

The lane nearest to Sebire's shipyard was known as Bordage until renamed First Tower Lane, long after Sebire had ended his shipbuilding business in the vicinity.

Across the way at St George's Esplanade, ships were built by Alexander Thom in a yard where today the Piette Hotel stands.

Launches were officially recorded as being from the Longstore, but undoubtedly they were from Thom's yard, which became de la Mare's from 1843 until 1878.

Old maps of the esplanade show a much narrower road than exists today, that widening owing much to the major gale in 1858 that wrecked the sea wall.

A consequential loss due to the redevelopment was the slipway that existed opposite the Piette in the first half of the 19th century.

From 1839, a second yard existed a few hundred yards along the coast and in a field opposite the Longstore.

Rankilor and Brouard built just one ship before handing over to Marquand and de la Mare, who launched their ships on the slipway that still is there today.

Above left
The demolition of Tower No. 2 in 1958
Left
The coastline tram service approaches the Red Lion corner in its heyday

"It's a bit of a pig for the tide and you have to put the boat on the outside moorings when the tide doesn't suit"

Ken Thompson

CHAPTER 15

LA SALERIE

Although it is seen by many as just a quaint corner and a car park used by many hundreds of commuters, Salerie Corner does have a rich heritage. Once it was a bustling little harbour when Guernsey exported salted fish.

SALT OF THE EARTH · HIDDEN DELIGHTS
THE GREAT FIRE

SALT OF THE EARTH

SALERIE is an adaptation of a French word meaning fish salting ground.

Were it up for renaming now, it might be given the French word for car park.

A plan of the old battery that sat proudly on this north-west corner of Town 170 years ago was headed 'Sellerie'.

Same thing as Salerie, just a mid-19th century adaptation of a word to describe the old salting trade which dominated this corner of St Peter Port's waterfront in mediaeval times. And, like the name, La Salerie has also adapted with time.

In the history of Guernsey it is more relevant than today's Tarmac-covered expanse of parking spots.

If only the old salters could see their little spot of Town now.

They would scarcely recognise the place, the only clue being the quaint and largely unaltered harbour.

Salerie in the 21st century remains, though, a nostalgic reminder of old town and on idyllic summer days, staring out from its most seaward flight of steps, which head down to the old 'cauchee' pier, one admits to silent shame in briefly once thinking that there might have been some merit in filling in this tiny segment of Belle Greve Bay to house a marina, or whatever else the developers envisaged in their 'lagoon' idea.

The sea views from the corner never

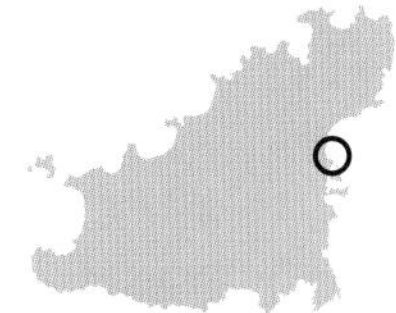

change.

But while 150 years ago you might have dangled your legs over one of its piers and heard nothing more than the gentle lapping of the incoming tide and the clip-clopping of horses' hooves exchanging one esplanade for another, now it is an unrelenting drone of traffic.

The old harbour is, and always should be, Salerie's jewel.

It is not as busy as it once was. The sailing ships of the past have given way to a flotilla of small fishing boats.

But those who operate those little craft would not want Salerie any other way, except perhaps to be dredged a little.

Like most island bays which permit boats to moor, Salerie and its Longstore neighbour has a moorings committee.

It is a committee of two and in recent times, with Tom Besnard laid low, John Turville is that body.

In a nutshell, he liaises with the constables and ensures the right boats go on the right moorings.

He said that Salerie has room for 25 moored boats and Longstore 14.

But in these times of wanting quick and easy access, the various marinas ensure that the Salerie-Longstore spread is far from being filled.

'A lot of people nowadays are nervous of going on a beach or are too lazy.

They can't be bothered to row out,' said John.

'They would rather be on a pontoon.'

It's not the expense, that's for sure. To keep your boat there costs a mere £5 a year.

It's a fairly safe mooring too, especially inside the harbour.

Only a big north-easterly will have the

Above
Moorings Committee chairman John Turville
Left
The Salerie has offered a safe mooring place for centuries

potential to cause damage and there is more likelihood of vandalism happening, as was the case in 2009 when John had the ropes to his boat, The Hero, cut and it was wrecked.

With that in mind, and the fact that nobody was ever identified as the culprit, John is not overjoyed when he sees youngsters larking about the place.

'In the summer we are plagued by the kids.'

'But don't they just jump or bombshell off the walls?' I asked.

'No, they swim out and get on board. They will take dinghies and set them adrift,' he replied.

That potential threat does not put off the hardy boatowners you will find down there.

Men such as John, Ken Thomson and Peter Dodd, who has held a mooring there longer than anyone else at Salerie.

He has had boats here since 1964.

Now 70, his major source of frustration is that there are so few fish to catch.

Two or three years back he came to the conclusion they weren't there in numbers any more.

'I was out Friday, Saturday and Sunday and caught nothing.

So I said to myself "no more".' Nowadays, he uses his boat for his own pleasure.

On this particular gorgeous afternoon he's popped over to Herm for a few hours and acted as a guard boat for the rowers, rowing being a sport close to his own heart along with darts, which three decades ago saw him play a key role in the success of the mighty Salerie Red team.

Salerie currently has 11 boats moored around the calendar.

'You used to have a waiting list of a couple of years,' said John, who has been associated with the place on and off for 19 years, the last seven unbroken.

John's new boat is a 24ft sturdy old fishing boat, Ken Thomson's a 22ft Channel 22.

Ken, 64, has had a fishing boat at Salerie for 30 years.

'I was brought up around here ...in St Clement's Road, just around the corner from the Foresters pub,' he says.

Nowadays he has moved as far afield as Les Amballes, near St John's Church. Salerie is still only a few minutes' walk away.

'It's picturesque and there is a nice crowd of people,' he says.

'It's a bit of a pig for the tide and you have to put the boat on the outside moorings when the tide doesn't suit,' he adds without a hint in his voice that that particular disadvantage is any real drawback.

Like his mooring neighbours, he reckoned the bay could do with being dredged, much of the silt apparently having been washed in from the middle of Belle Greve after the main Town harbour dredging deposits had been left there.

What else does he know about his Salerie?

'I know Salter House is where they salted the conger before they put them in barrels and ships would come and take them away.

'It used to be a well-known spot for octopus,' he adds.

But for sheer value for money, mooring in this corner of Belle Greve must rank as a steal.

You don't get the same safety as a marina mooring, but Ken is not complaining.

On the threat posed by the north-easterlies he said: 'We're quite good in here – it's the rest of them,' meaning those towards the Longstore.

'There you get the backwash off the wall. We lost a 16-footer only a few weeks ago. The swell hits the wall and meets another one as it comes in.'

Opposite
The Salter Street sign is a throwback to its days when it was just that... a street

Salter Street

HIDDEN DELIGHTS

WHEN the bulldozers came in and flattened the Salerie Inn in March, another historical chip was knocked off what was once one of the island's quaintest corners.

There is so little of the old Salerie left.

It took a while for yours truly to decide to add its story to the stop-off points in this ongoing natural and historical circumnavigation of the Guernsey coastline.

But dig deeper, just as you have to get through the mucky silt that has gradually clogged up its harbour bed to discover its true depth, and there is more to this most northern corner of Town than you might imagine.

The inn has gone the same way as the quarry which once yielded the island's blackest granite, the eperqueries [drying grounds for fish] and salting industry which gave the area its title, the tall sailing ships which came and went with their hulls full of conger and herring and, before we forget, a large chunk of the actual corner.

It's easy to forget that until the QE2 Marina arrived with its associated car park, the Little Russel sloshed in on both sides of Salerie Corner.

Now that tide comes and goes into the northern side of this natural bend in the eastern shore. Unless you are one of the few boat owners who moor their dinghies or little fishing boats inside the little stone jetty, or one of the children who 'bombshell' off its walls on a summer evening, it no longer matters much in island life.

It's a car park and one of many dumping places for tins, bottles and cardboard.

People start protest marches from there, or use it as a start or stopping off point on their fitness runs.

She, yes, female for some unknown reason, can still be a visual beauty, but like many other island places its grandest days are long gone.

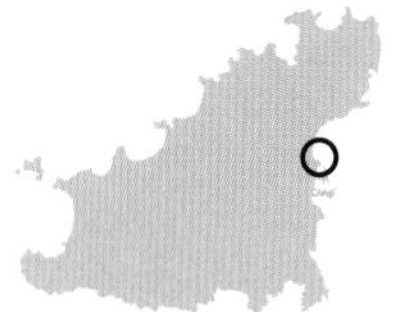

When Guernsey historian Victor Coysh wrote 37 years ago that La Salerie was one of the most picturesque corners of the St Peter Port waterfront, it very much was.

But that was pre-marina. He would also write that pre-1965 it was even more attractive.

But on 4 March of that year one of its two 'cauchees' was practically destroyed in a gale and the States, unhappily, did not see fit to restore it.

The ruins of the old pier remain, with its rounded extremity on which a post stands. The name comes from 'salting place', where fish were cured in medieval days.

In pre-Reformation times this commodity enjoyed greater demand than it does today and its preservation was important.

The men of La Territoire de Glatigny (a fishing village nearby) took their catches to this corner for salting and the name has endured.

The only salting it sees now is carried out by those with a bag of chips on their knees while soaking up the glorious views across the Russel.

There is little doubt that one of Salerie's two piers served the fishing community and, fortunately, at least one of them survived the battering of a storm on a wild March night 45 years ago.

The damaged pier, which is the one which points across the way to St Sampson's, was repaired some years later, but regular harbour user Peter Dodd tells of the remains of another old pier which is exposed on the lowest tides.

Peter may be a Salerie old-timer, but centuries before he came along, in fact, during the English Civil War, the pier was used by boats anxious to escape the fire from Castle Cornet's guns, which always threatened craft using St Peter Port harbour.

Possibly the existing jetty is not the original one, though it certainly wears an ancient appearance.

Left
Cheap and cheerful: it costs very little to moor at Salerie

The smaller repaired 'cauchee' was much more recent.

It was built in 1838 and the reason for its construction must have been to provide a place of embarkation and landing at a lower stage of the tide than the other pier permitted.

In years gone by one was referred to as 'the boys' cauchee' and the other as 'the girls' cauchee'.

This distinction would have been made by children of the neighbourhood, who used the piers regularly for bathing.

During the Occupation, the Germans removed the steps leading down to the smaller pier, probably for security reasons, and it was only in about 1950 that they were replaced.

In the times when fears of an invasion by the French were strong, the coast of Guernsey was heavily fortified and a battery at the Salerie was an obvious defence measure.

Traces of the fortification might well still be there if you know what to look for, but, unfortunately the old furnace used for the making of shot has disappeared.

The battery once mounted 10 cannon, but later the number was reduced to four.

The place even had a harbourmaster.

That was back in Victorian times and he was probably some sort of special constable of his time.

You can bet he had a beard and wore a guernsey.

It is doubtful if there is a man or woman alive who can recall the times when Salerie was also utilised as a place to legally skinny dip.

But that was the case in the early 20th century when a sign read: 'Bathing without drawers after 8am is strictly prohibited.'

Perhaps the best time to see the Salerie's journey through time is at very low tide.

Victor Coysh, to whom Guernsey will remain forever indebted for his research into the island's past, duly did and what he witnessed 40 years ago remains untouched.

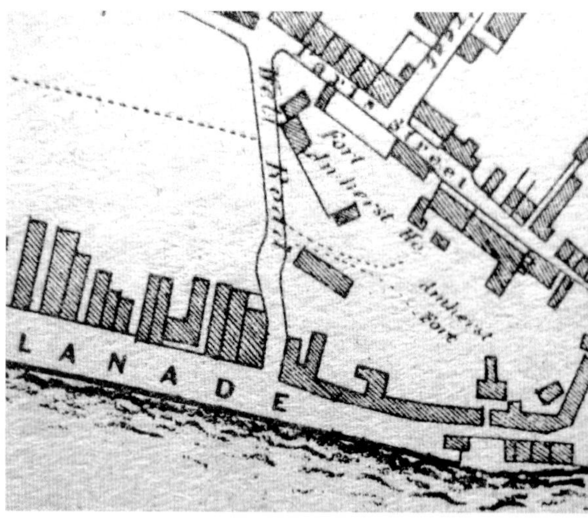

Right
An old Ordinance map showing Fort Amherst and Salter Street

Top far right
A summer's evening and local youngsters make the most of the high tide

Below far right
The main pierhead

The names of the boats have changed and the silt levels increased, but the masonry, little landing stages at various levels, steps, old paving stones and ancient mooring rings, remain.

It's a sun-trap for those who don't like getting sand between their toes, and some still regard it as a good bathing place, especially those youngsters who like to dive into its not inconsiderable depths at high tide in summer when amateur fishermen are normally busy minding their craft.

Above them will be a steady flow of traffic in and out of Town on a piece of road long ago widened out of necessity to the demands of Victorian traffic.

Close to the harbour, houses once stood on the seaward side of what is now the St George's Esplanade.

They were few in number and stood directly above the slipway, blocking the view down the narrow Paris Street.

It was named Salter Street but when the need for a tram track came along, down came the houses and Salter Street, simply too narrow for the steam trams, the horse bus and other traffic plying between Town and St Sampson's became no more and in time became St George's Esplanade.

A relic of this period is a plan of The Salerie Corner as surveyed in 1854 by Lyster and Brumell, who were also engaged in the construction of St Peter Port's new harbour.

It shows buildings at the seaward extremity of 'Glatney' Esplanade as well as on the sea side of Salter Street.

Four cannon are marked, as well as two piers and a slipway.

This plan also marks Fort Jolie, an old piece of defence, now disappeared, which stood in the vicinity of Well Road overlooking what was Sheppard's Wine Stores and the Salerie Inn.

Fort Jolie was also known as Fort Amherst.

When sailing craft used the area it must have been a visual delight.

To see such interesting gear as courges, pannier-a-co and wicker crab pots lying about the place, as well as sails and other gear, must have tempted many an artist to portray the scene, to say nothing of the early photographers.

And with the Piette shipyards no more than a hefty stone's throw away, the area must have been a nautical paradise.

If only we were able to go back in time and sample the sights and smells of an early Victorian Salerie Corner and its environs.

Today's traffic is non-stop, but back then it was never dull, with the shipyards, the coming and going of fishing craft, the launching of ships, the rumble of steam trams and, later, electric ones, plus the sound of horses' hooves as their rival, the omnibus, went by, together with the ordinary horse-drawn traffic between the ports.

As Coysh so rightly noted, 'put it all together and it must have lent this region a sense of activity which the rush of today's motors does not impart in anything like the same degree'.

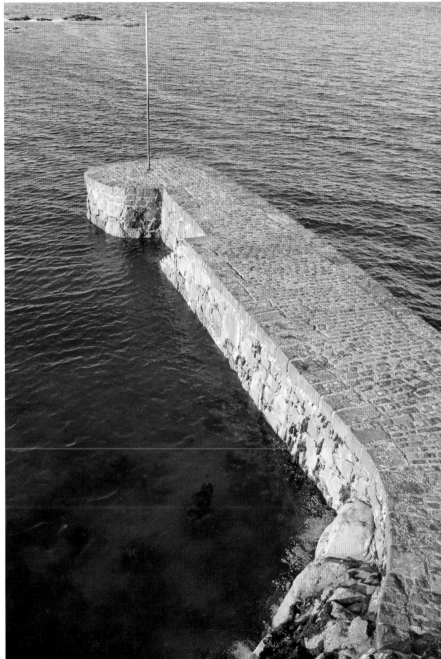

THE GREAT FIRE

GIVEN what was to come a decade or so later in the German death camps, describing the 'Great Salerie Fire of 1929' as a holocaust would be regarded as insensitive if it happened today.

But such was the ferocity of that blaze of all Guernsey blazes in March 1929, the published subheadline was not wrong in its use of the 'H' word.

After all, the Oxford Dictionary refers to 'a case of large scale destruction, especially by fire or nuclear war'.

They described it as 'one of the greatest fires ever known in Guernsey', raging all night, lighting up large areas of Town and pulling in hundreds of islanders to watch the battle to save the large box factory owned by J. W. Huelin and Co.

'Hell on Earth' was how one witness described the engulfing of the whole of the disused quarry site, measuring around 400ft by 120ft.

In describing the scene the journalist concerned went to Town and back.

How about this: 'Meanwhile with such combustible matter within the factory, a holocaust was in the awful throes of vigorous birth.

'Angry flames were shooting like great tongues into the sky, and the corrugated iron roofing was crumbling.

'Sparks were carried hundreds of feet upwards and at 11 o'clock, seen from Richmond Corner, the fire was like a blazing sunset, reddening the whole of Belle Greve Bay, and colouring even the plaster front of houses over a mile away.

'Hundreds of people from the upper parts of the town were drawn by the glare to the Cotils Belvedere, where they were able to witness the full extent of the great blaze.'

The heroes were not restricted to the Fire Brigade who parked their wagons in Well Road for the night-long hose-a-thon.

The choir boys of St Stephen's Church played a starring role, helping to evacuate babies from nearby houses.

'One of his [Father Hopkins] boys lives at the Castel.

He awoke and saw the glare in the sky, dressed like the wind and ran all the way to the scene of the fire, arriving somewhat breathless at 2.30am.'

Meanwhile, our intrepid news hound was, like the fire, waxing lyrically out of control on his weighty typewriter:

'At midnight the scene was an eerie one. Paris Street contained hundreds of persons, whose faces were all ruddy in the reflected glow in the quarry some 50 feet away.

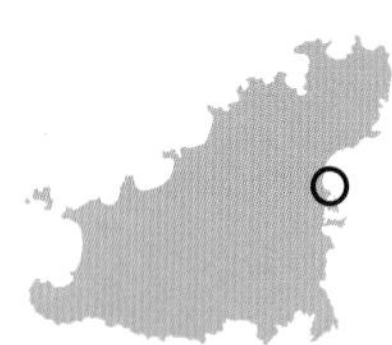

Left
When Salerie burned: a montage of the 1929 fire when Huelin's box factory went up in flames

Here one met lawyers, priests, doctors, the beau monde and the general public, all attracted by the glow that had made the sky lurid to the zenith.'

An exhausted fire service eventually won, but not before the factory was destroyed.

More than 50 men were immediately put out of work, while our unknown Castel schoolboy went back to sleep.

Thirty-one years later and with the whereabouts of that 1929 child Clark Kent unknown, the area was again hit by a massive fire.

The blaze that destroyed the Piette Saw and Planing Mills on that night in 1960 was described by the fire service as the biggest since the war.

For the second time, St George's Esplanade discovered daylight after dusk as £25,000 worth of damage – a lot of money back then – was caused by the fire that swept through the machine shop and into the large timber store. Eighteen firefighters fought the flames which produced a monstrous lit matchbox effect.

At the height of the blaze, about last orders time in the nearby Salerie and Foresters pubs, sparks were flying in all directions and 'Salerians' were too frightened to go to bed.

Heavy rain helped firefighters in their bid to stem the danger, but it still required 750 gallons of water a minute to finally quell the fire, the glow from which could be seen at St Peter's.

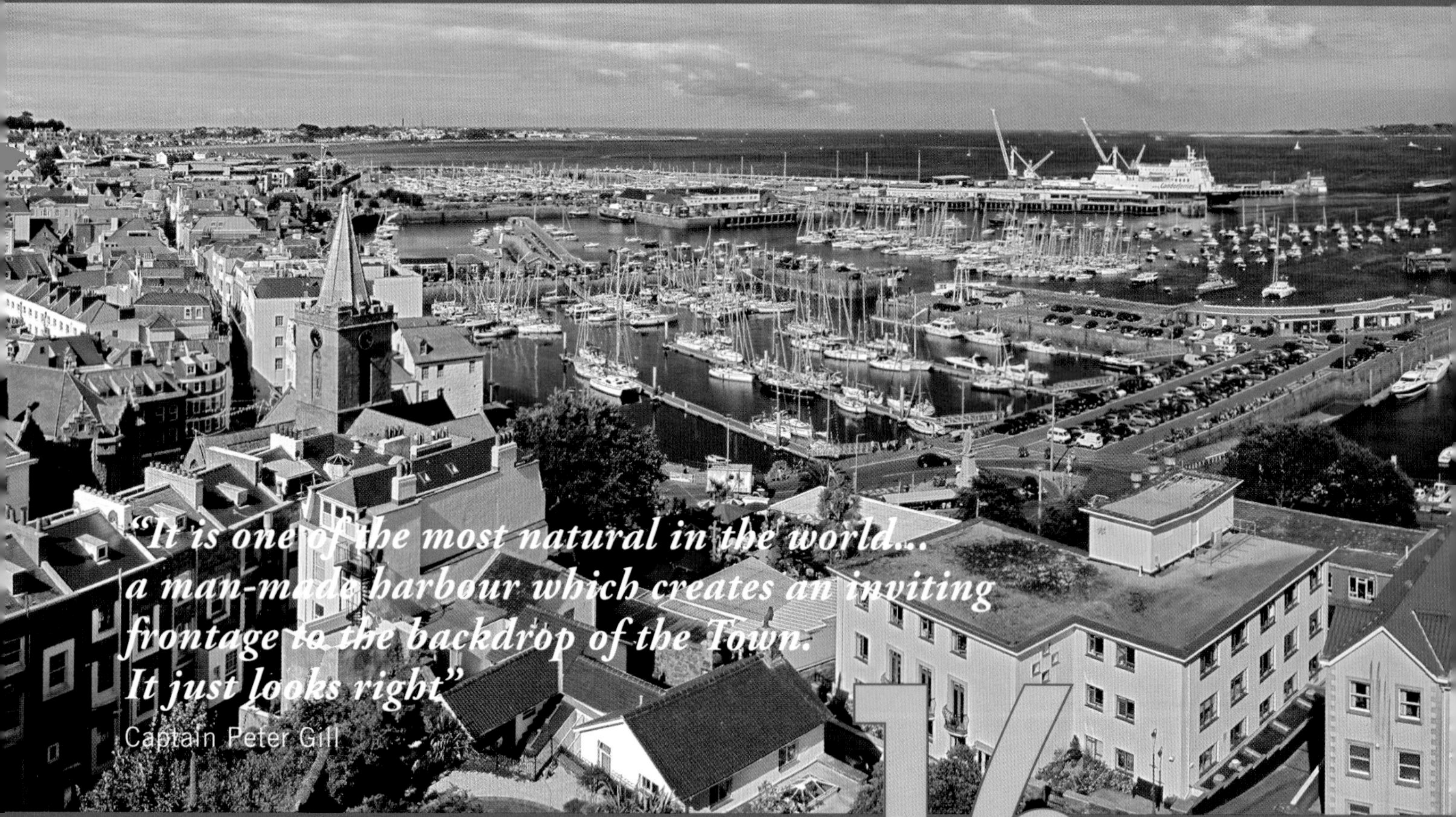

"It is one of the most natural in the world... a man-made harbour which creates an inviting frontage to the backdrop of the Town. It just looks right"

Captain Peter Gill

CHAPTER 16

ST PETER PORT

A jewel of a port with a rich and long history, forever changing and never losing its gloss in the process. Sea transport of both passengers and freight may have changed over the years but our harbour remains a place to be proud of.

SQUARE ROOTS

ST PETER Port Harbour breakwater has been a fishing Mecca for local anglers since the day it was built.

Steve Huxster, one of the island's most successful, has been fishing off the 'square' for all but seven of his 46 years. He has no doubt it's the island's hottest spot.

'If my life depended on catching a fish, I'd go from there. There is always something to be caught,' said Steve, who has twice landed Bailiwick-record fish from the area.

The only trouble is, as he explained, it is too good and too popular. It is not uncommon for 30 or 40 anglers to be fishing from it on a summer evening, which makes it all a bit cramped.

'I've seen 20-odd rods fishing the bottom for bream and others casting over the top of them,' he said.

'You try to keep it organised, but it's not always easy.'

The 'square', a raised area on which the lighthouse sits, also produces a wide variety of specimens.

Between 1966 and 1998 it yielded an incredible 32 Bailiwick records, covering 16 species.

'Last week there was a smooth hound caught, a cod and two double-figure [lbs] bass,' said Steve, who like so many islanders learned his angling skills there as a boy.

'When I was a kid we would stay there all day and all night.

'It's a good learning spot. I learned there and many of our top anglers cut their teeth there.'

But popularity brings problems – and ones related not only to space.

A couple of years ago, the harbour master threatened withdrawing use of the breakwater if those frequenting it continued to leave so much rubbish.

Steve said the situation had improved.

'We try to educate people to clear up after themselves,' he said.

'It's not the proper fishermen, but the ones who come down for the odd evening and chuck their rubbish down.'

Steve's seen some funny things there over the years.

'I've seen people cast out other people's rods and people's coats and there was one guy who had a hook through his ear.'

In terms of idyllic fishing spots, Guernsey has many better ones, but Steve said that while overcrowding often kept him away, he has a favourite time for casting out from there.

'Fishing for mackerel early mornings in the summer. Idyllic.'

There is perhaps one man who fishes the harbour breakwater more than any other.

Colin Help works at the harbour and given

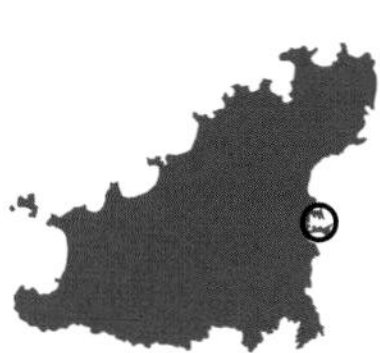

Left
Thousands flock to the breakwater every year, most with a rod in hand
Below
Angler Steve Huxster

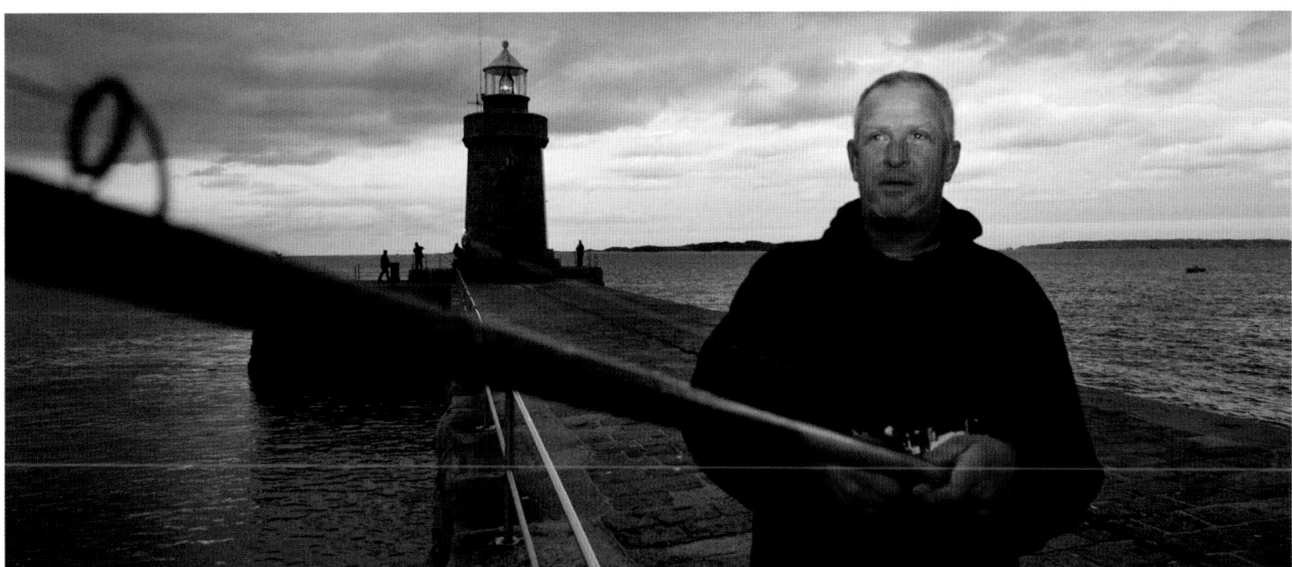

half a chance and decent weather, he will be dangling his rod over the side.

'It depends on the weather, but I'll fish there perhaps three or four times a week. And if the weather is good, almost every day.'

PETER'S PORT

PETER GILL has his dream job.

The 15th St Peter Port harbour master had eyes on the job 40 years ago while he was still at school and his dream came true when he succeeded Captain Robert Barton in 2005, following 38 years spent working for Shell.

The job description is extensive and he is responsible for most sea-related matters in island waters – the only aspects not part of his remit are fisheries protection and looking after the beaches.

It's a big task, but one he revels in despite the always-lingering political influences on maintaining a key part of Guernsey's heritage and the biggest port.

St Peter Port Harbour has developed into its current state over many centuries.

The first reference to it was made as far back as 1060 and now, nearly 1,000 years on, it's bulging at the seams, literally creaking under the weight of its own importance.

It's a sad fact that 58 years after 10,000 islanders swarmed over the White Rock to welcome home Guernsey's Muratti heroes after their first win since 1938, 12 years

Below
Harbour Master Capt Peter Gill dreamt of holding the post whilst still at school

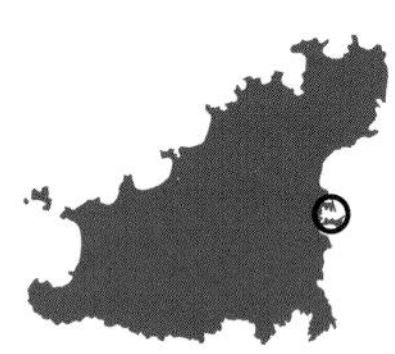

earlier, the harbour simply could not accommodate anything like it. The top walkway on the outer arm, which until two years ago enabled islanders to walk to within spitting distance of the port control office, is closed to the public, deemed too dangerous to use.

Close examination under the harbour master's guidance highlights why. It's crumbling, propped up from underneath.

Yes, there is an underneath to what on the face of it appears to be a solid mass of granite put carefully in place 140 years ago.

Peter revealed that a tunnel runs along most of the arm onto which number 6 berth was built – and it is not a nice place to go.

'To say there are rats down there is an understatement,' he said.

'I have been down once and I didn't stop itching and scratching for a month.'

The entrance to the damp interiors, long deemed of no particular use, is via a manhole

Above
The slowly crumbling No. 6 berth
Left
The Signal Station light dates back to 1868

cover in the buckled, dilapidated sheds, which stretch along the berth. The tunnels are barely deserving of the word, having been created, it seems, purely out of necessity to keep the wall from falling into the Little Russel.

No sooner had the pier been built than it was revealed that it had not been done so on solid foundations – instead, it stood on quicksand, with the bedrock 17ft below that. It was too heavy for its own good and four years after its completion, 400 tons of granite were removed and replaced by open sheds.

'Great chunks I'd imagine were taken out to reduce the weight of it,' said Peter.

'I'd love to have public access but it's just not possible.'

He is quick to defend its construction in the knowledge that it was being criticised from virtually the moment it accepted its first passengers.

'Number 6 berth wasn't a clever idea but it was better than nothing. Previously, ships would anchor and dinghy passengers ashore. It was a step forward – a massive improvement.'

Above right
Cranes have been a part of the Town skyline for a century
Below
A century old winch is testament to the harbour's old ways

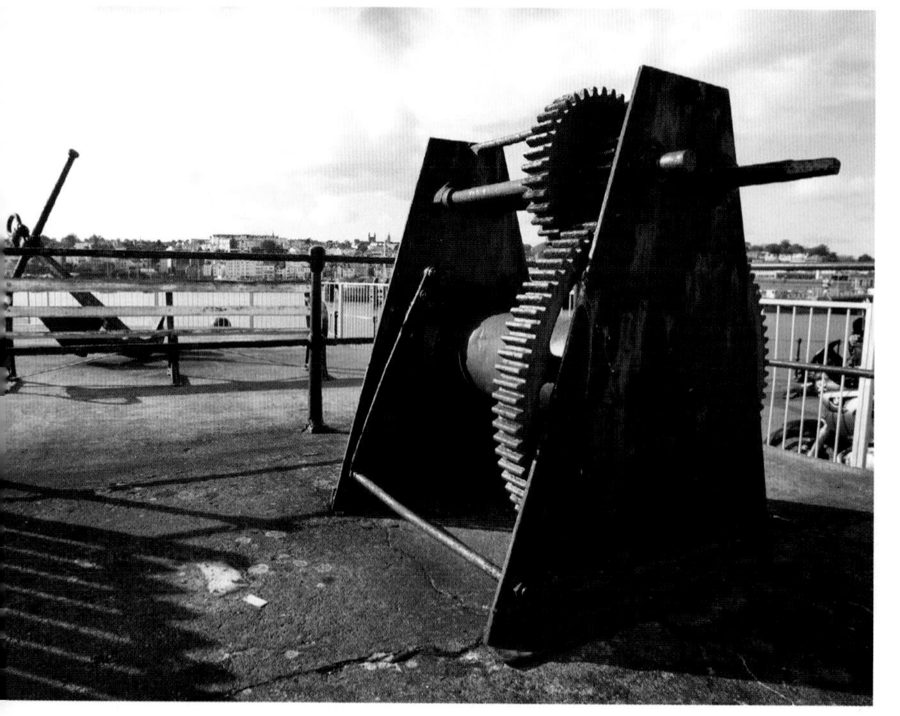

That said, it is impossible to imagine a similar project going ahead today, regardless of the results of seabed analysis.

A pier that services passengers only from below half-tide up would not be regarded as value for money. The depth here at low water is about a metre, while the lowest level at the New Jetty landing, built in 1928, is 5.5m.

Another still-visible reminder of the days of sailing ships is the winch sitting on the pier head below the port control office, built in 1946.

It dates back to the turn of the 19th and 20th centuries.

Long before the days of side propellers and modern techniques of manoeuvring high-speed cats, on entering the 650ft-wide harbour mouth a rope would be thrown ashore and attached to the winch.

Used in tandem with a series of anchor blocks and buoys situated in the harbour, the ships would be guided into position.

All told, the harbour master is boss of a full-time staff of 77, 10 of whom work in the port control office.

They are highly sought-after jobs – and it's no surprise. A working day at a busy and beautiful harbour such as St Peter Port is seldom the same.

'Once you've got a job here, you don't want to lose it. People stay for a long time.'

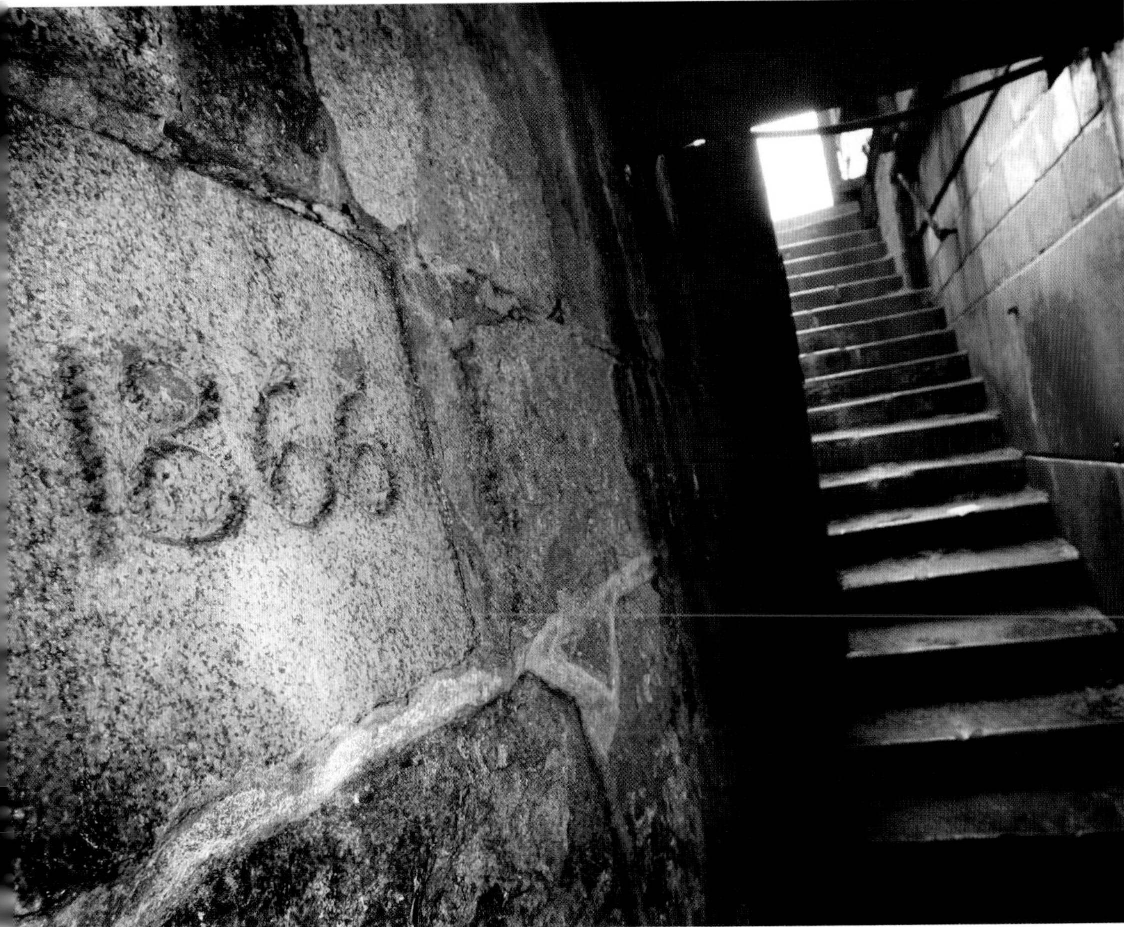

Above, left and overleaf
The No. 6 berth was built in 1866

HARBOURING A DESIRE

THE White Rock would have looked altogether different had plans put forward in 1903 got the green light.

With traffic on the increase, States engineer Mr Duquemin was ordered to produce plans for an enlarged harbour, with his terms of reference being to increase the deep-water landing accommodation outside the existing north and south breakwaters.

This is what he came up with:

1 Extend St Julian's Pier in an easterly direction for 750ft with a width of 90ft and a return arm in a south-easterly direction of 500ft with a width of 65ft.

2 The proposed length would give exactly similar shelter as existed previously and an entrance channel of 500ft.

3 His plan took into consideration the 'enormous amount of stones' deposited along the outside of the White Rock Pier and number 6 berth. The engineer proposed removing some of that and building another berth over the remainder to compete a basin of six-and-a-half acres with deep-water berthing of 1,590 feet and low-tide depths varying from 24ft to 11ft.

4 The whole of the new outer face would have a raised-terrace promenade under which would be goods sheds. It would, he suggested, be built using 30-ton concrete blocks, 31-35ft wide.

5 The lighthouse, the one which stands in the same place today, would have to be demolished and rebuilt on the new pierhead. And all for just £328,000.

Why did it not happen?

The influential railway companies wanted improvements but considered the plans as

Above
The ultimately spurned 1903 plans for the harbour
Overleaf
Waves crash over the breakwater

simply too grandiose.

It died a natural death, deemed a white elephant.

Today's harbour master, Captain Peter Gill, and his deputy, Tony Pattimore, were shocked to see Duquemin's plans for the very reason that such a layout would be an answer to their 21st-century prayers.

'That would have served us for the next 200 years,' said an enthusiastic Peter, who had not previously seen them.

'The principle of it was rock solid,' he added, calling it visionary.

Tony said Duquemin's layout would have rendered it needless to have built the New Jetty and would have allowed just about most ships in, including liners.

'That would have taken ocean-going ships.'

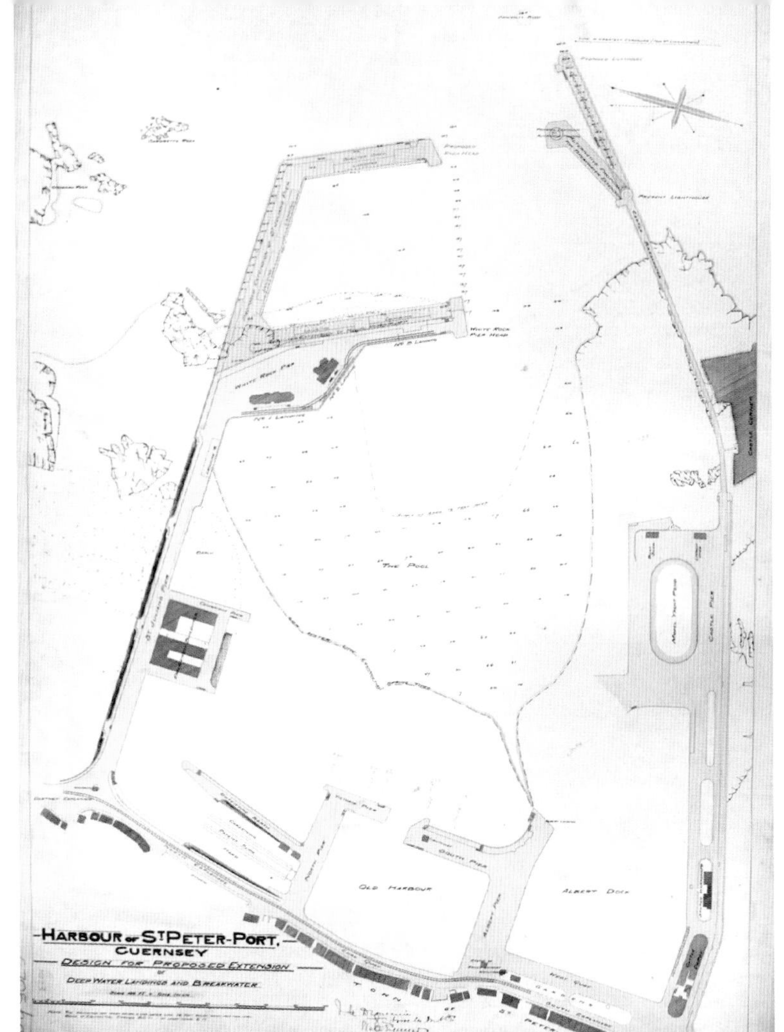

USER-UNFRIENDLY

EVER thought the Model Yacht Pond was outdated and a waste of space?

For a start, think of all those potential car-parking slots that could be filled were it taken away. I'm sure the Town planners have.

Not for one minute would I advocate the introduction of another ugly car park, but for many years islanders have been eyeing the area for alternatives to floating little boats.

In the late 1940s it was being touted as the ideal site for Guernsey's first lido and serious consideration was given to providing the island with what its competitive swimming fraternity has long wanted – a 50m pool. Only, it would have been outdoors.

Between the two world wars, it was argued that Guernsey's lack of a lido was its biggest handicap in satisfying the needs of both tourists and islanders.

The Castle Emplacement pool was one idea. Another was for something along the same lines in central Town.

In the early 1930s a syndicate came forward with serious plans to transform the Careening Hard – which had lost its patent slips to St Sampson's in 1921 – into an open-air pool.

In addition to a large swimming area, a children's sandy beach was planned, as well as hot and cold baths and a cafe.

Even diving stages and chutes were proposed, besides cubicles.

The 170ft pool width would have afforded 5ft more than the 55 yards then recognised as suitable for world-class competition.

It never came to fruition, no doubt to the disappointment of many a water polo player, who, during the long period when the Careening Hard was the main venue for their sport, were

Below
Hundreds would surround the Careening Hard to watch water polo

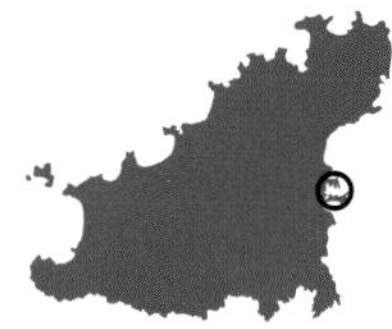

For many years island swimmers have deplored the fact that there are no facilities for swimming all the year round. Our picture shows a suggest ed scheme at the Castle Emplacement which came forward some years ago. Although the need is just as great, nothing has been done to make provision in the island for such a pool.

forced to splash about in water often contaminated by sewage.

Veteran swimmer and water polo star Mike Banfield recalls the experience of occasionally coming across the unexpected and the virtue of keeping one's mouth shut.

'There were quite often floaters on the pitch,' he said.

'There was a sewage outfall right alongside it.'

He stressed that it was not the norm to be faced with the most ugly of pitch invaders and it did not detract from what was a fine venue for the sport that entertained hundreds.

'It was great. People used to sit on the edge of the paths and on the wall as well. There were often people three deep, the full length of the pitch – or more.'

David Langlois, who served as secretary of the Water Polo Association during the sport's heyday, also recalled the downsides of playing in the poo-ey pool.

'The problem arose on spring tides when the sea got into sewers and brought the muck down. It was pretty unpleasant, but we survived.'

He recalled on one occasion Bill Green telling players that it was their duty to Guernsey to go down into the polluted water to play.

The main argument against the Careening Hard pool plan was the presumed danger of coal dust flying off the steamers unloading in the Old Harbour, although a bit of dust seems a lot less of a hardship than sewage.

All told, there were three schemes embracing better swimming facilities, including improving the main pool at La Vallette.

No less a distinguished man than W. H. Arnold, who was to become Bailiff between 1959-73, pushed for the Castle Emplacement lido, while Gervaise F. Peek gave his heart and mind and the power of the press – he owned it – to persuading States members to go with the Careening Hard venture. They commissioned an artist, a Miss Cheeswright, to depict the pool in front of Glategny Esplanade.

But their contrasting views weakened the overall argument for improved facilities.

The States fell between three stools, were left bewildered and plumped for none of them.

Above
Some would have turned the Model Yacht Pond into a lido

SAFE HARBOUR

BEEN to St Helier lately?

I wish Charles Brett had. He wrote a wonderfully factual account of 'Buildings in the Town and Parish of St Peter Port Harbour'.

His criticism of the parish buildings could be withering and when he got to sum up our seafront, he observed that 'the harbour area as a whole is rather a mess' and that 'the normal sea-port jumble has got out of hand'.

That was 1975. Just think what's happened to our dearly beloved St Peter Port since, with the filling in of North Beach, the creation of a car park to satisfy our lazy habits and the completion of the Queen Elizabeth Marina.

Old Bretty would have hated it, especially combined with the new builds along Glategny Esplanade.

And what about our roundabout, with the rigging straight out of the Onedin Line?

But I reckon Brett was wrong. Very wrong.

As are all the old historians who have charted the development of the harbour and sniffed at the new ways.

'What will they do next? Turn the Careening Hard into another marina?'

The answer is, quite probably, 'yes, mate'.

Well, I happen to conclude that as town fronts go, the St Peter Port of 2010 is a stunner and puts seafronts like that of the Jersey capital not so much into shade but behind a black curtain of architectural mayhem.

Our Town front is something to celebrate, particularly in the summertime, when the French yachties arrive by the dozen and park their motor homes outside Creasey's.

VisitGuernsey may do some things wrong, but ensuring Town is dressed to impress is not one of them.

One of the best places from which to see the collective beauty of the harbour is the car park at the former St Barnabas Church.

Imagine what the same vantage point would have offered in terms of vista 250 years ago.

Right
The roundabout at the bottom of St Julian's Avenue complete with its new iconic mast

To the right would have been the south beach, with a rolling sea stretching right up to where the esplanade gardens offer sanctuary to...I am not entirely sure, but it looks nice, anyway.

There was no breakwater stretching out to Cornet Island and its old castle, while at low tide Vermiere rock stood out proudly, ripe to serve as a link to the mainland by way of a breakwater.

Down in front of St Barnabas would have been the roofs of the properties which would have sat behind the narrowest of old quays, and the stinky Le Galet Heaume beach in front, where anything and just about everything went.

The new pier of 1750 was viewed by all as work of wonder and a vital addition to those keen to see the maximising of St Peter Port's positioning as an ideal harbour, but in this case, nothing was set in stone.

Indeed, the dry-stoneworked pier allowed the sea to flow through easily, thereby urging on any wave surge, and a tunnel allowed the

passage of carts at a time when the foreshore at low water acted as the main thoroughfare linking the north and south of Town.

Messy and smelly, it did nothing to hold back the sea when high tide came to wash up through the alleys and threatened the High Street. Interesting vision, that.

Unsurprisingly, the late 18th-century powers considered that this was no way to run a harbour front and in the four years between 1775 and 1779 an 18ft-wide quay was built, the forerunner to today's hectic frontage, which sees thousands of cars track their way north or south every day of the week.

Like the pier, the new quay was a dry construction and faced by wooden piles.

It ended almost before it started in front of what we know as Quay Street.

There was a problem, though.

It was cut off from the original pier to its south and in 1783 they remedied that by throwing a bridge over La Rue des Vaches which, by coincidence, was the point where the town sewage poured straight into the harbour.

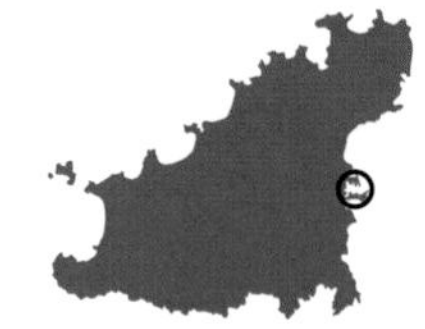

HARBOUR TIMELINE

1060 Earliest reference to a harbour, 'Sancti Petri de Portu'.

1250 Castle Cornet 'completed'.

1329 497 foreign ships pay dues at St Peter Port.

1350 18 February. King Edward III orders that St Peter Port be walled for protection, Jerbourg castle 'having fallen into hopeless disrepair'.

1563 Queen Elizabeth I authorises construction of a pier and orders the Royal Court to account for dues collected.

1590 South Pier completed, measuring 360ft x 35ft high and 20ft across at the top.

1642 Reference to round house/beacon at end of South Pier, St Peter Port.

1685 North Pier begun but abandoned.

1703 Recommended building HSPP North Pier.

1775 West Quay started.

1779 West Quay completed to Quay Street.

1783 West Quay joined to South Pier by bridge over Cow Lane.

1819 Lower Inner Quay added to South Pier.

1821 Storms damage every ship in the harbour and demolish Glategny Esplanade. Royal Court convenes on site to review damage and organise repairs.

1822 Extensive repairs to and beautification of South Pier.

1830 Petition by 187 merchants to Bailiff for a new harbour. Strong propaganda in local paper for same.

1831 Bailiff Brock strongly recommends building of new harbour: committee set up. Gas replaces oil lamps on quays.

1832 28 February. Lighthouse lit on South Pier head (now the Victoria Marina red light) to replace original wooden building. Known as the 'Pharos' or the 'Globe'. First recorded harbour master John de Carteret.

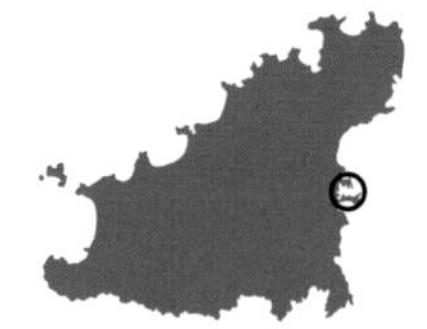

HARBOUR TIMELINE

1838 Pier heads adjusted and improved to make entrance 68ft at base (from 40ft). Wooden crane installed for shipment of cattle. North Pier head adapted for landing of passengers.

1846 Queen Victoria visits. Prince Albert asks why the harbour had been built on dry land.

1847 Harbour committee reappointed to look at new plans.

1851 Rendel's plans debated by States – £195,000 includes breakwater from Havelet to Vermiere (the site of the Model Yacht Pond) and sewer outfall at St Julian's Quay. States decides to build breakwater from Havelet rocks to Vermiere rock, rebuild existing quays, build Havelet esplanade and run main sewer through the new West Quay to outfall at St Julian's Breakwater.

1853 Contract for new Castle Emplacement breakwater awarded to Le Gros and De La Mare of Jersey. 24 August, foundation stone laid at base of wall below the North Havelet slipway, the ceremony cost £363 4s.2d. The pier to the lighthouse would cost £300,000. Lavoir at bottom of Havelet removed to allow junction with new esplanade. Second harbour master, John Du Port.

1855 States agrees to construct Careening Hard, extend the esplanade through to Glategny and build a North Quay of floating dock as far as the old South Pier.

1856 St Julian's Breakwater converted from a talus (sloping mass of rock) to vertical wall. Pier steps connected to High Street. Start made on St Julian's massif as a talus.

Town, quaint old town, may have been bustling and busy, but sweet-smelling, no.

Looking to the north from St Barnabas would have offered an unhindered view of the original White and St Julian's Rocks, long since buried by piers.

In the case of St Julian's Pier the plans usurped the original idea of it merely being a walkway atop a sewer embankment and also out of the window went the idea of adopting the quite sizeable St Julian's Rock as a ladies' bathing place.

Town was changing for the better and it has barely stopped in what's now approaching a century-and-a-half. Progress has rendered some parts of it obsolete.

The Careening Hard has long since served its purpose and it is understandable that consideration is given to utilising it as an additional marina for visiting yachtsmen.

Under the castle, the Model Yacht Pond is an odd link with Victorian ideals.

But as Henrietta Tupper noted in the second edition of her father's History of Guernsey, what was once a 'miserable harbour containing an area of about four English acres, we now have one of the best harbours in the Channel, enclosing a space of about 80 acres, with deep water berthage, we have wide esplanades forming a good harbour frontage, we have healthy and accessible marine promenades and we have the sewerage of the town conveyed far seaward into deep water'.

That was written in 1876.

Harbourmaster Captain Peter Gill is more qualified than most to answer that question.

A Guernseyman to the core, he loves what he sees when looking south from his first-floor office, situated where those ladies might have had their bathing place and where the original, natural model yacht pond existed.

Was Brett right in saying that the harbour had become a mess?

Jumbled and out of hand?

His studied assessment is that few mistakes have been made in developing the harbour to its capacity.

'Still, even today, it continues to do just what is asked of it and for something that has stood 150 years, I'd say that is pretty good.

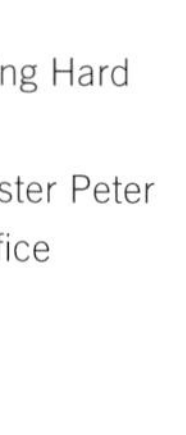

Right
The Careening Hard
Opposite
Harbour Master Peter Gill in his office

'It is only now that we have reached the end of its capability of the past and we need to modify for the future.'

The captain praises to the hilt the decision makers of the past.

'It was such a huge leap of faith for the States to make such a huge investment when they did, but without it the members of the Chamber of Commerce knew it could not develop.

'It created a massive safe area.'

Nowadays it is remarkable to think that 2,500 boats of various sizes and shapes use the harbour regularly and that is down to maximising its area.

'Because of the advent of ro-ro we have been able to compress the commercial side into less than a quarter of the whole harbour,' he said. Its purpose, Capt. Gill underlines, is not simply to look good but to make money and it does that very well in modern times.

While he looks down on an aerial photograph which shows the harbour's full workings and the outcrops of the rocks on which it has been built, the harbour master points out the various 'small but significant changes' which have given the pool extra breathing space, such as the fish quay.

As for the harbour as a whole, its master is clearly besotted with it.

'It is one of the most natural in the world...a man-made harbour which creates an inviting frontage to the backdrop of the town. It just looks right.'

No wonder, he says, the cruise liners can't stay away.

'The view of Town for us on something like the Herm Trident is one thing, but if you get up that extra 100ft, as the liners do, it is an altogether different view.

'You can see over the sea walls. It is a different perspective and a good one.'

Below
The modern day fishing fleet

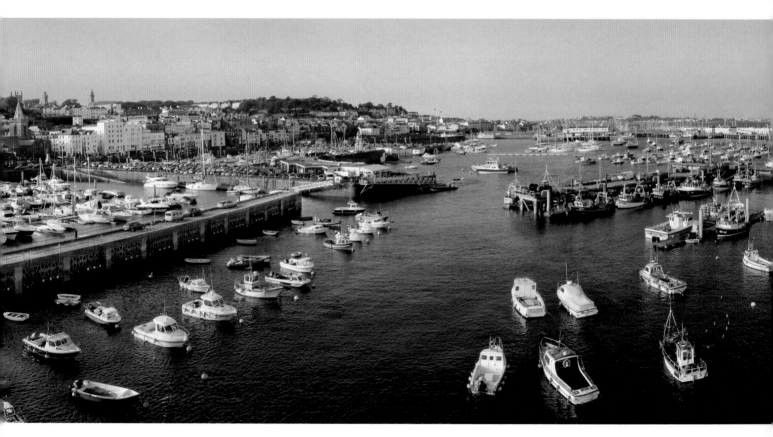

From my point of view, I would not wish it any different.

The second-floor canteen at Creasey's shows off the harbour better than most vantage points.

You can almost see the faces of those on the top deck of a Condor ferry when the wave-piercers are raised clear on a high tide.

Sure, the days of 'steady as they come and go' cargo ships have long gone, but the harbour has cleaned up immeasurably with the absence of coal and other goods.

All of the decisions relating to it over nearly 200 years have not been taken overnight and were preceded by years of debate.

Looking at it with the benefit of hindsight, we have got most of it right.

'What it does deliver is a huge variety of construction styles,' sums up Capt. Gill, and who am I to disagree with the master.

Ten out of 10, St Peter Port.

HARBOUR TIMELINE

1858 North Quay extended and adapted as mail-boat landing stage. Passengers land by gangway for the first time. Esplanade from Havelet to Glategny completed. Dredging of Old Harbour commenced with a view to installing a lock.

1859 Steps to west of Careening Hard built. Breakwater Castle to Havelet completed. Third harbour master, John Fleure, appointed and sworn in at States.

1860 Fourth harbour master, Nicholas Le Messurier. New quays in Old Harbour 'designed to be three inches above highest known tides'. Deepwater pier proposed. Heated discussion as to location north or south of harbour. Balance of opinion favours north side.

1861 Ten-ton crane erected at St Julian's Pier: allocated to London boats, SS Elk the first vessel to use it.

1864 No. 1 berth at the White Rock completed. Weymouth steam packets could now berth alongside at all states of the tide – long before they could do so in Jersey.

1866 Roadway and terrace to White Rock finished. Guernsey Evening Press announces the discovery that its pier head is on quicksand with bedrock 17ft below. The seabed is in fact soft vegetative alluvium, deposited from the streams over many years.

1870 Serious settlement along White Rock pier: 400 tons granite removed, replaced by open sheds. Hundreds of tons of rock blasted from inside Castle Breakwater dumped to form beach at White Rock. First mobile steam crane.

IT'S ONLY NATURAL

THE marina operation in the old harbour has come a long way since a group of impatient Frenchmen could wait no longer to berth in front of Woolies.

They came off their pontoon in the main harbour pool and, in a race resembling a photo-finish in the Olympic Games 100 metres, the fleet of yachts motored towards their overnight destination and managed to wedge themselves stuck across the 80ft or so entrance into what we know as the Victoria Marina.

It was one of the more memorable incidents in Graham Trebert's long career around the harbour, which culminated in his elevation to head of marina operations.

With more than hint of pride in his voice, Graham says he is the original marina attendant.

Prior to that he had worked as a harbour attendant, joining the staff in 1963 when small pleasure craft still littered the old Albert Dock and cargo boats unloaded in the old harbour alongside Boots.

It is strange to think that was still happening into the 70s.

The Victoria Marina came first in 1972 and two years later was followed by a transformation of the Albert.

That first season, a mere 80 yachts visited the Victoria Marina but once the word got round as to what St Peter Port had to offer to the restless yachtsmen of France and the south coast of England, it became jam-packed and has been at the height of summer every year since.

By the 1980s the Victoria had become a visitors-only operation.

On average 225 boats can be accommodated at any one time, the exact number dependent on the lengths and draughts of those wishing

Right
The old harbour
Opposite
Graham Tanguy, head of marina operations

HARBOUR TIMELINE

1873 Fault in 500ft of foundations of the 'forearm' (now White Rock Pier) discovered. Heavy tie rods inserted.

1881 New lifeboat house completed on Castle Emplacement. John Lockett relocated to eastern end of Model Yacht Pond, which remained the launch site until 1929, from which date lifeboats were moored afloat. The 'Castle Slipway,' now known as the Old Lifeboat Slip, constructed.

1890 Cross berth built for inter-island steamers.

1894 Buildings erected on Albert Pier – restaurant, ladies' room, harbour store, gauger's office and a room 'for selling little pigs'.

1903 St Peter Port Harbour debt of £360,000 cleared.

1906 Small patent slip at Castle Emplacement built (now known as Boatworks+).

1909 Cambridge Berth completed, incorporating former boat harbour at east end. New steps built at eastern side at a cost of £15,500.

1920 The void in the North Pier head (between sea wall and jetties), previously covered by timber, replaced with reinforced concrete slabs. Access today is from a hatchway in the toilets adjacent to Sark Shipping offices opposite Nos 5/6 berth.

1921 States agrees to dismantle both patent slips at Careening Hard and transfer the engine to St Sampson's.

1923 14 August. Regular 'Sea Eagle' flying boat services inaugurated by Captain Henri Charles Biard between UK and Guernsey, initially at L'Ancresse, but later at St Peter Port.

Right
Castle Cornet has dominate the ever-changing harbour for centuries

to moor virtually bang in the centre of Town.

It has been a phenomenal success story as well as an aesthetic one.

The income generated from the Victoria alone is reckoned to be in the region of £350-£360k a year, while the whole spend in the Town marinas is into several millions of pounds.

'We probably get in 11,500 to 12,000 boats per annum, says Graham, whose job is to make sure they are all well catered for, managed and that when they leave, they depart with the thought that they will return and plough more of their euros into the Town coffers.

The marinas are manned by nine full-time staff who provide 24-hour coverage seven days a week and are supplemented by seasonal staff.

Graham says that the average stay of a visiting yacht is about a day-and-a-half, all paying about £2 a metre for a night's stay.

'When I started, they were charged between 50p and £1.'

Nowadays, if your cruiser-yacht is 20 metres in length that will set you back £41 per day.

In addition to the visitors, there is the not inconsiderable matter of the 980 resident boats in the Queen Elizabeth Marina, which brings in the largest revenue stream of the whole marina operation.

But back to those mad Frenchies. How did Graham sort them out?

'They were wedged across the entrance as they fought with paddles to get in. There were three or four of us in dories, running around trying to get them organised.'

It still amuses him to this day.

But even more amusing to Graham is the time the harbour launch St Anne managed to get itself stuck atop the steel gate as it looked to exit the Victoria on a falling tide.

Now, that was very embarrassing. Then there

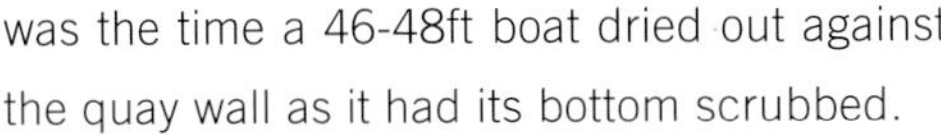

was the time a 46-48ft boat dried out against the quay wall as it had its bottom scrubbed.

'They let all their ropes go in preparation for refloating, when a young child on board called out to the rest of his family that he'd seen crabs down below in the water.

They all moved over to see what he was excited about and the boat keeled over on its side.

'We were very close to an enormous catastrophe,' Graham recalled.

But for a harbour that has so many thousands of people moving through it over the course of a year, serious incidents, or potentially serious ones like that near-disaster adjacent to the quay, are increasingly rare.

Graham is happy to blow his own and his staff's trumpets for that.

'It is so well controlled these days that it could be down to the quality of the staff that we don't get the number of incidents.'

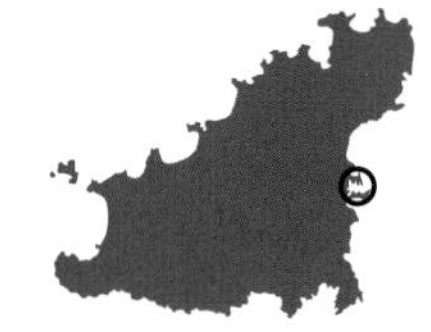

HARBOUR TIMELINE

1929 Passenger service using Calcutta flying boats established from Castle Emplacement.
1 September, last timber ship to use West Quay: SS Piroy from Riga.

1929 22 March. New Jetty commissioned. SS St Helier the first ship.

1932 HSPP recorded as having 17 electric cranes and two hand cranes of five- and 10-ton capacity. A branch post office opened on the New Jetty enabling letters, registered mail and parcels to be posted 15 minutes before sailing (previously two hours).

1935 The upper promenade over the North Pier head removed: known colloquially as 'The Pulpit'.

1945 Steel net fitted across pier heads. Alleged that more than 900 ships anchored in roads at one time. By end of November, prepared demolition charges removed from White Rock berth, Cambridge berth and New Jetty, including two torpedo warheads, 10 parachute mines, 600 French landmines, 207 27cm shells and three depth charges. Some 19,000 tons of ammunition dumped at sea, mostly in the Hurd Deep.

1946 Lifeboat house built to the east of St Julian's Emplacement. Port Control, a single-deck lookout, built on top of German bunker at White Rock pier.

1947 London ships cease to use St Julian's Pier, which is turned over to general cargo activities. First recorded instance of the harbour being 'full' for visiting yachts, which were required to moor elsewhere. Resumption of use of tanker berth in Albert Dock.

THE NUTS & BOLTS OF IT

THERE are an awful lot of people who are grateful for the commercial success of Guernsey's Town harbour.

It goes without saying that many a restaurateur would be the poorer, or not in business at all, but for the marina trade.

But there are other ancillary businesses that depend on St Peter Port's many thousands of keeled visitors and local boatowners and top of that list are the marine engineers, firms such as Boatworks+, Herm Seaways, AB Marine and Arun Marine Ltd.

Keith Duquemin, boss of Herm Seaways, whose workshop and showrooms are next to the Slaughterhouse, has lived his adult life off the back of the harbour.

Now nearing retirement age, Keith started out working for Moitier, marine engineers who operated from close to the Model Yacht Pond where today the marine craft stop for fuel.

If you count his school holiday part-time work, Keith has headed to the harbour daily for 50 years of his working life.

Herm Seaways exists from the remnants of the combination that came from the one-man Herm ferry operators just after the war: men such as Herbie Renouf and Bert Petit.

The operator Herm Ferries Ltd, which in turn became Herm Seaway Ltd about 35 years ago, worked from above the slip opposite the Town Church. It was around that time that Herm Seaways opened a workshop on the Castle Emplacement, on the spot where 100 years earlier Trinity House prepared the stone for the Hanois lighthouse.

The workshop owed its existence to the need to support the company's ferry boats and it was then that Keith came on board as a shore-based engineer.

'Over the years we took on outside private boatowners' work and ended with what it is today – eight employees, a retail shop and five service vehicles on the road, plus a couple of fairly prestigious dealerships.'

In time the ferries were sold off to Trident Charter, but Herm Seaways flourished and reacted to the constant changes of the harbour environment.

'It continually changes,' says Keith.

'Over the years it has changed phenomenally. Personally, as a marine engineer, we used to

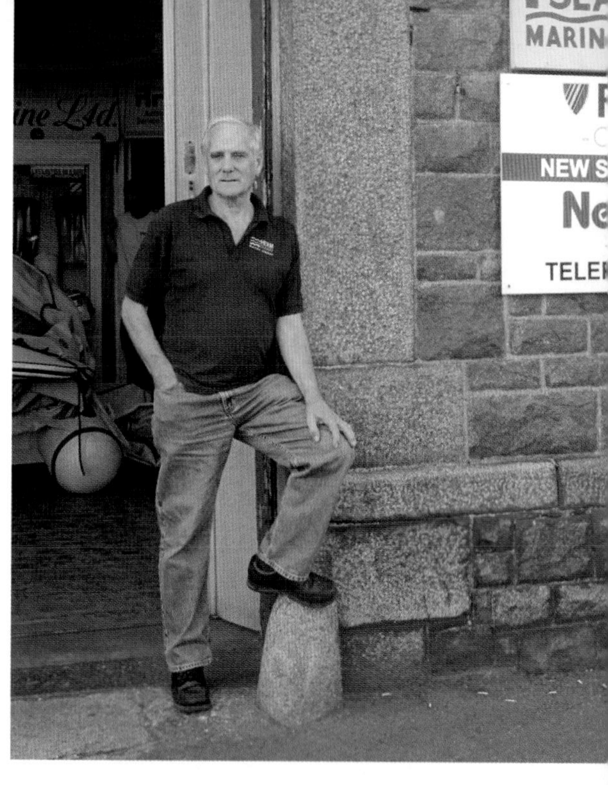

Above right
Keith Duquemin outside Herm Seaway's showroom on the Castle Emplacement
Below
The Fishermen's Quay

have to go out in a dinghy to the boats we were working on in the harbour.'

Now, of course, it is a case of walking down a few steps onto a pontoon.

While Keith has a keen sense of heritage and fondly recalls the pre-marina years, he appreciates the changes, both economically and aesthetically.

'It [the marina] gives us more business than a conventional harbour.

'We can walk to the boats now, which makes life a lot easier as far as working conditions go, plus the fact that the boats stay afloat all the time.

'I think there is a lot to be said for the look of a conventional harbour but our business very definitely revolves around the marina facility.'

A big chunk of his company's work is general breakdowns.

In the quieter winter months, there is a great emphasis on fitting engines.

'To do be honest we don't do much visitor work, because we have such a big local client base.'

As for the harbour's future, he hopes that whatever is decided the powers will strike a balance between old and new.

'It has been utilised to its capacity.

'Traditionally, it would be a shame to see the Careening Hard go – other than that, there has been talk of doing something with Havelet Bay'.

HARBOUR TIMELINE

1948 Ninth harbour master, Frank Nicolle (previously deputy harbour master). 4 February, St Patrick arrives. A very popular passenger ship.

1950 The Castle bridge or viaduct (1888), rebuilt in concrete: replaces 1868 wooden version.

1951 21 March. Last tanker to discharge at Albert Dock, MV Energie. The storage tanks, situated on the grass to the west of the bunker, were removed in May.

1952 The old lifeboat slip extended. Offices for Tomato Marketing Board built on the north side of St Julian's Pier. New harbour master's office built in timber on top of New Jetty building, north end, immediately above its predecessor.

1955 Flashing buoys introduced to mark the fairway.

1961 13 May. Passenger services from Southampton come to an end after nearly 140 years.

1962 Signal Station extended.

1964 'Flying Christine II' launched by the Bailiff. Tenth harbour master, Captain John Allez. 'Condor 1' arrives, a 33-knot hydrofoil, built in Messina, Italy. 1 May, the start of the fast ferry business.

1969 No. 6 berth set aside as 'dedicated' Sark one.

BAILIFF BROCK'S HARBOUR PLANNING

NOW I have the utmost respect for our Bailiff. Sir Geoffrey Rowland is a good and popular man who happily involves himself in all things community based.

He's a very sound judge, you could add.

But I would not expect him to be submitting plans for the mooted development of the Careening Hard as an additional marina.

Go back 172 years and his predecessor, Bailiff Daniel de Lisle Brock, was putting plume to paper and coming forward with his own diagram as to how the then very basic St Peter Port should develop as a harbour.

Indeed, everyone was having a pop at it. Colonel de Havilland had a go, as did a Captain Hide and a chap by the name of Walker.

They all submitted drawings in 1838, which, thankfully, were never taken up.

Brock's effort was a decent one, it has to be said, if only for the fact that he recognised the huge potential of building a long southern pier all the way to the castle.

But instead of utilising the natural foundational rockbed of Vermiere, he went south of it and straight to Castle Cornet.

None of the would-be architects recognised the potential of the St Julian's and White rocks in the process and nor did Mr Rendle, who made his own, more professionally drawn, proposals 13 years later.

Rendle also ignored the castle and St Julian's with his initial plans, but his reports were not ignored and within three years his ideas had been embraced as part of a new proposal by Messrs. Lyster and Brumell, which did take in piers all the way to the castle and White Rock.

Ultimately it was a further improved scheme that was adopted in the States of 1860 and we have not looked back since.

Above right
Bailiff Daniel de Lisle Brock had his own ideas for the development of the harbour
Below
The Model Yacht Pond and Castle Cornet

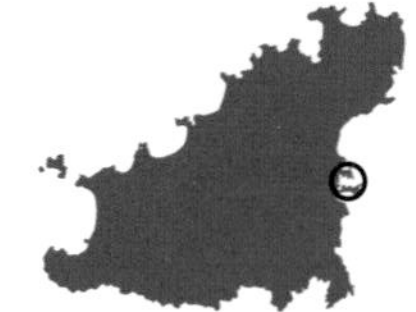

HARBOUR TIMELINE

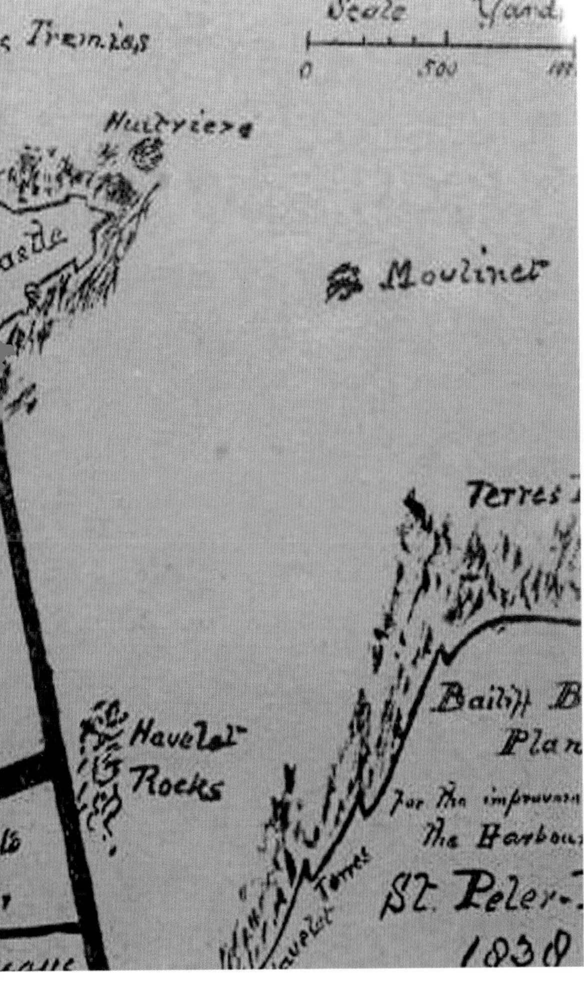

1972 Foundation stone at Victoria Marina laid 14 June. Cranes moved from New Jetty to 4 and 5 berths.

1973 12 May. Victoria Marina opened. Designed for 118 local and 160 visiting yachts.

1974 8 April. Foghorn moved from White Rock to Castle Breakwater light.

1975 Introduction of ro-ro by 'Svea Drott' car ferry, renamed 'Earl Godwin' during the same year.

1976 South end of the New Jetty becomes active again, known as the Cross Berth, for hydrofoil 'Condor 1'.

1977 8 November. Sealink starts a ro-ro service from Portsmouth. Eleventh harbour master, Captain Harry Wolley.

1981 Twelfth harbour master, Captain John Petit.

1987 Thirteenth harbour master, Tim Spencer.

1989 23 May. Queen Elizabeth II opens the new marina in her name.

1993 Condor 10 (74m Incat Catamaran, 580 passengers, 90 cars) starts service from Weymouth to the islands.

1997 Fourteenth harbour master, Captain Robert Barton.

2002 A project started to repair the New Jetty.

2005 Fifteenth harbour master, Captain Peter Gill.

"The tower is roomy and would house quite a number of men. The occupying Nazis restricted themselves to making their stay as comfortable as possible by lining the barrack rooms with beaverboard"

Victor Coysh

CHAPTER 17

LITTLE RUSSEL
& BREHON TOWER

More than simply a watery approach to the island's major port, but a once hazardous stretch made safer by modern technology and a line of cleverly placed marks. And in the middle of it all, the oval-shaped Brehon.

SMALL BUT DEADLY

DAY in, day out, no matter what the season, islanders crank their necks and gaze out over it.

For many, it's a quick check to see if it is rough, smooth, up or down.

If the glimpse is not enough and they need more, they will park their car, cross their arms and soak up the view.

I'm talking Little Russel, that stretch of water that separates us from Herm and Jethou.

But just where does the Little Russel start, where does it end?

Where does it become the 'Big' one?

On the first question, don't go by the official charts,

It may show the Little Russel stretching north from roughly St Martin's Point to Sark, but the most important man in modern-day sea matters, harbour master Captain Peter Gill, has his own view on the matter.

'In practical terms, I would say it starts from Brehon Tower upward.

Below that it is relatively open water.

'But there's not a start and finish as such.

'It's not a precise geographical description.'

So if Brehon is Captain Gill's starting point at the south end of the Russel, where does he consider it ends in the north?

'Once you're clear of Platte Boue rock you are out of the Little Russel. Take a line from Platte Boue to the Grand Brayes and you are then in open water.'

Before then, though, watch out. There are an awful lot of rocks about.

The most dangerous of all is Platte Boue itself, a rock never seen, just feared . . . a lot.

'It's the one thing you can't see, but it's the most dangerous rock we've got.

'According to Ronnie Munson it has claimed 78 ships.

'It gives me nightmares. For a sailing ship master it provides the ultimate fright.

'In truth, a book could be written on the

Right
Mid channel marks including Platte Fougere and Brehon

history of this rock alone, as it is arguably the most notorious rock in the Bailiwick,' said Capt. Gill.

A long time ago Platte Boue was marked by a buoy, but it became so difficult and costly to keep one in position, the authorities conceded defeat on that one.

'In the first six years of operation, the buoy had broken adrift and been found five times.'

Then, when the States Supervisor gave instructions to keep the retrieved buoy in a cattle shed and not risk another loss, the rock claimed one of its most famed victims.

On 5 June 1873, the South Western railways steamship Waverley, under Captain Mabb, struck the rock in fog and was a total loss.

Two years later, the Havre hit it in good visibility and after sliding beneath the waves came to rest on top of the Waverley.

The two ships remain adjoined today.

More buoys were fixed, but none stayed in position long and for more than a century this nastiest of rocks, just 12ft in diameter at its peak just 3ft below the lowest of ordinary spring tides, has remained unmarked.

Thankfully, as the sailing ships were replaced by steamers, the Platte's capacity for death and damage waned, yet as recently as 1990 a cargo ship is known to have 'slid over it' and managed to continue.

Nearer port, there are many more rocks that warrant staying well clear and, in the odd case, have been shaved to reduce their danger.

One is the Crabiere, bang outside St Sampson's Harbour, two other sets being the Agenor and Trois Grunes, slightly to its north.

Back in 1923 the Guernsey Press gave its readers a vivid description of the mountainous horrors that lay out of sight of ships drifting upon them.

To combat the problem of these rocks lying so close to the transit points of incoming and outgoing ships, the decision was made to blast away much of the rock – the very least they could do, argued the critical Press leader column.

'Vessels carrying 500 to 600 passengers induced to the island, and travelling at a speed of 20 knots, have been obliged to rely on aids of navigation which would have put a port a tenth the size of ours to shame,' blasted the paper, which petitioned every ship-maker using St Peter Port for improvements.

The authorities caved in and the States voted £6,700 (about £1.3m today) for work to be done, but in presenting the Harbour Board's plan for the work involved, the paper questioned the worth of simply blasting.

'We cannot seriously think that the Harbour Board contemplates making this passage safe by blasting. If they do so it will certainly be another case of exceeding the amount voted.'

The Press called for a buoy to mark the Agenor's threat and urged against 'a serious waste of money' being outlayed.

A light buoy would be best, argued the paper, but blast away they did that summer and, in so doing, divers came up with two cannon discovered on the Grune au Rouge.

By the end of the summer's blasting both sets of rocks were declared to be safe to any ship from half-tide up.

At Grune au Rouge there was now 30ft of water available at half tide.

'They [the cannon] may have been used as an anchor for a buoy,' considered an interested Capt. Gill, unaware of the Agenor and Trios Grunes blasting operations.

All these years on, he has sympathy with the 1920s' Press viewpoint.

'In sailing ship days they were more of a problem,' he said, and to ram home the paper's viewpoint that a little blasting is no guaranteed way of keeping ships from going aground, seven years later the coal boat Beauport hit them at low tide and sank.

This was no ordinary shipping disaster.

Although there had been no loss of life – she had a crew of 12 – the Beauport hugged the news for months as she sank, was raised, moved, sank a second time and then came to rest just outside the harbour mouth having been blasted almost to bits.

It is still marked just off the Town breakwater on the latest charts.

The £50,000 Onesimus Dorey-owned ship was chock full of coal but remarkably hit the very rocks which seven years earlier had been blasted to make the Russel passage safe.

The Press of 1930 revelled in its position of having 'told you so'.

Beauport's skipper, Capt. Christian, had been under the impression that his ship, drawing 12ft at the bow and 14 at the stern, would be well clear of Agenor, which had been cleared by the blasting some seven years earlier.

Oh, how wrong he was.

The Press leader of 22 February 1930 made hay of the situation.

'We maintain it is a waste of public money to reduce a rock by blasting 18 or 19 feet [away] while there are other dangers on the same line, one of which only has six feet of water at low water equinoxial spring tide.

'This, unless the whole group be removed, will in effect be but digging a hole in a group of rocks. To remove a small portion only of the dangers, and the buoy marking the whole group, will leave a state of things far worse than at present.'

The argument, of course, came too late for the Beauport and the attention switched to how to salvage the ship and its holds of coal.

For months strenuous efforts had been made to save the cargo boat and finally, four

Right
The wreck of the Beauport in 1930

months after it had sank, the Beauport was brought to the surface with the aid of two new submarines acting as pontoons, each with a lifting capacity of 600 tons.

The ship was then hauled to within 100 yards of the White Rock, where it was left to settle in comparative safety, the plan being to plug the holes, refloat and bring the vessel into port.

That was the idea, anyway.

Two months later the salvagers were still being frustrated.

The ship had embedded itself in soft sand.

Big crowds gathered on the promenade to observe the exercise, however, there was no applause.

It just wouldn't move.

By October, nearly eight months after it hit Agenor, the salvage exercise came to a conclusion as the final blasting of it sent it from view altogether.

The only people who were benefiting now were the interested amateur fishermen who had been sent hundreds of stunned fish, courtesy of the explosions.

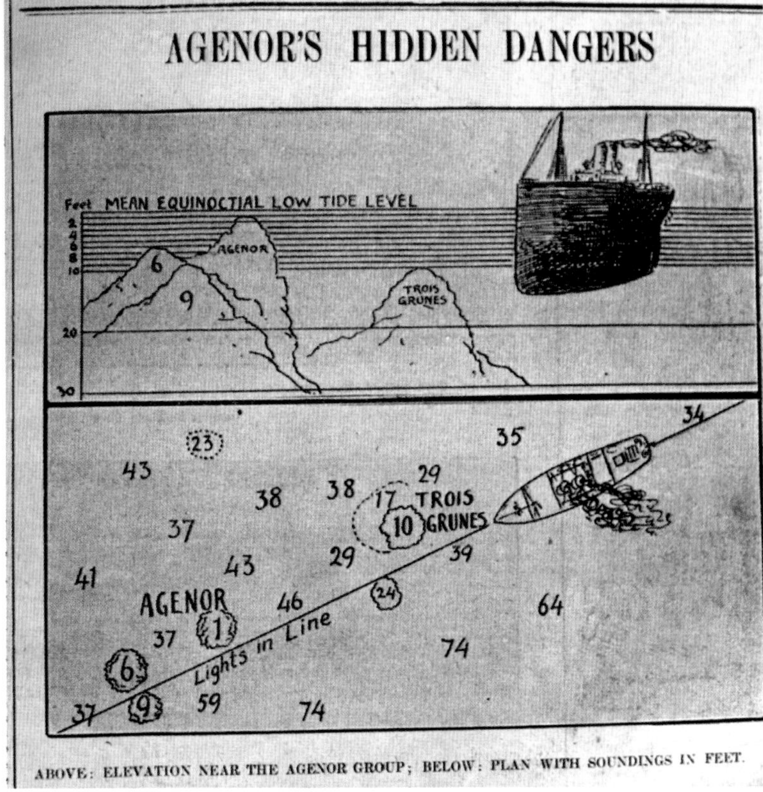

ABOVE: ELEVATION NEAR THE AGENOR GROUP; BELOW: PLAN WITH SOUNDINGS IN FEET.

Close views of the wrecked Beauport, from different angles, all taken by "Press" photographers at de ad low tide Sunday afternoon.

THE LIGHTHOUSE FAMILY

A LIGHTHOUSE it may be, but the 100-year-old Platte Fougere has never had an in situ keeper.

But until the 1970s it did have shore keepers, and they shared the big white house which sits across the draughty car park from Fort Doyle, staring eastwards the mile out to sea where possibly the least attractive lighthouse in the world stands proudly above the waves.

Graham de Jersey's family is steeped in Platte history. His father, Ernest, was a lighthouse keeper for 24 years until his retirement in 1973.

And before the war, his grandfather, Nick Ingrouille, was also a keeper for 14 years.

Both Graham and his surviving mother, who brought a family up on a headland which can one moment be idyllic and the next positively Arctic, have many memories of life on this north-east Guernsey promontory.

'It was lovely down there,' recalled Graham.

'But in the winter it was bloody cold,' he added.

As Guernsey dwellings go, the old keeper's house is about as exposed as any on this little rock of ours.

The house stands a world record triple jump from the sea and Graham has seen some big ones – 30ft swells – down there.

Nor has it always stayed within the confines of the beach.

'Peter Tostevin, who was living there in about the late 60s, got up to go to the outside toilet at two in the morning one night and found

Below
Graham and Winnie de Jersey

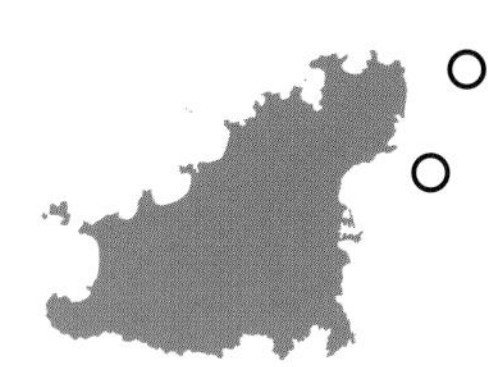

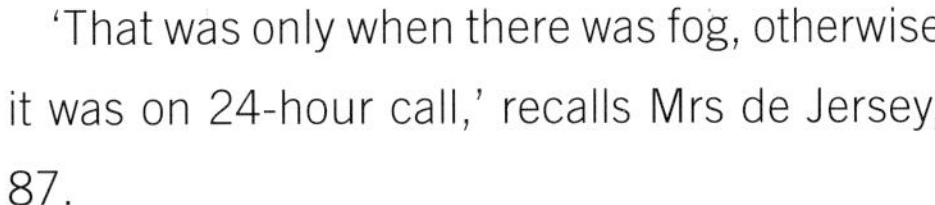

himself washed off his feet in the yard.'

Those were same toilets which, much to the de Jersey family's annoyance, became a popular stopping off point for desperate tourists, sometimes preventing the family from using it themselves.

'They'd say "get to the back of the queue",' recalls Graham.

Being a lighthouse keeper at Fort Doyle was not particularly exciting or taxing.

The tasks were basically to keep an eye on visibility and ensure that the on-land compressors which powered the foghorn did not shut down and cause the cable to blow.

When fog was about, the keeper would be 12 hours on duty, eight hours on relief, followed by another 12 hours on duty.

'That was only when there was fog, otherwise it was on 24-hour call,' recalls Mrs de Jersey, 87.

'It was an easy job when fine but you couldn't go anywhere as you always had to be close to the lighthouse,' she added.

Although the light fell under the jurisdiction of Trinity House, the building in which the de Jerseys lived was owned by the harbour authorities.

It was built to go with the lighthouse and, at the risk of being unkind, it's about as exciting as the car park beneath its windows.

The de Jerseys lived in the upper floor and they will never forget their telephone number – 44897 – which St Peter Port would dial to tell Ernest de Jersey that a fog bank was on the way up from St Martin's Point and it was time to start the horn.

And when the Platte horn failed, which it did very occasionally, a reserve one, atop Fort Doyle and operated by another compressor, would replace it.

Looking out on a stormy spring day towards the Platte, it is almost unimaginable to think that in its early days a diver, dressed as if he had stepped out of Jules Verne's 20,000 Leagues Under the Sea, walked the mile across the sea bed to check the cable's position.

'It's sand all the way,' Graham assures me. 'There's a passage that goes through the reef. My grandfather was there when he walked it.'

Legend has it that on one such occasion the diver pulled on the rope attached to him as a safety measure.

He was duly brought to the surface and Graham takes up the story.

'He wouldn't go back down for two or three hours. He saw something which he said he'd never speak about,' recalls Graham.

Perhaps it was Captain Nemo, aka James Mason, himself.

LITTLE RUSSEL'S LEADING LIGHT

THERE will be no candles in the Little Russel wind, probably no great ceremony at all when, next year, the ugliest lighthouse in Channel Islands waters celebrates its 100th birthday.

To reach its century is no mean achievement for the Platte Fougere, especially for the Yorkshire firm that 100 years ago this year, with the help of skilled local men, began to construct the 83ft of concrete octagonal inelegance that keeps navigators blinded by fog off a notorious reef.

After just 10 years in existence there was serious concern that the tower would not make it through to 1910, let alone 2010.

The January Billet of 1909 noted the acting States Engineer's consideration that it was in immediate danger of collapse.

But patched up and bulked up to withstand the force of the raging tides that run down the Russel, it has somehow made it.

It cost £10,000 to build, but would they attempt it today?

Probably not, says harbour master Capt. Peter Gill, while at the same time not underplaying its importance to maritime safety.

'Is it still a fit and appropriate aid to navigation to meet future requirements?' queried the harbour master, who rightly points out it is not going to stand forever without much remedial work required.

'It's necking at the bottom. If you have to rebuild it, it's not going to be cheap,' he added. He even went as far as saying: 'Do you need a foghorn there?

'We haven't had a serious incident at the Platte for quite a number of years and you can put a lot of that down to the Racon transmitter on the beacon, which keeps ships away.

'Of all the passages we've got, the Little Russel is the most dangerous, and it would be foolhardy to remove the protection without ensuring an adequate safety replacement.'

That might mean operating something similar to the Roustel beacon, a little further south down the Russel.

'I'm bending towards replacing it with something that is a shorter-range lighthouse with a Racon. Whether we need a foghorn I'm not quite so sure.'

A century ago the building of the tower was, naturally, hailed as a great achievement.

It is one and a half miles off the north-east coast and was the first lighthouse to be unattended and to be controlled from the shore by a submarine cable.

It remains one of the most important navigational lights around our shores and is one of the leading lights for shipping approaching the Little Russel from the north.

Before the lighthouse was built there was a wooden beacon, on top of which were the letters PF.

Then the States decided to erect the lighthouse and the contractors who got the job were Messrs. Arundel Brothers from Yorkshire.

Among the locals used was a 15-year-old local lad, Adolphus Brache, who in 1975, aged 82, sat down and told Carel Toms, the late Guernsey historian, just how they did it.

Still full of enthusiasm, Mr Brache remembered how well he and his father, the late Adolphus Brache, became involved.

Mr Brache senior was a carpenter who served his trade with J. D. Robilliard in the Truchot. Young Adolphus followed in his father's footsteps.

Working alongside Irish, Scots and Yorkshire men, Adolphus Brache's first job was to get rid of the vraic and clean up what could be seen of the rock at low water. In all there were about two dozen men on the job in addition to several local labourers and boatmen.

Mr Brache recalled how the work started and the fact that after three weeks it was found

Right
The construction of Platte Fougere was a feat in itself at the start of the 20th century
Overleaf
The St Peter Port lifeboat heads past La Platte and Roustel Beacon

impossible to keep the concrete on the rock. It was simply being washed away.

The manager, a Mr Swift, became desperate for a solution and it was Mr Brache's father who was able to assist.

The diameter of the octagonal base was 17ft and Mr Brache constructed an iron framework of 3/8in thick sheet steel. This was made in four parts and bolted together on the rock.

The framework was made in a forge on the Southside, which was used for making anchors, chains and other items for sailing ships.

Before this frame could be shipped to the rock, holes had to be drilled 8 or 9in into the granite. These took 1/2in thick pins, which secured the metal frame before concrete was poured in. Much of the work could be done only on neap tides and the hours were long and arduous: starting at 7 in the morning and going on until 6 each evening, except on Saturdays when they finished at 5pm.

There were no paid holidays other than bank holidays and the wages were 3s 4d per day for labourers and 4s a day for master men.

Building went on apace and the little steam tug, Pioneer, owned by Martel Brothers and in charge of Captain de Carteret of Sark, was employed to ferry the men and supplies from Southside, St Sampson's.

All the concrete was mixed by hand at a yard at Southside and was put into hessian

sacks for easy transportation. But it was far from easy to transfer these heavy sacks of wet concrete by derrick from the ship to the rock, especially when there was a sea running.

As the building progressed, a wooden framework was made from 6in square pieces of pitchpine, to which 7in wide and 1in thick boards were fastened. This shuttering enabled the concrete to be held until it set hard.

When the base reached a height of about 7ft above high water spring tides, holes were bored into the new concrete and into the rock to take 3in. steel rods, around which liquid cement was poured.

Below
Building the Platte Fougere in 1909

As the tower increased in height longer hours could be spent on the site. At times it was necessary to use flares, while on occasions it was impossible to land on the rock because of the weather.

Slowly, the tower rose and when some 30ft was completed in solid reinforced concrete, and a perpendicular ladder placed alongside, the rooms were built to house the equipment necessary to operate the light and fog signal.

Day after day the Pioneer steamed out to the rock and almost nudged the structure in order to get as close as possible to unload concrete which was hoisted up on the derrick, five bags at a time.

Once, when the Pioneer rolled in the swell, the chain holding the sack snapped and there was a great splash as the bags dropped into the sea, gone for good.

Landing was sometimes very difficult when there was a swell.

This was always done by dinghy and at times an inexperienced man would jump on the ladder at the bottom of a swell and before he could clamber up, the sea was up to his waist.

After the Braches' job had been completed young Adolphus recalled how the submarine cable was laid from the shore and how it was secured to the gully below the rock with tons of liquid cement and concrete.

This cable, in fact, lasted until 1950 when it was replaced with a new one at a cost of £10,000, as much as the States paid for building the original lighthouse and laying the first cable.

The original cable weighed 70 tonnes and was 11in in diameter. Its replacement weighed 57 tonnes and was just 4 1/2in in diameter.

The top of the tower is 50ft above high water mark and 83ft above low water.

NAUTICAL DODGEMS

JUST imagine the maritime mayhem in the northern approaches to our main ports were it not for the string of beacons that stand amid the waves down the Guernsey side of the Russel.

There's Brehon Tower, which has sufficient history to have had its own dedicated Coast feature, the black-and-white hooped Vivian, the green-topped Platte Light, the chequered Roustel and the yellow-headed Corbette, all guard the closing stretch once past Platte Fougere and, above that, the fearsome white-topped Brayes, the big ones and the little 'uns which stand out from the blue with their blonde tops.

In their various guises and location, they all make the mariners' lives so much easier and safer.

They are where they are as a result of major mishap.

The Platte Rock beacon, not to be mistaken for the Platte Fougere to the north, was, back in the 1800s, a mast painted white and black with a round top 5ft 1in. in diameter.

That, in time, was replaced by a 'beacon with ship's lower mast', but for the last 60 years it has resembled a truncated granite cone.

But it is more than a lump of green stone.

Fitted with a wind generator and solar panel, it makes for hairy maintenance work.

Boats have to be capable of finding a location within the current flow and to have their engines in neutral while maintaining a constant position.

It has been hit by many a ship, but not since 1899.

Roussel, an isolated rock in the middle of the Russel off Bordeaux, has not been so lucky.

In 1923, the cargo ship Ulrica struck the rock and it was only then that the powers that be gave in to the mariners' insistence that a beacon should be erected there.

George Le Couteur was awarded the contract to erect a concrete tower which survived a number of hits, before in the winter of 1970, the Winchester all but destroyed it.

As a result of that incident the tower was reduced in height, the stone base sheathed in GRP, painted with black-and-white chequers and topped with a stainless steel lattice structure with a black top mark.

Outside Noirmont headland stands Corbette, which has been marked as a beacon for the last 150 years.

Today it has a yellow stone truncated cylinder with pole marked 'O' on top and over the years it has largely been avoided, although in 1881 the two-masted schooner Ulysses, loaded with stone, left St Sampson's and struck Corbette before immediately sinking.

Above and left
Corbette Beacon and Vivian are two more vital marks for mariners

DISCOVERING BREHON

IT SAYS something about the uncomfortable congestion of Guernsey life that it is quicker to travel by motorboat from the QE2 Marina to Brehon Tower than it is to get out of the Salerie car park at a quarter to five.

In fact, you could speed out twice to the landmark more quickly than it takes to drive by car from the Salerie to the Bridge during Guernsey rush hour.

More, at three knots, the speed of the tide flowing north of Brehon is quicker than the stream of traffic edging along Les Banques when islanders are leaving work.

But the upside of being stuck in the east coast traffic on a beautiful late August afternoon is that you get to admire Brehon Tower at a little more leisure than normal.

And what a structure it is, albeit one which has turned out to be more of visual value than of a practical one.

In essence, it's a chunky, extra-large Martello tower stuck out on a rock, a particularly nasty piece of rock as it happens.

It is unwise to get too close to the reef on which it sits and the days of anyone and everyone stepping ashore for a nose have long gone.

A slick downstream tide of about six knots from the Petit Creux mark towards the tower takes me to within 150 metres of the elliptically-shaped 19th century building, the closest I ever may get, unlike my brother-in-law and navigator who, as a Scout four decades ago, occasionally rowed there from St Sampson's on a summer's evening to have a look at the place and the rats famously said to exist there.

How the rats ever managed to exist is a mystery, unlike the tale of the tower itself.

Below
The Little Russel's most treasured mark

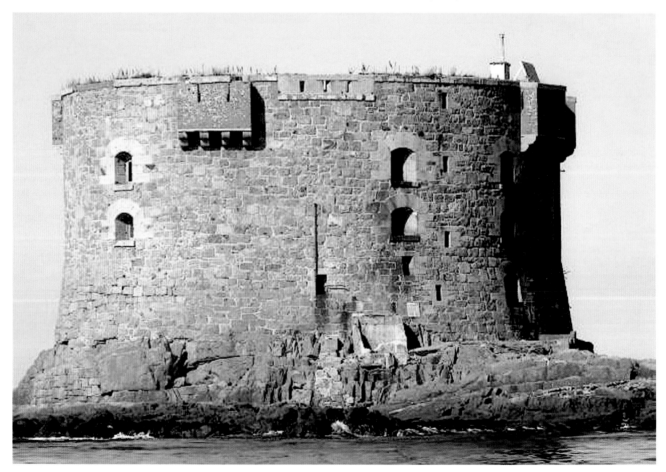

TOWER HAMLET

WHAT'S fat and round and, as history has proven, has very largely been a waste of time and money?

Why, Brehon Tower of course.

You look at the stout granite tower and wonder why it was ever built.

But at the same time, I suspect just about everybody is glad that it was.

A Little Russel without Brehon would be like Cobo without the Grosse Rocque.

But study the background to Brehon's presence and you will probably agree with most historians that have delved into its origins, that here is one of the Bailiwick's first white elephants.

Not as useless as Alderney's breakwater, but all things considered, not really required.

Its very existence can be blamed almost entirely on two things: the French, and panic by the mid-19th century British Government. Even after Napoleon had popped his French clogs in 1821, the Brits were so concerned that their nearest neighbours would strike again that forts and batteries began popping up everywhere across the Isles de la Manche.

Brehon has existed as we see it since 1856, but it had been of important navigational use to mariners for half a century previously.

From as early as the turn of the 18th and 19th century, the great slab of Guernsey rock had been used as a mark for shipping, with a stone obelisk erected on it initially.

Peter Gill, the St Peter Port harbourmaster, confirms that it was one of our very earliest navigation marks.

'It was well described by Deschamps in the early 1800s and there is a picture of it in The Harbour Master's notebook of the 1850s.

'It would be difficult to imagine the Little Russel without some form of mark on this reef [because] Brehon Tower is used both directly and indirectly as, for example, it is a striking transit for a number of other rocks, and it also provides a guide for clearing marks and anchorages.'

Above
The Brehon reef's original structure was an obelisk

The initial obelisk, or Deschamps Tower, was more than 40ft high and 34ft in circumference at its base.

It stood for 30 years until hauled down and replaced by the elliptical stone one we all know.

But an 1803 report by Colonel J. McLean highlighted to General Doyle, the then Lieutenant-Governor of Guernsey, that even from its very early days as a fairly useless shipping mark, its military potential was being considered.

McLean's report read:

'This rock is situated abreast of the Channel through the Little Russel within a quarter-of-a-mile of the passage for large ships.

'It is 2,300 yards from Vale Castle and about the same distance from the island of Herm.

'Between the rock and Herm there is no passage, except for boats, although it is reported that vessels now and then are carried by the current into this channel, and pass safely through it.'

Two hundred and six years ago McLean described the rock as 'perfectly naked' except for the small obelisk which was erected upon it 'some years ago'.

He noted, too, that 'the greatest part of it is overflowed at high water and the spray flies over the whole rock in stormy weather, but not with much violence'.

In other words, the soldiers won't drown and their muskets be filled by saltwater.

Interestingly, as nobody since 1856 has seen the true shape of the rock, McLean wrote: 'The summit, which the seat only thus washes at times, is composed of large masses of rock and in dimension measures about 40ft in diameter, being somewhat of a circular figure'.

But McLean, perhaps at the Lt-Governor's request, played on the significance of Brehon as a shipping mark and outlined why it may be very useful in terms of an early warning military battery.

'At this eventful period of a more serious war with France than ever Great Britain was yet engaged in, it becomes, however, a question of some consideration whether this rock might not be occupied as a post for night signals, to give notice of vessels passing through the Russel, which are not usually observed by the ships in the road until they are actually abreast of the Town.'

McLean goes so far as suggesting that it might be very beneficial to have a small guardroom with the means to make hand signals to shore built.

He also suggests a signal staff upon which lanterns might be suspended and, as a support system, the 'non-commissioned officers of the guard would, of course, be furnished with a good-speaking trumpet to hail all vessels and boats passing within hearing'.

He also wanted to throw in a guard boat in case of any urgent necessity to get over to Herm or to headquarters, Castle Cornet.

That boat, he suggested, could be hauled up on the rock and out of the way of surf thrown up by bad weather.

McLean's suggestions of 1803 fell on deaf ears.

In 1805 the French fleet limped away from Trafalgar badly beaten, and not too many years later Napoleon was out of the equation – finis.

But half a century later the reawakened threat of French invasion prompted the decision – there can be no other valid reason – to demolish the obelisk and erect what we see today.

Building it was not without incident.

In the autumn of 1855, with work well under way and 29 men working on the rock under the direction of employer Thomas Charles de Putron, a vicious storm blew down on them.

The Comet of 29 October 1855 told the full story in answer to growing rumours that several workmen had been washed away to their deaths at the height of the storm.

'This was happily not the case but the habitants of Brehon did not fail to experience anxiety on their own account, for the sea beat with considerable violence against the base of the tower which is in course of construction there, mounting to the altitude of 30 or 40 feet above the high water mark.

'Neither the masonry nor men have suffered. The work was too solid: and the workmen took refuge behind a large pile of bricks, near the north-west part of the tower.

'The damage caused to Brehon consists of a portion of the gantry, the gear and materials carried away by the sea.'

Another major gale in September 1856 saw masonry and scaffolding washed away.

Thankfully, none of the 20 to 30 men working

on the project were hurt.

Once up, it was never likely to come down again, a testament to its safe positioning, sheer girth and the best of Guernsey granite being used.

But with hindsight, it was never much use other than as an architectural delight to islanders and those slipping up and down the Russel on the water.

There have been times, though, when Brehon has been substantially armed – just in case.

The Star of 1859 reported the logistical difficulties on introducing several new 68-pound cannon to the fort, which was being prepared for the introduction of troops.

'This morning a 68-pounder, weighing five tons, was being lowered over planks, the upper end of which rested on the slip, the lower end on the bottom of the barge.

'On reaching within a foot of the boat's bottom, the tackle was let go and the boat, with four men in it, instantly capsized.

'The 68-pounder sank the boat with it, but the four men happily escaped with no greater injury than a ducking.'

Needless to say, the men were not wearing high-vis waistcoats and safety helmets.

Alongside a garrison of up to 35 men, the guns stayed mid-Russel for half a century before the place was demilitarised in the early 20th century.

Sadly, the obsolete weapons did not remain in the island and were sent back to the UK by the War Department.

But of course, Brehon got a new lease of life with the Germans' invasion of Guernsey.

Now its main use was that of anti-aircraft battery.

Were we permitted access today, evidence of the Germans' occupation of the fort would be impossible to avoid.

Nearly 70 years later, it is navigation that is the primary reason for Brehon's continued requirement and low maintenance.

Its navigation light is maintained by Guernsey with one eye on its new inhabitants – birds.

The harbourmaster confirmed that in looking after the equipment provided, including solar panels, Guernsey Harbours limits the timing and frequency of maintenance schedules to take into account the significance of the site to wildlife.

Above
Generations of sailors have used Brehon as a navigational aid

Overleaf
Brian Green's aerial shot clearly shows the old gun batteries

UNSUCCESSFUL EXPERIMENT

Above
Naftel's painting of Experiment going aground near Brehon

GIVEN the fortress's position and modern navigational aids and warnings, it would seem fairly unlikely that any boat or ship would hit Brehon in the 21st century.

But a century and a half ago, it was a different matter and on Sunday 16 March 1850 the Brache family of pilots made the headlines.

Nicholas Snr was on board his pilot boat Mary and saved 20 from the cutter Experiment on the Boue Petite rocks north of Brehon.

But despite Brache's work, a Captain Le Cocq and eight passengers perished.

In recognition of this the Lieutenant-Governor, Major Bell, presented 'a handsome blue bag, on one side an anchor, the other a branch of laurel' containing 1,899 francs (£75) which had been subscribed.

The recipients were Nicholas Brache Snr, his two sons, John and Nicholas, John William, James Henry, Nicholas Brache, Charles Bichard, Peter Le Poidevin, James Langlois and Thomas Renouf.

A painting was also commissioned by P.J. Naftel, a reputed local artist, which was also presented.

To put this into some historical perspective, this was the very same year that the first visit was made to Guernsey by a screw steamer the SS Collier.

INSIDE STORY

LIKE the sea and the wind, we have tried and tried.

But with the stubborn resistance of the fort against nature, every attempt made by the Coast team to view the inside of the 154-year-old fort has been resisted by the people who nowadays are ultimately responsible for Brehon – Treasury and Resources.

In a nutshell, people aren't wanted on the rock and, most definitely, not inside where, it is said, the stairways and remnants of rotting wooden floors are a danger to all.

These days few people other than the Guernsey Harbours men, who carry out basic maintenance, know the extent of the obviously grim picture within its round walls.

There is also the nature aspect.

As all semblance of human life disappeared, the birds moved in.

Even Jamie Hooper, bird lover and conservation officer for La Societe Guernesiaise, has not stepped ashore on the rock and his insistence that it is a level playing field for everyone in terms of an entrance ban makes me feel a whole lot better about being denied a snoop.

'The landing restrictions are there to give birds who need places to breed an undisturbed place,' said Mr Hooper.

Below
The internal layout of Brehon Tower

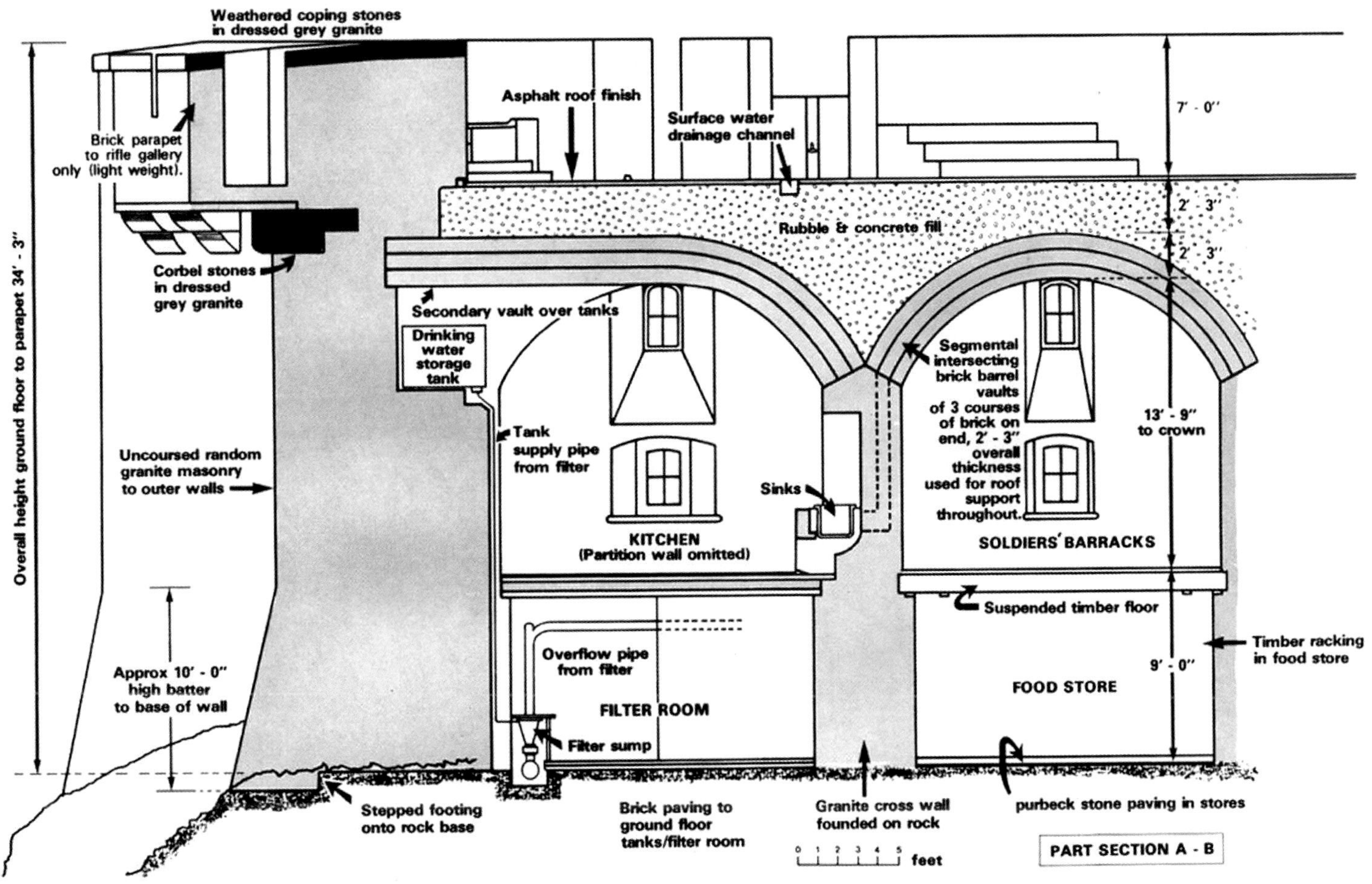

'I've never been there,' he added, but he knows all about the common terns that have.

'It is an important common tern colony, but they are a temperamental species and it doesn't take much to scare them off.'

And it seems that just that has happened, with Mr Hooper reporting that they have now moved to a little islet off Herm.

But, he insisted it is important that Brehon's seclusion is preserved.

'There are great efforts to make sure the place is suitable for when they come back.

'If people were to land regularly the terns wouldn't consider it an option.'

Previous Guernsey Press correspondents have, however, enjoyed the experience of a mooch inside and in 1952 the paper gave readers some idea of the misery within in a feature headlined 'Inside the grim fortress of Brehon Tower'.

Even then, 57 years ago, access was via the lowest window, some four or five feet above the ground.

The wooden stairway used by the Germans only seven years previously had all but disappeared.

The main entrance, eight to 10ft above rock level, is crowned by a granite lintel bearing the inscription VR 1856.

The visitor, almost certainly historian Victor Coysh, took a close view of the masonry and formed the opinion that it followed the pattern of the Martello towers and even of the Elizabethan and mediaeval stonework of Castle Cornet.

'Near the top are several brick projections, like the "oubliettes" of mediaeval castles,' he wrote.

'These are open at the base and were apparently intended to harass an enemy who, having landed on the rock, made an attempt to breach the walls or force the windows.'

Right
The ins and outs of Brehon: a disused battery and a decaying cooking range

But what about inside?

'The tower is roomy and would house quite a number of men.

The occupying Nazis restricted themselves [though] to making their stay as comfortable as possible by lining the barrack rooms with beaverboard.

'A spiral staircase against the overall leads to the top where there is a battery site.'

It was the 'splendid newel staircase' which the late Coysh regarded as its best feature.

It leads from the ground floor to the roof and twines around what were the living quarters, magazine and storerooms for the gunners.

All the interior work is German, including what was a fine brick fireplace in an upper room.

But, even half a century ago, when Coysh visited the tower it was very much a case of 'careful where you put your feet'.

He wrote then: 'Striking matches, we cautiously explored hidden depths. Everywhere, we trod warily, not knowing what pitfalls awaited us or whether or not the floors were rotten. The place is big and there are many rooms in it.'

There is also a concrete tablet on which the inscription records the names of two soldiers who were killed there, within a month of each other, in early summer 1943.

It is surmounted by a swastika and laurel leaves.

BELEAGUERED BREHON

THE tower was never bombed during the war but invariably attracted interest from the RAF.

And while not bombed it was most certainly machine gunned, which accounted for the two dead Germans.

How servicemen of the 19th and 20th century managed for fresh water is something of a mystery, but most likely it came from the two big cisterns which collected rainwater.

Access to fresh water on the rock is, in fact, one of two popular questions that need clearing up.

And the writer of the Guernsey Society's review of Brehon in 1951 was clearing his own mind both in terms of water supplies and the rats which are said to riddle the place.

'A deep well is said to exist there but, in fact, there is no water supply, only a huge storage cistern.

'As to the rats which, it is said, exist in large dimensions and plentiful supply? This is doubtful, what would they live upon?'

The last residents of the fort were German, for one unexpected night only, on a bleak January one in 1946.

Twelve German prisoners were put ashore with the solitary task of removing the Nazi ammunition.

But as they worked, conditions deteriorated, and the landing party was unable to retrieve them before dark.

The Deutsche dirty dozen was forced to spend the night in the empty granite cylinder and to keep warm made a fire from the vast amount of wood left in the abandoned fortification.

When they left the next day, the fort said goodbye to its final non-feathered inhabitants.

Forever? Who can tell.

Below
Commemorative tablet bearing a Swastika and laurel for two German soldiers killed on Brehon Tower

INVADERS? NOT QUITE...

THE horror scenario of the French landing at Brehon did, in fact, happen.

Well, islanders imagined it did, with the help of pranksters.

One day in 1892 the French tricolour was seen flying from the fort, which naturally sparked mild panic among locals fearing Napoleon's evil was at work.

Customs men were sent to investigate and on arrival they found nobody at home – not a Frenchman, not even a proper tricolour, merely strips of coloured fabric sewn together and hung to the flagstaff.

On it were the letters: 'ECLMGG', the initials of two mischievous young Guernseymen having a lark.

WAS CREVICHON HANGMAN'S ISLAND?

FOR non-nautical types who don't their Crevichon from their Grande Fauconniere – it sounds like some sort of Guernsey French insult, doesn't it? – here's a little geography lesson.

Everyone who has travelled to Herm has passed Crevichon to the right on the way there, and to the left on the return.

For Crevichon is the unusually mis-shapen island immediately west of Jethou.

Surprisingly, it totals three acres and, like its mate to the Sark side of Jethou, is crowned by six feet of whitewash to help those at sea avoid mishaps.

But surely nothing happens there?

That's sort of true. Nothing happens there any longer, but there was a time...

That grand old writer Victor Coysh once described it as a perfect sugarloaf, like Le Grande Fauconniere, but with a chunk bitten off.

But, of course, it was not always so.

Until the need to build St Peter Port Harbour in the manner we see today, Crevichon was that perfect dome.

Then came the quarrymen and out came ton upon ton of its granite, destined to make the long arm from Havelet to Castle Cornet.

While there is no doubting that Crevichon played a key role in the development of St Peter Port, three miles away, you are entitled to raise a querying eyebrow to believe Coysh's speculation that once upon a time, when the Crevichon cone had been untouched by human hand, that it was the place where we executed pirates.

Proof, please?

Coysh reckoned so, after studying a mediaeval Guernsey map in which Crevichon is well drawn and shown to house a watch-house and signal post.

Jethou was, said Coysh, reputed to be where pirates were hanged in chains and as Crevichon is officially and legally recognised as part of Jethou he was ready to believe and propagate the theory that the baddies were marched at low tide across Crevichon's sandy beach, exposed by the low tide, to their death on the islet's higher ground.

Fact or fiction, it is an interesting theory, but Crevichon has seen proven incident, and more recently.

In 1905 the passenger ship Courier practised for its fatal demise a year later by hitting a rock in the Percee Passage.

Seriously holed, enough to make limping into St Peter Port impossible, the captain grounded the ship on Crevichon's sandy spit.

From there she was temporarily repaired and towed to Town, before hitting rocks again in 1906. This time the vessel sank to the bottom and lives were lost.

Above
Crevichon off Jethou

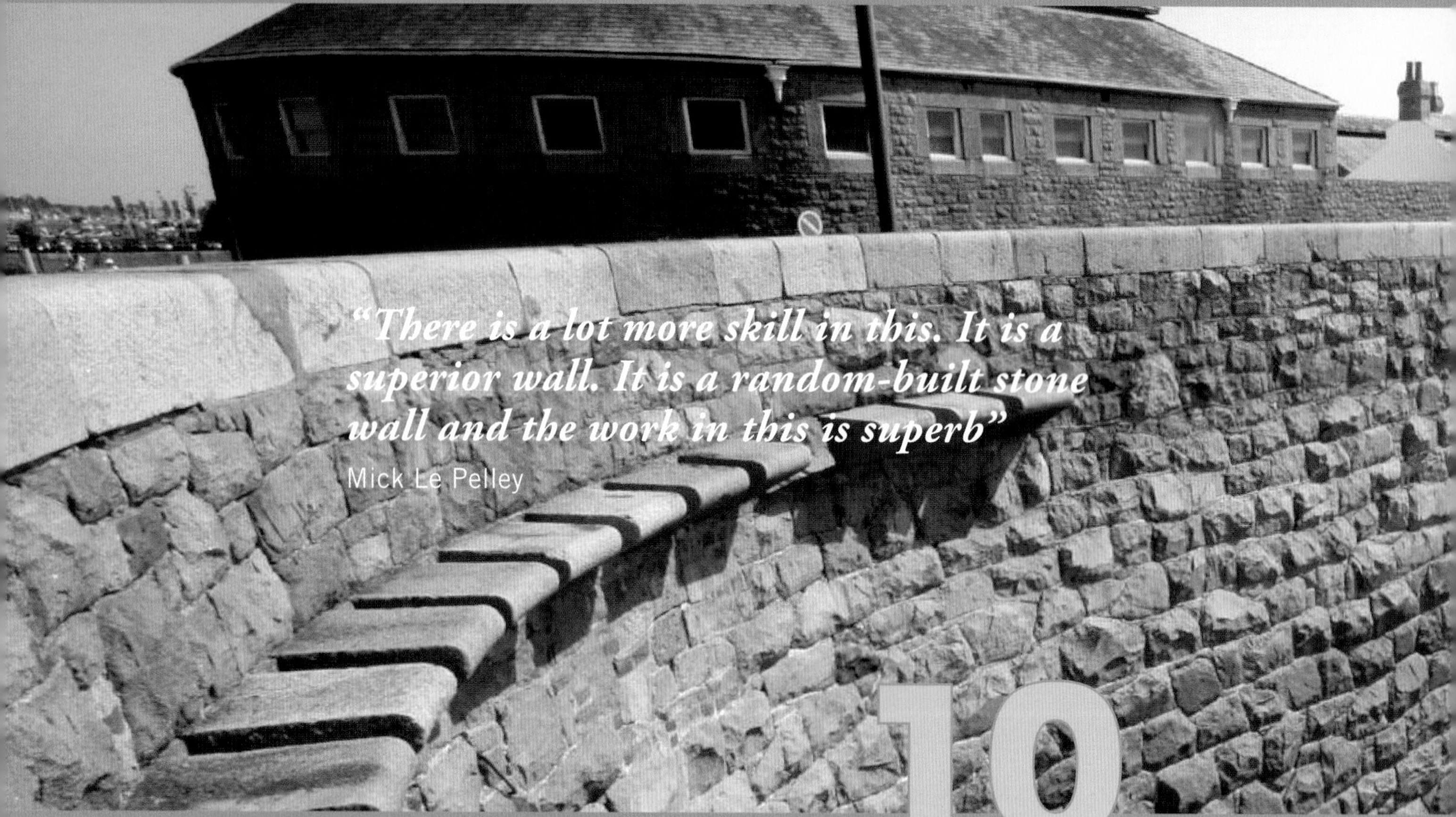

"There is a lot more skill in this. It is a superior wall. It is a random-built stone wall and the work in this is superb"

Mick Le Pelley

CHAPTER 18

HAVELET

With its long wall out to Castle Cornet, reclaimed South Esplanade and bathing pools underneath the old fort, the bay has come a long way since its time as south beach and shipbuilding heritage.

BIGGEST AND BEST · POOL TO POOLS
PLENTY MORE FISH · KEEP YOUR DRAWERS ON
AROUND THE HORN

BIGGEST AND BEST

WHEN it comes to knowing your stone and, particularly, Guernsey granite, Mick Le Pelley is about as knowledgeable as they get.

So who better to ask about the splendour of our top wall, Stone de Croze's answer to the Great Wall of China?

The retired stonemason, so instrumental in building the North Beach wall and QE2 Marina, takes a long, studied look at the Castle Emplacement structure and a stream of superlatives flood out.

The sheer straightness of it has him oozing bewilderment. 'It's mind-boggling how they kept it so straight,' he says.

He points to the square-angled granite dowels driven between each one-ton coping stone which lines the sea wall stretch and utters: 'They wouldn't bother with that today.'

The dowels are no more than 3ins by 3ins but are one piece of stone and fill the entire 18in depth of each coping stone, locking them together.

They will probably last until kingdom come.

'Every one of those dowels would have taken a long time to do,' says Mick.

In pure Guernsey terms, it is a wall not only bigger than anything else constructed here, but prepared beautifully. Nothing compares, certainly not the newest construction at the North Beach.

Mick is quick to admit it. 'There is a lot more skill in this. It is a superior wall. It is a random-built stone wall and the work in this is superb.'

Around 1,000 yards away, close to the weather-beaten and relatively small plaque to

Below
The Great Wall of Guernsey: a wonderful feat of engineering

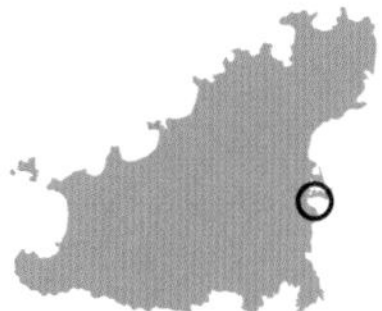

mark the laying of the foundation stone on 24 August 1853, he studies the stonework at the point where the wall hits the slipway across from the slaughterhouse.

This time it is the two, perhaps three-ton granite rounded stop-end which impresses him.

'I dread to think how long it would have taken [to do]. It probably had two or three men on it.

'You bet your life the diameter of it is perfect.'

I'm intrigued to know where the granite facing and coping would have emanated from and Mick gives me a quick answer without knowing the historical details of this impressive construction.

'There's a fair old mixture of stone, but most of it would have been from Herm or Jethou. Certainly, some of it is from the Chouet quarries – the grey granite with a deep black speckle is a particular of Chouet.'

And following a visit to the Island Archives, where Nathan Coyde has unearthed the full story of the evolution of St Peter Port Harbour, the work of author E. W. Sharp confirms that, back in the late 1840s, labourers were sent

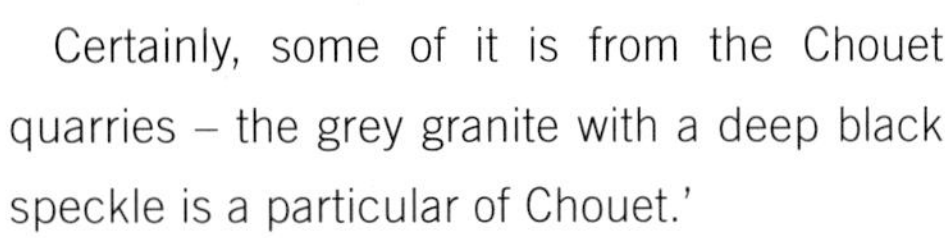

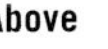

Above
Stonemason Mick Le Pelley explains how the granite blocks were laid

Above
Mick Le Pelley admires the stone work at Havelet
Right
Jumping for joy: Town lads often use the big wall to 'bombshell'

to Jethou and the rock known as Crevichon was hammered to pieces to supply the biggest single development Guernsey has known.

They did it with not a single laser beam, pneumatic hammer or theodolite in sight.

Exactly how many were involved in the construction is unknown, but the man who created Granite Le Pelley expects they ran into hundreds.

'They would have had to have their tools sharpened daily. They would have had to have masonry blacksmiths working alongside them all day.

'Each coping stone would have taken a mason a couple of days to prepare.'

Placing the stones would have been a major exercise in itself and he points to the now-rusty hand-drilled holes which feature in the top of each one, which would have enabled them to be raised and dropped into place.

'With the size of those stones there would have had to be some sort of gantry.'

Sharp's informative story of the harbour's evolution confirms the theory of wooden gantries, hand cranes and winches, horses and carts.

Construction began at the landward end and, while barges fed the stone for the facings and copings alike, the stone infill came via a narrow-gauge railway from Les Terres.

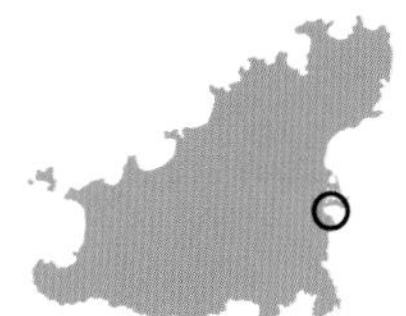

Now for the bad news and something to remember if the Havelet or Castle Emplacement walls were to fail to survive the test of time.

They were partly built by two Jerseymen, Messrs. Le Gros and de la Mare, who won the original tender.

They didn't last the distance, but surely our big blue wall will.

Liberation Day apart, Guernsey people surely have not gathered in a greater number in one place than during the lunchtime of 24 August 1853.

Staggeringly, 20,000 were present to see the laying of the harbour foundation stone, the cavity of which acts as a time capsule to this day.

Stuck in there are coins, almanacs and local papers of the time and special editions of the Guernsey papers were printed, The Star carrying a visionary piece of journalism in its leader column.

Bearing in mind that it was still a time when islanders in the northern parishes took their holidays down Pleinmont way and there was great inter-parish rivalry and suspicion, the paper's editor might have been considered to be away with the fairies when he wrote: 'We foresee that long before the date of the stone's disinterment our ships will have been superseded by aerial machines which will require no harbours, but perhaps be moored to the spires of churches...'

Below
Where it all started: the foundation stone is buried as a time capsule beneath the wall (bottom left)

FROM POOL TO POOLS

TAKE a summer stroll along the La Vallette promenade and there are parts of the grand old bathing pools which look every bit as venerable as their 150 years.

And until a few weeks ago, the gem of the four-pool complex, the ladies' pool and its tired-looking changing and refreshment facilities, struggled to stand out from the battered and worn features of the men's and horseshoe pools which precede it as you walk along the promenade from Town.

Enter Adie Locke, a man who knows an awful lot about pool – though not so much about the plural form.

Many years ago he saw an opportunity to supply island bars with pool tables and now he has turned his attention to reviving the bathing places that remain.

Having taken on a long-term lease, Mr Locke has wasted no time in polishing the gem.

The makeover is barely half-complete and it will be 2010 before it is finished, but he has made a dramatic impact on the area and, in particular, the building from which he feeds and quenches the thirst of swimmers and non-swimmers alike.

Suddenly, the place is sparkling again and among those who approve are the Polar Bears swim group and regulars such as Tom and Ruth Walsh, who have lobbied long and hard for Culture and Leisure, and the Recreation Committee before it, to spend more money on the public facility.

Ruth, 71, has returned virtually daily to La Vallette in the 63 years since she learned to swim there.

Below
Bathing Pools proprietor Adie Locke
Opposite
La Vallette regular Ruth Walsh

Above
A rather sad-looking Horseshoe Pool
Below
La Vallette's new-look

She is thrilled to see the sudden improvement. 'It is absolutely brilliant what he [Mr Locke] is doing.

'It is something we have been waiting to be done for years. He really is getting the place spruced up. The terrace is the best I've seen it in over 60 years.'

A long-term critic of governmental attitude to the area, she is encouraged by recent redevelopments.

'The States seem to be getting a bit more interested and keeping them a bit more clean. Things are getting better.'

Mr Locke is certainly revelling in the challenge of breathing new life into the once esteemed saltwater bathing spots.

He pulls no punches as to what he thought of the place when he took over.

'It was an absolute disgrace. It really was.

'It was suffering after 20 years of neglect.'

When asked to give reasons for its demise following the glory years when hundreds flocked to watch galas and a similar number, particularly townies, would use it to safely splash about, he raises three fingers.

'It was a triple-whammy,' he said.

'There was the opening of Beau Sejour, the removal of the diving boards and the closure of the amusement arcade in the aquarium.'

And although none is set to return, Mr Locke oozes belief in the area's rejuvenation potential.

He is seeing a revival already and when the main pool and its sidekick, the children's one a few yards to the south, are fully repaired, he expects to see a steady surge in numbers.

The latter, which holds 500,000 litres of water and is about six- to-seven feet at its deepest point, has already had its bed cleared of unwanted rocks.

Next on the agenda is the main pool, which holds 1.5 million litres when brim-full.

'The actual pool is in good repair,' says the new leaseholder.

'We have plans to get the digger in, but it will take two days to empty it and the tides have to be right.

'It won't be done this year but we're certainly

looking to do it for next season.'

Its perimeter staging is, in parts, looking sorry, with cracked cement in need of more repairs.

It will be done in good time, promises Mr Locke, who speaks with an air of confidence that anything is possible, except the reintroduction of the high boards.

There remains about 8ft of water beneath where the old 10m board stood, but there is not much more the other side of the wall where submerged boulders would surely be in range of anyone diving, or of foolhardy tombstoners.

But with the 150th anniversary of the pools only four years away, thanks to Mr Locke and new-found encouragement from Culture and Leisure, there is real hope that it will be a birthday worth celebrating and not hidden.

Ruth, for one, is 100% behind them.

For her, the pools have been a second home for virtually her whole life.

'From the first time I went down there, I thought it was a magic place,' she says.

Can they survive another 150 years?

She is more confident now that the pools will be around for a while yet.

'They have been the Cinderella and been allowed to deteriorate.

'But if there's the will, with some good stonemasons, I think they could still be saved.'

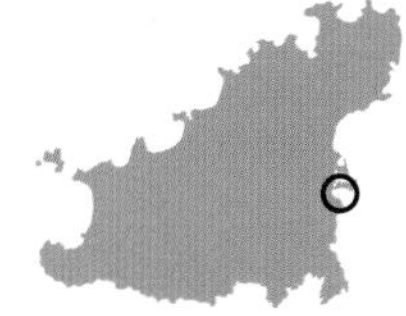

PLENTY MORE FISH

Above
Mackerel...the fish flooded the pools in the summer of 1953

THE biggest haul of fish the island has ever seen arrived at La Vallette and as far as Town in the summer of 1953.

Sea walls, piers, slipways and rocks were packed with islanders and holidaymakers gawping at the magnitude of a mackerel glut not seen before or since.

Chasing whitebait, millions of mackerel came ashore, to the extent that people were not catching them with rods, but buckets and bare hands.

It even caused frantic efforts to salvage a planned Guernsey Swimming Club gala, with hundredweights of fish being cleared from the main pool.

The men's pool situation was worse. When the attendant opened the stopcock to let the water out, only a quarter of the fish went with it.

He tried to sweep them through the outlet with a broom but they were so numerous that they had to attempt it a second time the next day.

But while everyone feasted on mackerel fry-ups for days on end, legend has it one clever islander had other ideas and targeted what had led the mackerel ashore in the first place.

It's said he scooped up so much whitebait and sold it on to Billingsgate in London that he was able to buy his first boat with the proceeds.

There was so much mackerel to go around that much of it was left to rot.

GOING SWIMMING? KEEP YOUR DRAWERS ON

Above
The way they were... hundreds used to flock to the main pool to watch galas

IT'S strange to think that going swimming on Guernsey's coast is relatively new.

For those like me, who have an unwritten rule that I never swim before 1 August, if at all, would have been in the vast majority a century-and-a-half ago.

I guess we owe early 19th-century visitors and the States of the 1840s for islanders' modern view that the sea is something to be enjoyed and good for your health and not just something to ice your tenderest parts.

But back then, the few who did take a dip were either skinny-dipping men or women clad in old dresses fit for the sea and not much else.

Indeed, well into the 20th century a sign stood proud above the Salerie mini-harbour, aimed very much at the men.

'Bathing without drawers after 6am is strictly prohibited.'

The swimming revolution went hand in hand with the foresighted government of the time which, with one eye on the precious crumbly rock at La Vallette to infill the construction of the new harbour, thought it would be lovely for Guernsey folk to enjoy a leisurely and scenic walk along a new marina promenade.

Much of the original scheme bore fruit.

Vast quantities of filling was needed for the harbour and the soft cliffs south-east of Town were ideal.

The wisdom stretched to installing bathing places and the first to appear was in 1844 near the Black Rock, immediately before what we know as the men's pool.

The paths and steps remain but the pool was demolished after just 15 years and in its place came the horseshoe pool, built to the designs of the new harbour engineer, a Mr Lyster.

They must have gained immediate popularity,

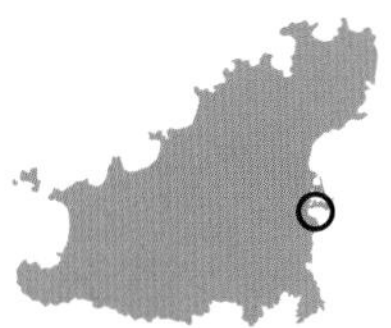

That in turn lasted until just after the Liberation when it was again replaced by the stage which lasted until a few years ago.

The four-pool complex was in place until 1977 when the States Recreation Committee called time on what the April Billet referred to as 'pools one and two'.

They brought in no income, were costly to repair and should be allowed to fall into disrepair before, on safety grounds, being demolished.

Three decades on, the disrepair is ongoing as the granite takes all the heavy seas thrown at it but refuses to budge.

because by 1870 the ladies had one, too.

It took fours years to build and cost £1,260. The men's pool, which cost £550, arrived a year later.

In 1887 the Guernsey Swimming Club formed and set up a diving stage off the site of the original pool off Black Rock in 1911.

It was given the name Black Stage: appropriate because of its situation and the fact that the smaller one at the nearby men's pool was painted red.

Also known as the kitchen, for as seemingly bizarre a reason as the close-by Cow's Horn got its name, it was built by the Guernsey Railway Company and a wooden bridge was used to access them.

Diving competitions were held there until the First World War put a stop to them and in 1925 it was dismantled and re-erected at the ladies' pool.

Above
A bird's eye view of the action from the top board in the 1930s
Left
The old Black Stage platforms c.1913
Overleaf
The pools as they were in 1960

AROUND THE HORN

PARKED cars which flank both sides of the stretch from the Half Moon Cafe south-eastwards have rid it of much of its charm.

But even without horses and traps and ladies in sweeping dresses, hats and parasols hanging on the arms of gentry or garrison officers, the reasons for creating La Vallette's promenade one-and-a-half centuries ago were surely fairly obvious.

One was the spectacular view out towards Sark and, secondly, something had to be done to repair the ugly scars caused by the quarrying of the soft, crumbly rock beneath Terres Point in order to provide infill for much of the harbour development we see today.

Les Promenades des Terres was the name given to the 19th century by-product of the harbour construction and, as successful as it was, the full intention was something much more spectacular – a roadway or promenade all the way to Fermain.

That had been the plan: a rock-cut esplanade or corniche at shore level until in stepped the military authorities.

The War Department ruled that if the promenade stretched southwards across Soldiers' Bay, it would compromise security at Fort George.

Shame? The thought of such a promenade stretching to Bec du Nez and beyond does have its appeal.

But what about Ozanne Steps?

Where do they sit in this fated proposal to change the shorescape of the eastern section beneath Fort George and Village de Putron?

I have heard various theories for the construction of the steps – all 90 of them by my count – which you will now find fighting years of neglect.

One theory linked the steps with the concept of the Fermain-bound promenade. Wrong.

Another was that they were built by a

Right
The author at the foot of the Ozanne steps

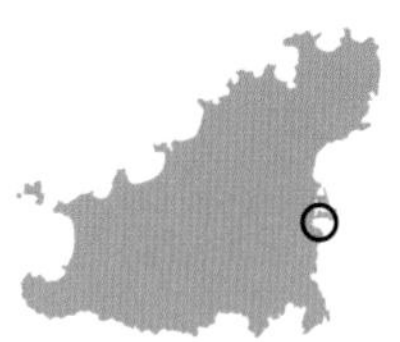

Lt-governor as a gift for his wife so she could stroll down from Belvedere House for a quiet and private swim in the tiny bay which is revealed at low tide. Wrong again.

C. P. Le Huray, the late author of the King's Channel Islands and that fount of local knowledge, the archive section of La Societe Guernesiaise, came up trumps.

Simply, the steps were built for one reason only: for the pleasure of those living in the Village de Putron estate in early-Victorian days.

And the instigator was, indeed, an Ozanne, Albert Thoume Ozanne to be precise.

The steps, complete with a gazebo-cum-lookout at the top, were part of his grand plan to build a mansion directly above.

He got as far as the steps and more granite ones as part of a path above the now public footpath, but then it seems he ran out of money.

The States took ownership of the land in 1907 and there was a serious intention to build a lunatic asylum high above the sea looking eastwards to Jersey.

Not surprisingly, there was much opposition and the project was never begun.

But the Ozanne Steps were and are a prime example of what the well-to-do could achieve in times of cheap labour.

Today, the cost of such a building project would be comfortably in six figures.

The steps are, to be frank, a mess.

The approach by sea suggests something charming and special.

Up close, they are tired, unkempt, overgrown and a relic of the old days.

Where the gazebo once stood lies a roofless top deck where the Ozanne coat of arms, once set into the plaster, has gone, along with the dozens of ormer shells which decorated the walls.

Back along the coast past Soldiers' Bay where, you guessed it, members of the garrison cooled off and where today a few naturists take advantage of the privacy afforded by the rocks, lies a small, unnamed stone beach, into which the back-end of the aquarium drops.

And the Cow's Horn named as such because... Well, no one I can find seems clear about its current title, which at some point succeeded the proper name, Terres Point.

Now, I can see the lion shape in the Lion Rock at Cobo, but for the life of me I can't see a cow or a horn at Terres Point, where the well-kept Clarence Battery once offered protection against those dastardly French.

But forget the cannon. The Cow's Horn has long held a less-than-distinguished reputation in island life and probably has done so from the days when randy servicemen were stationed at forts George and Irwin.

There is one Guernsey-French word to sum up what was going on at the Cow's Horn in the early part of the 20th century, barely a mile away from the notorious green-shutters district on the southern end of Town.

The word is pernaques and, translated, means antics. Whether the pernaques are still as frequent you will have to tell me.

Below
What's left of the old Clarence Battery
Opposite
The small beach behind the Aquarium

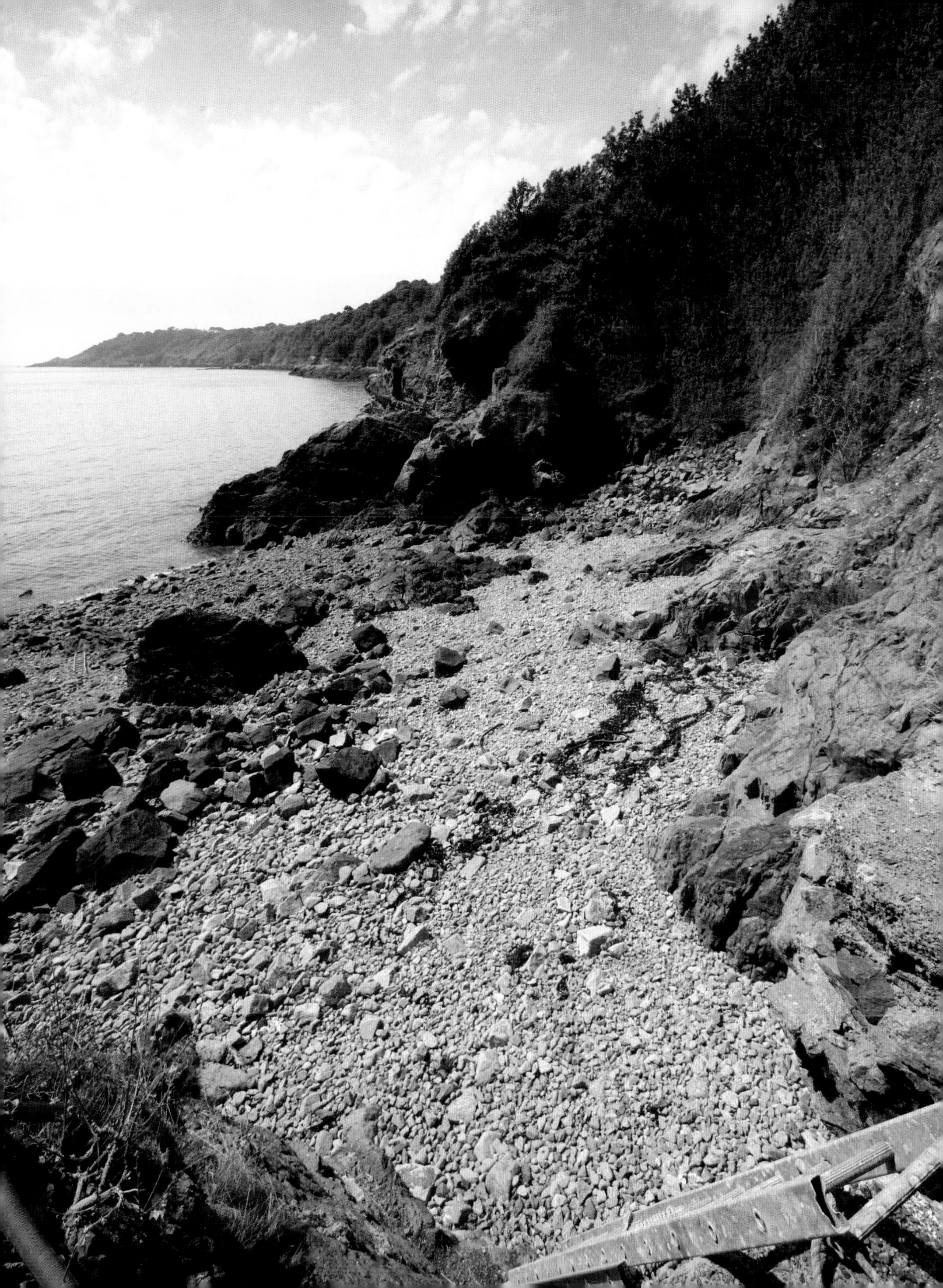

"I can see the logic in it. It [the proposed breakwater] could have easily been supplied by sea from St Peter Port, which is only a short way away and protected from Fort George"

Gary Thoume

CHAPTER 19

FERMAIN BAY

Once one of Guernsey's most popular destinations with the regular summertime open-top ferry service from town.

HARBOURING DOUBTS · VALID VIEWPOINT
FASCINATING FERMAIN · ON THE DEFENSIVE

HARBOURING DOUBTS

GUERNSEY history and its geography are littered with a series of ifs and buts. In the north, what if Doyle had not got his way and the Braye du Valle had remained a waterway dividing mainland Guernsey and the Vale?

I shut my eyes and imagine a nautical paradise with water skiers being pulled the width of the channel, sailing boats gliding down the narrow estuary and waterside restaurants.

So pretty, so different from what we have today.

As for the east, what if the invasion-fearing UK Government had got its way and built the 917- yard breakwater it had planned to run north-east from Fermain all the way out to Anfre beacon?

Again, I shut my eyes and see Guernsey Yacht Club dinghies tacking down the Russel to their traditional southerly mark and coming face to face with one long granite wall the likes of which Jersey has to put up with at St Catherine's – only longer.

The words 'white' and 'elephant' also come readily to mind had the long, solid arm of Fermain borne fruit and turned the quiet coastline under Village de Putron and towards Soldiers' Bay into a great harbour refuge to safeguard the British Navy from those nasty French gunships of Napoleon.

But it nearly happened and had it so this section of lovely east coast would not be the tranquil beauty we enjoy today.

The government-driven Fermain scheme was of such proportions that the States, in its plans for enlarging St Peter Port Harbour in the last century, held its fire until the Government had arrived at a conclusion about Fermain.

The plan had much going for it, not only providing a fine stretch of deep water but approaches that were relatively safe.

To defend the harbour of refuge, Fort George was to be modernised, and Brehon rock, in the Little Russel, was to be fortified and associated with the Guernsey plan was the scheme to build other harbours of refuge at Braye in Alderney and St Catherine's in Jersey.

In the event these harbours were constructed on rather a modified scale, a tower was built on Brehon, the coastal defences of Guernsey were improved, but no harbour at Fermain was constructed.

Phew. It was largely because of what the French were doing at Cherbourg that the UK Government had become nervous in the first place.

It was felt that the great fortifications and harbour works at Cherbourg constituted a threat to the UK to which it needed to respond.

Right
How Fermain might have looked with the giant breakwater

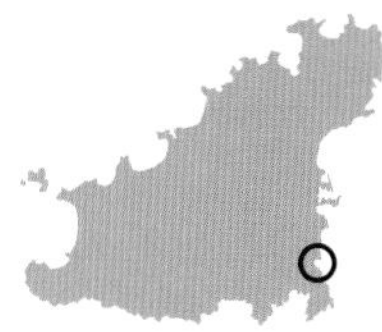

Part of that response we see today at Portland every time Condor sails into and out of Weymouth.

But it wasn't regarded highly enough by the paranoid Brits and from the early 1840s the commanding royal engineer at Fort George was involved in the plan to build a large harbour at Fermain, one which could be protected from hundreds of feet above on the cliffs.

There the British Navy would be fully protected by batteries that could readily be constructed at a variety of levels on the slopes of the cliffs facing France.

The cost of this little operation? A whopping £400,000.

The surveyor reckoned his Fermain plan would provide 60 acres of well sheltered water with an average depth of five fathoms.

A fleet of steam ships or ships of the line could be readily accommodated.

And where would the stone for all this come from? Some could come from the nearby Fermain cliffs, but the bulk of it sat three miles away in Herm.

Convict labour from Portland would be used to quarry it.

For 12 years the Fermain plan was on and off the building agenda, before finally all idea of it was abandoned.

Simply, they had dithered too long. Land in the Village de Putron, vital to the harbour plans, had been privately purchased and developed.

In addition, the French had receded and the UK had other military matters on its mind ... the Crimea.

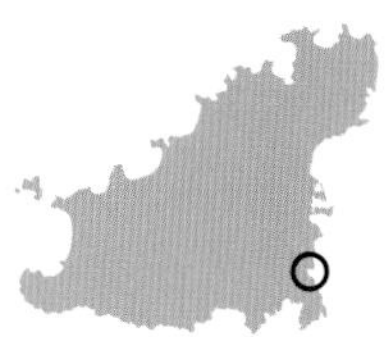

VALID VIEWPOINT

WHO better than a former naval man and the bay's moorings committee representative to have a view on the UK Government's plans for a massive breakwater at Fermain.

Gary Thoume, whose family links with the area date back centuries, was shocked to hear of them, but having studied the architect's plans and seen our artist's impression of the harbour that never was, could see the logic in the scheme.

Gary, who doubles as the Guernsey Boatowners' Association representative for nearby Bec du Nez, said that had Fermain developed in such a way, it would have had massive repercussions for the surrounding area, one he described in the recent parish magazine as 'the most beautiful place in the world and the only part of Guernsey left untouched'.

'They would have had to build a roadway up and along the cliffs coming out along Calais. It would have transformed the whole area, definitely for the worse. It would have knocked Calais for six.'

That said, it would have made sense, such was the threat of the French in the mid-19th century.

'I can see the logic in it. It could have easily been supplied by sea from St Peter Port which is only a short way away and protected from Fort George.' But would it have lasted?

'On a south-east wind it would have taken a hammering, worse than Alderney's breakwater. It would have needed to be built to the standard of the old breakwater from the castle to the lighthouse.'

As for the tides, Gary doesn't feel it would have affected the drift which from Town to Anfre flows outside the latter.

'It's a beautiful spot now and this probably wouldn't have enhanced it.'

Then there would have been the massive repair bills.

Left
Moorings Committee representative Gary Thoume
Overleaf
Fermain as boat-trippers remember it

FASCINATING FERMAIN

MENTION Fermain today and people think of the award-winning cafe-restaurant by the beach, Le Chalet Hotel halfway up the hill and the Fermain Valley Hotel, which has brought new life further up since Healthspan bought La Favorita and the Fermain Hotel and transformed the area.

The name has also been in the local media in the past year because of the narrow lane that runs down the valley and the traffic that uses it.

Perhaps the best way of looking at Fermain is to start in the present and work back through history.

So, today it's full of restaurants and hotel rooms, with the beach a bit of an afterthought for many people.

But in the 1950s and 60s and even into the 70s, this was one of the island's most popular with swimmers and sunbathers (it's never been much good for games, being pebbly until low tide and then wet and uneven).

What made Fermain unique, though, was the ferry service that brought boatloads of visitors around from Town.

If you fancied a little adventure on the sea with the feeling of island-hopping – even though you would be stepping back onto the same piece of land and going only about a mile as the crow flies – it made for a different day out.

The small matter of getting the passengers ashore, originally done by dinghy, was later addressed by a rolling landing stage, a wooden structure in several parts on big carriage wheels.

Three of those wheels – all that remain of a contraption that was once known island-wide – now stand in the cafe grounds, novelties that most visitors would hardly notice.

The main part of the landing stage stood perhaps 8ft high, sloping down to half that,

Right
The ferry Fermain III arrives from Town c.1950s

PERMAIN III

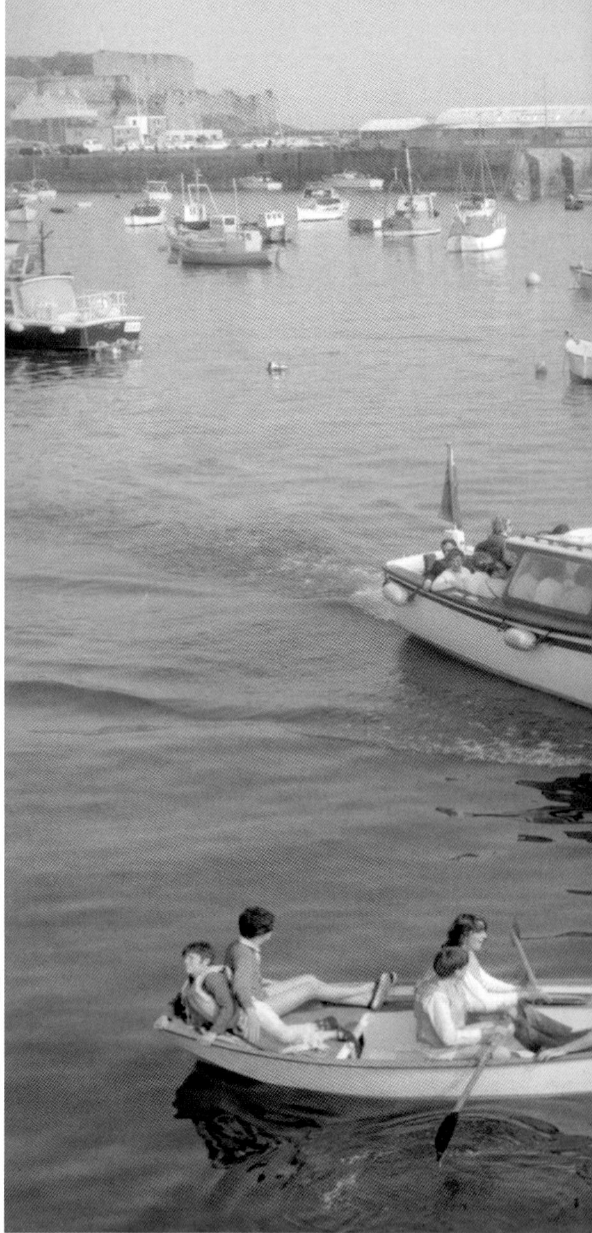

where it would be met by a low-slung, flat unit, also on wheels, which would suffice at most stages of the tide, with a simple wooden walkway taking passengers onto the beach.

At exceptionally low tides, with the water shallow and the boats unable to come in too close, more of the walkways would have to be employed, sometimes propped up on stones as the landing stage staff improvised frantically to keep customers' feet out of the water as they 'walked the plank'.

It was a classic example of the kind of quaint, makeshift approach that never hurt anyone but would certainly not be allowed in these safety-conscious, insurance-ruled days.

Nor, it seems, would the whoopee floats, the raft-type individual pleasure craft that amounted to two long boxes linked by planks on which to sit and propelled canoe-style by paddles.

The ferry service was run by the Ferguson family, a previous generation of which had lived in the Martello tower in the 1860s.

The Malletts had run a tea room from the magazine (ammunition store).

The building that now houses the acclaimed Fermain Beach Cafe was built as a much less ambitious kiosk.

The ferry service began operating in 1928.

John Elliott, now principal of the Guernsey Sailing Trust, was involved with both the Fermain boats and the cafe in the early and mid-1970s.

Starting as an engineer for the boss, Percy Ferguson, on Fermain V, an elegant, open vessel which had famously taken part in the Dunkirk evacuation during the Second World War, John went on to skipper Fermain VI for four years, before taking over the running of the catering operation.

Fermain V had previously been called Silver Queen and was built in 1926 in Southampton for use as a harbour launch.

Hardly ideal for crossing the Channel, it was towed across to Dunkirk, where it was used to ferry soldiers from the beach to the destroyers and transport ships waiting offshore.

Boats of its type were considered expendable after the operation and there was a report that it had sunk but been refloated before being brought to Guernsey and a new career making the short trip from St Peter Port Harbour past Castle Cornet and Soldiers' Bay to deliver and collect passengers, its minimal (2ft) draught enabling it to be brought relatively close to the shore at low water to meet the landing stage, even on those problematic spring tides.

It could certainly get in closer than Fermain VI, the propeller of which would create craters

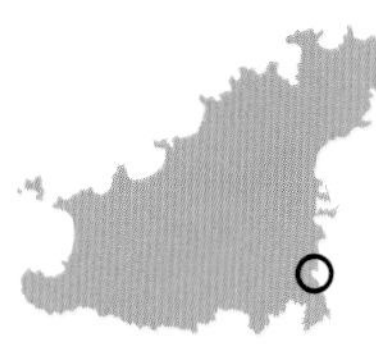

Left
John Elliott's Fermain VI returns to St Peter Port harbour from its namesake

in the sand as it reversed to avoid running aground as the tide retreated still further.

When the ferry service ceased in 1996, Fermain V was laid up ashore for three years and had begun to deteriorate when the Dunkirk Little Ships Restoration Trust came calling.

Suitably repaired, the boat was based at Tilbury, in London's docklands area, for two years and used by sea cadets for boat-handling training.

Then, after taking part in the 2000 Commemorative Return to Dunkirk, it was rehomed on the Thames at Shepperton.

It still takes part in Dunkirk-related events.

The high wall that separates the land from the beach in front of the cafe at Fermain used to be matched by another on the southern side of the slipway, but this has now been lowered to a less vertigo-inducing level.

The change came about because of landslips during the mid-1990s, when a Board of Administration spokesman said: 'The whole south side of Fermain is moving.' It moved so much that the wall collapsed, but then came the assertion that the 150-year-old structure hadn't been a sea wall at all, but 'a masonry skin over a rubble and earth cliff face'.

Reducing the height was the answer and in 1995-6 the States spent £240,000 rebuilding it, only for the granite facing that masked the concrete armour to be ripped off by the power of the sea.

A section of the cliff path was dangerous, too, and Mr Ferguson donated some land further up on which to build a replacement.

That is just part of a long list of changes that have taken place there over the centuries.

Old postcards from the collection of Village de Putron resident Anne Woodington show the valley largely without trees, with a building some way up on the right as you look upwards, the remains of which can still be found among the trees and undergrowth.

Some also show what was apparently a small hotel near the top of the slipway, past the tower.

A feature of the valley is the presence of what is generally referred to as 'giant rhubarb' but is actually gunnera, a South American native that was probably introduced during Victorian times, when the plant was very popular.

The origins of the name, 'Fermain', are as obscure as many local place names, but Marie de Garis' book on the subject suggests 'stony, iron-strong, probably a fortified strongpoint'.

Another school of thought is that it could be taken as what many would consider a clumsy and too obvious translation of fer (iron) and main (hand).

One who doesn't object too much to this interpretation is Jenny Seth-Smith, who runs the officially approved guided walk in the area and calls it Tales of Smuggling and the Steel Hand.

While the valley has a damp, jungle feel today – the stream that runs down it marks the boundary between St Peter Port and St Martin's – the north side was at one time planted with barley (the lane being called La Ruette des Orgeries meaning lane of the barley fields) to supply the brewery at South Esplanade.

Jenny's walk goes from Sausmarez Manor through Le Varclin, where she talks at length about the properties in the area, including distinguished old farmhouses and the more recent (19th-century) but distinctly grand Bon Air.

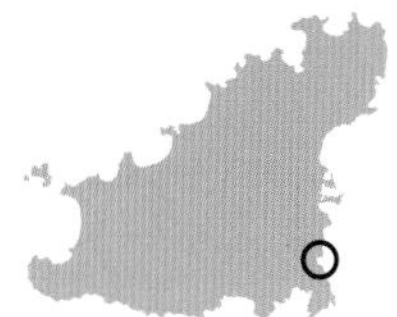

It goes down Calais Road, named after the de Calais family, and left into a tiny lane that gives way to a footpath.

At the top of the path there is evidence of quarrying, with a rather crumbly kind of red granite.

Halfway down is a small clearing with a seat, providing a clear view of the bay.

This appears to be the vantage point for the vast majority of Anne's postcards.

The path, the lower part of which has been altered in recent years, comes out further above the slipway than it used to.

Because it offers good shelter and is close to Town, Fermain has, over the centuries, been considered as a possible harbour, although by today's standards it would clearly be too small.

According to some sources, under the sand there is evidence of an ancient wooden harbour.

More recently, Fermain was used by smugglers, for whom the proximity to St Peter Port might not have been such a boon.

Their presence may, though, have been partly responsible for the abundance of spooky tales concerning the lanes above – a headless man carrying a coffin and so on – because spreading such tales was one way in which shady characters up to no good could persuade people to keep well away from the area.

Even before the smugglers, a hazard of living in Guernsey was the island's vulnerability to pirates and one who is reputed to have sailed into Fermain under the Jolly Roger in 1337 is Madoc of Wales.

With or without eye patches or parrots on their shoulders, Madoc and his crew attracted so much attention that 87 men are said to have tried – unsuccessfully – to repel them.

A house a few hundred yards away in Les

Top left
The old Fermain tea room in the 1920s
Bottom left
A modern scene of the bay

Hubits is called Mare Mado, which may indicate that this band of cut-throats went for a walk and made an impression on the residents there.

The bay was the scene of a famous episode during the English Civil War, when Guernsey was for the Parliamentarians and only the Governor, Sir Peter Osborne, supported the Crown.

As the governor's residence at the time was in Castle Cornet, that was where Osborne stayed, besieged, for eight long years, supported by troops brought in from England by sea.

During this time, cannon fire echoed across the water in largely harmless exchanges.

This was before the building of the castle breakwater and it was possible to get to and from the rock only at low tide.

One day, three jurats – referred to as parliamentary commissioners – were tricked into meeting a Captain Bowden, whom they knew as a Parliamentarian, on his ship, Bramble, at Fermain.

Once he had them on board, Bowden revealed that he had changed his allegiance and took them to the castle, where they were imprisoned.

The resourceful trio managed to make ropes from flax they found in the room below the one in which they were held, reach it, and escaped down the outside walls.

The tide was out and they made it to dry land.

Fermain has several interesting features.

Just below the cliff path as you go towards St Peter Port can be found the Ozanne Steps, now apparently in the middle of nowhere but built for the convenience of a family living in a property above.

At the top are the remains of what is thought to have been a tiny chapel in which fishermen and their families could pray or give thanks for a safe return from the sea.

The roof and two walls have gone, but indentations are still clearly visible where it would seem that ormer shells had been used for decoration.

The steps may originally have been called the de Putron steps after the family that owned a huge estate in the area, including what was to become the Village de Putron.

In the 1930s, this was bought by the States with the intention of building a mental hospital there, before the Le Vauquiedor site was acquired – although that became the Princess Elizabeth Hospital, while the mental health unit was based at the former Country Hospital, now the Castel Hospital.

The States sold the land to a developer.

Meanwhile, back up the main Fermain hill, we return to the hotels.

Built early in the 20th century as a private house, Le Chalet has one of the most fabulous locations in the island, perched on the hillside overlooking the bay and with the alpine aura for which whoever chose the name must have hoped.

The house was owned by an innovative man with a practical bent, who installed a dynamo in a summer house down the hill and used the power of the stream to generate electricity.

It is thought that the house was the first in the island to use electricity for lighting.

Just up the hill, the Fermain Valley Hotel is a combination of La Favorita and the Fermain Hotel, the latter, at the top of the hill, having been demolished and now serving as a car park.

La Favorita was once a 'gentlemen's club'.

It served as accommodation for officers during the German Occupation and became a hotel after the Second World War.

Run for many years by Simon Wood, it was recently bought by Healthspan and transformed into a thoroughly up-to-date establishment that, happily, retains much of the exterior

Above
Rooms with a view

character of the original.

The area has an interesting architectural theme, with private houses and the nearby nursing home, Chateau du Village, being built in a Gothic style.

While that does not apply across the road at the Fermain Tavern, that is a pub that has played a considerable part in the social life of the generation that was out 'socialising' in the late 1960s and '70s and into the '80s.

With its unusual configuration of a dance floor and stage that is lower than the main bar area, the Tavern has throbbed as a disco and reverberated with live music.

Today it has a devoted crowd of regulars in the public bar and concentrates on serving food.

Undoubtedly the most famous face to peer up at the beer-swilling crowd was that of Elton John, who appeared there in the late 1980s as a favour to Beechy Colclough, the Irishman who had been one of the most charismatic singers to perform in Guernsey 10 years earlier, before confronting his own addiction problems and using the experience to set up a clinic in London, where Captain Fantastic sought help.

The Elton gig was part of a series of Saturday afternoon shows in which names well known in rock circles made the trip to Guernsey more for the social side than as a moneymaking exercise.

This was a time when British soul singer Paul Young (Wherever I Lay My Hat, Every Time You Go Away, etc) was a frequent visitor to the island and his musical director, Ian Kewley, had a farmhouse in a lane near the Longfrie, complete with recording studio.

The driving force behind the Fermain Tavern gigs was sound engineer Alfie Barton, a friend of Young and Kewley, and with an address book that could bring seasoned performers to the island to play in a pub: the figures surely didn't stack up at all.

Former Rolling Stone and John Mayall guitarist Mick Taylor played there, ignoring a mouth abscess that eventually made a hole in his cheek, while blues veterans Chicken Shack came over, as did former Small Faces and Humble Pie frontman Steve Marriott and Snowy White, an itinerant guitarist and one-hit-wonder solo artist (Bird of Paradise) who spent some time with Thin Lizzy.

ON THE DEFENSIVE

FERMAIN still has impressive defences, though they pre-dated the Victorian era. Across the landward approach to the bay, a sturdy bulwark of stone is still to be seen, acting as a retaining wall today.

There is a Martello tower nearby, while on the cliffs on either hand the remains of batteries are to be found.

On Le Becquet, where the 'pepperpot' stands, were further guns and an observation post.

Fermain, indeed, was a vital link in the chain of anti-Napoleonic fortifications.

Below
Sitting in the dock of the bay...the imposing house on the left was built in the late 1800s but no longer exists
Bottom
'The Pepper Pot'

The Germans made use of this locality in their scheme of defence, though happily few signs of their ugly works remain.

But the history of Fermain goes further back than the Occupation, the 1842 proposals and the gun positions of two centuries ago.

In the days of the Civil War, a ship, the Bramble, cast anchor in the bay and her master, a Captain Bowden, sent a boat ashore to collect three Parliamentary Commissioners.

It was thought that the ship was a Parliamentary vessel, but it was just the reverse and the three Guernseymen were seized and handed over to the Royalist Governor of Castle Cornet, Sir Peter Osborne.

How they escaped from the fortress is a thrilling tale which has often been told and which plays no part in the Fermain story.

More pertinent was an event of the 18th century, when a Royal Navy press gang party landed at Fermain with the intention of pressing islanders into naval service, something which was illegal in Guernsey.

The sailors reached the Hubits and seized three young men of St Martin's by force, carrying them to their ship.

The Royal Court protested at such action and two of the men were returned.

The third remained in the Navy, possibly having come to like it.

Fermain, in days gone by, was rather a vulnerable inlet.

Enemy ships could easily anchor in its sheltered, deep waters and the valley was simple to scale.

So it was that a bulwark was built and guns mounted and, even if these had failed to repulse the French, Fort George was near and horse, foot and guns would doubtless have surged down the glen to drive the invaders into the sea.

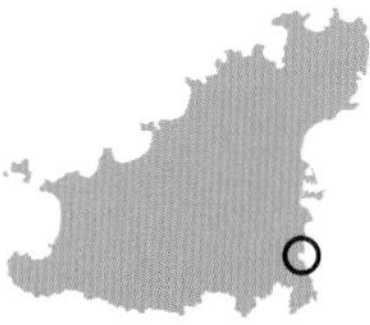

The 'pepperpot' (so called because it resembles one of the Victorian variety) served as a sentry box and a sea mark.

Today, it is still a recognised mark for mariners.

A little way above the tea house (itself a former powder magazine) once stood a comely house, a product of the late Victorian era.

Old photographs show this stately residence, whose ruins can still be found by those willing to battle with dense scrub, which conceals the building's remains.

To stand on the headland of Le Becquet and gaze down onto the cove is to behold one of Guernsey's loveliest views.

The greenery of the opposite cliffs is reflected in the deep, clear water, upon which many a yacht rides.

Had matters turned out otherwise, the visitor might well have been dissuaded from peering down upon a naval roadstead, whose environs bristled with guns and barracks.

Happily, this proposal never bore fruit and Fermain remains its old sweet self.

Above
Tower of strength

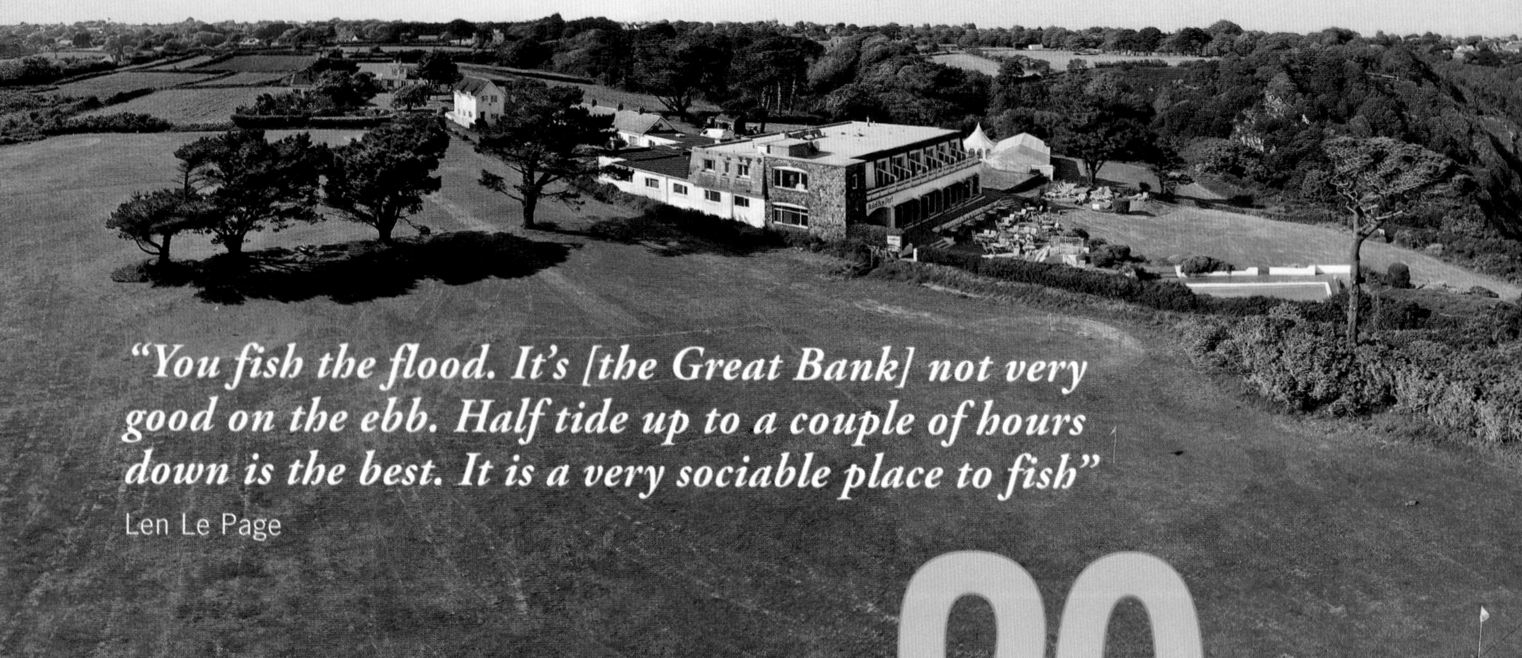

"You fish the flood. It's [the Great Bank] not very good on the ebb. Half tide up to a couple of hours down is the best. It is a very sociable place to fish"

Len Le Page

CHAPTER 20

MOULIN HUET
BEC DU NEZ & ST MARTIN'S POINT

Renoir could hardly get enough of it, but Moulin Huet and the south-eastern corner of Guernsey have much more to offer than just outstanding views. They have also got pretty good places to fish.

POINT PROVEN

A GLANCE at the Bailiwick boat-fishing records will see two words crop up time and again. More than three dozen times, to be exact. Great Bank.

On a fine summer's evening it has not been unusual to see more than 100 boats fishing the mark above the large sandbank, which stretches down the Russel roughly to the point to the harbour.

'The reason it's so good is that it's so easy to get there,' said the most famous man in local fishing, columnist Len Le Page.

'People go out of the harbour and turn right. I can get there in 10 minutes and, in a slow boat, 20 minutes,' he said.

'In summer, you can load up with fish there.'

Most of the fishing is done at the southern end of the bank where it rises from 45 metres to 10, or less on rare occasions.

The area is two nautical miles south of St Peter Port and half-a-mile east of St Martin's.

It's a particularly popular place for mackerel hunting but bass sometimes make an appearance on the east side along with John Dory, more so in recent years.

'You fish the flood,' says Len. 'It's not very good on the ebb. Half tide up to a couple of hours down is the best.

'It's a very sociable place to fish.'

For more details on fishing in Guernsey, read Len Le Page's Angling in the Bailiwick of Guernsey.

Below
The stone beach at Moulin Huet

FIVE CHOICE ROCK MARKS

Le Rico or 'Lerico' Facing north, Lerico is an awkward place to reach and the nearest spot to park your car is towards the south end of Calais Road. Situated on the cliff path between Fermain and Jerbourg, take a small, steep path through the bracken. Care is needed during the final 20m down onto the rocks. The rock on which to fish is reached across a narrow gully and you fish from the slightly higher one looking into Fermain. Bottom is sand but take care on spring tides as the rock covers. Safe on neap tides in calm weather. Best tide: Two hours up or two down.

Bec du Nez Here you can fish off rocks or the pier as you face either east or north. Park by Doyle Column and walk a short way back down Bouvee Lane before bearing right through the field and onto the cliff path. Turn left and follow the signs. Total distance from car to spot is just 800m, albeit a pretty steep half-mile. Good for a wide variety of fish. Rocky bottom off the pier and sandy off the main rocks and to the right. Safe on neap tides but a narrow gully fills for the two hours either side of high tide. Best tide: One hour up or two hours down.

Marble Bay To reach it initially, take the same route as if fishing Bec du Nez. The total distance is just 350m. The fishing spot is the big rock outcrop on the south side of the small bay and the bottom is varied with rock and weed close in, sand straight out. East facing, access over the rocks is awash on big springs. No problems on neaps. Best tide: One hour up to two hours down.

Divette Very similar to that of Marble Bay but the spot is reached by traversing a man-made, rubble mound causeway, referred to in Perry's Guide as Divette Pier. No problems on neaps or in settled weather but great care needs to be taken on high water springs or in rough weather. Best tide: One hour up to two down.

St Martin's Point Ample parking at Jerbourg from where you descend 300m towards the fog and signal station. Take a first turn before reaching the foot where the battery (a saucer-shaped grassy area) faces you. To the east the bottom is rock and weed, to the south and north there are sandy areas. Can be fished in strong southerlies if you tuck yourself in on the north side. Best tide: Half tide up through to two hours down.

A BEACON OF NATURAL BEAUTY

MY OPINION might change if it were two in the morning in the middle of a southerly winter gale with waves crashing over the steep sided rocks.

But it wasn't dark.

Instead, blue skies lit up the rising spring tide and despite it being 11 February, never was the contrast more typical of Guernsey's coastline in different weathers.

It was my first visit to the signal station and foghorn at St Martin's Point and I had better not leave it another 50 years to return.

All four of us – two cameramen and our host from the Harbour Authority – were struck by the 360 degrees of brilliant natural imagery, even though all we had come to see was what was inside a small concrete block not much bigger than two old-fashioned outdoor lavvies.

Richard de la Mare, the maintenance man from the harbour, insisted it was not always so hospitable but was nonetheless waxing lyrical about how great it was to be alive and able to witness such a view.

He goes back long enough to recall the nights when some fault or other had rendered the station useless and the necessary two staff had had to all but crawl on their hands and knees over the short causeway which joins the two most southern outcrops at St Martin's Point.

'I can assure you it's not very pleasant,' he says.

Nor is the inside, to be honest.

Step in and all you see is a room of peeling white paint, some electrics, a shaky metal ladder and a 42 x 30in. blue metal box fixed to the facing wall.

Inside: a foghorn with the sound level of 133.6 decibels at one metre.

To be truthful, the actual foghorn and its three small 'speakers' sit atop the building with the audio outlets pointing towards Jersey.

And barely a yard-and-a-half away is the warning light which marks the southern end of the Little Russel.

Right
Richard de la Mare tends the Jerbourg Point light

The bulbs are of the size you might find lighting up your home oven, but they are mightily more important than those in your kitchen.

The station flashes red and white sectors at a range of nine miles every 10 seconds.

Stay in the red sector and you're heading for trouble – you are all right on the white.

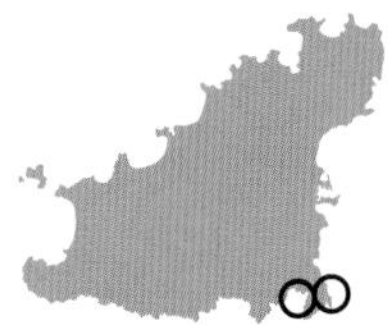

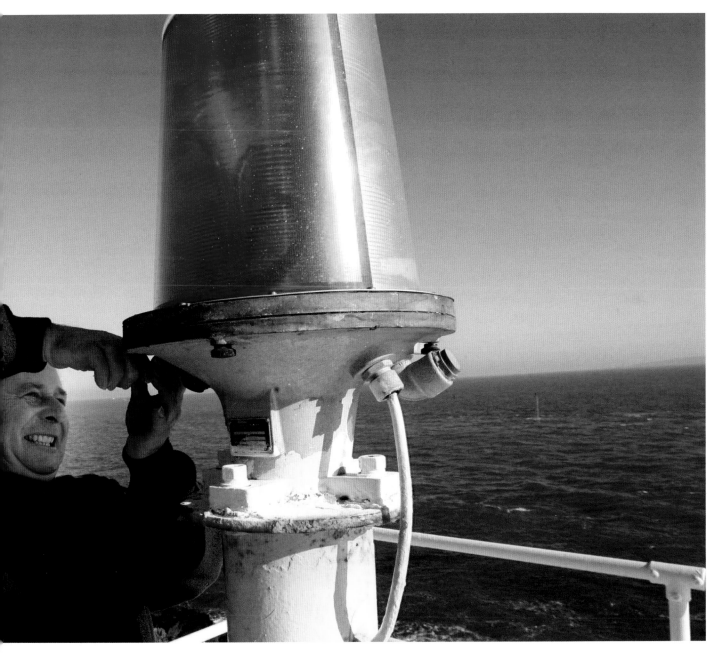

The light marks the dangers both northwards and southwards on the east coast, notably Gabrielle Rock and the Grunes de Jerbourg respectively on the west side of the Little Russel.

These days the foghorn is turned on and off electronically by Port Control or St Peter Port Radio, the link being a wee aerial attached to the railings atop the station.

And while the horn is quiet for long periods, the lights never go off.

The days of blowing bulbs and regular trips to the point to replace them are happily confined to history.

These days the light features automatic changeover bulbs and maintenance trips to the point are few and far between.

The station is pre-Second World War, having first been debated in the States as early as 1915.

QUIET CORNER

WHAT comes to mind when you hear the words, Moulin Huet?

A quiet, largely secluded beach, maybe.

Renoir's watercolours, Cradle Rock, the Dog and Lion rocks, the Pea Stacks or possibly the pottery, the home of one Guernsey's finest-ever sports stars, squash player Lisa Opie.

The French artist loved the place so much he painted about 15 views of the bay and its surroundings on and following his visit to the island in September 1883.

Eighty or so years later, Rex and Robina Opie moved into the valley and began operating their successful pottery.

Rex says the fact that the bay never changes is part of its beauty.

'Nothing has changed down there. It's still the same as in Renoir's day.'

Like all the south-coast beaches, they are left in relative peace with the gradual decline of the tourist industry.

'Years ago it was a popular bay for visitors and there were floats and a tea room down there,' said the renowned potter.

'But what I like about it is that it's not over-populated like the west-coast ones.

On one side you have the sand, the other the stone.'

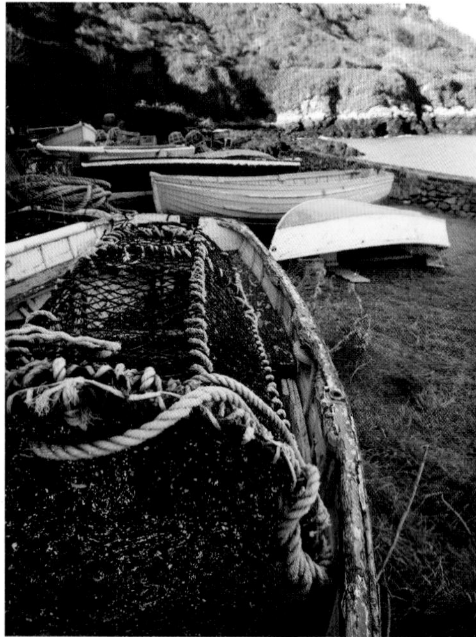

Below
Idyllic Bec du Nez
Top right
Crab pots above the slip at Bec du Nez
Right
The stone hut is a testament to the days of smuggling

SMUGGLERS' COVE

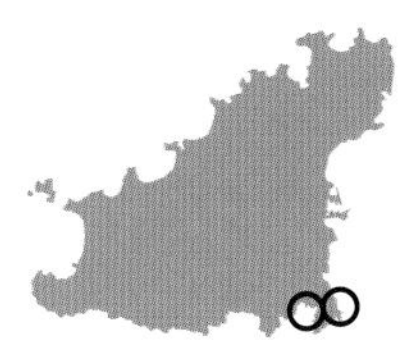

I CAN'T clarify if it provided the inspiration for the now-burnt-out Idlerocks Hotel's popular 1970s disco, Smugglers, but with its proximity to some real-life smuggling, it is nice to think it was.

It's only a couple of miles from St Martin's Point to the quiet, half-hidden Bec du Nez slipway and landing stage, but it happens that 200 years ago it provided Matthieu de Sausmarez with a nice little side business.

The little mooring quay, with its steep and tortuous land path, was part of the Fief du Sausmarez until Matthieu opted to sell it, together with the quarrying rights, to the British War Office in 1803 on the condition that the stone hut a few yards away remained his.

And why?

It wasn't to allow ivy to grow uncontrolled, which is all the visual evidence you will see today, but to store illicit wine, which Matthieu was accustomed to bringing in from France on the quiet.

Using Bec du Nez as a nocturnal landing spot, he would initially store the barrels in the hut before moving it to the Fermain Tavern and then on to Sausmarez Manor.

But for generations the moorings have been put to better use by families of part- or full-time fishermen, one of whom is today's Guernsey Boatowners' Association representative for Bec du Nez, Gary Thoume.

It was a role his father held and one that delights him.

'It's the best place in the world and the only bit of untouched Guernsey left,' he says of its steep, granite slipway and small landing to bring small boats ashore and store safely above sea levels, which alter alarmingly on big spring tides.

But this is Guernsey at its most charming and Mr Thoume is only too happy to continue his family tradition of fishing out of there.

'At the moment we've got 12 boats, but at one time there were up to 25.

'This year [summer] we should have 16 – that's dinghies and those on deep-water moorings.

'The majority of people mooring down there have been doing so for years as have generations before them, mainly people from St Martin's, but I am getting people now from all over the place wanting to go down there.'

And as for the access?

It doesn't worry a hill-hardened man like Gary.

'We've been doing it since we've been kids, so it makes no difference to us.'

GONE FISHIN' ... FOR A MONSTER

GUERNSEY'S south-east corner offers anglers numerous hotspots and on a quiet October night in 2000, Paul Carre's favourite yielded the catch of his life.

Fifteen minutes to midnight and on his birthday, he snagged the biggest fish ever to be landed off rocks in the Channel Islands: a 65lb 14oz conger.

Over the years Bec du Nez, tucked away between Fermain and Jerbourg, has brought much peace and contentment to the Bucktrout's worker and leading angler, but in terms of satisfaction, nothing beats the night when the monster conger took his bait.

He was fishing for bream at the time and was not rigged up to snare big eels, which made the catch even more remarkable.

'I was bringing it in and I knew it was something big,' he said at the time.

'It was staying pretty deep when I pulled it and in the light, I had difficulty working out what it was.'

The conger made a strong initial fight before coming to the surface in a subdued state, which was just as well, as Mr Carre was shaking with the excitement of it all.

Looking back, the man who once fished every day of the week but nowadays restricts himself to around four said it 'was the best birthday present' for which he could ever have wished.

'It was a nice clear night and an hour after high tide. It was probably an 8m tide.'

Paul will be eternally grateful for the assistance he received from fishing partners John Holdaway and Geoff Le Page, who helped him with the gaff.

'John had a conger rod out with mackerel bait, while Geoff had two rods out for conger. But without the help of both them, there is no way I could have landed the fish.

'The whole experience left the three of us

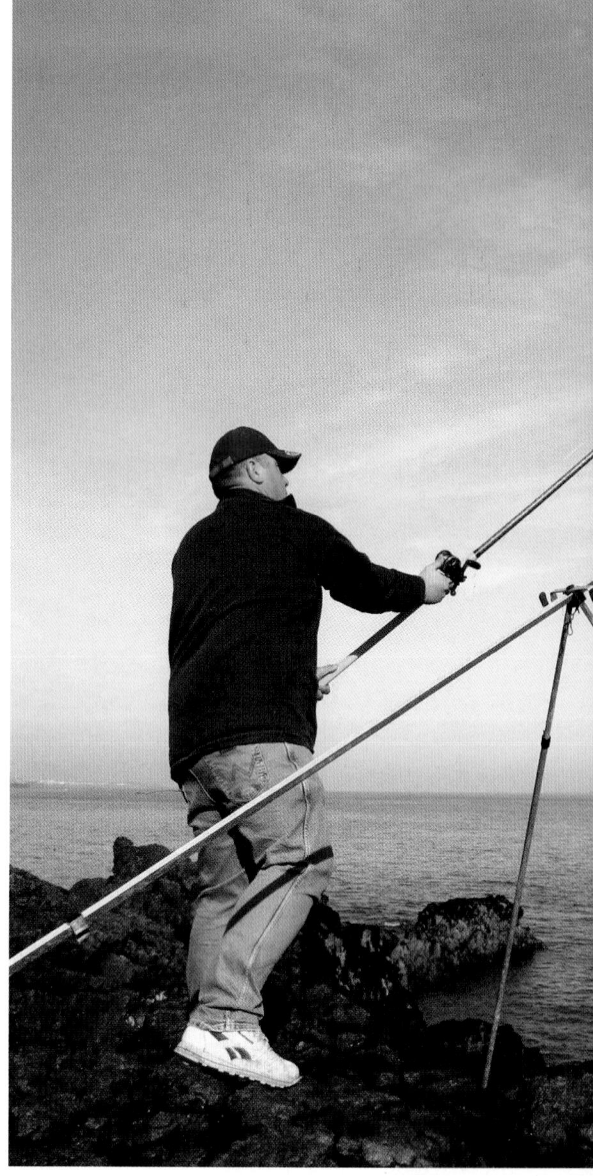

Above right
Conger-catcher
Paul Carre

shattered and it was at least an hour before we recovered.

'The adrenaline rush was amazing. My legs went to jelly, I was shaking so much.'

Which is not what you want when there is an angry eel about and a steep, lung-stretching climb back up the paths and fields to the car park adjacent to the Doyle Monument.

But the trudge from the peaceful rocks to the main road is about the only downside to the spot, which our conger catcher views as his favourite.

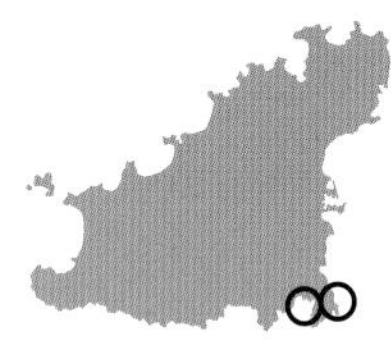

'It's a lovely place – so peaceful.

'You don't get so many people down there and the view is fantastic.'

I can vouch for that, having spent an hour with him on the same rocks on the most beautiful, unseasonable Sunday afternoon in February you could ever imagine.

He has his own views on why the area is so good for fishing and on a still afternoon close to low water on a 9m spring tide, the evidence lies with the reef only a few hundred metres away.

Paul is sure it is the reason behind the angling spot's scaly treasures.

Between the reef and the rocks from which Paul nonchalantly flicks a 60m-plus cast is a large stretch of sand.

'The congers come off the reefs and like to feed off the sand. That's my opinion. Others have their opinion, but I think they go on to the sand to feed.'

Not that catching fish is the solitary reason for Paul popping down to the Bec du Nez.

'I don't care if I don't catch anything. It's just nice and peaceful. Nobody can shout at you down here.'

He regards August onwards as the best time to fish the area, with a wide variety of potential catches.

'I'd say there are about 20 different varieties down here. When it comes around to the specimen hunt, this place will be very busy.

'The other good thing about the spot is you never know quite what you are going to catch. Even at low tide there's quite a depth of water and you've got the Great Bank so close.'

There is nothing secretive about the Bec du Nez hideaway, but I guess many will be put off by its isolation and the descent and climb back up, which are particularly testing in the dark.

The night Paul caught his once-in-a-lifetime conger he had several rods and 80lbs of gear with him.

Not surprisingly he decided it was asking a bit much of himself to carry that and nearly five stones of conger in a sack.

He did it in two trips.

Bec du Nez is one of several renowned fishing spots in a short stretch of south-east coast, but it is the one Paul likes most.

'I think I'd rather come here or Marble Bay [a short distance away] or Divette. There's more sand here. On a clear day you can see Corbiere lighthouse in Jersey.'

THE HIGH PRICE OF BEAUTY

THE story of Guernsey's coastline would be incomplete without reference to its cliffs and those men and women who are called out to save the lives of those who have underestimated them.

Cliff rescues date back to the dawn of time, but it's in only the last 40 years or so that they have been a perennial problem for the St John Ambulance & Rescue Service.

Recorded figures prove that the stretch along the south-east corner is as dangerous as any.

Of the 87 rescues in the 30-year period between 1975 and 2005, Petit Bot and Jerbourg provided the backdrop for a third of them.

Icart featured five times, Saints four and Moulin Huet three.

Back in the 60s, every week in the summer months seemed to see some rescue or another.

Often it was a dog which had chased a rabbit that little bit too far and fallen.

On many other occasions it was youngsters who had thought it would be fun to take the unconventional route from the bay to the top, or had become trapped on rocks with a rising ride and saw the cliffs as a way out of trouble.

But the good news is that the A & R cliff-top service is being called upon less and less.

'Perhaps it's education, perhaps it's a lifestyle change,' said head of the service and former rescuer Neil Tucker.

What is more surprising is that in nearly half-a-century of rescues, nobody has lost a life who had not gone out intentionally to do so.

'Most of our rescues are just people who have got stuck,' said the chief ambulance officer.

'The cliffs can look easy from the bottom,' he added.

'It's like a tree to a kid.'

Neil cannot recall a single fatality, though.

'Touch wood, I don't think we've had any serious injuries even.'

That the number of incidents has fallen is also good news economically.

He has worked out that, on average, it costs £2,000-2,500 per rescue.

But savings are not what it is all about, as he highlights.

'The service's aim is to help those whose lives are at risk, or who are suffering from illness or injury, to receive the highest standard of immediate care, wherever they may be.

'People may be injured in sewers, on cliffs, in quarries or other inaccessible locations and over the years the service has developed teams to reach casualties in those areas and give immediate on-the-spot ambulance treatment.'

Some services in the UK are now following Guernsey's example by setting up teams of ambulance staff to access casualties in difficult situations, or by training paramedics to respond with lifeboat crews to marine incidents.

He says Guernsey's service gives distinct benefits for casualties, which are not available elsewhere, as well as economic benefits for the island.

He gives the example of a patient who fell on Guernsey's south-east cliffs.

'The island's cliff rescue team responded to the incident and since the team is provided by the Ambulance & Rescue Service, the first rescuer to reach the casualty was a paramedic: someone who was able to assess and treat her injuries with the skills and experience of a full-time professional paramedic.

'In that particular case the paramedic was also a member of the inshore rescue boat

Opposite
Dramatic 1970s rescue at Telegraph Bay. Sean Goddard hangs on to the cliff face for dear life whilst at the foot volunteers hold a blanket should the 11-year-old fall the 70ft. After an hour-long ordeal he was rescued from above.

crew, so he was able to use his knowledge of the abilities and limitations of the inshore boats to decide that lowering the patient down the cliffs into the boat was the best evacuation in the light of both the sea conditions and her injuries.

'Once he had assessed her condition and made her safe, he accompanied her as she was lowered down the cliff and since he was a member of the inshore rescue team himself, accompanied her on the boat for the journey to shore.'

He added: 'When the boat reached land, he assisted with her transfer into the ambulance and then climbed in himself to continue treatment en route to hospital, since that was his normal daily working environment and its crew his own work colleagues.'

The fact there were only two services involved in a complicated rescue – the Ambulance & Rescue Service and the Police – meant an efficient and effective use of resources.

Especially since the rescue aspects of the first are provided at no cost to the States.

But the benefit for the patient was more important.

'From the perspective of a frightened and injured casualty, in fear for her life, the first person to reach her was not just a climber but also a qualified paramedic, who could arrange her evacuation in full consideration of her injuries.

'He was able to comfort and care for her and then instead of passing her on to another person, the same caring hands stayed with her throughout her ordeal, down the cliff, on the rescue boat, in the ambulance, to a handover in A&E.

'In this way he was able personally to monitor any changes in her condition and provide a continuous, reassuring presence as the various elements of the rescue integrated.'

Right
Neil Tucker closes in on Sean Goddard during the dramatic rescue in the 1970s

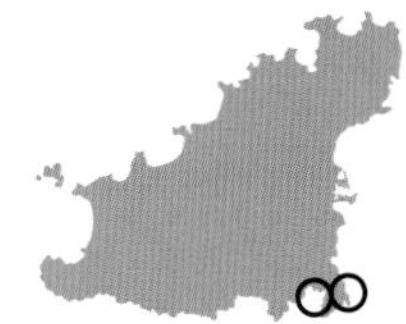

HIDDEN HOME

TO THE Cadastre it has the title 'Mecca'.

To the Ogier family it is simply known as 'The Shack'.

Only a small proportion of the island know it is there, sitting atop the cliffs between Moulin Huet and Petit Port, an occasional home to the Ogier family, who have owned it since 1960.

And as far as the Ogiers are concerned the fewer who know its whereabouts probably the better. The family have done very good job of hiding it.

The hedging camouflages so well at path level you would not know it is there, only a hop, skip and jump away.

It is a place of sheer bliss, its situation and views a stark contrast to its grey wooden casing which may look like asbestos but most definitely is not.

Claire Ogier is unsure when it was built but 'we have a feeling it is the hut you see on one of the Renoir paintings,' she offers the view.

If that is the case it pre-dates 1883 when the legendary French artist put brush to canvas.

It was bought by Tom Ogier, her father-in-law, when he returned to his native island from Trinidad and caught sight of it as he involved himself with the Natural Beauties Committee of the time.

The man who was to become something of a legend in Guernsey politics and, more specifically, for his steadfastly prickly leadership of the Island Development Committee, would often take afternoon tea at The Shack with his wife Kathleen while sampling a view that must rank as one of Guernsey's finest five.

'It is a great place to study or write and heavenly to stay there,' said Clare, whose late husband Roland had to repair the building when it was battered by the vicious 1987 hurricane.

'The hurricane scooped the left side of the roof off and the bed was deposited up on the hill on the Jones' property.'

But it survived and more than two decades on offers the Ogiers and invited friends a sanctuary few in this ever-crammed island could ever hoped for.

Inside, you will find a bed, a kitchen table and a few chairs, but nothing more than that and a few old cups and plates.

It has no electric, gas or running water, just a view to soak up and feel grateful that you are alive.

'We still stay there,' says Claire.

'It is like upmarket camping.'

Left
The Shack above Moulin Huet

"It's a superb place. A great area to train.
The sand is so firm and flat it is unbelievable"

Colin Renouf

CHAPTER 21

PETIT PORT

You need strong legs and a good set of lungs to climb in and out of the bay, but on low tide this bay underneath Jerbourg Point opens up to be a beach and almost spirit-level straight firm sand of significant proportions.

PITCH PERFECT · WARTIME HEROES
OPERATION AMBASSADOR · ULTIMATE CLIFF-HANGER

PITCH PERFECT

NOW here's a question.

Which beach best suits full-scale football practice?

Old St Martin's football greats Colin Renouf and Henry Davey will give you a quick and definitive answer as they have plenty of experience of its flat, rock-hard sands: Petit Port.

Officially part of Moulin Huet Bay, Petit Port has gone through a rollercoaster existence in terms of use and popularity.

The great Saints side of the 1960s often trained there under the eagle eye of Sgt-Major style coach Frank Mackwood.

Running up 321 steps with a stone in each hand was not Davey's idea of great fun, but the latter-day St Martin's AC president loves the area for its quality of pure-white sand and idyllic shelter when the summer sun is burning down and a northerly is blowing.

'It's a beautiful, beautiful beach,' said Davey who loves nothing better than to take his little boat into the oft-protected bay.

'It's a bloody long way up though,' he added, recalling the days when Mackwood would have the team run there from their Blanche Pierre HQ a mile-and-a-half or so away.

'The sand is rock hard and we used to play proper sized games down there.'

Saints would use jumpers for goalposts and when it was all done, Mackwood would order his men to run up the steps, in various painful manners.

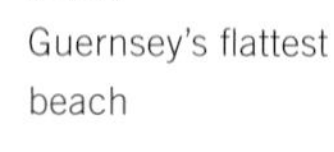

Below
Guernsey's flattest beach

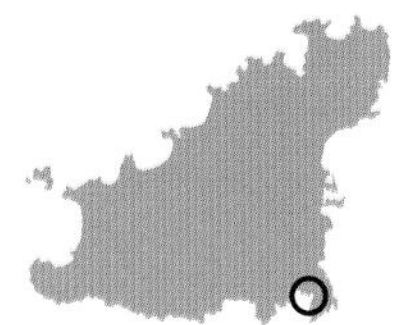

'You used to have a stone in each hand and you might have to hop up one flight on one leg, and the next on the other.

'Frank would physically hit you with a gym shoe if you were lagging behind,' recalled a player not renowned for his athletic prowess.

'Jack Martel was running into Blanche Pierre and I was still coming up the steps,' Davey laughingly recalled.

Colin Renouf, indisputably Guernsey's finest non-professional footballer, has a particularly special feel for the beach as it was there where he spent much of his childhood kicking about.

'As youngsters, we'd spend high tide at Divette on one side and low tide at Petit Port.

'It's a superb place. A great area to train. The sand is so firm and flat it is unbelievable.'

On climbing the steps, he said, 'Sometimes we'd have to do it with two feet placed together.

'But, believe it or not, it doesn't take too long to run up, about three minutes.'

Guernsey hockey, too, is indebted to the bay's immaculate sands.

Long before all-weather synthetic surfaces came along, the local club would use Petit Port when its grass pitches were out of action.

Former jurat Tony Spensley recalled the delights of a flat pitch and the pain of lugging all the equipment down those steps.

'I wish I had a £5 note for all the times I carried the goalposts and nets all the way down those steps,' he said.

'We had some great times down there.' Hockey's use of the beach was very much weather and tide dependent.

'We used it when the grass pitches were waterlogged, which they often were.

'It was a beautiful surface and we would have to adjust the width of the pitch with the tide. It was great fun.'

Above
The great St Martin's football team regularly used Petit Port for training

In other eras, the footballers and hockey players would have had no access to the beach. Until 1911, when local building firm and J. and S. Rabey built the steps for the parish of St Martin's, only the canny fishermen would know the way down there and across the rocks.

In its heyday, Petit Port would attract hundreds to its clean sands and quiet beauty.

It was popular enough to warrant whoopee floats being stacked for use near the cave on the left of the beach as you look down.

There was also a little cafe down there.

But in 1991, seven years after their ownership moved into the hands of the Board of Administration, the steps were closed after a series of landslips of gravel and small pieces of rock from the right side.

Some considered it a total over-reaction and continued to use them and, in 1993, the States agreed to fund an £85,000 project to install a flight of steps in a different area.

They were opened in September 1993, but to many regular users it was obvious that the new route was ill-advised and dangerous.

Within a month of completion tons of rocks came crashing down on them, two flights from the bottom.

Thousands of pounds were spent in a vain attempt to stabilise the area, but further falls rendered the new section completely blocked after spring 2001.

St Martin's douzenier Patrick Symons, who lives above the bay, was particularly indignant.

'He was like a terrier after a rat,' said parish deputy Francis Quin, who recalls that Symons made it something of a crusade to get the old route reopened.

He eventually won the argument and the steps reopened, allowing regular beach lovers like himself access once more.

FOR 22 years Patrick Symons has lived above Petit Port beach, his lounge window overlooking Moulin Huet and, in the distance, Saints Bay harbour.

But it's Petit Port, the little sandy inlet around the corner from Jerbourg, which is his geographical jewel.

Patrick, a relatively recently retired St Martin's douzenier, treats the beach with as much care as if it were his own garden.

He is full of facts and anecdotes on the area, which, at its lowest tide, is said to be large enough to house five full-size football pitches.

'It is probably the cleanest sand in Guernsey,' he boasts.

His reasoning is the effect gales have on it.

'In a south-westerly gale the beach level can drop three feet.

'Yet it will all come back in the following few weeks.'

The sand was of sufficient quality to attract the interest of the Occupation forces in the war.

All pictures
Three views of Petit Port

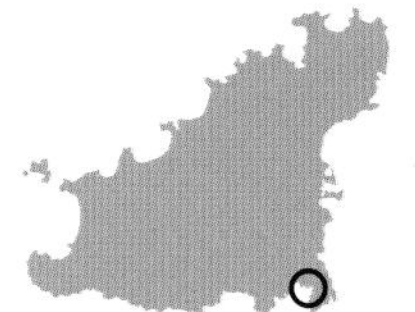

'A lot of sand was taken from Petit Port by the Germans and put in Havelet Bay for their submarine pens.

'So most of the sand you see there now came from Petit Port.' Patrick suggests that La Mouliere rock, which stands in the middle of the bay, may have taken out a First World War German submarine.

It's an unsubstantiated tale, but, he said, 'I'm not sure if it is true but there is a big metal boiler which appears after a gale sometimes.'

The beach certainly keeps him busy.

'It probably also collects more rubbish than any other in the island,' he said, referring to the large amount of wood and plastic which is blown ashore with the tide.

'In the winter months you get the most rubbish, but you do get some good plans occasionally.'

And with the days of the States sending a barge around to collect the debris long gone, it's left to Patrick to burn what he can.

WARTIME HEROES

PETIT PORT is one of those beaches that many islanders may never visit in their lifetime.

All those steps, for a start.

No facilities either.

But, per square inch of exposed sand, the first south coast inlet west of Jerbourg point possibly has more tales to tell than most of our island sands.

It has seen smugglers, silver mining on either side of its steep slopes and boasts a beach even Winston Churchill once got to hear of as he scratched his bald head, dragged on one of his mighty cigars and supped his scotch, wondering how to defeat the Germans and to protect his 'dear Channel Islands'.

Never mind A Bridge Too Far, Reach For the Sky, Dambusters and bouncing bombs off German lakes.

What about Nicolle and Symes or Operation Ambassador, the failed 1940 commando raid on Petit Port?

The first is a story worthy of Sir Richard Attenborough's directing talents.

But what did we get?

Island at War – six episodes of sanitisation and falsehoods – set on a fictional island called St Gregory which looked remarkably like the Isle of Man.

Their tale of Sarnian born and bred commandos Philip Dorr and Eugene La Salle coming ashore on a reconnaissance mission, is said to have been based on the escapade of two real-life Guerns – Lts Hubert Nicolle and James Symes.

The real heroes came ashore at Petit Port at 3am on 3 September 1940, Nicolle having surreptitiously visited the island only a few weeks earlier, on that occasion arriving by canoe at Le Jaonnet, further along the coast.

Before that excursion to see what the Germans were up to, he was summoned to the admiralty on the instructions of Churchill and

told in no uncertain terms, 'If you do this and are caught, we don't want to know you. You are on your own. You will be shot and that will be the end of it.'

Being a hero, traits which Nicolle showed from his days at the Elizabeth College, where he broke the school 100 yards record with an electric dash of 10.6sec., he accepted the mission on the spot.

The mission was successful and he was soon back for a second with Symes.

Dressed in plain clothes and landing by motor torpedo boat, Nicolle and Symes scooted up the rocks, probably the old

Above
Covert mission in 1940: landing craft brought ashore Commandos who climbed the cliffs at Petit Port

fishermen's path, utilising knowledge of the area gained from childhood.

The TV series had the pair gunning down Germans, but that was as far from the truth as St Gregory was from St Peter Port.

This time, Nicolle was to be on his homeland for longer than he would have wished.

The Navy's return taxi never arrived and, stuck, they went into hiding for weeks.

In the film, La Salle was shot.

In reality, Nicolle and Symes eventually gave themselves up and became POWs in the east.

Nicolle was an enthusiastic tunneler and is said to have made many escape attempts.

He dug his way out of Spangenberg, only to have to surrender as four German Shepherd dogs set upon him.

Even when he was released, he had the misfortune to endure, but also the luck to survive, his plane crashing at Brussels airport.

Half a century later Bill Bell, the Guernsey politician, wrote a book on his life.

It was entitled, 'The Commando Who Came Home to Spy'.

Sadly, Nicolle, who had read and approved the script, died before its publication.

Awarded the Military Cross, he died in St Martin's in 1998.

OPERATION AMBASSADOR

Below
Local hero Hubert Nicolle as a PoW following his failed reconnaissance mission
Opposite
Rough seas overturned a dinghy on the botched commando mission

IT WAS still the early days of the Occupation and Churchill's government were undecided as to how to react to the occupation of the Channel Islands.

A full-scale attempt to overturn the German invasion was quickly deemed foolish.

However, it was worth a look to see the extent of the occupying forces.

The reconnaissance operation was divided into two phases.

Hubert Nicolle was at the heart of the first two, bracingly titled Anger, while the name Ambassador was given to the third and most ambitious.

Petit Port was the focal point of the landing of 140 men of the No.3 Commando and No.11 Independent Company.

They were brought to Guernsey by two destroyers, the Saladin and the Saracen, and were transferred to seven air-sea rescue launches off the south coast.

The plan was for three separate landings, all to be made as Anson aircraft flew overhead to drown out the noise of the landing craft.

One party was destined for the airport via Point de la Moye to destroy planes on the ground, petrol stores and aerodrome installations.

A second was earmarked to land at Le Jaonnet Bay to intercept any German troops and the other deployed at Petit Port to attack a machine gun post and German billets.

It was pretty much an unmitigated disaster.

Already postponed for 48 hours due to bad weather, when Ambassador was finally given the green light tidal conditions were far from perfect.

In short, the party of 11 heading Le Jaonnet were taken to Sark and did not land.

The group bound for La Moye and the airport encountered a series of boat problems.

The Petit Port team did get ashore but they failed to find any of the island's 469-man German garrison.

Patrols were sent out, even a road block set up and the Jerbourg peninsula was thoroughly searched.

But the Germans were nowhere to be seen.

What is more, the commandos' exit proved more hazardous than anyone could have planned.

Ordered to re-embark, disaster struck as a launch was badly damaged and a naval rating made several trips into the bay to claim three at a time. On his fifth trip, the dinghy over-turned in heavy breakers and a soldier was swept away, presumed drowned.

The few men left on the beach were ordered to swim, but three non-swimmers could not make it and were stuck, left for another day.

ULTIMATE CLIFF-HANGER

FOR nearly half a century, responsibility for the upkeep and maintenance of the Petit Port steps and cliff face has been the responsibility of the States of Guernsey.

Nowadays, States Property Services employees undertake regular inspections of the steps and adjacent cliffs, the most recent being in March, when for several days Devon geologist Richard Gould and Derbyshire safety access expert Peter Cresswell could be seen dangling from ropes on the cliffs.

Peter is employed by the Industrial Rope Access Trade Association (Irata), who has a 10-year contract with Geomarine to provide qualified rope access operatives to assist geologists from Frederick Sherrell Ltd in their inspection of the cliff face.

During inspections, the geologist identifies any areas which require scaling and the whole cliff face is systematically scaled by Geomarine.

The Petit Port cliffs are prone to gradual weathering and loosening of fractures causing flakes of rock to occasionally become detached and fall onto the footpath and steps.

Wholesale meshing of the rock face would control the rockfall hazards but this has been ruled out due to the adverse visual impact it would have on the outstanding natural scenery.

Geologists such as Richard need to identify at an early stage where rockfalls might be developing and take remedial action, which often means scaling with hand tools to remove loose rock.

Most of the damage normally occurs in the winter (storms and ice wedging) and the inspection is normally carried out in the early spring ahead of the tourist season.

In some parts cliff scaling alone is insufficient to control the rockfall hazards and additional support is needed in the forming of meshing,

Right and far right
Saving face: a recent cliff inspection

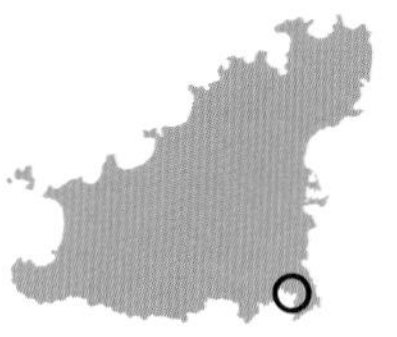

rock bolting and rock catcher fences.

Richard has been climbing cliffs for 24 years and thinks nothing of it.

'It is a very safe process and very closely regulated,' he said.

'We always use two ropes: a main working line and a secondary line.

'You have to have a head for heights, obviously.'

The rock face at Petit Port is formed of a band of very hard vein quartz, which is pale grey in colour and forms a distinctive rocky crag at the top of the cliffs.

The rocks to the north of the quartz vein are different and comprise granite-augen gneiss of the Icart type.

A geological fault forms the contact between the two.

Most rock types are dissected or broken by naturally occurring fractures, including bedding planes, joints, faults and shears.

Geologists measure the orientation and conditions of these fractures, which are collectively referred to as the geological structure of the rock.

Petit Port has a complex rock structure and in exposed cuttings they need careful evaluation.

Richard has been visiting Petit Port for the last eight years and thinks the cliff face is in better shape now than when he first inspected it.

'It's a nice, clean face and pretty straightforward [to descend].'

But, as he acknowledges, he is very much in the hands of people like Peter Cresswell.

'I'm qualified to do it [climb] as well, but as a geologist you rely on the specialist to set up the ropes and make the right health and safety assessment.'

At 70m the Petit Port cliffs are as big as Richard works on and he regards the task as a joy.

'It's a fantastic view. I say every time I go, this is my office for the next three days.

'It is a process of familiarisation and the long-term assessment is important.

'It [Petit Port] is definitely something that is improving.'

That, along with expert assessment, is down to the meshing and insertion of stainless steel bars ranging between 1.5 and two metres in length.

Richard does not insert them himself.

'I tell them [Geomarine] where to put them.'

He does not envy their task.

'The logistics of getting stuff to the rock face is horrendous. It is not good access to the top of the cliff and it is very difficult work for the guys who put the bolts in.'

Below
St Martin's douzenier Patrick Symons (foreground) fought hard to have the steps reopened. With him are Martin Gavet and Dave Parish.
Opposite
Pretty as a picture in early June

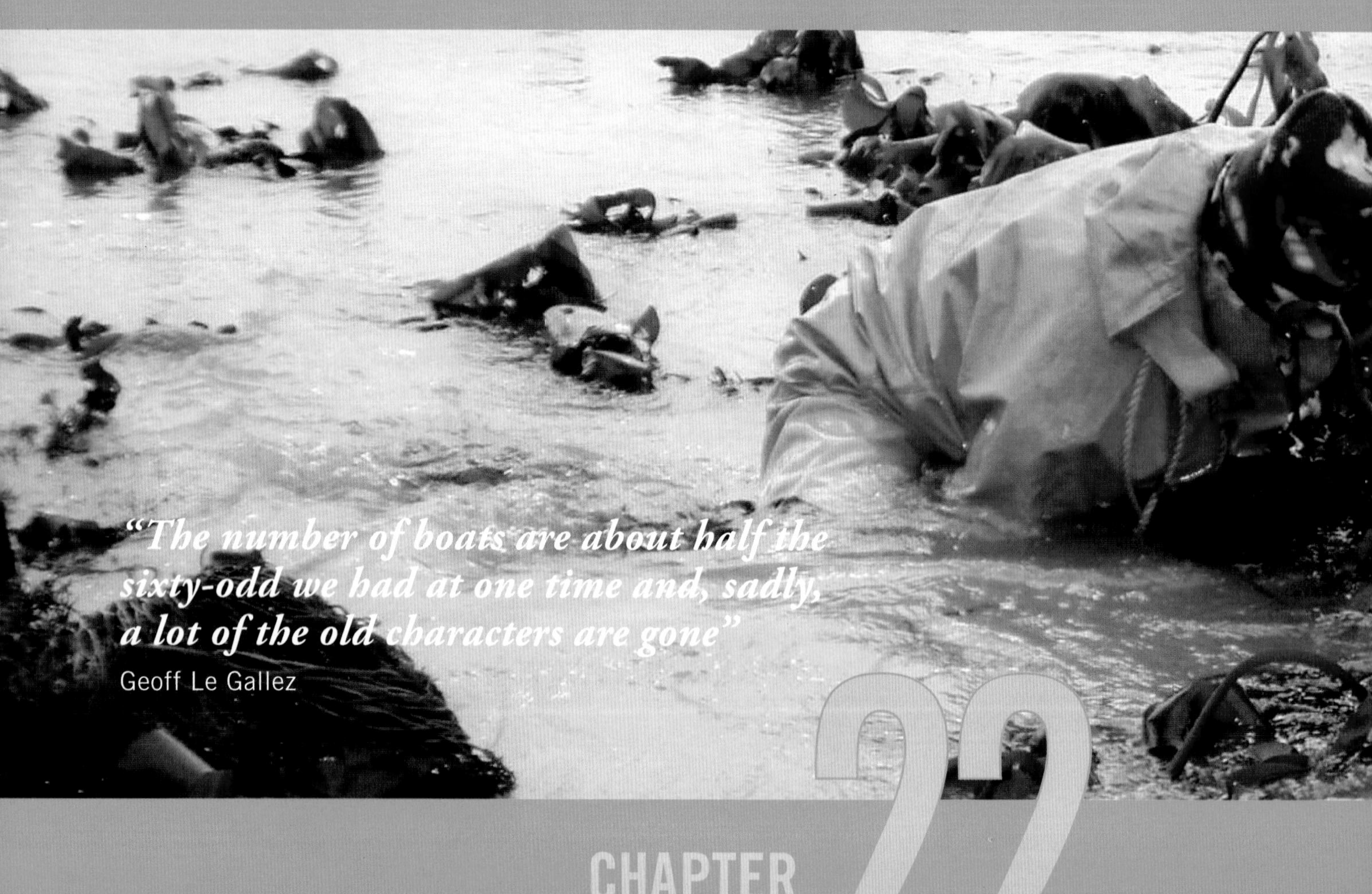

"The number of boats are about half the sixty-odd we had at one time and, sadly, a lot of the old characters are gone"

Geoff Le Gallez

CHAPTER 22

SAINTS BAY

With its quaint little harbour and small part-time fishing community 'Saints' has lost none of its old charm, even if like other bays it has lost its regatta.

ORMERING MADNESS · THE ROCKS SHOOK
DECEMBER GALE · MONUMENT RESTORED
BLANCHELANDE FIEF · BEGINNING OF THE END

ORMERING MADNESS

I CALL myself a Guernseyman and here I am, just about 50, and never eaten an ormer, let alone submerged myself in freezing water in an attempt to catch one of the little green blighters.

Whether you are eating them or catching them, this ormer business really is not for the squeamish and faint-hearted.

Geoff Le Gallez, special constable of Saints Bay, is neither of those, but he is a little bit odd.

The man is prepared to wallow like a great yellow seal in the cold winter sea for the pleasure of giving them away – free – to others.

'The family love them, but not me. I'm not keen,' he said on the day he and brother Billy claimed 27 juicy big ones off their favourite beach.

'I give them away to the old people. I love to see their faces.'

For the first spring low of March, I joined Geoff and his youngest brother on the rocks at Saints.

They try the spot every now and then. It was to be Jerbourg the following day but for now their beloved Saints did not disappoint despite a strong wind and big swell.

Two hours of rummaging among the largely submerged rocks and between them they had more than two dozen to take home.

Long before the end of their mission, Billy was looking forward to his traditional Guernsey meal.

'It's more like meat than fish,' he says to my question of how they taste.

'It's the steak of the sea.'

It's a 0.4m tide on the day in question and when I arrive at the bay, two hours before low tide, for a minute I struggle to pick out the man who has served as constable for the past 10 years.

Then I spot him, sitting in his bright yellow waterproofs among the rocks.

With the temperature just 4C and black skies depositing large hailstones, it was not a morning to see Saints at its best.

My man is the only human in sight.

'Born and bred in Saints Road,' says the second of five Le Gallez brothers, as I start my nosiness.

He has had a boat moored in the bay since 1983 and simply loves the place.

'The number of boats are about half the 60-odd we had at one time and, sadly, a lot of the old characters are gone,' he laments.

'My jurisdiction is all of this,' he says, while opening his arms wide.

'I'm also in charge of the east and west pathways to Saints and the whole of the shoreline which stretches from halfway to Petit Bot and Moulin Huet.'

In the summer months and when the tide is up, local youngsters will be seen jumping and bombshelling off the harbour. Geoff got the T-shirt for that nearly half-a-century ago.

'It's a safe beach because there's always someone down here.

'Only when the wind is in the south-east or south it's bad in here.'

But it happens and not always in winter.

'Three years ago we had that freak weather in August and it wiped out most of the boats,' he said. 'It caught everybody napping really.'

And talking of napping, just what was that captain of the President Garcia doing that night 40 years ago?

By simply closing his eyes, Geoff can still see the hulk of iron stuck on the rocks in front of the slip and the ship's stern sticking out at an angle into the bay.

'Saints Road was chock-full of cars. There were people everywhere.'

'The night the tugs pulled it off, they bent it [the ship].'

The 56-year-old maintenance electrician at the PEH admits to being a shade mad to go to

Right
Geoff Le Gallez ormering at Saints
Overleaf
Geoff with brother Billy

GEOMARINE

such lengths to catch the crustacean, but will not miss an ormering tide, despite his aversion to feeding on them.

'I don't crave to eat them, I crave to catch them.'

That day and despite less than favourable conditions – low pressure and a swell – the result was a good one for the brothers, who began by predicting a double-figure catch.

'It's a 9.8 high water today but the wind is going to spoil it. We'll end up with a dozen between us if not more.'

Watching them duck into the sea – particularly Billy who had only a pair of jeans, jumper and light yellow waterproof for protection – I concurred with their admission of a precarious mental state.

'When I used to go with my father, we've had up to 15 dozen, but you don't get that now,' says Geoff.

'Last year the three of us had 86 here.

But there's still plenty out there in the deeper water.'

Billy agreed in between reaching for a hidden ormer.

'As long as you've got layered stones, you've got a nursery,' said the younger Le Gallez, who earlier this year was ormering on his own in the same area and was hit by a wave out of the blue and was washed up among the rocks.

'I turned around and I couldn't see the horizon.

'I don't know where it came from,' he said.

The big rollers were, ultimately, to spoil that particular mission.

Time and again the brothers would be already up to their necks in the slate green sea when a roller hit them.

But the catch more than made up for the watery chill.

'There were plenty of big ones. Down this end you get some big ones.

'To get that many like it is and the pressure like it is, was good.

'Also we saw lots of small ones, which is good news,' said Geoff, who was part of the team who restocked the bay in the late 1990s.

'The parish bought some ormer seeds from Dick Tostevin at Pleinmont and we put them down around the coast.'

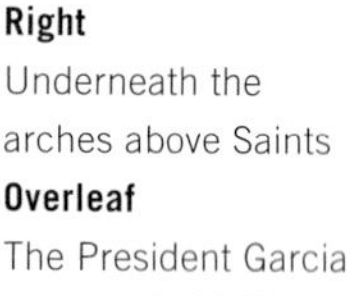

Right
Underneath the arches above Saints
Overleaf
The President Garcia aground in 1967

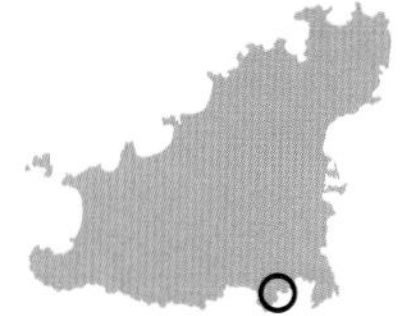

THE ROCKS SHOOK

THE sun had long gone down on a scorching summer's day, but as midnight approached on 13 July 1967 it was still stiflingly warm – high 20s – and not a breath of wind.

Out at sea it was misty, bordering on fog. The heat and the stillness suited Pam, a waitress from Staffordshire, and her local boyfriend, Jim.

'We'll have some peace and quiet down Saints,' he might have said as the amorous couple headed down to the harbour in his car.

Meanwhile, not so far away, deep in the bowels of a 7,687-ton cargo vessel steaming northwards en route to Rotterdam, the old captain, Fredricko, was dreaming of his beloved Manila or perhaps it was Imelda Marcos, as he dozed aboard the old President Garcia with a hold full of copra, dried coconut kernels used to make oil, some 42 days out of the Philippines.

Up the hill at his house in Saints Road, Evening Press photographer Brian Green was struggling to sleep on the uncomfortably hot night and down in Town reporter Herbert Winterflood was checking harbour movements and having a chat at the watchhouse.

Then it happened.

The earth moved, not only for the couple, but also for old Fredricko who had gone to his quarters confident – why wouldn't he be? – that the boys up top and the autopilot would steer the old tub safely past the Channel Islands and up the Channel towards their destination.

That was the plan, anyway. The officers on duty had seen the warning lights and knew where they were going, even if it was a bit foggy.

What they didn't know was that the lighthouse they could see in the distance was not the Hanois. It was the one at St Martin's Point. Oops.

'Hard to port,' was the translated order.

The red St Martin's light was seen as a danger signal, but a sharp left would see them back on track in the open sea. Wrong.

Instead and at 12 knots, the President Garcia ploughed straight into Saints Bay, to give Pam and Jim the shock of a lifetime.

Instead of a torch beam shone into their faces accompanied by the words, "Ello, 'ello, 'ello, what're you two youngsters up to?", the jump came from the sound of thousands of tons of iron scraping across the rocks a few yards away.

'I had my fingers in my ears,' said Pam to reporter Herbert, who was quickly on the scene.

'But I could still hear the crunch as the vessel struck the rocks. It was an experience that I never want to go through again,' she told Herbert.

Jim's version of events was not too different.

'It really made a bang when it hit,' he said.

The couple had initially thought the ship was heading for the Peastacks.

'Then she turned in a bit as if she was heading into Moulin Huet Bay. She then turned in sharply and didn't seem to slow down at all,' Jim said. But slow it most certainly did.

'It shook the cliff as it crashed,' said the couple.

Nearly 8,000 tons of it settled onto the rocks near the foot of the slipway. It was to remain there for nearly eight days and thousands came from all over the island to see the Philippine President Lines ship. El capitano, meanwhile, had been given the shock of his own life and as he realised the extent of his error, the thought must have crossed his mind:

'That's my captaincy career over.'

Over the next few hours and the coming days, Herbert was to get quotes from all and sundry. But he got nothing from Fredricko. The old man was saying nothing.

PPL
PHILIPPINE PRESIDEN

LINES

When the media went aboard the following day, its master cut a disconsolate and sad figure.

He sat attending to his paperwork but refused to say anything about what had happened in the lead-up to the accident.

Outside, it was chaotic in the area around Saints.

The small bay had never seen anything like it and the narrow lanes were not built for hundreds of cars coming and going.

The police made special arrangements and a field was opened for use as a car park, with the proceeds suitably going to the RNLI.

Out in the bay, where incredibly not one moored boat had been hit by the lost ship, boatowners from all over the island chugged in to have a closer look and swimmers donned masks and snorkels to take an alternative view.

What the salvagers saw was a ship virtually wrecked by at least four gaping holes.

Three of them had already been repaired from within the ship but the other, in No. 2 hold, could not be reached because of the cargo of copra.

The crew, meanwhile, were not certain where they were – some thought they were in France.

A week later they were off again.

Two powerful Dutch tugs finally hauled the boat off its rocky perch and life for Saints watchers and users returned to normal.

As for the ship, it is understood it went to the breaker's yard after eventually reaching its destination with 9,000 tons of copra on board.

Back on the beach all that was left was a nasty smell of oil and, as an unnamed little boy said in earshot of the Press: 'I don't think she did much damage to the rocks.'

Right
Stuck well and good

Looking back on the fateful night, the Guernsey Press's man on the spot, Herbie, recalls driving down to Saints fully expecting to see a yacht in trouble, which was the report received at the watchhouse.

'I went out and when I got there it looked like the Royal Hotel had appeared from nowhere.

'There was so much light coming from it, I couldn't believe my eyes.'

The short-term legacy of the President Garcia's unscheduled Guernsey excursion was the invasion of millions of bright blue copra beetles.

Inadvertently released through the ship's holds, they plagued the Saints area for several days. They got everywhere and left many with bites and bumps.

Francis Quin, who was running a beachfloat and deckchair business from Petit Bot at the time, recalls the infestation.

'The Board of Administration told us to shut the bay down, but they paid us for our lost week after filling in the necessary insurance forms,' he recalled.

'But as quickly as they came, they went.'

DECEMBER GALE

THEIR parish football team has had many a bad December night. But nothing to compare with the disastrous one the St Martin's fishermen suffered in the winter of 1868.

A fortnight before Christmas, the present they all had been waiting for and which was all but ready for use was blown away in front of their eyes.

It was to be in the form of a long-awaited breakwater to protect the ever-increasing number of fishing boats moored in Saints.

Nothing had been done for the parish's fishing fleet for 32 years but with its number up to 50, a petition to the Bailiff to get the States to make good the funding for a breakwater did the trick.

But a north-easterly gale put paid to all their dreams. Although in place, the stonework was not consolidated and combined with a spring tide, the breakwater was swept away.

Their big chance had gone.

After nearly a decade of procrastination, the Saints people got a second head of steam on the issue, but this time lost out to their counterparts at Rocquaine who had their own harbour plans.

Faced with a requete from the western parishes, which was signed by 90 men of the sea, a swell of constables and douzeniers of Torteval and St Peter's, the States took the safe option – they did nothing.

Our forebears had an early sign of the fence-sitting we have become accustomed to in recent times.

It was not until 1909 that Saints finally got a quay, all 50ft of it, and at a cost of just £750.

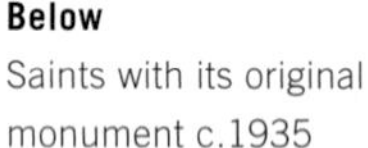

Below
Saints with its original monument c.1935

MONUMENT RESTORED

WHILE at one end of the island the people of the Vale were mounting a whopping piece of granite atop of L'Ancresse to mark the millennium, the Saints Bay users had their own hefty project to mark the ticking of time and the 20th century being replaced by the 21st.

The Lefebvre Monument was erected to mark the involvement of Captain Lefebvre, a former Lord of Blanchelande Manor.

He had contributed £500 to the cost of building the breakwater and it had stood above the harbour for all but a century when the Germans arrived in 1940 and ditched it into the sea below.

For nearly 40 years it remained sprawled among the rocks until 1975, when the obelisk was restored close to its original spot by Bill Simons and a team of divers, minus its top.

Twenty-five years later, on 1 January 2007, a small team led by Roger Berry restored the pyramid section to the monument.

'We retrieved it, dug it up and using blocks and tackle we pulled it up on ropes,' said Geoff Le Gallez, constable for the bay.

'The granite ball on the top was missing, though, and we don't know where it has gone.

BLANCHELANDE FIEF

THE Bailiff of Guernsey has so many hats you might suggest he opens a shop.

Only joking, sir.

But one of his lesser known responsibilities, especially for those outside St Martin's, is his role as head of the court of the Fief of the Abbot of Blanchelande.

For the last 20 years this particular court, which has among its number officers such as a seneschal, greffier, vavasseurs, a grenetier and a sergeant, has met once a year to oversee the 600 or so vergees this fief, dating back to 1154, covers.

Its coastal link is simple in that all the cliffs of St Martin's come under its administration.

And while the States of Guernsey happily forks out for the upkeep of paths and steps, the fief does have important roles to play as well as several that hardly apply in the 21st century.

Twice a year the court distributes money to needy families in the parish.

But behind the scenes, the fief also strives to oversee the rights of rabbit shooters.

And if anyone in St Martin's wants to dry fish, cut furze for their ovens or graze sheep, the court of the fief de Blanchelande is the people to see.

Left
In 2004 Bailiff de Vic Carey unveiled the stone that marks the place of the original Fief de Blanchelande

BEGINNING OF THE END FOR SAINTS' REGATTAS

FOR Saints boat owners such as Ray Simon, little changes around the bay.

In Ray's case there has been only one significant change in nearly 50 years of mooring his boat there – the sign-of-the-times end of the annual regatta.

A summer at Saints would never be quite the same.

Great water-filled days of fun for the kids, boatowners and parishioners ended when, like elsewhere, people could no longer be trusted to behave.

In the days of legendary Guernsey policeman Noel Trotter, fun never seemed to get out of hand.

But, as Ray said, the writing was on the wall 'when we started to get people coming down and getting a bit boisterous'.

There was nothing out of the ordinary about the regatta, just good, clean, watery fun.

Dinghy and rowing races, swimming competitions and a good old party in what is commonly known as 'The Vot', the tunnel situated at the top of the long, steep slip.

Utilised by the Germans as barracks, the Vot remains a vital store and safe house for

Below
The moorings at Saints

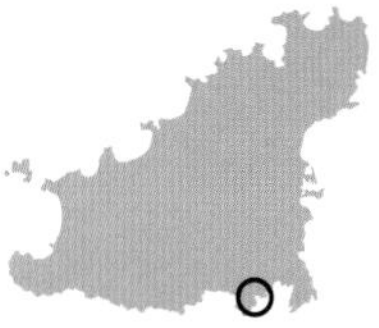

the boatowners.

It is also the place to winch boats to safety when the weather gets a little hairy and there is not enough time to make a run for Town.

Boats nowadays total about 20: 40 years ago there were double that number.

It remains a haven of peace and beauty for Ray Simon and his like, even though modern habits make it a little less charming than it once was.

'Once upon a time you could keep anything down Saints, but today you can't even leave a boat unchained.'

Above
Ray Simon's photographic recollections of a nasty day at Saints in the 1970s. Above, divers assist in rescuing boats but nothing could be done to save Grace (top) which was sunk by two big waves on the same day

"Few sights beat being down at La Moye at six on a summer's morning with the sun coming up. It's beautiful"

John Torode

CHAPTER 23

ICART
PETIT BOT & LA MOYE

Its network of coves and caves has long fascinated nature lovers but there is much more to this magical piece of coastline than its picture postcard views.

SOUTHERN BELLES · PATH MINDERS
DRAMA IN THE VALLEY

SOUTHERN BELLES

YOU need a strong pair of lungs and legs, but the pain of the climb back up is worth it.

Le Jaonnet and La Bette had eluded me for half a century, and if I ever get myself fit, I may make a quick return.

Even in early February and with the tide high enough to prevent strolling through the rocks from one small bay to its neighbour, it's easy to see the appeal of the small coves on the eastern end of the peninsulas which have Icart Point at one end and La Moye at the other.

Icart Bay takes in Portelet, Petit Bot, Le Jaonnet and La Bette, the latter two joined by the same steep approach from the cliff path, which is no more than a half-mile stretch from Icart car park.

Peter Jackson, who manages the States Works' cliff path team, is old enough to recall a descent into Le Jaonnet without the benefit of steps.

He remembers surfing in the mouth of Le Jaonnet, which is a summertime haunt for those who like an all-over tan.

It also has one of the, if not the most, impressive caverns in the island, Le Creux des Chiens, or Dog Cave for short.

Across the coastline, close to Petit Bot, are more caves backed by sheer cliffs.

Some of them are accessible by foot, but only at low water, and exploration without expert guidance is not recommended.

West of Petit Bot is Portelet Bay and under the magnificent Les Sommeilleuses cliffs can be found an impressive archway.

Victor Coysh, the former Guernsey Press historian, reckoned this section of coastline to be equal that of Sark's best.

The rocks are multi-coloured, the cliffs richly covered in vegetation and the sea deep blue and clear.

There is a savage beauty about the gull-haunted coast the further you inch west.

Right
Looking down on Petit Bot

Indeed, the gulls and the height of the drops bring back to mind the eerie and most effective advertisements Channel TV has probably ever come up with, the 1960s campaign to warn against the dangers of climbing cliffs.

It spooked me every time I saw it and ensured I stuck to the bays on which you could play cricket and pick up an ice-cream and get it back to your mate before it melted.

Before reaching La Moye and the steepest imaginable boat launch contraptions you are likely to see, there is one more piece of impressive nature: the Fontenelle Caves.

Russ Sarre, a veteran of the cliff path team with more than 20 years' experience of quietly beavering away from the public eye, helped replace the dinghy slide at La Moye nearly 20 years ago.

It almost cost him his life, as the bright idea to roll one of the heavy beams down the cliff face to the landing point above La Moye did not go quite to plan.

'It rolled all the way down into the water, just missing the boats, and it ended up in the [nearby] cave.' Nowadays, the only boat to be seen there – upside down, safe under the wall, is the one owned by John Torode, the sea fisheries officer.

He said that few sights beat being down at La Moye at six on a summer's morning with the sun coming up.

'It's beautiful.' John just wishes more boat owners would join him down there.

'I had a boat down there as a nipper. I then had a bigger one in the harbour before reverting back to La Moye.'

Why did he go back?

'It's a place I grew up with and I had good memories from those times.

There's also some good potting areas pretty close.

'Also, at any state of the tide you can pull your boat in and off you go. You don't need to have a dinghy.' Full-time fisherman Micky Saunders recalls the not-so-distant days when up to a dozen boats were kept down there.

He called it a 'Jekyll and Hyde' place.

'When it blew you sometimes couldn't get to it for weeks.

But when the sun shone it was a beautiful place.' Visitors are often drawn to the landing and see what he refers to as 'the skids'.

Fishing out of La Moye was always a bit back-breaking though.

Micky fished there for more than 30 years and while he now has a boat in the harbour, La Moye retains fond memories.

'When you're fishing spare time it is the sort of place you'd want to be when you leave work at five o'clock.'

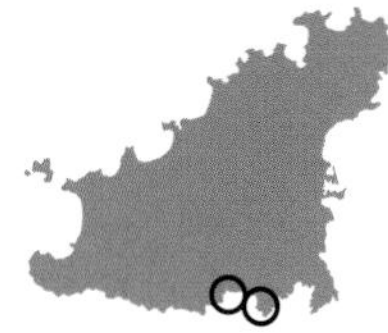

Above
John Torode is the only surviving boat owner at La Moye

Left
Petit Bot as seen from the water

Overleaf
The old Dingle's Hotel at the foot of Petit Bot pre-war

PETIT BOT before GERMAN OCCUPATI

ON C.I.

PATH MINDERS

'ARE you prisoners?'

Just one of the questions that has been known to come the way of the people responsible for the upkeep of the island's cliff paths.

'Do you do this voluntarily?' is another gem of an enquiry that has been forced on the ears of Russ Sarre and Kim Wilkinson, two of the most experienced of the States Works Department's eight-strong full-time cliff team.

Russ, 23 years on the cliffs, and Kim, who's been working on them for 10, do not appear to me the sort to be offended by innocent enquiries.

Working there has several pluses, particularly in the summer months, but even though the scenery is undoubtedly stunning and the solitude welcome if you like being tucked away on your own, it is backbreaking enough work to warrant a good hourly rate.

Peter Jackson, the departmental manager, points out that the whole cliff system for which he is responsible is 26-and-a-half miles long.

For management and recording purposes the area is broken down into 26 sections.

Men such as Russ and Kim are some of the most knowledgeable around when it comes to knowing the hidden paths into the lower reaches of this beautiful but highly dangerous stretch of coastline. And when you stare down the face of a 100ft drop you can understand why they would not want to spill the beans on a secret pathway to the stony shores of the south. The Guernsey Press archives are littered with tragic stories of cliff deaths, so why should anyone want to add to the danger? The life of a cliff path worker is more varied than you might imagine.

Apart from the basic path and step maintenance there is the small matter of 260 viewing benches to paint and 91 bird-boxes to look after, as well as run-off gullies to be kept clear and unblocked.

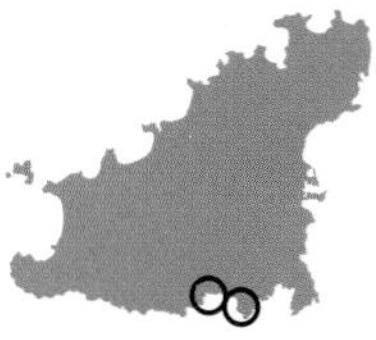

But cutting back the pathways is the most time-consuming job and is tackled from the beginning of May until the end of October.

And you can forget using a strimmer.

'Ninety per cent is done by French hook, purely to protect the environment.

'You can imagine the noise eight men with strimmers would make,' said Peter, adding:

'Anyway, these guys are experienced with hooks and cut a section as quickly with them as doing it with a strimmer'.

The team's core staff of five has nearly 70 years of experience between them, which clearly demonstrates it's not such a nasty job that men run away from it.

Russ loves the quiet it provides.

'The day flies – times goes so quickly,' he adds.

'It's a big garden to look after,' chips in Kim.

They also meet more people than you might imagine.

'A lot are complimentary,' Kim adds.

You certainly need to be fit to do the job.

The steps leading up from the depths of Le Jaonnet are lung-busting and enough to turn knees to jelly. But are they the worst?

The men consider the question.

'The ones up from Saints harbour and at

Above and left
Maintaining the cliff paths is a year-round job for Peter Jackson and his team

Petit Port are very steep with short treads,' says Kim.

'Don't forget Jerbourg, up from the foghorn,' adds Russ.

'There's also the nightmare steps in the Prevote valley ... 100 each side but very steep.'

Such is the remoteness of many areas that popping home for lunch, or down to the nearest shop for fags or a cold drink, is out of the question.

'Everything goes with you for the day,' said Lee.

There is enough versatility in the job that when the weather is at its worst, the gangs can take relative shelter in spots protected from the elements.

But at the height of summer there are times when it is just the opposite. Too much so.

'In some of the valleys it can get very hot It can be up to 8C warmer in the bottom of them,' reckoned Lee.

If there is an irritation, it is the quantities of dog poo they encounter, but generally the men find people polite and appreciative of their work.

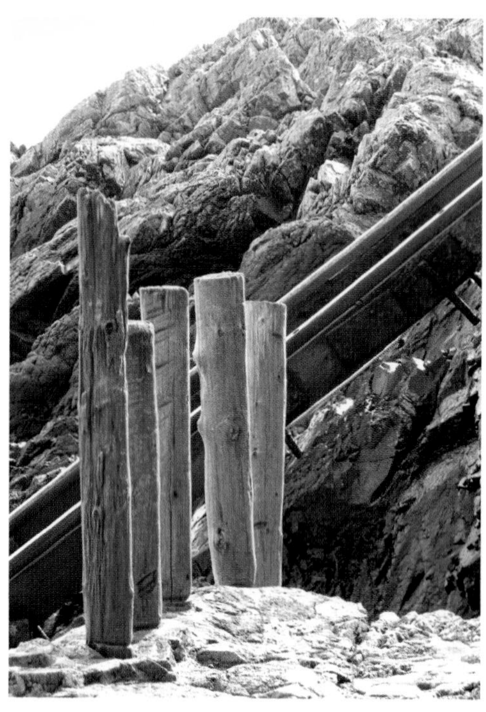

The boss said that history shows no matter how well they maintain paths there are times when erosion wins the day.

'A lot of paths have had to be abandoned and re-directed because they have become unsafe.

'But that's rare. Fermain was the last one, more than 10 years ago.

Right
The final few steps into Le Jaonnet
Top right
'The Skids' at La Moye
Opposite
St Claire Battery at Portelet

DRAMA IN THE VALLEY

HOW green is my valley?

In Petit Bot's case delightfully so, unless there's a big fire about.

And in the case of the tranquil south-coast valley, there have been a few.

To lose one beautifully situated hotel at Petit Bot was a setback.

To lose a second within two years was plain careless.

As vistas went, the one enjoyed by visitors to Dingle's hotel, probably known as Petit Bot Hotel, must have been an impressive one.

Sure, unlike our west-coast hotels it didn't have a glorious sunset to polish off a summer's day and there is no view of the Little Russel, which is always a bonus of staying in one of the big Town hotels, but situated plum next to the beach and with a clear view out to sea, Dingle's two-storey hotel had a lot going for it.

It stood for 20 years.

Dingle is said to have built it amid acrimonious circumstances in 1920.

He had upset the authorities with some illegal quarrying operations, but as a peace offering he built the short stretch of road which, for nearly a century now, has linked the beach exit by the Martello tower and the main road down the valley.

Old photographs show an impressive building with two terraces in a situation to die for, cut into the cliff.

But in about 1940, the hotel was razed by fire and with the Occupation finally behind the island, rather than rebuild it the remnants were demolished and the area was laid out as lawn, with seats for the public.

And that's how you will still find it today.

As an area, Petit Bot has not looked after its prime properties well.

The impressive mills of yesteryear were either partly or completely destroyed and the South View Hotel went up in smoke in the

Top right, bottom right and overleaf
The Bessin family come to terms with the loss of their South View Hotel to fire in 1938

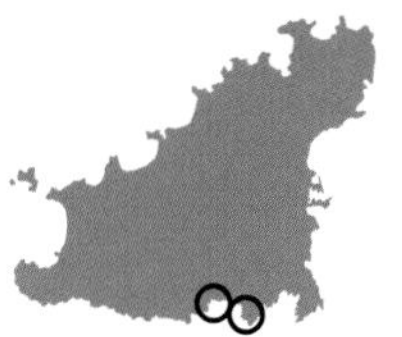

summer of 1938.

The lower mill house was rebuilt after the Occupation and today houses the tearoom, Las Tapitas.

South View might have been an ideal name for the hotel next to the beach, but in fact it was situated much further up the valley, just down and across from the Manor Hotel.

Despite its name, the view must have been much less impressive in comparison with its rival establishment down the valley.

Also two storeys high, it had been built by Frenchman Rene Bessin only five years earlier.

The top floor was either wooden or asbestos.

Mr Bessin, a builder, left his wife Mary to run the hotel, but in late July 1938 it is thought she left the cooker on while she visited her mother next door and the place went up in flames.

In not much more than half-an-hour, the 17 residents and the Bessins lost everything.

The Fire Brigade was acclaimed for doing a superb job and its alert work prevented the next door property, Kermarten, from meeting a similar fate.

There was sufficient sympathy from locals to set up a fund to help the unfortunate holiday-makers and the neighbourly hotels stepped in to put a roof over their heads.

Seventy years on, a fine open market property stands on the site where South View offered the Bessins a living.

Mrs Bessin, a relative recalled, was left with just the dress she was wearing and when war broke out she took her two children, Margaret and Basil, to the UK.

Husband Rene remained here and lived among the ruins of the hotel's first floor.

They were reunited to run a guest house in New Road, St Sampson's, after the war.

"It [the restored Battery Dollman] has been a labour of love and certainly not a money-making scheme"

Ian Brehaut

CHAPTER 24

LE GOUFFRE
CREUX MAHIE & PLEINMONT POINT

Deep and dangerous cliffs lurk beneath the cliff paths between the scene of a once popular old coastal hotel and the south-west tip of the island.

TOWER HAMLET · TRACKING HISTORY · FIELD WORK
COUNTESS PLUNGES · PARISH PUMPS · ROCKING THE BOAT

TOWER HAMLET

WE LIKE to consider ourselves more English than French.

But the maps of Guernsey, from the very earliest to the modern-day Perry's Guide, occasionally suggest the opposite, and that is certainly the case at our most south-westerly point.

Pleinmont has not always been known as that. Back in the 16th and 17th centuries, it was Plymouth.

And along the south coast you might come across Corby, which in time became Corbiere.

But by the mid 18th century, the island maps showed Guernsey becoming altogether less English.

Plymouth became Plein [the French expression for open air] Mont and, in time, Pleinmont – the name we have long used for the point at the tip of Torteval.

It remains a pretty bare place, but atop the cliffs, where the motocross community has developed a racetrack at nearby Rue de la Trigale, there is rarely a shortage of open air.

Too often on race days, the air comes at you as quickly as the fastest of the motorbikes hurtling around the track.

The area is as exposed as any in the island.

But there is much more to this stretch of coastline than meets the eye.

There is plenty of history out west, but much of it belongs to the distant past, most recently, of course, involving Adolf's men, whose concrete legacy is nowhere more prominent than on the Pleinmont headland.

The island's older generation will no doubt – and with good reason – wish the German fortifications had never been built.

But 64 years after the Occupation ended, things just would not look the same without some of the giant towers.

They are 'must-see' structures for tourists, but there is little doubt that Guernsey's authorities a long time ago missed a trick in making a real attraction of the visual proof of the gloomiest period in the island's history.

Thankfully, others have not given up on what is a key element of the island's relatively recent history.

Festung Guernsey, Richard Heaume, Guernsey Armouries and The Occupation Society work to their own agendas, but collectively they are preserving structures along our coastline.

Ian Brehaut has spent countless hours over many years working between Festung and Guernsey Armouries, the latter being responsible for the nearly completed restoration of Battery Dollman, which peers out towards the Hanois.

For the past 12 years, he and a small group of colleagues from Guernsey Armouries have spent much of their spare time restoring the battery, which was entirely covered shortly after the war by spoil transported from Best's quarry in St Andrew's.

'We started on the site in 1997,' said Ian, ever present in a fluctuating group of helpers.

'There's been a hardcore of five, I suppose. Apart from me, there is Dave Malledent, Tony Froome, Paul Gaudion and Mick Lanyon.

'It's a hobby that's become a passion – if not an out-of-control one.' Twelve years on, the restoration job is all but done, with only one bunker, comprising two rooms, still to be completed.

'We will probably make a start in the spring,' said Ian.

'We've still got a couple of years up here and the maintenance [of the site] is ongoing.'

It was back in 1997 that the Guernsey Armouries group selected gun pit no. 3 to be resurrected as an example of a German coastal artillery battery.

After negotiations to secure a lease on the site and get permission from the relevant authorities, work began on excavating the back-filled trenches and pit.

All told, 1,000 tons of spoil were removed, many of those by hand.

Opposite
Paul Gaudion and Mick Lanyon having a blast at the restored Battery Dollman

Overleaf
L'Angle German observation tower looks down from the cliffs at Pleinmont

The steelwork was shotblasted and repainted, the original wiring in the bunkers replaced and the walls repainted.

On top, with tips from a local Occupation survivor, who had at one time been forced into working for the Germans, the restorers relaid the camouflage of chicken wire with wood-packing straw dipped in cement.

'It's been a labour of love and certainly not a money-making scheme,' Ian said of a group who plan two or three open days in the summer, when they will fire a blank charge from the huge cannon rescued from the foot of Les Landes cliffs in Jersey.

'All the German heavy artillery was dumped over the cliffs there, whereas in Guernsey all ours went for scrap.'

Indeed, the 1948 States initiative Operation Coastal Cleanup resulted in 10 lorries being utilised for three months to fill an estimated five miles of trenches, bunkers and associated works on the various Pleinmont batteries.

TRACKING HISTORY

TWENTY-FIVE years of motocross at Rue de la Trigale, Pleinmont, was celebrated last weekend.

And as the Guernsey Kart and Motor Club's 25th championship season gets under way this coming one, members can reflect on a satisfying quarter-of-a-century of operating on the headland.

The club, which has now bought the land, still yearns for more opportunity to race there, but at least it can operate on a measured basis, which is more than can be said for the instigators of banger racing in Guernsey.

Before the scramblers came along, the autocross club pushed hard for its own race track at Pleinmont, only to be thwarted at every attempt and being forced to switch its attention to Chouet.

Today's circuit is longer and more technical than the original and, of course, if the spectators ever get bored with the racing, there is always the view.

Below
Much work has been done to carve out a motocross track above Pleinmont
Right
The building of the Dollman Battery

FIELD WORK

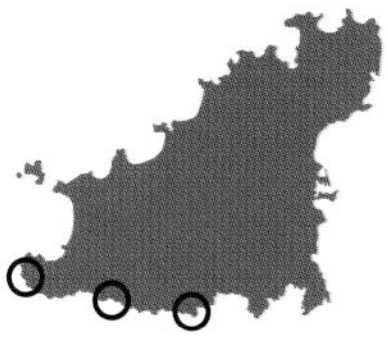

BACK in 1941 the fields off Rue de la Trigale were a mish-mash of site offices, workshops and a mess for the men who were building the four batteries in the Pleinmont area.

Labour comprised many continental civilian tradesmen and labourers, both volunteers and enforced. Some locals, such as the man responsible for the chicken wire camouflaging, were also employed.

After the survey work, deep pits were dug for the gun emplacements, reserve ammunition bunkers and personnel shelters.

The ground was kept for landscaping or simply thrown off the cliffs.

The main gun at Battery Dollman could hit targets 15 kilometres away and through a 360-degree field of fire.

But directing these large, 22cm K532f weapons was another matter and to solve that little headache a series of multistory Marinepeilstaden und Messstellen (naval direction and range-finding positions), known as MP towers, were planned.

One of them – MP4 – stares down over the renowned Le Tas de Pois d'Aval (Gull Rock), the other – MP3 – towards the Hanois and across Rocquaine.

COUNTESS PLUNGES

BLAME it on the Occupation if you like, but Le Gouffre is not what it was.

The sartorial splendour of the place in the late 19th century and early 20th ended when the occupying forces chose to ransack the once popular hotel that stood at the head of the valley.

It's said the compensation for ravaging the three- and four-storey building never amounted to enough to permit a like-for-like rebuild and on its site now stands the cafe we know as L'Escalier, formerly The Hollows.

Le Gouffre's history was always of great interest to Babis Kalamis when he and his late wife, Cathy, ran The Hollows.

Now at The Rowan Tree on Glategny Esplanade, Babis still talks enthusiastically about Le Gouffre, one of the four Forest valleys – the others being Le Bigard, Les Fontenelles and Petit Bot – which run toward the south coast cliffs.

Babis's recollection of Le Gouffre folklore includes a prosperous hotel in the late 19th century and a watercress farm up the valley – a clear indication of how clean the water is around those parts.

'Even in the worst droughts, the springs were very active,' said the former Hollows restaurateur.

A century ago stables stood across the way from the hotel.

Today, the building that housed them is the home of the Clifftop Shop.

Walk east around the cliff path and you quickly come to a low wall at La Moye Point, where once the fishermen of the parish loaded their carts, having hauled their catch from the beach below.

Stare south towards the horizon and if the visibility is good, you will pick out the towering Roches Douvres lighthouse, its 58m. tower shrunk to a fraction of an inch by the intervening 20 nautical miles.

Right
Le Gouffre, with its old hotel, c.1900

Legend has it that a woman was once blown off the cliffs to her death at Le Gouffre.

The stretch of cliffs westwards towards Pleinmont and the Tas de Pois d'Aval – the official end of the south coast and the curve to the north – is far less frequented than those at the eastern end of the island, but they are no less attractive.

Fewer people mean fewer attempts are made to climb the precipices and the number of cliff rescues there is far lower than at the bays at the other end of the southern stretch.

But there is one infamous incident that claimed the life of a young countess.

In early August 1954, 19-year-old Irene

Countess Blucher from Austria decided to take a break from her holiday sojourn at Havilland Hall and climb the 300ft cliff above Belle Elizabeth Bay at Pleinmont, near the Mont Herault watchhouse.

Her brother Nicholas, a far more accomplished mountaineer, accompanied her, but at around three o'clock that Sunday afternoon, as she followed him up a 60ft crag, the Countess became stuck, unable to go up or down.

In an attempt to move, she grabbed a piece of rock on the crumbly cliff face, made worse, ironically, by the Germans during the Occupation.

The countess fell 60ft to the beach and despite a mercy dash by the Flying Christine, she died of severe head injuries as it headed into St Peter Port Harbour.

The cliffs may be steep but back in 1940 the German forces, like the islanders fearful of Napoleon a century earlier, considered them to have vulnerable spots.

One of those was above Havre de Bon Repos and the result was the big, grey, ugly La Prevote Tower.

Swing westwards again and you come to Creux Mahie, which has, at the foot of its cliffs, the largest cave in the island – 200ft long, 40-50ft wide and 20-60ft high.

But by its very situation, it's a cave seen by very few and if Creux Mahie has a reputation at all, it is for what you might sniff in the air rather than what you cast your eyes on.

PARISH PUMPS

CREUX MAHIE Foul Water Pumping Station.

You may or may not have seen it, but if you have walked the cliffs, there is a fair chance you've smelt it.

For 40 years it's taken the processed particles of Guernsey's most south-western parishes – 5-6% of the island's total treated sewage – out of Pleinmont via a 300ft-long underwater pipe out to sea.

The scheme comes to an end this summer and the local rabbits and rats will be left with a more appealing natural fragrance than the normal hydrogen sulphide – aka rotten eggs – blowing in the wind.

Permitted a site visit before its imminent closure, one thing immediately struck me about this operation.

Where on earth is it? It may have been in operation since the summer of 1966, but it is cleverly hidden away.

The dumping point is barely 100m. from the local garage, but the station itself is tucked away down the valley, well out of sight.

At first glance it resembles a tatty bungalow, but as States Works' Nick Nicolle explained, the centre has changed drastically over the years.

Initially the operation came with a purpose-built, granite-faced building on a ledge near the foot of the Creux Mahie cliffs, where two pumps fired water up the cliff to the station up the valley.

That disappeared one long, wet and windy night.

'The pumps, everything, was gone,' said Nick.

Looking at it now, in its final throes of operation, it is difficult to imagine Creux Mahie as a pathfinder.

But back in 1966 it was the first electrolytic sewage-treatment plant to be opened and run on a commercial basis and the first using elec-

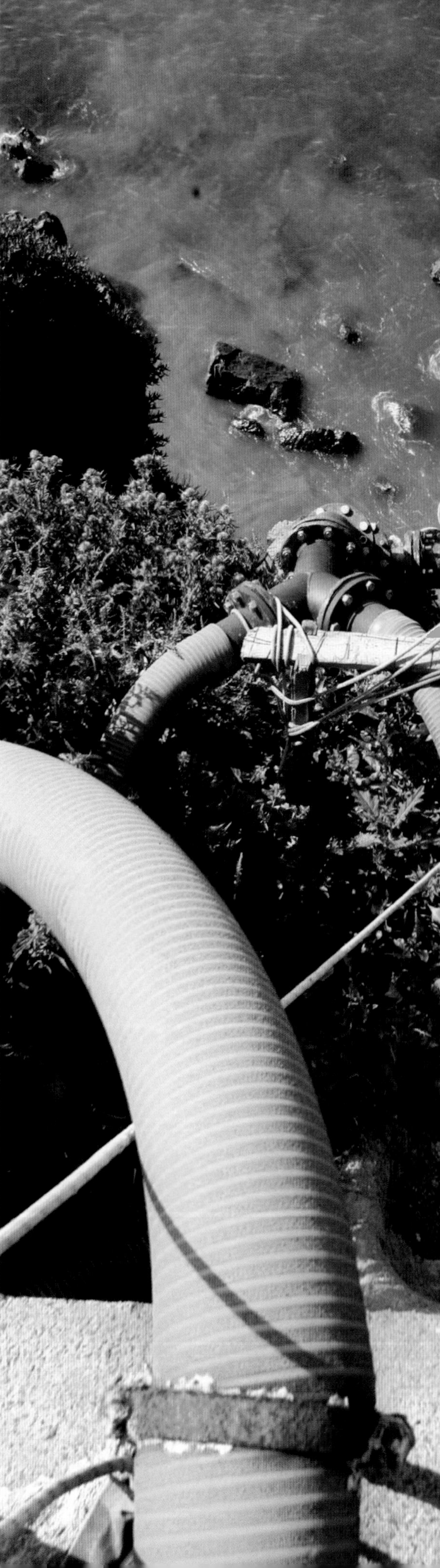

Right
The Creux Mahie foul-water pipes
Far right
The fishermen's road from La Moye to Le Gouffre

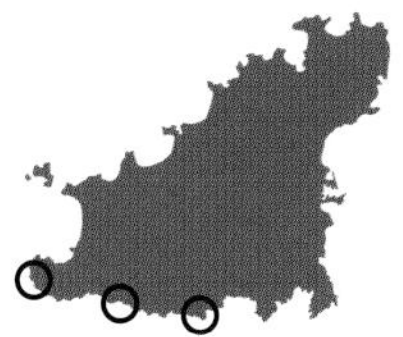

trolysed seawater in the United Kingdom.

All at the cost of £95,000.

Forty years on, it is one of the smallest of the island's 65 pumping stations and, for that reason, won't be missed.

As Nick explained, the sewage process system, here and elsewhere, has to cope with much more than the obvious.

We know it can rain cats and dogs, but it can also process cats and dogs.

'You name it, we've had it,' said Nick, in reply to a question about the effectiveness of the macerators against less-than-natural wastes.

'The odd cat or dog has found its way in. Belle Greve is a popular one for cats.

'We pulled out an exhaust system once at the old Cobo sewer under the mound by the Cobo beach kiosk.' Creux Mahie won't disappear altogether when the operation grinds to a halt this year.

The tatty bungalow – which, if it ever goes on the housing market, should attract decent offers given its solitude and vista – will stay untouched in case of emergency.

The associated pipework will be kept, too, but to all intents and purposes, the Creux Mahie plant has served its time.

ROCKING THE BOAT

SAINTS BAY had the President Garcia.

And Le Gouffre, or, to be more precise, the rocks of Fond du Valle off the end of the Bigard Valley, had its own unexpected night arrival, 54 years earlier.

Admittedly the French Dundee rigged vessel, Jeanne, was a less spectacular sight than the copra carrying cargo ship which parked itself at Saints, but it was big news in early May of 1913 when fog was a pest for all in the English Channel.

The Jeanne was heading from a Spanish port to Dunkirk with a cargo of bar zinc.

For nearly two days, the ship had drifted in dense fog and with no sun to make observations, all bearings were lost.

As soon as the captain heard the sudden cry of 'land ahead', he endeavoured to turn the little vessel, but a strong tide, aided by the wind, drove her over some rocks, which left her absolutely cradled as though in a graving dock made for her.

The Jeanne's bowsprit almost touched the precipitous cliffs just half a mile to the west of Le Gouffre.

Her back was broken and she had a slight list to port.

The crew, comprising the captain, mate, two hands and a lad, stepped on to the rocks below Le Bigard and remained there all night, with not a clue as to where they were.

Were they on a small, isolated rock or on some mainland – or on one of the larger islands of the archipelago of the Bay of Avranches?

But at about five o'clock the following morning, the crew heard the welcome sound

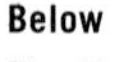

Below
The Fond du Valle rocks at the end of the Bigard Valley

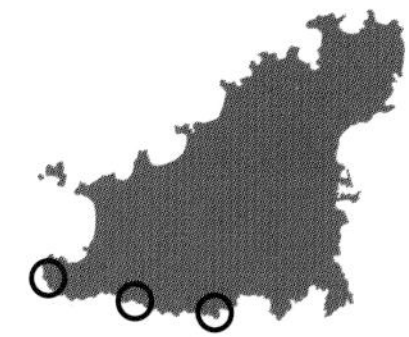

of a cock crowing and knew they were near habitation.

Encouraged, Captain Le Quillec, with one of the hands, managed to scale the dangerous cliff and, guided by the voice of chanticleer, made for the house of a Mr Gorvel, across gorse, cliff and potato patches.

The Frenchmen were walking straight across the latter when Mr Gorvel first saw them and learned of the disaster that had occurred on the coastal stretch immediately beneath the site of his dwelling.

Information as to the ship's whereabouts was given in exchange for details of the wreck and the Jeanne men departed, delighted to know that not only were they on an inhabited land, but that a French consul lived in Guernsey.

Later that day, Le Quillec returned to the Gorvels and asked how he could communicate with his consul, who by now should be awake.

Mrs Gorvel, a Jerseywoman, at once offered to send her son, Francis, a smart lad of eight, to show the path to Le Gouffre Hotel, half a mile or more to the east.

While Francis dressed, Mrs Gorvel made tea, which was very welcome, the captain having been chilled to the bone after a long night on the rocks in the cold and fog.

He and a colleague were offered food as well but would have nothing but the refreshing tea before departing in search of the consul.

Arriving at Le Gouffre, Captain Le Quillec at once informed Baron de Coudenhove, who lived at La Falaise above Petit Bot, of the wreck and of his men's condition.

Later, the consul arrived and was given all the details before heading to Town and despatching telegrams to the proper quarters.

The vessel was French-owned, Captain La Quillec being one of the owners, and insured with a French insurance society, which was just as well, given that it was seemingly beyond repair.

Above
The Jeanne goes aground at the Fond du Valle in 1913

During the morning, the Lt- Governor heard of the disaster and, as the Guernsey Evening Press reported, 'with that consideration for others which characterises him', at once telephoned for particulars to Mr J. W. Lucas, the senior constable of the Forest.

He also requested that Mr Lucas see that the crew and ship were duly protected and looked after.

The Lt-Governor visited the scene the same evening and interviewed the constable, Captain Le Quillec and a Mr Richards of Le Gouffre Hotel, who was told that any food required should be supplied to the crew.

The captain explained that delays caused by the fog had meant they had run short of provisions and there would be barely enough fresh food for another day.

During the night, the crew made themselves as comfortable as they could on hammocks on the rocks, watching to see that no one interfered with the little vessel and its contents, which, a week or so later, went up for auction.

The sale, conducted by W. W. Fuzzey, was held on the cliffs above the rocks but quite what happened to the broken ketch does not appear to have been recorded.

"The farthest the water would come up the Hanois was spray at the kitchen window [level six]. That was with a north-westerly"

Gordon Brown

CHAPTER 25

HANOIS
& ROCQUAINE BAY

Land's End to islanders and until the lighthouse arrived in the late 19th century, a watery deathbed for hundreds of stray seamen. Onshore, this quiet corner of Guernsey remains a draw to holidaymakers and locals alike.

MISTY-EYED · TOWER OF STRENGTH
MUSSELING IN · A REASON TO CELEBRATE
THE DRIFTERS · ALL AT SEA

MISTY-EYED MEMORIES

AN HOUR after the spring high tide and the power of the sea is such that salty froth is everywhere at Pezeries point.

Propelled by gales only marginally weaker than the hurricane-force winds that hit the island 10 days ago, the froth is driven up narrow gullies in the splintered granite rock or, elsewhere, flies through the air 100 metres and beyond.

It is both spectacular and a reminder of the power of the sea where Guernsey's south coast meets the west.

Only a mile or so away, the Hanois reef is swallowed by massive rollers, the 33m tower alone against the force of nature.

Along the coast in Rocquaine Bay the coastal wall has crumbled for the first time in many years and the road is like a bombsite.

But whether it is against the power of nature or modern development and new ways, Rocquaine fares better than most and a strong case could be made to suggest it is the least altered part of our wonderful west coast.

Over the last 200 years, Rocquaine has won and lost.

The building of the Hanois was a victory for hundreds of seamen who no doubt would have perished without guidance from Trinity House.

Another significant victory was the saving of our beloved Cup and Saucer, known otherwise as Chateau de Rocquaine, Rocquaine Castle or Fort Grey.

Built in 1804 to bolster sea defences under threat from those nasty Frenchmen, it was splendidly restored in 1976 and turned into one of our leading tourist attractions.

But had individual entrepreneurs had their way, it could have been lost to visitors and islanders and developed for private use.

About 40 years ago there was a threat that a Mr W. D. L. Theed would develop the castle into a super-home.

Plans for a two-storey open market development were drawn up but thankfully thrown out by the Island Development Committee in December 1969 and the authorities vowed to renovate it into a 'gem of the west' tourist attraction.

Perhaps the biggest decision to affect the area came in the late part of the 19th century when the States gave the thumbs down to detailed plans for a harbour at Portelet, which would have altogether altered what we see at the quiet and quaint little bay beneath the gaze of the Trinity House cottages.

Much like the ultimately disregarded plans to build a huge breakwater at Fermain in the mid 1800s, had the Portelet proposals gone ahead – and they were very serious ones – they would have had a profound effect on the area.

The Billet of November 1877 copied a letter from the States Surveyor's office to accompany detailed plans drawn up with the input of pilots, fishermen and 'others on the spot'.

'The pier to start from the point of land under the rock called La Varde and to be carried in northeasterly direction for a distance of 380ft when it would return in an easterly direction for a distance of 2,130ft, this return to be at extreme low water of equinoctial spring tides.'

The pier, it stated, would be 30ft wide at quay level and should have strong walls bound together by cross-walls every 30 feet.

The outer one was supposed to have had a parapet and the quay, comprising stone rubble, would be paved.

Had it gone ahead, it would have cost around £8,600.

The surveyor also produced an alternative pier running 190ft further north, which would be built into about five feet of water at low water of the equinoctial spring tide.

All for just another £1,400.

Right
The proposed Portelet harbour would have been more than 2,500ft in length
Overleaf
Perfectly Portelet

Behind the plans was the expanding quarrying industry, but ultimately the plans were left to gather dust and we were left with a petite pier inside Portelet that is often underwater.

At the top of the beach above a short granite slipway is the former oil store built out of Cornish stone by Trinity House.

Purpose built, it has long been of little use and plans to turn it into a small residence have got nowhere.

Richard Tostevin, who lives around the corner from the Imperial Hotel, sold it by auction to Tom Scott after being frustrated in his hopes to make something out of nothing in the modern world.

These days the narrow road to the point is closed off to general traffic and the heavily wooded headland above is difficult to equate to late 19th century images of a barren area behind and to the west of the Trinity House cottages.

Vehicle access was, though, still permitted in March 1971 when a production crew arrived to film one of the final episodes of the long running British television science fiction anthology drama series, Out of the Unknown.

Spread over four series, Pleinmont was utilised for one of the very last episodes to appear on national screens.

Entitled The Last Witness, the murder yarn starred nobody of great fame and told the story of a man waking up in a hotel bedroom after being washed up on the nearby beach.

Among the cast, and the only local credited as being an official member of it, was Milton Brehaut, who played the part of a bus driver.

'I actually saw it on TV and it was on again a few years ago. Somewhere, I've got the original cheque from the BBC and never cashed it.'

Of the 49 episodes of Out of the Unknown that were made, only 20 survive in their entirety, mainly from season one.

It is understood only 33 seconds of the Guernsey episode remains.

Even 40 years ago, Pleinmont was an entirely different world from the halcyon days of the mackerel drifters and the fishermen's cottages ringing Rocquaine Bay.

It was not, after all, so long ago that the principal spoken language of the area would have been patois and virtually every property around the bay was the home of a good old 'Guern', many of them with strong fishing connections.

That no longer applies. But the beauty remains.

TOWER OF STRENGTH

HE SHARES his name with the current British Prime Minister but for the moment, Guernsey's Gordon Brown has one thing the PM has not – an MBE.

And while the Scot is better versed in running a national treasury, the Sarnian knows far more about lighthouses.

It was for services to Trinity House that Guernsey's most eminent lighthouse keeper was officially recognised by Her Majesty in February 1994, nearly a full 12 months before the born-and-bred Sarnian stepped ashore from lonely lighthouse duty for the very last time.

Nowadays, his room with a view is at his quaint old Guernsey house overlooking Bordeaux, but for 39-and-a-half years the view was one of unremitting seas from some of the most famous and notorious lighthouses in the Trinity House chain: towers such as Longships, Bishop's Rock, the Smalls and Lundy Island, not to mention closer to home on the Casquets

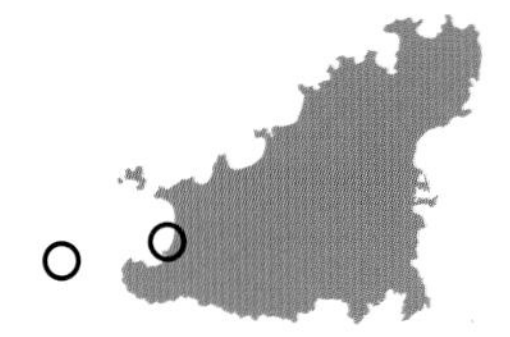

and just a mile or so off the south-west tip of Guernsey, the Hanois.

Gordon spent a five-year stint serving at Guernsey's south west tower from 1959 to 1964 and then became head keeper in 1975 before he headed off for spells in Sark and the Casquets.

In keeper's terms, the Hanois was a doddle when compared with the likes of the Smalls, 18 miles off the Pembrokeshire coast, and Bishop's Rock, four miles west of the Isles of Scilly.

'The advantage of the Hanois is you had very little overdue,' said Gordon.

'The most we ever had was five days.' Overdue is when bad weather prevents the keepers enjoying a well-earned one-month reconnection with everyday community life after two lonely months out at sea.

'On the ones off Cornwall you can get loads of overdue. Once we had three months. We went out in November and came off in February.'

The fear of acute loneliness was never a problem to the qualified electrician, who was working as an engineer in the Army when the possibility of a whole new career was suggested to him.

'I was lying in the wing of a Vulcan bomber when one of the lads [reading a paper] said, "Here's a good job for you. Lighthouse keepers wanted".

In no time he had talked the subject over with his wife, Margery, whose immediate concerns were how it might affect the bringing up of their two young children.

But off he went to an interview at Holyhead, got the job and after lengthy training (22 months) began to sample the solitude of life in houses off the Cornish coast.

There were spells, too, in land stations, but after just three years in the job and short stints on the Smalls and Longships, he got his first posting to the Hanois.

As with all lighthouse postings, he was one of three men.

Taken to the rock by George Le Couteur, who for many years acted as handling agent for the lighthouse, the stints were always two months on, one off on the nine-level tower.

So what was life like at the Hanois?

'The bedroom [level seven] contained four bunks, which came around in the shape of the tower.

Left
Tripping the light fantastic: Gordon Brown overlooks his former temporary home on the Hanois

'In the kitchen [level six] you had a small table by the window. But you couldn't swing a cat in there. It would have hit the walls.

'We also had an old Guernsey range.'

Apart from the general supplies, each man had his own meat stored in paraffin-powered fridges.

There was no phone, no television.

Watches were divided into three.

The morning one was four to midday, the afternoon noon to eight.

The man on the early morning stint would return for the eight to midnight spell and the midnight to 4am watch was in the hands of the man who had been on duty all afternoon and early evening.

On duty, the men did their best to keep themselves busy with regular tasks.

'You'd clean the kitchen, wash down the stairs and every couple of hours you would wind the lens up and check the light.

'Once the light was out, you cleaned the burner and the lamp, replenished the paraffin tanks, cleaned the brass.'

'You just did the jobs to keep yourself occupied.'

There was always one with 24 hours off, filling in more time in a place where the clocks seem to tick slower than anywhere else.

Gordon's utilisation of non-working time was varied.

'I used to do quite a bit of fishing or go cricking for crabs.

'There were always passing boats with local fishermen too.'

Fishing off Les Hanois was always rewarding, he recalls.

'Plenty of pollack, but you could never catch mackerel.

'We'd get those from the fishermen who would throw them to us.' Making model boats was another of his pastimes, as was playing

Above right and below right
Inside and out on the Hanois

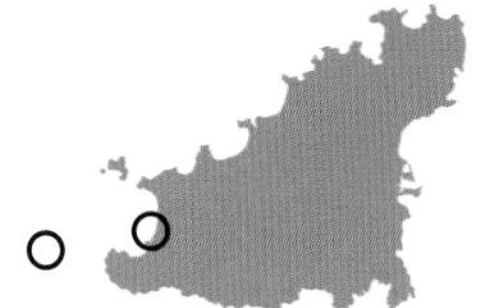

chess or crib.

And while there was no more an idyllic spot than Les Hanois on a low tide on a hot summer afternoon, it could also provide some wild and dark nights.

'The farthest the water would come up the Hanois was spray at the kitchen window. That was with a north westerly.

'But normally you could get down to the entrance doors at low water.'

Such relative calm was not the case at Longships, 1.25 miles off Land's End.

There 'the green water would come halfway up the tower'.

Lying in his bunk at night, he would hear a resounding thump as the seas struck the tower.

'The ones off Cornwall is where you had most of the bad weather and on those you did not know when you'd get off.

'For a fortnight you might have the sea going over the top.'

Normally, Margery could contact her husband with semaphore flags from their Trinity House home, looking down from the point at Land's End, but such was the deterioration in conditions one day she allowed herself to be momentarily spooked.

'The new vicar phoned to say the lighthouse had gone. "It's gone, it's gone," he said. I thought, oh no. But it was only a squall.'

Margery, oozing pride in her husband's career, described the Trinity House years as 'a wonderful life'.

'You lived off some of the most magnificent rocks in the country.'

The downsides included being parted for key dates in the calendar, including Christmas and New Year.

Remarkably, Gordon went nine years without a Christmas ashore.

'The last one I spent at Longships I cooked on

Christmas Day and we were short of supplies.

'We had just eight potatoes left.

I did a cottage pie and a Christmas pudding out of suet, which had cocoa in it.' After 13 years of retirement he still regards his spells at Longships as his favourite, although he admits Les Hanois had one advantage.

'It wasn't often you couldn't get out onto the landing.'

But the latter was the tower from which he required his own emergency rescue.

That was in November 1961 when, while working on the lantern, the handle of the manual winding mechanism sprung back in his face, badly lacerating his lip and giving him suspected concussion.

The accident occurred in the middle of the night and his two colleagues quickly decided he needed medical attention.

A radio telephone call was put through to St Peter Port signal station and having discussed the situation with Dr J. Garrett, it was decided to evacuate the patient.

That was not to happen until midday, George Le Couteur advising that it could not possibly be undertaken until the tide had gone down.

Far worse fates have befallen keepers around the Trinity House chain.

In showing off one of his favourite framed pictures of notorious towers, he tells the tale of a chap called Nichols falling to his death while cleaning the lantern on the Longships rock.

Fourteen others, he says, have been simply washed away by the sea.

The Smalls has its own spooky tale, which brought about a change in lighthouse policy in 1801 after a gruesome episode.

Right
Whipping up a storm off Guernsey's major lighthouse
Below
A more settled scene from Rocquaine with the Hanois in the distance

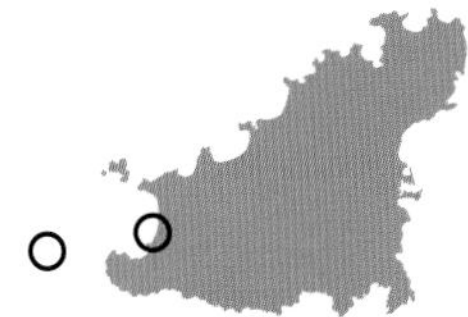

The two-man team Thomas Howell and Thomas Griffith were known to quarrel and when Griffith died in a freak accident, Howell feared that he might be suspected of murder if he discarded the body into the sea.

As the body began to decompose, Howell built a makeshift coffin for the corpse and lashed it to an outside shelf.

But stiff winds blew the box apart and the body was fixed in a macabre, beckoning pose.

By the time the usual service boat arrived, several months later, Howell was apparently white-haired and driven mad.

Thereafter lighthouse teams were changed to rosters of three until the automation of all British lighthouses in the 1980s.

MUSSELING IN

THEY couldn't farm the sea, so they have brought the sea to them.

That's the strange but oddly successful story of Torteval's newest and potentially biggest ever sea farmers, Lucy Kirby and Peter Witham.

From an old farmhouse storage shed at least half-a-mile from Rocquaine Bay, the couple are farming 200 kilos of juicy Bouchot mussels each week and it could be as many as 800 by the height of the summer.

The enterprise has been running for nearly four months and so well has the business developed it seems an obvious contender for the local version of Dragon's Den.

Under the banner Rocquaine Seafarms, pony-tailed Peter and the red-haired art and photography teacher at Ladies' College have stumbled across a potentially lucrative entrepreneurial venture that is attracting great interest from more and more local restaurants.

Right and far right
Peter Witham and Lucy Kirby have built a successful mussel-farming business at Rocquaine

'I've always wanted to run my own business and secondly we liked the idea of doing something which involves you in the community,' said Lucy.

Unable to farm out of the bay, the fledgling sea farmers grow the mussels in seawater drawn from it and tractored up the hill to fill four large blue tanks, which could also house cockles and oysters.

And when the water has done its job, it is returned cleaner than ever to Rocquaine due to the Defra-approved depuration system.

Everyone's a winner.

In a nutshell, the Rocquaine operation is a holding system, which replicates the sea.

'Only ours is a hell of a lot cleaner,' said Peter.

'We only go for top-quality mussels,' explained Lucy.

'They have, on average, 45% meat content. Every mussel is absolutely full, none of this all-shell-and-no-meat,' she added.

'We searched hard for suppliers and only deal with those with that level of meat content.' The joy of this backyard aquaculture is summed up nicely by Peter.

'We're not influenced by bad weather, storms or pollution.

As long as we can collect our water.

'These systems are the way it is going in the UK. It's more efficient and we are not held back by tides.'

And restaurateurs are voting with their fingers, dialling up for more supplies at all hours of the day and night.

'It really is starting to take off,' said Lucy.

'The Deerhound is taking six times as many as it was before.'

The couple are grateful for the support of parishioners, in particular veteran sea farmer Richard Tostevin, who has encouraged them

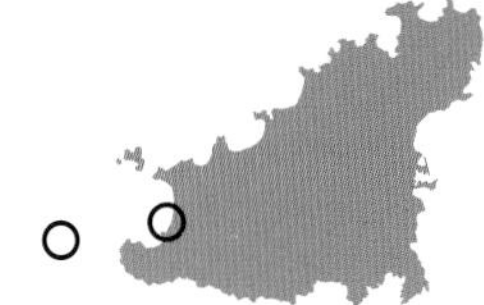

ensure it runs smoothly, seven days a week.

'It was a huge ask for us,' says Lucy.

'Sea farming takes over your life. It takes up so much time, but it's been worth it.'

Bivalve molluscs such as the mussels reared by Rocquaine Seafarms are filter feeders, extracting food from the water around them.

Purification involves the transfer of the mussels from the harvesting area into purpose-built indoor tanks containing clean seawater brought straight from Rocquaine beach.

Here they continue filtration and normal digestive activity and over a period of about two days purge themselves of any bacterial contamination present.

The system loading and water flow conditions must be such that sufficient clean seawater of the correct quality, temperature and dissolved oxygen level is circulated to all the mussels within it.

all the way.

'Richard has been absolutely wonderful. He has mentored us all the way through to where we are now.

'He was the first person to get to try them. We're incredibly grateful to the parish as a whole.'

The idea was conceived early in 2007 and it took many months to get the business up and running.

They identified a gap in the market for top-end mussels and bought the Bailiwick's only mollusc purification operation.

Once the live mussels have been shipped in from Brixham, they are put into the Torteval tanks and over 48 hours any impurities, such as sand and bacteria, are removed.

The system doubles up as a holding facility.

It's a full-on operation and with Lucy a full-time teacher, the pressure is on Peter to

A REASON TO CELEBRATE

ONE HUNDRED years old in two summers' time, the Rocquaine Regatta is the last bay-community celebration that remains as part of Guernsey heritage.

Not that it has been plain sailing and without interruption.

After making its debut appearance in the summer of 1910, it was suspended through the Great War and on its resumption appeared only every other year until 1928 when, in the words of current regatta secretary Hugh Lenfestey, it 'more or less expired'.

'One of the main problems was fund-raising,' said the former States archivist, who has served the event since 1972 and from the following summer has been its secretary.

But for 43 summers either side of the Occupation it simply did not happen, other than an attempt by early organisers, men such as George Le Couteur and George Paint, to revive it in 1948.

Back in 1910, the regatta comprised mainly sailing boat events. Face painting, tug-of-war, five-a- side football, beauty contests, sand castle competitions and live bands were the property of future generations.

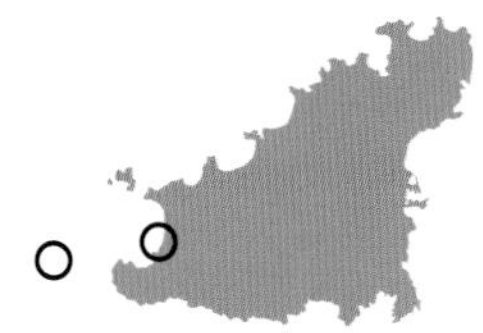

This was an era of mackerel drifters and other sailed fishing boats.

The comparisons can be extended to the ever-popular greasy pole competitions.

In the early days, they were conducted off the bowsprit of the old sailing ships.

'You have to have a fairly large vessel for that,' says Hugh, adding: 'Now the pole is covered with soft soap rather than grease.

It is also done on the sand with mats rather than the sea below.'

John Andrew Le Couteur and Tom Brouard were the two men most responsible for the regatta's modern revival, the Le Couteur name a link to the very early days.

Asked why he has remained event secretary so long, Hugh responds: 'It's continuity, that's all.'

Today's regatta committee comprises a healthy group of 20 and last year it became a company, limited by guarantee.

'It protects members to a certain degree,' says Hugh, who plainly loves the involvement.

'It's special because it is happening locally. Apart from the regatta, the West Show and now the Torteval scarecrows, nothing else happens out west.'

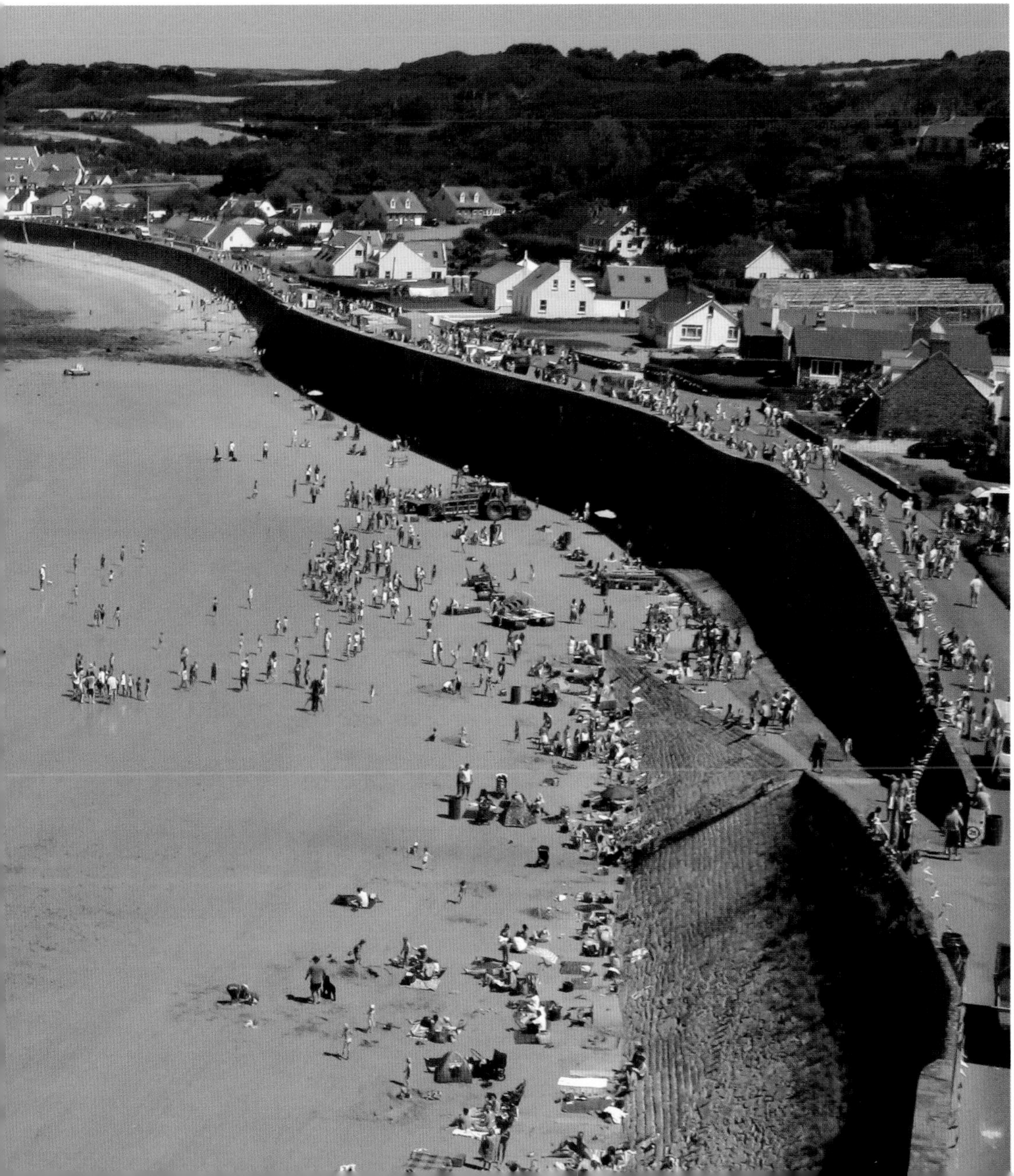

Left
Summertime at Rocquaine

THE DRIFTERS

FOR 60 years spanning the latter part of the 19th century and the early decades of the 20th, mackerel fishing dominated the everyday summer lives of Rocquaineers.

Catching onto the initiative of the Cornish fishermen who saw our shores so yielding, the mackerel drifters largely fished out of Rocquaine and as far north as Vazon.

At the centre of it were the Le Couteurs, who not only built drifters from their base at Alderbaran at the bottom of Le Coudre, just a stone's throw from Fort Grey, but dominated the fishing workforce.

At one time 24 drifters, each containing up to six men, worked the west coast, scooping up tons of the copiously available shoals of mackerel and pilchards.

Generally considered to have been started by the family, who hailed from Jersey but had moved here as wholesale merchants in the 1830s, two brothers, Edmund and George, spotted the business opportunities.

Edmund had the business head and George was the skipper who went to sea with their fleet of 9-10 boats, many of which were built in the Alderbaran yard, where an old barn, called 'La Halle', stored the tackle required.

The Le Couteurs became suppliers of nets and gear for fishing boats operating from Portelet, north through Crocq du Sud, La Creve, Le Douit de Moullin, Perelle and Vazon.

The drifting season ran, in the main, for 12 weeks from May to August, depending on the mackerel shoals' whereabouts.

The Le Couteurs' boats had their own colours: black on the top, green below the waterline.

They would fish anywhere from between 10 and 25 miles of the south-west tip of the island with nets as long as 1,500 fathoms, pieced together in 30-fathom lengths.

Once ashore and long before refrigeration, the fish would be dried or salted and it was a common sight to see gutted and split-open mackerel hanging on lines all along the west coast or atop thatched roofs.

And while George and Edmund ran the business, a skipper with a propensity for drinking pubs dry built his own reputation on the water.

Tom de Carteret or 'Le p'tit' as he was known in the area, lived at Les Issues cottages and

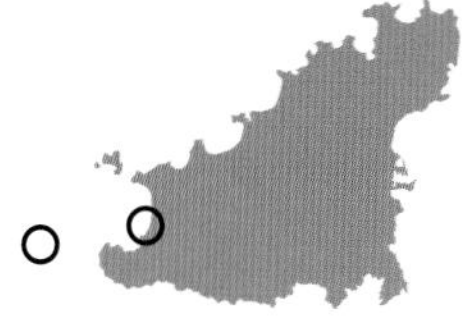

was said to be the ace mariner, when sober.

With a particularly wrinkled face and a love for chewing baccie, he would often have to be dragged from his favourite bar to go out to sea on GU140, Rosalind.

Although its skipper, legend has it he was often so pickled that he had to be tied to the mast for his own safety.

Alderbaran, which also operated as the Rocquaine Commercial Hotel in the 1800s, catering for picnic parties and tourists, remained with the Le Couteur family up until 1986. By then mackerel drifting had long since died.

By the 1920s and the advent of petrol rigs, catches were failing and with the gradual decline of sail it all died a salty death.

The Le Couteurs thereafter concentrating on stonemasonry.

That's a story for another day.

Left
Mackerel drifters would work the coast from May to August in the 19th century

ALL AT SEA OVER ROCQUAINE

MOST of us prefer to simply watch it.

But the sea has been – 'in a nutshell' – Richard Tostevin's life.

Most of Rocquaine's old characters have passed on, leaving the man who lives a mere shot-put from the sea wall and the Imperial's back bar across the road as a link with old times down on the bay.

Not that he's particularly old at 68 and has lived at Pleinmont all his life.

He isn't and hasn't.

It's just under 40 years since he built his own seaside bungalow fit for a fishermen, but since those swinging 60s he has been close to the centre of much that goes on underneath the lounge windows at the Imperial.

He has dived the area, trawled it, ran a hugely successful ormering farm and took on the supply boat duties for the Hanois after the death of George Le Couteur.

'It's my workplace and it means a lot to me. It's my home,' says the man whose talents have now embraced building Romy sail rigs, two of which can be found in his back garden.

And while Guernsey forever changes, Richard refreshingly reports that Rocquaine is doing better than anywhere else in retaining its charm and looks of old.

'It hasn't changed an iota, other than the sand [levels] moving up and down on the beach.

'Portelet has always been my bay,' added Richard, his first introduction to it coming as a toddler on an outing from nearby Forest.

'My first recollection of it was in 1945. I came down as a five-year-old and was fascinated that a heavy, flat-bottomed boat could float in two inches of water.'

The sea has transfixed him ever since.

For years he took from the nearby seas, whether it be as a diver, trawling for scallops or potting for crabs, but he built a reputation for his sea farming on the little beach under the gaze of the old Trinity House cottages.

'Farming ormers was a bit of a learning curve, but we mastered it.'

Its success is both a source of satisfaction and regret to him.

'If we'd done it 20 years earlier it would have been embraced by the Guernsey people and the States [Sea Fisheries].

But it was too late.

'I did that for the best part of 20 years. It started as a hobby and it got more and more serious and we got very good.

'We made it work and viable.'

At its peak his submerged hatchery was yielding so many ormers that there was a need to utilise only half of the 20 x 40ft area.

Twenty-six one-ton rigs each contained 4,000-5,000 ormers, which were sold locally and to the Chinese community in the UK.

And to insure against his farming secrets being lost for good, as were his late mother's technique for making pure white curds, he has them recorded on an hour-long video and manuscripted, 'so the method won't be lost'.

'They [the curds] were perfect. She was taught the old way.

'So the lesson to me is to not to hog it [the information] all to yourself, because eventually it will be lost.'

He has even gone to the trouble of placing an introduction on ormer farming on the web at www.abalonefarming.com.

Nowadays he leaves the sea farming to Lucy Kirby and Peter Witham.

He has afforded the couple every encouragement.

'I think they are doing it very well and it's very professional, the way they are doing things.

'They have improved on what we used to do.'

Opposite
Rocquaine resident Richard Tostevin

"They used to come here on charabancs for lobster teas. The local kids ran behind the charabancs and pleaded 'one penny please sir'"

Hazel Ozard

CHAPTER 26

L'EREE
& LIHOU ISLAND

On land, the modern home of the West Show and Guernsey's first aerodrome. Some had ambitious plans to dominate it with a holiday camp, others just stripped it of huge quantities of sand. Offshore, the delight that is Lihou.

SUN, SEA AND SAND

L'EREE Bay has changed more than most west coast beaches since the Occupation.

But the locals are adamant.

No Guernsey beach receives more sunshine than their beloved stretch of sand.

Whether there are any statistics to back up such a claim I doubt, but indisputably the small drop from road level to beach does allow sunseekers to make the most of the rays from early in the morning until the sun drops over the western horizon.

What cannot be denied is that it is one of the island's smellier beaches.

And while I might say that is a shame for a bay that has gradually lost its island-wide appeal over the 20th century and into the 21st, hotel proprietor Mark Frost would probably use the word, disgrace.

During his 10-year occupancy of the biggest coastal hotel in the area – one that dates back well into the mid 19th century and perhaps longer – he has consistently groaned about the lack of regular beach cleaning.

He is not referring to litter, but the altogether more stinky vraic which gets dumped by the ton by the tides.

The weed may have been welcome and a source of income 100 years ago, but today it is a plain nuisance, keeping holidaymakers and locals off a fine stretch of flat sand.

'It's the nicest beach in the island and what's more, it's a safe beach,' agree old L'Eree friends Una Mortimer and Hazel Ozard.

'But it would be better if the States cleared it more,' adds Una, who, like her 91-year-old, sharp and witty associate Hazel, has lived in the area virtually her whole life.

The vraic situation is a big bone of contention for Mr Frost.

'I have four to five thousand stay in the hotel each year and that [the smell of the vraic] is always among the highest number of

Right
An aerial view of modern day L'Eree with Lihou in the distance

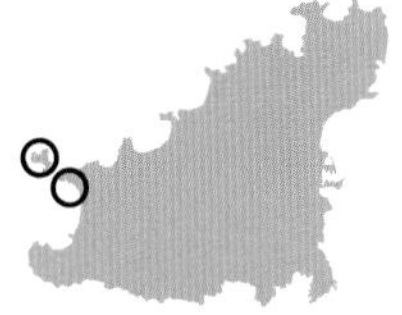

complaints.

'It's been ongoing since I've been here.'

The proprietor can't understand why L'Eree fails to receive the same attention as other west coast beaches, notably Vazon and Cobo.

'It transforms the whole look of the beach when it has been dragged.'

The outfall pipe is not a crowd-puller either.

'As soon as the tourists see the pipe and smell the vraic, they think it's a foul beach.

It is really let down badly.

Old times at L'Eree:
Top
The beach in 1964
before the wall was built
Middle
Plane sailing at the
old aerodrome
Bottom
The L'Eree Hotel in 1867

WHY WE NEED THE WEED

ENVIRONMENT minister David De Lisle said that seaweed is an indicator of a healthy marine habitat.

It reaches maturity during midsummer and is washed off rocks onto the beaches.

L'Eree collects more seaweed during July and August than its neighbours because it lies in a rocky basin which holds it close to the shore.

'Left to its own devices, nature will clean L'Eree at each high spring tide and whenever possible the department's policy is to allow that to happen.'

But clean-ups do take place periodically if a significant strand line is left after spring tides during hot weather.

Deputy De Lisle added that the department has also responded on several occasions to calls from the community to clear weed and will continue to review the situation each summer.

He pointed out that L'Eree's strand line seaweed is a valuable food resource for wading birds and particularly important for turnstones, oystercatchers and other breeding species.

'The reason for the steady decline in the number of wading birds on British beaches has been largely attributed by conservation organisations to the increased use of mechanical rakes,' he said, adding that Environment's approach to management of the strand line is supported by La Societe Guernesiaise, English Nature and the Marine Conservation Society.

He also mentioned the local community's annual 'spring clean', which prepares the beach for summer use.

The cost of clearing seaweed would also be prohibitive.

Daily removal would cost the taxpayer many thousands of pounds over July and August, said Deputy De Lisle, and the use of heavy machinery damages the structure and natural organisms of the beach.

And despite the weed, people still flock to L'Eree.

'It is well known locally as a safe beach for bathers and was featured in the 2007 Good Beach Guide published by the Marine Conservation Society,' said the minister.

Right
Burning seaweed above L'Eree
Far right
The smell of seaweed is unpopular with holidaymakers

LOOKING BACK

HAZEL OZARD'S association with L'Eree dates back to just after the First World War when her parents – the Browns – took over the running of the hotel and pub.

She arrived in 1920 aged four and left with them at 15.

'Before we came, my uncle, a Mr Partridge, ran it, but he left for the Queen's, which belonged to my grandfather.'

In those days the L'Eree pub and its entrance were right on the road and the section where today's pub pulls in the locals was a skittles alley.

Just a small stretch of road away lay the lovely, natural sand dunes which were to stay in place until the beach defences were strengthened in the early 1960s.

The 1920s was still a period when the more well-to-do islanders would spend summer holidays in the most south-westerly stretch of Guernsey.

And when they were not on holiday, the rich still came for other tasty attractions.

'They used to come here on charabancs for lobster teas,' recalls Hazel.

'The local kids ran behind the charabancs and pleaded: "One penny please sir".

'My mother used to say to me: "You're not to go after those charabancs".

"Of course not mum", I'd say.'

But one look into her sparkly, still young eyes and you know the young Hazel did.

The dunes were useful for many things and not just for sunbathing.

'When the men got boozed [up] they'd go over to the sand dunes to sleep it off. It was

Below
L'Eree's oldest resident Hazel Ozard dresses up for the West Show

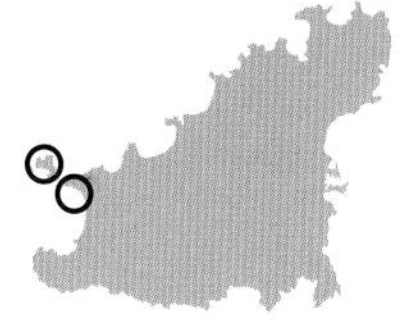

full of fennel. Willie Guilbert would fall asleep in it and stink of fennel,' says the grand old lady of the area.

'You often couldn't see the road for sand,' she adds of a time when the West Shows were being held by the St Peter's arsenal.

Una and Hazel laugh as they recall the shipwrecks of L'Eree's past.

'First of all the wine ...everybody was drunk then,' Una recalls of one, probably the Briseis, which came ashore at Vazon.

Hazel chips in: 'They were clever, these L'Eree-ites. They found out that some barrels [of wine] were better than others.'

As for other wrecks?

'Another one was full of candles and oranges, then there was the Enterprise.

'It was going to America with Christmas presents.

'We had to go behind Lihou, because that's where the stuff was coming in. They were queuing at the causeway to go over.'

That was still an era when there were no buildings between the hotel and Rocque Poisson, a few hundred metres south.

Hazel also recalls a large worked sandpit close to where the large White House property stands and, like many other west-coast locals such as L'Eree Hotel proprietor Mark Frost, has heard of the rumours of gas chambers where today stand the hotel's staff headquarters.

But German Occupation Museum owner and respected war historian Richard Heaume says there is no truth in the stories.

'The Germans used L'Eree for barracks and it was no more than showers and latrines.'

Above
Aerial view of L'Eree and its marvellous dunes in the 1920s or 1930s

Left
L'Eree local Una Mortimer

HI-DE-HI L'EREE

L'EREE as the Skegness of Guernsey.

It's difficult to imagine, is it not? But 70 years ago it very nearly became reality.

Had a dozen more men in the States of Deliberation uttered 'pour' instead of 'contre' on the morning of Wednesday 13 November 1946, the entire history of tourism in Guernsey would have changed forever.

Billy Butlin wanted his Redcoats here and where previously stood an aerodrome, and where West Show tents go up and down every August, plans were drawn up for a massive camp housing 2,000 holidaymakers.

It was on the recommendation of the Tourist Industry Enquiry Committee and its president, Jurat Pierre de Putron, that the Bailiff Ambrose Sherwill called upon the States to make the momentous decision.

Writing in the November Billet, Jurat de Putron observed that while the glasshouse industry had made a good start, 'the fact cannot be disregarded that a setback would have far graver repercussions on the islands in the absence of supplementary industries'.

'The tourist industry,' he wrote, 'is a source of income which is capable of considerable development and an increase in the number of visitors coming to Guernsey appears inevitable.' Butlins on the west coast would, he argued, lengthen the holiday season and the total number visiting the island could double.

Sir Billy, or plain Billy as he was then, had an exciting vision of L'Eree which included a swimming pool, rock garden, golf course, theatre, bowling greens, children's playgrounds, ballroom and dining halls, boating lake, 10 tennis courts, shops and a sports complex to house eight table tennis tables, 15 billiard tables, lounges, a gym, darts and card rooms.

His and tourism's plans were even welcomed by the island's Natural Beauties Committee and the layouts were said to compare favourably with those at Filey and Skegness, which had been up and running for a decade.

'Taking everything into consideration, particularly the type and demeanour of the persons in the camp and the facilities provided, we see no reason why a camp established at L'Eree, with a capacity of 1,000 expanding later to 2,000, should be detrimental to the island as a whole.'

Ahead of the big vote, the island's Finance and Advisory committees duly sat on the fence.

They refused to be drawn publicly and the Advisory Council's resolution recommending

Far right
Far-fetched plans for a holiday camp came to nothing
Right
An artist's impression imposed on an aerial picture of the area
Overleaf
Old L'Eree

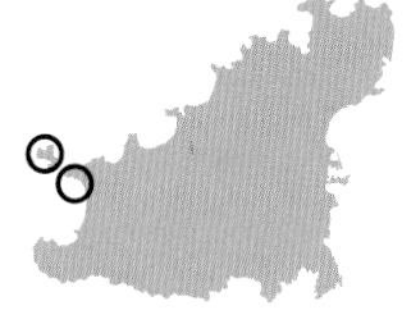

the adoption of the tourist committee's report was carried by the casting vote only.

All the while pressure was growing on the States to say a combined 'contre'.

The hotel and boarding house owners attacked the tourist report, claiming it was 'bristling with inaccuracies' and that the camp would be detrimental to island life.

Come decision day, the plans were thrown out by 35 votes to 13.

Only two jurats voted for, six were against and all the island's rectors gave the idea the thumbs down.

Of the deputies present, six supported the plans, 10 did not.

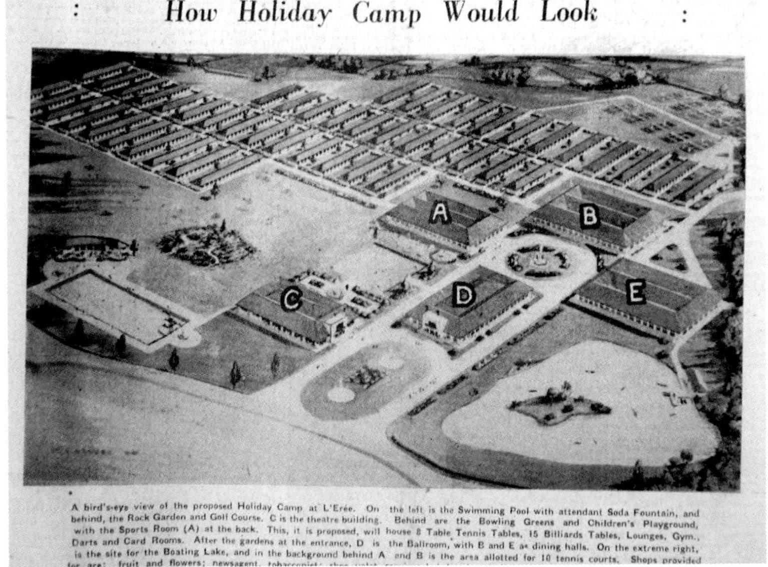

How Holiday Camp Would Look

A bird's-eye view of the proposed Holiday Camp at L'Erée. On the left is the Swimming Pool with attendant Soda Fountain, and behind, the Rock Garden and Golf Course. C is the theatre building. Behind are the Bowling Greens and Children's Playground, with the Sports Room (A) at the back. This, it is proposed, will house 8 Table Tennis Tables, 15 Billiards Tables, Lounges, Gym., Darts and Card Rooms. After the gardens at the entrance, D is the Ballroom, with B and E as dining halls. On the extreme right, is the site for the Boating Lake, and in the background behind A and B is the area allotted for 10 tennis courts. Shops provided for are: fruit and flowers; newsagent, tobacconist;

SMALL BUT SIGNIFICANT

A FLICK through the office archives on the Bailiwick's seventh island – Lihou – suggests a reassessment of the pecking order may be necessary.

The 18-acre rock that separates L'Eree and Perelle may not have full-time inhabitants like those of Brecqhou and Jethou, but it certainly has attracted more news over the years and its heritage is rich and, at times, quirky.

The States, on the taxpayers' behalf, bought the Lihou house for £430,000 in 1995, although I dare say that had every islander been asked whether they wished to contribute to its purchase, the population would have cried a resounding 'non'.

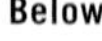

Below
The house on Lihou

But like it or not, we have got it and since late 2005 it has been leased to the Lihou Charitable Trust for a peppercorn rent, the States feeling flush enough to turn up its nose at an offer of £16,500 per annum from an unnamed individual.

Twenty-one months later, the newly refurbished house was opened by the Bailiff, Geoffrey Rowland, and, said the new warden, Richard Curtis, the emphasis was to be on the young.

'Youth groups will pay the bare minimum so the corporate groups will be helping to fund them,' said Mr Curtis at the time.

'The house is open to all, but the bias will definitely be in the direction of youth groups and young people.'

Five months down the line the warden is delighted with progress.

'It's going incredibly well. At least once a

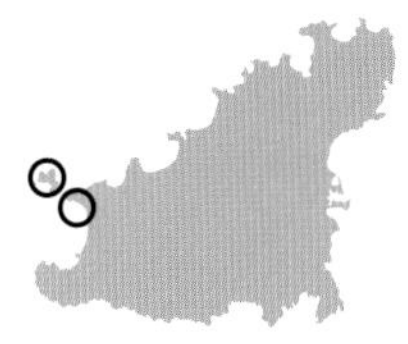

week we have someone [a group] over there and already we have 58 bed nights booked for 2008.

'We also have half-a-dozen schools booked, most of them for multiple-night stays.'

Lihou's past is variable, to say the least.

The current building is sited on what was formerly a large farmhouse.

That is, until the Germans came along, looked out from L'Eree and asked what their Panzers could practise shooting at.

They quickly came up with the answer – the house on Lihou.

Iodine from seaweed was also made there until the war years.

Lihou has never had a large settlement, even when the Abbey of Mont St Michel took temporary possession of it in 1415.

At one stage Henry VI granted Lihou to Eton College, but after the Reformation, the priory fell into disrepair.

And then came the Wootton years.

Lt-Col Patrick Wootton was founder of the Lihou Youth Project, an organisation catering for the needs of youth.

His vision was admirable enough, even if it would be considered a shade cranky if his ethos were put across today in the manner in which it appeared in the Guernsey Evening Press and Star in late 1969.

His stated aim for the project was to create 'a constructive pattern for living in this difficult age, centred around a spiritual outlook to life, a scientific interest in life and a sociological responsibility for life'.

He would also go about halting the 'further decline in our already unhealthy lifestyle'.

Faith, purpose and enthusiasm were his key words for the future.

In his 14 years on Lihou, the colonel was seldom out of the paper and these are just a small selection of the Guernsey Press headlines during the Wootton era:

- **Compromise over causeway post box**
- **Boathouse plan submitted**
- **Tibetan refugees may visit**
- **Plans for shop on island**
- **Row between Post Office and Wootton over Lihou stamps**
- **Lihou Youth fellowship nominated for**
- **Belgian award**
- **Windmill to be erected on Lihou**
- **Seaweed-eating sheep for Lihou delayed**
- **Actress Jenny Runacre spends 48 hours on Lihou for TV Times**
- **Dig uncovers Lihou's secrets**
- **St Peter's parish to fight Wootton's threat to close Lihou for part of the year**
- **Wind shatters vaulted arch of Lihou Priory**
- **Two ormerers find live German shell**
- **Is Lihou part of St Peter's?**
- **St Peter's to sue Lihou tenant for non-payment of rates**
- **Lihou rams sold for slaughter**
- **Last night on Lihou for Woottons (1983)**
- **Lihou sold for £274,000 (1983)**

Today, the island's seven hectares is rich in flora and fauna, with around 170 flowering plants recorded.

In addition, it is a sanctuary for birds and birdlovers due to its relative remoteness and peace. At high water it is a roosting site for waders and gulls.

In autumn, Lihou is a stopping-off point for small birds on migration, while just around the corner at the shingle beach the seaward side of the shingle bank is used by breeding seabirds such as ringed plovers and oyster-catchers.

Banks such as this one were formed when the sea rose after the last Ice Age, pushing the stones from the bed of the English Channel in front of itself.

This shingle bank was mined for stones during the German Occupation for use in fortifications.

BEST-LAID PLANS

BILLY BUTLIN has not been the only one to see his plans for the area know as La Rousse Mare and La Claire Mare fail to get off the ground.

It might have been our airport, it might have been a housing estate, a race course or the site for a 200ft wind turbine.

Two of those sets of ambitious plans came courtesy of L'Eree landowner the late Colin Best.

In 1993, he announced grandiose plans for a 200ft high wind generator that was to rise above the nearby German tower at Fort Saumarez.

It was not one of the Island Development Committee's most testing decisions. Best considered the small hougue opposite the shingle bank at L'Eree to be the ideal site for a turbine which could harness winds from 10mph to 83mph.

If it was a success, more could follow, he said.

Then there was the race course, which also got to the planning stage, but no further.

"He loved doing things people said he couldn't do," recalls Susie Farnon, daughter of the man who bought the land at auction for £40,000.

"He was very serious about it. But it was pretty obvious in the political climate of the time that he wasn't going to get permission," she added.

Seven furlongs in length, the remnants of Colin Best's canny plan for an alternative to the restricted L'Ancresse circuit can be see on the raised ground which runs parallel with the shingle bank close to the main road.

Raising that section of what is notoriously wet farmland got Mr Best into trouble with the authorities.

Below
Colin Best hoped to turn L'Eree into a race course and this is how it might have looked

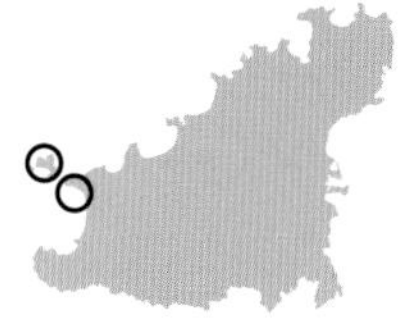

But it was the embryonic stage of the course, reveals his daughter. He knew that he had to raise ground levels and it was his way of doing it. Only it did not get very far.

Nor did L'Eree Estates Limited with plans to develop the area.

Back in the 1960s it was the company's wish to put extensive housing on the last large undeveloped expanse on the west coast which, back in the 1930s, was Guernsey's first aerodrome.

The Guernsey Aero Club of the time pushed hard for the area to be designated worthy of expansion into the island's main air passenger terminal, all to no avail.

The club had the whole area drained with a special conduit into the sea and they even had the support of a world-renowned aviator in Sir Alan Cobham.

The chief opposition to L'Eree was that it did not allow for misadvenutre.

In other words, there were too many houses on its doorstep and the margins for error were too small.

It was simply not suitable for reliable, year-round air services, being small and still subject to flooding.

During its short period of operation, L'Eree boasted three grass runways, the longest being just 500 yards.

As well as catering for club flying, including the famous Wee Mite high-wing monoplane of chief instructor Cecil Noel, L'Eree was the location for the first land-based air service to the UK, Cobham's Guernsey to Christchurch and Portsmouth routes.

The service was inaugurated on 6 May 1935 using tri-engined Westland Wessex planes, but after just eight weeks it ceased, with one of them crashing into the sea off Bournemouth.

PRIVACY AND ARCHAEOLOGY

WANT all-day round sand, sun and seclusion?

If so, the beach with no obvious name immediately north of L'Eree, tucked beside the car park overlooking Lihou, may just be for you. Especially if you like a spot of archaeology in between flipping over to get that all-over tan.

Guernsey's Heritage people have a keen interest in the narrow sand beach and it has nothing to do with the fact that it offers a bit of privacy for those who like to tan their white bits.

It could be argued that the L'Eree headland is one of the more prominent and historically important areas along the west coast of Guernsey.

Largely undeveloped, it possesses, as well as a fantastic view of Lihou, a well-preserved Megalithic passage tomb, Le Creux es Faies.

Situated towards the centre of the headland, it is well outside the influence of coastal processes but provides an indication of the archaeological importance of the area.

Nearby is the important and endangered prehistoric site on the southern side of the headland.

The low cliff at the rear of the beach contains layers of sediment that yield large quantities of pottery and flint and traces of stone and post-built structures.

Pottery from a lower layer appears to date from Neolithic (c. 3500BC) while higher up the sequence pottery of beaker type is date about 2000BC.

Potentially, this site could be one of the more important Neolithic sites in western Europe.

The low cliff yielding the pottery is presently prone to coastal erosion and important archaeological remains are being lost.

Below
The beach on L'Eree headland
Opposite
Coastal erosion is a major concern

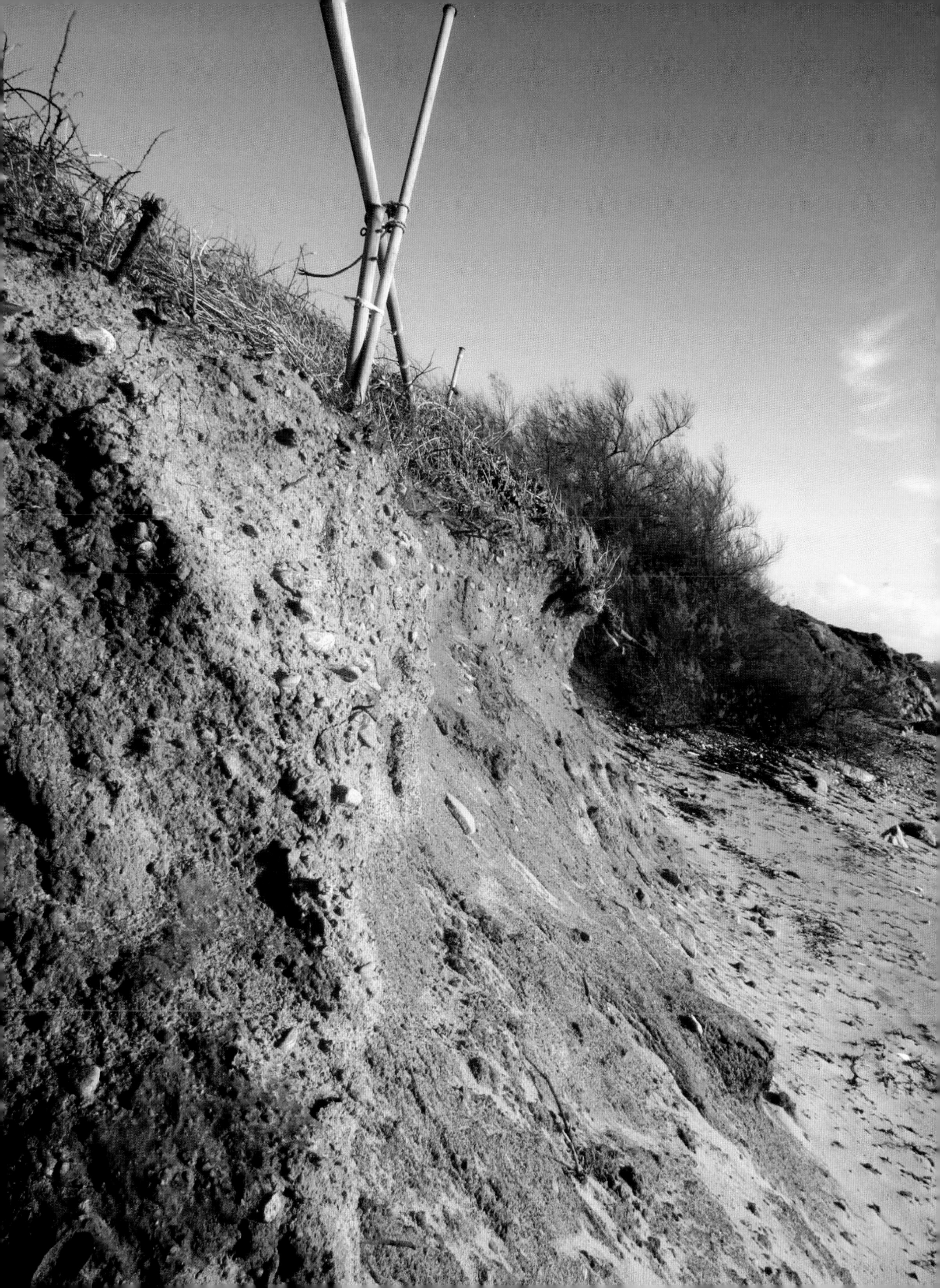

"I didn't like to see it [the Prosperity] when you think of the number of people who were lost. I have never been on that reef since. I don't know why. There's something about it"

Nev Robert

CHAPTER 27

PERELLE

Between the Le Catioroc and Richmond headlands lies a small bay that may have lost much of its old fishing community but can still yield many a tale.

STORMY TIMES OUT WEST

LIVING along Guernsey's coastline is an opportunity not to be missed. Natural beauty on your doorstep.

But in some spots, particularly along the west coast, one can occasionally be too close for comfort.

Two such men are Nev Robert and Bert Enevoldsen, whom you will often find gazing over the beach wall at Perelle, putting the world to rights just a few yards away from their back gardens either side of Rue des Crabbes, which hits the coast bang between their houses.

We speak on an idyllic mid-December afternoon, 48 hours after a weekend of near-hurricane winds hitting the islands.

The west coast had received another battering and the residual evidence at Perelle is a string of some two dozen stacks of vraic spread across the beach just 10 metres or so from the sea wall.

It's as if they have been planted there in much the same way farmers would stack hay.

'I haven't seen it piled up like that before,' says Nev, a Perelle man for more than 50 years.

'They were 15ft high the other day,' says Bert. 'But they have settled since then.'

It takes some believing that the seaweed stacks, around 6ft in height, are a 100%-unchoreographed product of the peculiar nature of the coast, as is the disappearance of many feet of sand that normally makes for a soft and appealing spot just beneath the sea wall on the south side of the bay.

Rest assured, the sand will come back – and so will the gales.

Nev, 73, has known many wild nights in this unheralded piece of coastline on which he has lived in the same house – a renovated 18th-century fisherman's cottage – for more than half-a-century.

One of the worst storms and one indelibly stamped in his mind is the night the Prosperity ran aground no more than half-a-mile from where he slept.

It was one of those nights when you wonder whether the roof will still be there in the morning. It was, but sadly he could not say the

Right
Perelle old boys: Bert Enevoldsen (left) and Nev Robert

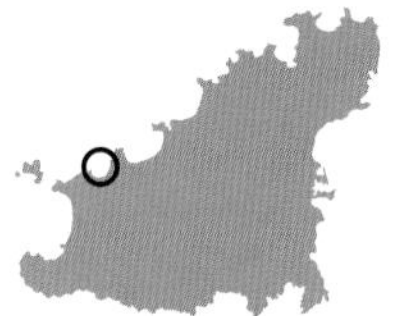

same about the fated crew aboard the Cypriot timber ship. All 18 had been swept to their death.

For days, many islanders clambered aboard the broken ship, but not Nev, who has kept a boat in the bay for decades.

'I rowed out there and went level with the big rock. But there was a funny smell around it and it put me off going aboard.'

He was, he admits, a tad uncomfortable with its presence.

'I didn't like to see it when you think of the

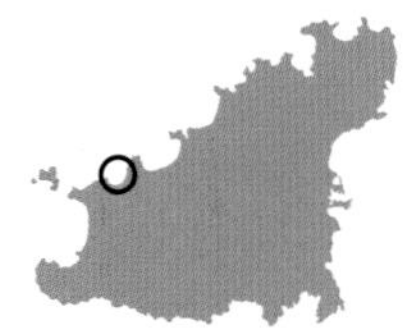

number of people who were lost. I've never been on that reef since. I don't know why. There's something about it.'

Ashore at Perelle, though, there have been worse nights.

'One of the worst was when the Orion went ashore. Here it was really bad that night.'

The area has also suffered from flooding.

'The water would come right up the road.'

For years, Nev worked at the nearby garage, which is in the firing line even more than his own house. One particularly bad winter the forecourts were flooded four times.

Latterly, boards have been put across the top of the slipway to alleviate flooding and in the main they have been a benefit to the neighbourhood.

'There are pros and cons with the boards,' said Bert. 'Because when water does get over, it no longer has anywhere to go.'

Nev's son, Colin 'Roob' Robert, has his own memories of stormy periods out west.

'There were many times it was so rough we would wait for the school bus in the telephone box [in the garage forecourt] to protect ourselves from the waves.'

Colin also has boyhood memories of trying to sleep with the sound of deep, rumbling waves filled with stone reverberating against the sea wall.

Nev's tales of Perelle are many and one of the more recent ones relates to the aircraft that ditched in the outer reaches of the bay in 2001.

'I was fishing just below the Conchee reef when I saw it coming down and then ditch into the water.

'There was then some smoke [flare] coming out of the life raft. I chucked away my pots and headed towards it but a cabin cruiser got there first.'

Piloted by Tony Rix, all aboard the Piper Arrow survived unscathed, which is more than can be said of the railway sleepers, in the area during the Occupation, which mysteriously disappeared in their dozens.

Bert had not heard the story before as Nev, with more than a hint of Guernsey pride and one-upmanship in his voice, described exactly where the Germans' supply railway ran through Perelle, including Bert's front garden.

'All the people along the road lost their front garden to it, but I remember before it was finished that the work had got as far as where Richmond Shopper was.

'They left the sleepers they were going to lay overnight standing up in two training wagons, but hundreds went that night.

'A lot went to greenhouses, others were used for firewood. The locals would bury them in the ground until they needed them for firewood.

'Me and my mate took some and a woman gave us a lump of sugar for each one. We gave her eight or nine. We were only kids.'

And talking of the Germans, Nev is happy to relate the story of their failed attempts to use a 'half-track' (half tank, half lorry) with tank-like rubber tracking to pull a large field gun up the beach and over the sea wall in front of where the Atlantique Hotel stands today.

'They were probably doing it to see if it was possible. Because if they could, so could the British landing forces.

'The sea wall was lower than it is now. They got the front wheels of this half-track over, but all the rubber tacks were spinning on the edge of the wall and they ripped off. In the end they had to abandon it on the dunes across the road.'

The Germans, Nev reckons, had learned enough. They built up the wall another four feet afterwards.

Opposite
Vraic stack after a particularly stormy December

Overleaf
Perelle is prone to onslaughts from the sea

PEARLS OF PERELLE

THERE are, apparently, 1,800 named rocks around the Bailiwick of Guernsey. That is a lot of granite and a lot of danger to those who like to splosh about on the sea.

Barry Paint – or should I say Captain Paint? – is sufficiently fascinated by our rocky outcrops that he is well into a project to ensure that the rocks keep the identity our forebears gave them.

As it happens, we are very good at changing the names intended and he can freely reel off a multitude of examples.

He is also fascinated with Perelle beach – and has been since the age of three, when he

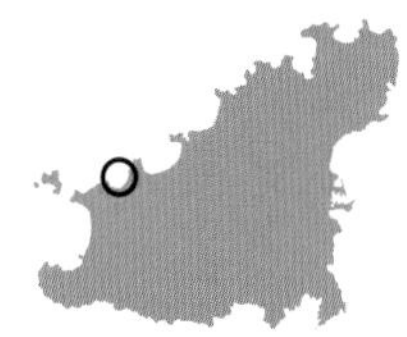

first stepped upon it.

To this eminent man of the sea, with probably unrivalled knowledge of the island's west coast, Perelle means beauty.

While at a low spring tide I see little else but ugly vraic – tons and tons of the stuff – the merchant seaman, skilled enough to be asked to steer the Vermontborg safely away from our coastline after it had run aground on the nearby La Capelle reef in early January 2003, is uplifted by its rugged beauty, quoting the Guernsey French names of rock after rock in the horseshoe-shaped bay, all with obvious love and enthusiasm.

'It's a wonderful beach,' he says. And the tales start flowing.

Looking out from our central vantage point close to the main slipway, his finger points right to the natural causeway linking the headland close to Fort Richmond and the Conchee reef on which the Prosperity crew, all 18 hands, perished in January 1974.

The reef is reachable by foot on a spring low and he knows it like the back of his hand.

'When I was 12 I went out there with my gaff and caught a big conger in a hole as well as seven dozen ormers.'

That was 1959 when the delicacy was so plentiful that he could afford to throw them away so he could carry the big eel home, a stone's throw away up the road.

'It was 30-and-three-quarter pounds gutted and I couldn't carry both.'

Perelle is in his blood, although he was born in the Grande Rue, St Saviour's.

'My father, grandfather and great uncle were all fishermen out of Perelle. As a boy I spent nearly every day of my life on this beach, fishing, swimming, rafting or just going out with the local fishermen.

'It's a very good mooring bay after half-tide. You've got perfect shelter.'

As a young boy and now at 60, Perelle has offered much to him, just as it has to generations of seaweed gatherers.

Two stretches of cobbled road beneath the sea wall on the south side provide lasting evidence of an era when horses and carts were a common sight on the rocky beach.

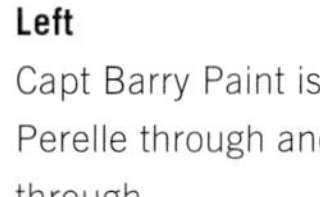

Left
Capt Barry Paint is Perelle through and through

'When I was a boy I remember periods when the whole beach was full of octopus – thousands upon thousands of them,' he said.

'I'd get them for the fishermen to use as bait and recall my best was 40 in one day.

'But the winter of 1962-63 slaughtered every single one of them. Today they would make a fortune out of them.'

When the tides were high, jumping off the sea wall that runs parallel with Rue du Catioroc, Barry and his mates had many a fun-filled hour.

And when the wind blows, Perelle is as spectacular a sight as most west-coast beaches.

At such times it is not best practice to be aboard a boat or ship of any size close to the mouth of the bay.

The Prosperity disaster is the obvious case in point.

Barry recalls the night very well, although he was many miles away aboard his own ship, doing his best to stay out of trouble at anchor.

'I was listening to it in the Bay of St Malo, just off Cancale, on the Commodore Trader.

'I heard the Greek captain of the ship, who kept saying: "We're going around, we're going around." But what he meant, of course, was "We're going aground." It was a hell of a storm.

'The crew should have stayed on the bridge, which didn't even get wet. But it's always easy to be wise after the event.'

The 2,000-ton Cypriot timber ship had lost power 20 miles west of the Hanois lighthouse in the worst weather for years.

The St Peter Port lifeboat was launched but was called back as it made slow progress in the terrible seas, which were being whipped up by force 11-12 hurricane winds.

The crew, including a woman and a 16-year-old boy, all drowned after abandoning the ship.

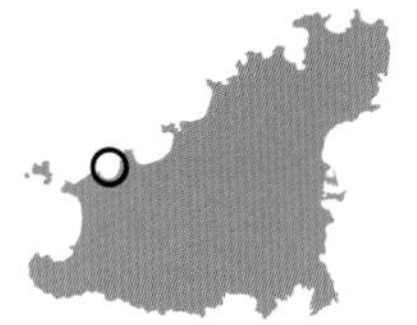

THAT SINKING FEELING

HE HAS sunk in the Bay of Biscay and experienced nightmarish seas, but in more than 40 years in an adulthood at sea, Barry Paint admits to only four occasions when he would have preferred to be home in front of the fire with his slippers on.

Not scared, mind you. Captains of the sea don't do that word.

He prefers to sum up such experiences with: 'I've wondered what I was doing out there.'

Twice it has been aboard the Commodore Clipper.

'Once off Cape St Vincent [south-west Portugal] we pooped and the sea broke over the bridge deck, about 36 feet above the V/I's water line in still water.'

On the same ship he found himself at the helm in the Bay of Biscay in the midst of hurricane force-12 winds.

'We travelled two miles in 36 hours.'

Another time he was off the 'Smalls', off the south-west point of Wales, on a trip from Liverpool to Le Havre.

'I was off duty and asleep when a huge wave hit the side of the ship and threw me out of my bunk.'

And the fourth occasion saw him looking at 190ft of ship disappear three times under seas off Start Point, Devon. The wind was gusting at 94mph and the Salcombe lifeboat was turned over.

Thankfully, the seas were relatively flat on the occasion his ship did slip under the waves, never to be seen again.

Hired in 1970 to transfer the old Spanish galleon, H'Ispaniola, from London to Spain with no more than a compass and a beaten-up radio, he broke down off the Pointe du Raz and then, fatefully, sank near Spain.

'We were off Santander in thick fog when she started to leak. We couldn't stop the flow and had to abandon ship. We spent 20 hours in a life raft.'

Opposite
1970s tragedy as the Prosperity goes aground on the Conchee Reef with the loss of all aboard

TUG OF LOVE

TWENTY-NINE years after the Prosperity disaster and just 1,050 yards away to the west, the new-hull Vermontborg stuck hard and fast on La Capelle reef.

The hull, worth close to £2m., was being towed from the builder's yard in Romania to the Netherlands for fitting out when it broke free of its lines in high winds and drifted inshore and aground off Perelle.

It would be there for 15 days and might have been there for a lot longer but for the efforts and local knowledge of Barry Paint.

'It was very well stuck,' he recalled. 'We needed a 7.7m tide to even start thinking about refloating her and it was stormy weather all the time up to the day we got it off.'

His job was primarily to pilot the tugs into the area, dodging the array of rocks.

'The biggest had a 21ft draft and I was chosen as the one with the most knowledge of the coast.'

For this reason alone, it was never going to be easy to get the 120m-long Vermontborg off and some doubted it would disappear at all.

Roger Berry, then president of the Board of Administration, said at the time: 'It is so far up the beach there is only a minute chance of refloating it.'

Barry said there were reefs that the tugs could not clear, although the ship could.

He recalls much tension among the salvagers, but he insists he remained calm throughout.

'I didn't feel pressure. Concern, yes. But I had nothing to lose.

'It was hell of a challenge and the chances of getting it off were quite slight.'

He says it was the most interesting project of his 20 years as a pilot – and one that paid him well.

It took three attempts on different days to free the empty ship.

'We started pulling at 25% power, which is a lot. It went 20 metres and stopped dead on the bottom. It was hard and fast again.

'She was floating on a bed of [pumped] air but as soon as it is disturbed, down she goes again.'

But, thankfully, the sea helped out.

'Another swell came along – a huge one – and she was off. There was a huge cheer. It was like being at a football game.'

All done, with the help of Barry's expert guidance, in 54 knots of wind. It had been stuck fast for 15 days, providing islanders with an attraction with a difference.

Harbour master Captain Robert Barton praised the work of all concerned and had special words for his two local pilots, the other being Andy Lowe.

Below, opposite and overleaf
The Vermontborg went aground on the La Capelle Reef in January 2003

515
515

44
42
40
38
20
18
16
14
12
10

DAUNTLESS ISLANDERS

CORONATION Street star John Savident, aka Fred Elliot, has a strong link with Perelle.

On 1 July 1940 his father, also John, was among seven islanders who sneaked out of the bay and Occupied Guernsey aboard GU44 Dauntless bound for the UK.

It was the first boat to escape the island during the Occupation and 16 hours after departing the west coast, the five men and two women arrived in Budleigh Salterton, east Devon.

Built in Rotterdam 13 years earlier, the logger with a four-horsepower engine was just 19.2ft in length with a beam of 6ft 7in.

The escapers comprised Mr and Mrs Fred Savident, their sons, John, Cyril and Joe, their son-in-law, Herbert Pike and his daughter, Monica.

It is understood they all returned to their native home, but it is thought they have all since died.

Ship pilot Barry Paint recalls Joe as the area's local cobbler and his workshop, on the road to Fort Le Crocq, becoming a meeting place for locals to gossip and chat. He also recalls Cyril, who owned a shop at St Sampson's.

As for Dauntless, it was left slowly to rot away on the beach at Budleigh Salterton, never to return to these waters, but having done its job to transfer seven desperate islanders to freedom.

WEST IS BEST FOR SURF

IT'S a reef not to be messed with and not only for those owners of huge empty hulls off to be fitted out.

Vazon may be the most popular place to surf locally, but for the purists and those who like to be tested, the same reef that had the hulking Vermontborg stuck fast for 15 days five winters ago provides wicked surfing when the tide is up and the wind is blowing.

A simple visit to the Beach Wizard website – 'by surfers for surfers' – confirms as much amid their blogs.

Here's one example:

'Some way the best wave on the island and certainly the biggest. It gets crowded but there are three or four breaks in this bay, which can be good.

'The right-hander behind Dom Hue is excellent. There is a dodgy rock on the inside, too. Use it to your advantage and you can get a good cover-up.'

But, as the man adds: 'It looks good but can be a bit dodgy on take-off and wipeouts.'

Kevin Hinshaw, veteran surfer when he is not performing his head-teaching duties at La Mare de Carteret Primary, confirms it is a place for only the experienced to sample.

'Unless you are a competent surfer, you shouldn't be out there,' he said. 'You wouldn't want to go out there without knowing what you are doing.'

Nor is he is about to disagree that Perelle provides Guernsey's best surf.

'It's consistently the best, biggest and best shaped waves. They hold their shape well, so you can get long rides.'

It's not Hawaii or Newquay, but the waves can be a decent size.

'I've surfed a right with about 12ft to 14ft faces – but it does break big,' says Kevin, who reckons it is not uncommon to have waves with 15ft faces at Perelle.

Beach Wizard reckons it to be of 'intermediate' difficulty, but it is given a rating of four out of five.

The ideal wind is, apparently, an easterly and a good swell, a westerly.

Ideal tide? Well, that would be a mid to high and the hazards, apart from the hidden rocks, are 'crowds and idiots'.

Opposite
The Dauntless carried several islanders across the Channel in 1940

DAUNTLESS

CHEEKY DEVILS' FRIDAY NIGHT FROLICS

LOS Angeles had the Valley of the Dolls and all the sex and debauchery that went with mid-60s drug-fuelled Flower Power, but listen to some and Perelle and the area of Le Trepied dolmen has also seen some wild sights in its time.

Back in the 16th century it was noted for some spicy goings-on, with the bored local women getting up to all sorts of no good while their fishermen husbands were out at sea.

Annette Henry, accredited guide and the hugely entertaining woman behind the Ghosts and Graveyards tours, has extensively researched local witchcraft and has some juicy tales to tell about this particular area, which overlooks Perelle and Le Catioroc.

Central to the guide's tale of Le Trepied are the Becquet sisters, Marie and Isobel, who spilled the X-rated beans in a 17th-century witchcraft trial that led to Marie being branded, having an ear cut off and thrown into the sea and banished from the island, while Isobel was simply burned at the stake.

Their trial revealed that the Becquets were just part of a regular gathering of west-coast women who fell for Perelle's version of sex-crazed Charles Manson.

Brought to trial by the Tostevin brothers, who accused the sisters of affecting them with ill health, the Becquets told their tale of pre-EastEnders Friday night rebelliousness.

Just what else was there for them to do?

'They [the Becquets] would paint their face with black ointment and fly from the Longfrie to Le Trepied to be with their devil,' said the tour guide.

And there, together with other 17th-century Desperate Housewives, they would allow themselves to be plied with black wine – 'a wine like no other wine before', said Mrs Henry.

This was no Cabernet Sauvignon, Shiraz or Zinfandel, but one probably laced with herbs and magic mushrooms and strong enough to have them happy to strip off and have their wicked way with an unnamed local man wearing a devil's mask.

It's a story that has long interested the guide, who lives locally and finds the whole story 'so logical'.

'They gave themselves a degree of anonymity by putting the paint on their faces.'

Ultimately, the then-Bailiff, Amias de Carteret, stepped in to end the Friday frolics.

His role is a part made for Edward Woodward, that most Christian of film coppers and star of the cult 1970s movie, The Wicker Man.

In that film he played the part of the Scottish policeman dumped in Summerisle to tackle the evil Christopher Lee who was lording it – nudge, nudge, say no more – over the devil-worshipping islanders, many of them scantily clad young women. In one scene, Swedish stunner Britt Ekland teases him by nakedly writhing against the bit of plywood separating their bedrooms. Unlike most, he resisted.

De Carteret, who was in office for 30 years from the start of the 17th century, conducted witchcraft trials to sort out those dastardly demonised local lasses who liked nothing better than popping down to Perelle on a Friday night for a spot of jigging around some big rocks in the name of devil worship.

An altogether tamer confessional story – but who would believe a witch? – goes that the devil, in the form of a black goat called 'Baal Berith' or 'Barberie', sat on the central capstone of the dolmen while the local lasses simply put aside their broomsticks and danced around in worship.

They were led in their revels, it is said, by the terrible Heroguiazes, shouting as they went 'Qui hou hou, Marie Lihou' in mockery of the shrine of Notre Dame de Lihou in the nearby island.

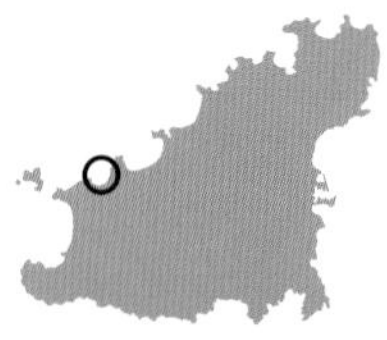

Mrs Annette Henry also reveals a somewhat sordid tale of the nearby Fairy Cave, aka the dolmen on National Trust land, in the lane to the Lihou headland car park.

It is an 'allée couverte' (hidden pathway) and a neolithic passage grave dating back to around 2500-3000 BC and was discovered by F. C. Lukis in the 19th century, complete with human and animal bones and gifts for the afterlife.

According to folklore, it was named Le Creux es Faies centuries ago. The 'fairies' used to come out and dance in the moonlight but the colourful modern historian says her research puts a different slant on what a 'fairy' was.

'As the young women of the parish would meet at Le Trepied to engage in debauchery, drunken antics, satanism, sexual activity, drug taking and witchcraft, they were not always able to or willing to make love to the "devil" who had plied them with black wine.

'In such cases they would signal to the pre-pubescent girls who met at Le Creux es Faies on a Friday night, who would then leave the cave and go to Le Trepied, where they would satisfy the [old] devil's need for younger, firmer flesh.'

The little people (fairies) were in fact young girls, willing to get in on the action. Just who was this 17th-century stud?

Above
Le Trepied was the site of devilish goings-on in the 16th century

RECHARGED BATTERY

PERELLE will be providing islanders and tourists with a newly restored historic site in the summer.

Mont Chinchon battery is currently undergoing extensive restoration, which Heritage Services' Helen Glencross is confident will further light up this picturesque corner of the west coast.

'We hope to have it open from early summer if everything goes to plan,' said the island's historic sites manager.

Also known as the Druid's Altar for its proximity to Le Trepied dolmen, the battery once had two Guernsey Militia-manned 20lb cannons pointing to sea to cover possible French landing spots at Perelle.

Work on repairing the battery and clearing the headland area above the coast road has been going on for a while and Heritage has been using the services of a UK stone conservator.

'The front section of the battery is complete and the area cleared.

'The turf laid on the top looks really smart and we might have some guns put up there,' said the sites manager.

The battery consists of a low, enclosing, granite wall to the east, south and west and a

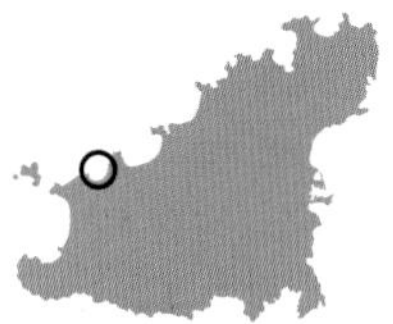

higher, granite-faced and lined, earth parapet to the north. Cut into this are two apertures, or embrasures, which are lined with brick, through which the guns would have been fired.

The hardstanding for the guns is made of granite slabs. To the south are the remains of a magazine.

The site was largely complete at the outbreak of the Second World War. However, it was dismantled by the Germans to make way for more modern defences.

A cutting for a railway line also meant the rear of the battery and the magazine were altered. After the 1940s, the battery fell into disrepair but restoration work started in 1990 when it was cleared by members of La Société Guernesiaise's conservation volunteers.

Materials for repairing the battery were also stockpiled and later that decade it was proposed by Noel Andrews, a building-conservation specialist from the UK, that the site be reinstated.

Due to other commitments he was involved in, primarily at Vale Castle and Lihou Priory, the project was never completed.

But in 2006 he returned to work at Mont Chinchon and since then has carried out three sessions on the site, with great success.

Left
Mont Chinchon Battery has been restored to its former glory

"The surfers of Guernsey are perhaps the best organised in the world. Get seriously stoked in Guernsey was the message and surfers have been doing so for 40 years. They come from all walks of life - and still do"

Peter Dixon

CHAPTER 28

VAZON

Once a forest, now the island's widest and most widely served bay. The home of surfers, sand and road racers and thousands of tourists each year. And at its southern end a few hidden secrets from Guernsey's distant past.

CHANGE OF SCENE

SHUT your eyes and just imagine you are atop a granite outcrop high above Vazon, where Fort Hommet lies today – only it is 2000BC and the fort and German concrete bunkers will not be built for thousands of years yet.

In front of you lies a beautiful, deep, V-shaped wooded valley – no beach whatsoever, no crashing waves.

Turn your head to the left and towards what we know as King's Mills lies a large inland lake.

Turn your head back 180 degrees to the right and the seashore runs in a line from Fort Le Crocq north towards the Grosse Rocque.

That was Vazon 4,000 years ago and it has been changing ever since.

It may be difficult to imagine, but where today we swim and surf once lay a dense forest, the remnants of which is still there at very low tide if you look closely enough.

The re-creation of Vazon to what we see today is a fascinating story, much of it expertly told by the late Peter Girard in his book entitled 'Guernsey', published in 1986. And when he was not writing about it he was telling the parish's children about it.

As a Castel schoolboy of the early 1960s, I well remember listening to my headmaster waxing lyrical on the geological history of Vazon, struggling to believe that there could ever be forestation where we kicked around on the beautifully white sand.

And where golfers today do their best to miss the small, fresh-water lakes at La Grande Mare, there lay one large inland lake which was to grow and grow until, more than 3,000 years later it was, by some judgments, two miles in circumference.

But back to 2000BC when Guernsey was a whole lot larger than it is today.

Girard's theory was that as the world came out of the Ice Age and sea levels rose, the natural consequence was that they ate into the land.

Barriers of pebbles were forced inland, burying and compressing vegetation all the way.

Ultimately the pebble barrier, something akin to what we today see between L'Eree and Perelle, clogged up the natural drainage and the stream waters no longer filtered away.

The lake grew and storms and erosion did the rest with the aid of rising sea levels.

The pebble ridges were pushed further inland over what had become a peat bog, the sheer weight of it compressing and consolidating the mass of peat and dead trees. It took many centuries for the pebble ridges to reach

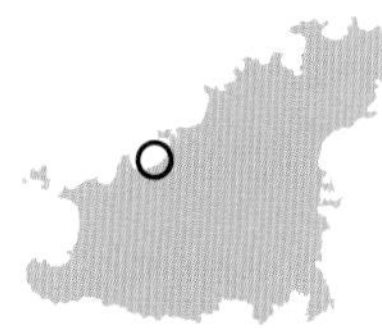

Left
Vazon from the air
Below
Wooden groynes remain a feature of the beach

where they are today.

The age of surface peat at Vazon has been measured at 1200BC and the surface of the peat below the sea wall near the drainage outlet dates back to around 2840BC.

The peat was to provide inhabitants with a form of fuel for hundreds of years, but you have to look very closely to see it these days.

By Girard's account, it was best found at the lowest part of the beach and when the tides were right, islanders would flock armed with iron rods, hoes and spades. It would then be loaded onto carts by children and women, carefully unloaded elsewhere and left to dry until fit for use as fuel.

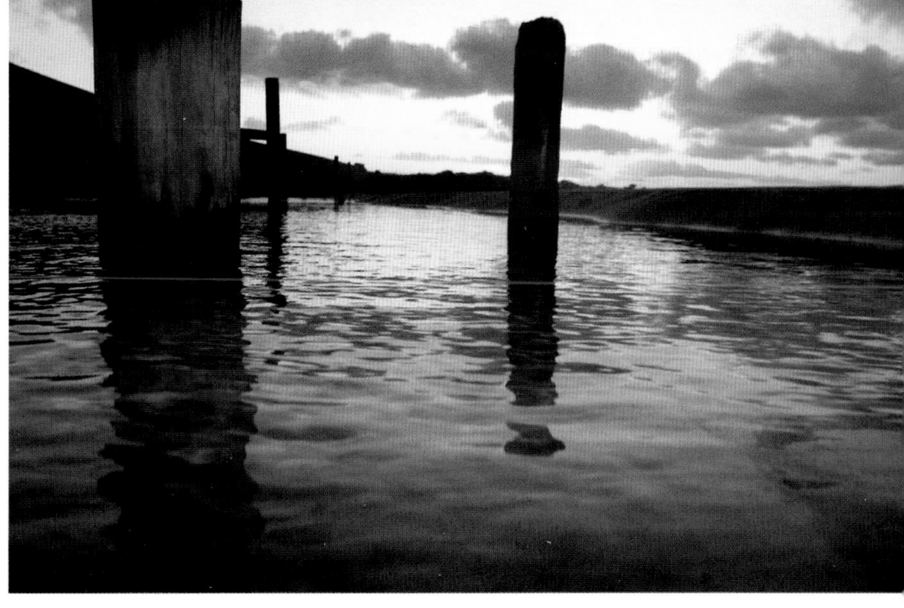

GUERNSEY'S LAKE DISTRICT

BY THE 16th century, La Grande Mare had developed into one very large carp-full lake.

Writing in 1677, author Charles Trumbull described it as being two miles in circumference.

By the mid 18th century, extensive drainage had taken place and the famous 1787 Duke of Richmond map showed the various drainage channels, a main stream and an outlet onto Vazon beach.

Marsh replaced lake and between the 20th century wars it had dried sufficiently to be set up by the new leaseholder, a Stephen Duquemin, as a racecourse. He diverted drains underground and built bridges over the main channels, but the racing authorities would not grant him permission and a licence to run flat racing.

In the Occupation years, the Germans had their own plans for the area.

What is now the golf course was a large sandpit, which the occupying forces emptied so they could get on with building their fortifications.

When the war ended the large pit was filled before being covered with soil.

For a time afterwards, horse racing finally went ahead on the area and farming continued until – as the 20th century neared its end – the new owners, the Vermeulen family, found an altogether different use for the land.

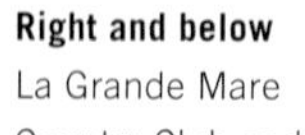

Right and below
La Grande Mare Country Club and Hotel has transformed Vazon's wetlands

GRANDE DESIGNS

IN 1976, the Vermeulen family bought 40 acres of land at Vazon, much of it an eyesore.

They had a vision which, although seen through, led to many uncomfortable moments for the family.

'We took the brunt of the argument unfortunately,' recalls Chris Vermeulen, one of Peter Vermeulen's two sons, who have run La Grande Mare Hotel since its opening in 1986.

'It was an uncomfortable time, but we have never looked back,' said an obviously satisfied man, who has seen their land ownership at Vazon more than double to 100 acres and a course steadily mature to the extent that it is now considered good enough to stage inter-insular matches.

At a time when Guernsey was desperately crying out for a second golf course and the authorities could or would not provide one, the Vermeulens stuck to their guns and pushed ahead with their ambition to provide their own course to sit alongside a fine hotel and time-share complex.

It is an understatement to say that not everyone was happy with the way they went about it.

'We battled for eight years to get golf. We fought because it was something we truly believed in.'

Golfers, hundreds of them desperate for somewhere to relax and play, are indebted.

The club, which opened in 1994, boasts 800 members. Add to that 600 health club members and 600 time-share owners.

It has all replaced land which had become untidy, fit for little unless you had wings. Bird-watchers squirmed at the development while golfers cheered.

The 'isn't it bad for wildlife' argument is knocked back by Chris, whose uncle, Tony de la Mare, once dug peat on the land.

He points to the black swan residing in one of the large lakes, which hold mira carp, carp and perch, and the Damsen flies.

'We have never had so much wildlife. There is no end of wildlife stopping off on their migratory paths,' he said.

'It is a green area saved from development. It was a low-lying area, poorly drained and wasn't managed. We have improved all the drains and managed it. We are extremely proud of it, although it has been a labour of love.'

A WAY OF LIFE

ROB OZANNE would surf every day if he could. He has felt that way for more than 20 years, since the day he was introduced to surfing, not at Vazon but at Portinfer, just down the road from his childhood home.

Now 35, Rob will go anywhere and everywhere to get his buzz. His work is fitted in around his desire to surf and if anyone locally lives a true surfer's life, then it's him.

Surfing is a year-round experience for him, not that he's alone in that. And while everyone has bemoaned the worst summer in living memory, Rob is not so harsh on the weatherman. For surfers, conditions have been better than the norm.

'We've been getting in quite a lot more than in recent summers,' said the man a day after he returned from south-west France and a short surfing break which was notable for the strong winds and rain which has beset the Guernsey summer.

To surf the best waves, a flexible lifestyle is priority, he said.

His job – at The Surf Shop – sees him put in the hours across weekdays and weekends. In return, when it's time to surf, he has the 'green card' to do what he loves best.

Like most things, practice makes perfect.

'It's quite easy to stand up [on a board] but once you start to do manoeuvres it gets very difficult,' he said.

'The waves are very quick and quickly close out. You have to pick and choose the ones with the best shape and with 30 or 40 guys sometimes in the water, it's difficult. With that scenario you've got to be able to go in during the week, when it's quieter.'

Vazon is like a second home to Rob, although he admits to preferring Perelle for the best waves.

'On its day it is the best – the right-hander.

'But you have to have perfect weather for that.'

For someone who, in a perfect world, would surf 365 days a year, it's a shade surprising to hear just how often he does.

'On average, over the year, I get out once a week,' he said, before revising that number to perhaps twice. 'It's quite a lot.'

The search for surf has taken him far and wide, with Morocco his favourite.

'We travel a lot to get better,' he said.

'In Morocco you've got a selection of four to five perfect right-handers, which is very good because I'm a natural foot which means

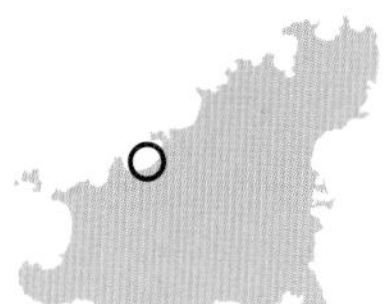

Left
Surfer dude:
Rob Ozanne

I surf with my left foot forward – going my natural way.

'There's one wave in Morocco that's two minutes long. A day's surfing there is like a year's surfing in Guernsey.'

Rob has now been to Morocco three times and other surf trip locations have included the Canary Islands, Barbados, Australia, Bali and Hawaii.

He is happy to admit that his competition days are over.

'I'd rather surf for myself and, anyway, all the youngsters are becoming very good. It's a progressive sport here and you need to stay very fit.'

And why surf?

'It's the buzz of getting out there and paddling into this wave that's going to push you along. You're with nature and you never quite know what you are going to get.'

And when he's not in the water, it's surf talk.

'It's a very sociable sport out of the water, but in the water you are for yourself, you are all hungry. But there's a lot of chatting done over a couple of beers.'

SURFERS' PARADISE

THINK Vazon, think surf. I do and I have never climbed on a surfboard. But having ploughed through the Guernsey Surf Club's 25th anniversary booklet, which was available at a reasonable £1 back in January 1990, I feel a tinge of regret. Cricket was good but these surfers really did seem to have a better time of it.

Vazon may not be the best beach in the world for surfing, but it is renowned for it and has been for some time.

Its origins at Vazon are not entirely clear.

The Guernsey Surf Club came into being in the mid-1960s and most credit for its introduction is given to the late Dave Fletcher, the man who founded Fletcher Sports.

The early boards were a monstrous 12ft-plus long and constructed from plywood on timber frames.

When dry they weighed 70lb, but they could pick up the smallest of waves, even if it only took you in a straight line.

The island was soon being put on the world surfing map by Peter Dixon of Malibu Beach, California.

In his book 'Where The Surfers Are' he covered the top surf spots in the world and on three pages devoted to the Channel Islands, he reported that: 'The surfers of Guernsey are perhaps the best organised in the world.'

Get seriously stoked in Guernsey was the message and surfers have been doing so for 40 years. They came from all walks of life – and still do.

The Guernsey Surf Club has had various homes, most notably the Green Hut in a field opposite La Mare de Carteret school, of all

Above
Peter Frankland is snapped at Vazon by mate and fellow photographer Alex Wallace in this magnificent surfing scene

places, and Fort Richmond.

The Green Hut was the place to retire to when the surf was not up or when surfers simply needed a rest from the whole exhausting exercise.

And when the hut was no more, the club moved close to its spiritual waves and a few hundred yards away at Fort Richmond.

Opened in 1969, the new HQ provided surfers with a coffee bar, 42ft clubroom, TV lounge, committee room, bunkhouse and showers.

But it simply cost too much to run and the responsibility of paying back a bank loan was not a surfers' thing as this brief extract from the club history shows: 'Guys were beginning to say things like, "surfing is about waves and the beach, not clubhouses and raising money" and that was true, even if hard to listen to.'

So the club moved away from organised surfing and in the 1970s returned to more of an 'I just wanna go surfing' movement.

The surfing options at Vazon are more varied than you might think.

There are five areas to surf. There is the beach itself and also the reef, when the tide is too high for the beach and the left-hander on the reef starts to break.

Then there is the Vazon Reef for right-handers, which comes into its own on a spring tide when the taller rocks are covered sufficiently.

The other side is a fourth alternative, which is made available on a big swell, and if they were not enough to lure you down, there is the centre reef which was regularly ridden in the 1960s.

PROFITING FROM TRAGEDY

IT'S human nature that few turn their back on profit handed to them on a plate, even if it comes as the result of death. No better example came than in January 1974, when the Cypriot timber ship Prosperity went down off Perelle in hurricane seas with all 18 lives lost.

Down at Vazon the next day you could not see sand for timber, so much of it had been spilled over the sides of the stricken ship.

Nobody knows just how many islanders benefited from the estimated 21,000-plus pieces of timber washed ashore, but it was many dozens.

'It was a fantastic sight,' described the Guernsey Evening Press, carelessly forgetting the tragedy that had gone on two nights previously.

The States acted quickly, sending officials and police to the scene. Vehicle numbers were taken and drivers were told that the wood had to be taken to the Phoenix Mills yard, in the Charroterie. The receiver of wrecks would then sort out ownership.

The total cost of the timber washed ashore was estimated at £250,000.

Many a new house was probably built with it and even though it was illegal to simply take it, there was only so much the authorities could do and were prepared to do, as civil servant Richard Kirkpatrick recalled on his retirement earlier this year.

He told of Louis Guillemette, his boss and the then States supervisor and receiver of wrecks, boasting how to stop the big wood loot.

'This is how you deal with it Kirk,' he said, before approaching a man who had just finished loading his trailer with the long lengths of timber. 'Take the wood to the States yard and you will get a receipt to claim salvage rights later.'

The reply was short and not so sweet.

'**** off,' said the man, who jumped on his tractor and set off to build himself a new life.

Above right and below right
Profiting from tragedy and the cargo from the stricken Prosperity

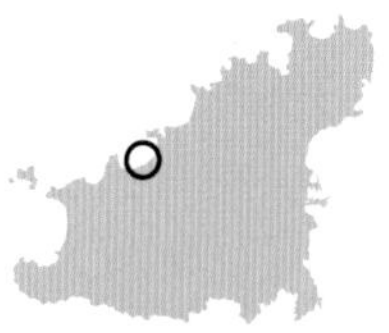

Above
The Prosperity aground

The whole question of salvage proved a thorny problem for Guillemette and the police, who came under fire from Guernsey Shore-gatherers Association president Helier Le Cheminant, for their handling of the affair.

The association asked what right the police had to stop islanders from profiting, when some were allowed to take wood and others were not.

Le Cheminant, quoted in the Evening Press, summed it up thus: 'The captain of the ship, in effect, threw away the timber when he abandoned ship and so people who pick it up can't be accused of stealing by finding.'

More than 33 years on, Richard Kirkpatrick said the GSGA man was way off the mark and that islanders were not entitled to take the wood.

'Some people did very well out of it, but some did badly, putting it on their roofs only to find later it split because it was covered in salt and had not been treated,' he said.

But he is not aware of there being any prosecutions.

'They came to agreements with the people concerned,' said the former civil servant. 'After the first 24 hours just about everybody did it by the book.'

And those who didn't? Some time later the Salvage Association, representing the ship's owners, went banging on people's doors, even hiring a helicopter to peer into west-coaster's back gardens in the search of poached timber.

SUPERB SEAMANSHIP WHILE FIGHTING FRENCH

Above
Battle scene featuring Admiral de Saumarez in the Crescent

A LEGENDARY sea battle was fought off Vazon in the summer of 1794. And its site could scarcely have been more appropriate for the man who was fighting in the British corner against the dastardly French.

The man in charge of the Navy vessel Crescent was none other than James Saumarez, who had been given special responsibility for the defence of the Channel Islands from Napoleon's ships.

Two hundred years ago the Iles de la Manche were a thorn in the French side, with privateers playing havoc with French merchant ships. The governor of Cherbourg referred to us as 'the despair of France'.

Napoleon referred to the Channel Islands as 'a nest of brigands and assassins'. No sitting on the fence there.

By the start of 1794 there were real fears of a French invasion of the islands and in June of that year Crescent and Saumarez were to clash with the French.

On 6 June, Crescent's commander was given orders to proceed from Plymouth to Guernsey and the following day they left port at 6.30pm. Twelve hours later they were faced with two 54-gun French battleships, two 36-gun frigates, a 12-gun corvette and a cutter.

Saumarez and his two accompanying frigates were in big trouble. Perhaps doomed.

Outgunned, Saumarez had to use all his sea skills to escape the French and ultimately it involved heading straight at Fort Hommet point.

With the French ships firing, Saumarez would rather be run aground on his own island than be captured and to the full view of islanders, including the then Lt-Governor, the sea hero steered Crescent, with its Guernsey pilot Jean Breton directing, for a narrow passage just off Vazon.

The French, lacking local knowledge, wisely chose to stay clear and Crescent, within a mile of the beach and an 18ft draught to contend with, avoided the potentially ruinous rocks before tacking north and to the safety of the Little Russel.

With no accurate chart to guide him, it was amazing seamanship.

It appears that Saumarez steered Crescent through a 200-yard-wide gap between the dangerous Grunes and Susanne reefs, two miles off Fort Hommet.

Legend has it that Saumarez asked his fellow Guernseyman Breton if he knew where they were in relation to the reefs and received the reply: 'Surely, for there is your house and over there is mine.'

LES DUNES

THESE days the biggest bikes on the Vazon sprint cover the quarter-mile from the Martello tower at its north end to the finish line approaching Le Gele Road, in less than 10sec.

Had those bikers tried something similar on the first Vazon coast roads they would have had difficulty in finding a quarter-mile to race along and if they had what they would have found was rough enough to bump them over their own handlebars.

As recently as about 150 years Vazon did not have a road to link the Albecq end with Richmond.

All that existed until then was a short sandy stretch of cart pathway which cut in from the Route de la Margion at Richmond and continued, tucked behind the dunes, in front of a small collection of old Guernsey cottages for a few hundred yards.

In time the path would be extended to join Le Gele Road, but until 1853 when the States of Guernsey voted to provide a much needed link along the island's longest bay, to reach Perelle from the north was by one of the old military roads which ran parallel with the bay and above La Grande Mare and beyond.

It's odd to think that at a time when the authorities talk in millions of resurfacing the Guernsey Airport, that Vazon's first coast road – 16ft wide all along – cost them less than princely sum of £236 plus the £40 the Castel parish agreed to chip in.

My great, great grandfather Nicholas Batiste, who lived at Les Dunes in those Victorian years, would probably have witnessed the first Vazon Road, no doubt a dirt creation which was splattered daily by the droppings of those equine slaves to the carriages and carts which clip-clopped the way up and down the stretch.

Walter, Nicholas's brother, still lived down the 'Doons' until he passed away in 1915, the year after Stanley Brehaut was born out St Peter's but destined to move to the Dunes and spent virtually his whole life there.

Stan Brehaut is a sprightly 96 and has now spent 77 years living behind those sandy verges on the west side of Vazon.

And, other than bemoaning the lack of upkeep of the Dunes, it is happy to hear him report that nothing too much has changes down his way in nearly eight full decades.

The old sandy cart path still runs in front of the cottages which, in latter years, have been joined by more modern creations, and while some additional 'drives' have been added to link the old road with the new one, Stan still wakes up every day, opens his eyes and sees the same Dunes.

But there have been subtle and some not too subtle changes over the course of the 20th century and generally for the worse.

The greatest loss is the splendidly named John Thomas slip which ran down the beach from the point where the Germans built the concrete bunker which today provides the

Left
Les Dunes' oldest resident Stanley Brehaut outside his home

little beach kiosk with shelter from the north.

Les Dunes' 'John Thomas' was, like many island slips, dismantled by the occupying forces, but it is marked clear as day on the old ordinance survey maps and, thanks to the local knowledge of Hugh Lenfestey, it is easy to envisage the slip when you are made aware that it ran in a direct line from the diagonal road which today links Vazon and Le Gele.

Mr Lenfestey is as knowledgeable as most on the area given that he is responsible for monitoring the interests on the land which lie on the old Fief Le Compte.

Who owns and is responsible for what down this stretch of coast is not always so clear cut.

'The best analogy I can give it,' said Mr Lenfestey, 'is the problem of the car park at Cobo. It is nearly the same situation.'

He stresses that there is no titled ownership of much of the Les Dunes and that the States, from time to time, give it the equivalent of a short, back and sides, but in the middle section much of the foreshore is land owned by Fief Le Compte.

Stan Brehaut, though, has no cause to wait for the Works department to keep his part of Les Dunes tidy.

His patch up to the main road is cut regularly and he just wished the rest of the stretch was as well looked after.

Here is a man who, when a boy at St Peter's School, recalls the horse carriages carrying King George V past.

'It was 1921 and the King came past in his carriage.'

He recalls the former Vazon Hotel as a farmhouse run by Mr Dorey 'facing the other way'.

Right
Guernsey's fastest stretch of road?

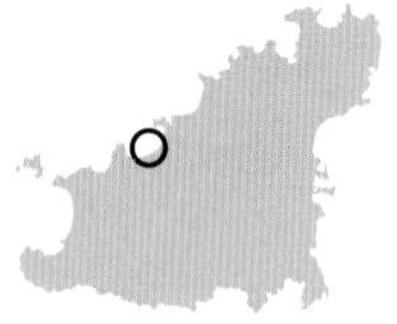

And at the Les Dunes he remembers a time when the locals would sit on the sea wall in summertime until late.

Out in front by the same seawall the farmers would dry their seaweed.

He has endless stories of old Guernsey to tell and life on the west coast, particularly Occupied Guernsey.

'The train was passing the Dunes when a bag of cement fell off. Grandpa [Edwin] Martel picked it up and put in the shed.

'The Germans found it and gave him six months in jail but the waiting list was so long he never went in because the jail was so full.'

One person he did get to see in jail was Andros Nicolle.

"The Germans put some barbed wire through his land where his heifers were.

'He came along, got his hay fork out and charged the officer. They took him away, threw away his shoes and walked him all the way to town.'

He recalls his trips to town in his grand-mothers carriage.

And while his memory remains sharp so do his eyes and thanks to the remarkable handiwork of his son Robert, he has a rather unique piece of back garden.

Robert, better known as Bob, the former Guernsey Muratti captain, has snaffled a patch to house his handmade miniature and largely granite versions of notable local buildings.

He has built his own version of the Hanois lighthouse, the Vale Mill, the original and current Torteval parish churches, the original Gardner's Royal Hotel, a Martello Tower, the old Tudor House and many more.

The granite chippings he used came from

This page and top right
Bob Brehaut has fashioned a remarkable miniature garden at Les Dunes

an old well on his Rue de Preel property.

He has used it wisely and skilfully.

'I started doing it when I heard a programme on Radio Guernsey asking people what they would do when they retired.

'I owned a little bungalow in St Martin's then and I saw an old Guernsey house opposite. I suddenly thought that I am going to build it in miniature form.'

But why Guernsey properties only?

'I built them to teach my grandchildren something of the history of Guernsey.

'It is a full-time job.'

Well, that is not quite true. It is full-time within his retirement years.

He has been working on this superb collection for 23 years.

But, recently, he has ensured a setback on the construction front.

Many of the miniature buildings at the house he shares with his partner were largely destroyed by an over-excited pet dog.

Indeed, as we talk in the garage of his father's small coastline cottage, he is working on repairing an old Guernsey house that existed in Cow Lane.

But the biggest Brehaut miniature construction is not for Les Dunes.

His version of the Vale Castle is just too big to take there, being 10ft high.

'The next biggest is the most amazing building in Guernsey,' he says,' the Hanois.'

His Vale Mill, complete with moving blades/paddles/arms, pushes it close for stature but I share his feeling for the Hanois which so many of us easily associate with living on this island.

Bob may now live away from Les Dunes but his passion for the area remains strong.

After all, this is where he grew up and he and fellow Muratti veteran, Vince Tostevin, played football on a Les Dunes which was kept

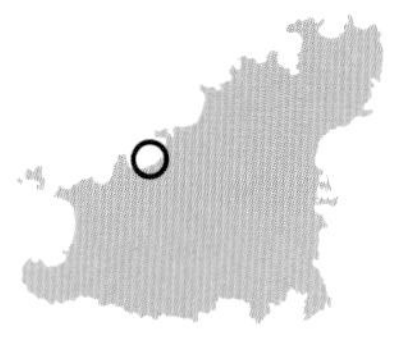

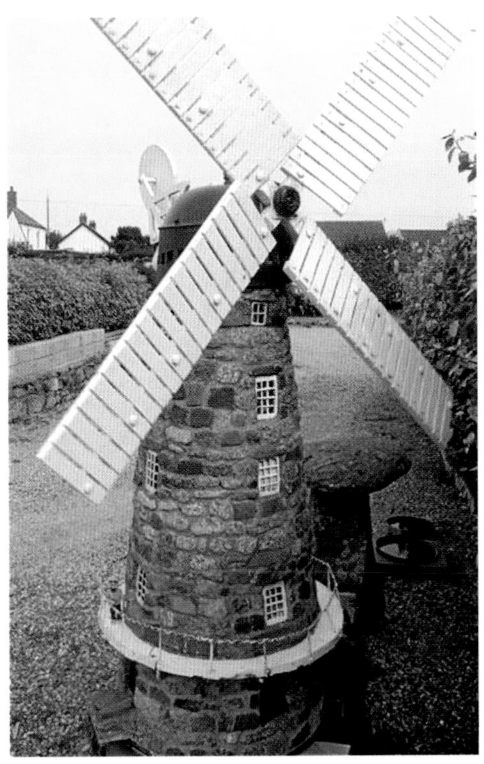

short by the grazing cattle.

Things have changed.

'Look at it today. It was almost a straight field when we played as boys.'

Today's Dunes has numerous driveways linking it with the main road.

Just a well-hit pass away on the Richmond slip, Bob stood in 1944 and watched, with others, German artillery target and hit an aircraft over Vazon bay.

The Germans cheered and when the engine fell off they thought it would go down, but it just carried on flying.

Over the next half-hour or so Bob takes me on an exploration of the Richmond headland.

Despite his obvious fondness for the play area of his childhood he is saddened by many things he finds there today, one of them being the existence of a huge slap of Todt built concrete which today blocks the exit from the old winding Le Crocq slipway until the war.

Much of the lower part of it still exists, but just as pronounced is the erosion of the headland. Some of the methods of remedying the onslaught by sea and wind have seen builders' rubble used at Le Crocq as landowners do what they can to keep hold of the land they imagined they had.

One such owner, George Allez, has known it all his life and seen much of the headland slip away.

'We [landowners] all tried to stop the erosion but to no avail.

'The whole area has changed, but to put a measure on it would be difficult.'

Pressed on the suggestion it might be as much as a yard a year, he baulks at that figure.

'I don't know about a yard a year but there has definitely been 10 feet lost in the last 38 years I've been here.

'Funny enough it seems to have stabilised a little but at La Marette [beach] you can see it has washed away a hell of a lot.'

And where will it all end?

My guess is the sea.

Left
Tom Le Prevost gets to grips with his seaweed fertiliser

THOROUGHBRED BEACH USERS

TRAINING race horses locally is going the same way as the collection of seaweed.

In terms of numbers – downhill.

But the one trainer we have got is as good as they get in the Channel Islands and the Vazon sands are as important to Tom Bougourd as is the hay he feeds his star mounts: King of the Beers and Garden Party.

'They've got to have a good blow out between races,' says Tom and there is no better place to get a horse at full speed than our widest beach.

These days the work is done by Jackie Bougourd, Tom's daughter, and star showjumping rider Emma Dorey, on what the owner calls wider Vazon. But until relatively recently it was the Richmond end that was Tom's preference.

'I'd still like to do it down here at this end but somehow it's got too rough to use.'

By rough he means stones and seaweed and ever since he returned to training after 13 years away from the business of nursing winners, he has had to dispense with this end of the beach, which he regards as a shame as the sand is better for his horse's legs. It has more give.

The stretch he would utilise was half-a-mile in length. But there was a time, he says, that there was enough sand under the outflow pipe near La Grande Mare, that the horses could go the full length of the beach.

'The going wasn't so hard on the legs as it was at the other end', and many a trainer has recognised that.

'Some of the island's most successful horse trainers, people like Stan Ephgrave and Commander Poynder, used to use it too.'

Nowadays he has use of a field with a good sized circuit on it, but the field does not allow speed work.

'In a field you can only do a certain amount. At 40 miles an hour it does not take long for a horse to get from one end of a field to another.

'When you do the fast work to get their breathing right you've got to open them up and Vazon is right for that.'

When Richmond was operational for his horses the jockeys would slowly walk their way down from his nearby fields looking down on Les Dunes.

Now it is a case of taking them in horse

Right
Vazon's wide expanses are perfect for training flat racing horses such as King of the Beers and Garden Party ridden by Emma Dorey and Jackie Brehaut respectively

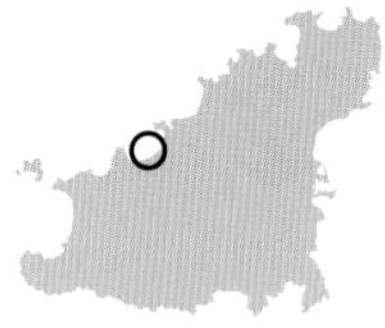

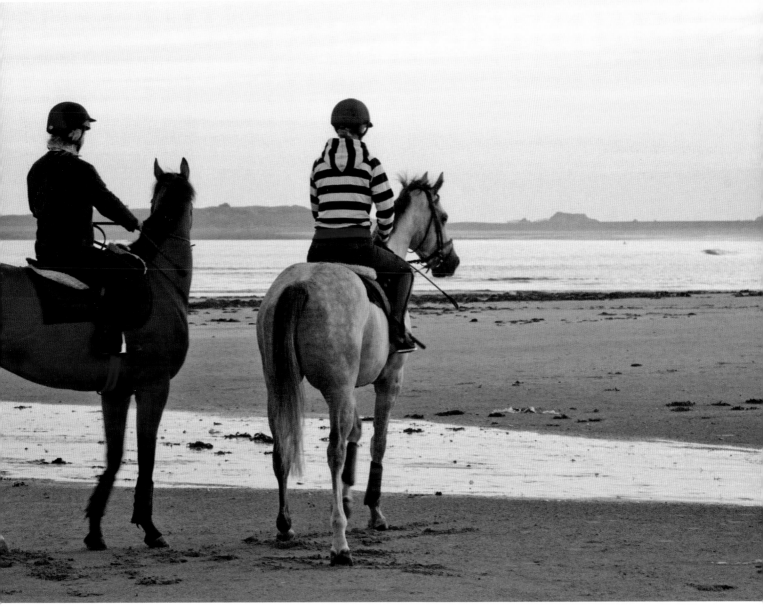

boxes to the main slipway and taking them from there.

'We always like to be down there at dawn – people-wise that is a good time.

'We always walk them around first to see for stones, soft spots and pot holes. We never go down and gallop straight away.'

Another negative to using the Richmond side of the beach is the allowance of dogs on it, which is not allowed summertime at the other end.

Racehorses and dogs are not a good mix.

'We've had dogs jumping up and grabbing their tails. I'll tell you it's not funny.'

But at the time they go nowadays that is not likely to happen.

Yet Tom still hopes for a change in the beach's characteristics to allow a return to using the end closer to his stables.

'I'm hoping it will come back.

'They [the experts] tell me it changes in cycles.'

SLIPWAYS

Above and opposite
Guernsey's finest slipway at La Marette

IF THERE is a place which signifies the island's forgotten past it is the Richmond headland.

Tucked away between Vazon and Perelle is an area which had its golden years in the monochromic days of vraic collecting with the use of horse and cart.

Look closely enough and you will see what I'm talking about.

For a piece of coastland which cannot be more than a half-of-a-mile in length it had five slipways, if you count the two existing and working ones on the extremities of the headland.

But, like with other parts of the Guernsey coastline, the Germans intervened and now you will find just one still readily usable, the other two having either been part destroyed or largely cut off and left to the tides, gradually no doubt to steadily fall into disrepair.

The most northerly of the trio at Le Crocq is the one which intrigues most, La Marette facing west that catches the eye.

Until the Germans arrived and Bob Brehaut, born and raised of these parts, can testify that the slipway exited the headland perimeter to meet the main coast road.

'It was one of the places where the old farmers went out to cut the bobble vraic,' says Bob.

Seventy years on, the impeccably built blue granite structure is just a slip of its past glory, the Germans having taken away the top half, and the old cart path is blocked by a whopping piece of Todt designed concrete which is situated on private land.

It was a slipway with a difference.

This did not simply climb straight off the beach in a direct line, it wound its way parallel to the coastland before climbing out.

Barely 100 yards away to the west you will find another slip. This remains in one piece from its base point in the rocky beachline, only the exit onto what would have been the old road has narrowed to the degree you would barely get a horse through let alone a cart or a wagon of any sort.

The whole headland is, sad to write, a bit of an eyesore.

It is eroding badly and with that coastline being in private ownership the States have no inclination to lay out taxpayers money for its upkeep.

The result?

Landowners having to dip into their own pocket to shore up the bottoms of these most natural of gardens with all sorts of builders rubble. It is neither pretty or what you would wish to see.

Bob makes a plea, in hope, rather than expectancy, that the States do something to do their bit to stop the steady erosion which, he estimates, is up to a yard a year in some parts.

"The nicest time was in the winter when the elements were throwing everything at you. It was absolutely amazing"

Noel Le Tissier

CHAPTER 29

ALBECQ

Spectacularly pink, simply gorgeous and with a coastal road carved out of Cobo's finest and most distinctive granite. What better place to view from afar the start and finishing point of this coastal story.

ON THE ROCKS · ROOMS WITH A VIEW
END OF THE ROAD · AXE MURDER · RECHARGING BATTERY

ON THE ROCKS

THERE are rocks and there are special rocks.

Albecq has the latter in spades.

To many islanders, there is no more striking and beautiful stretch of coastline than the quarter-mile up and around Albecq headland.

And for the hundreds of motorists who pass over it each day of the week, it is one snatch of road in our forever choking transport system that is always a delight to navigate.

Many moons ago, National Geographic magazine recognised Albecq's natural beauty with a full-page colour spread showing local youngsters splashing about in the 'Randall' and wherever you cast the eye at Albecq,

Below
Lion Rock

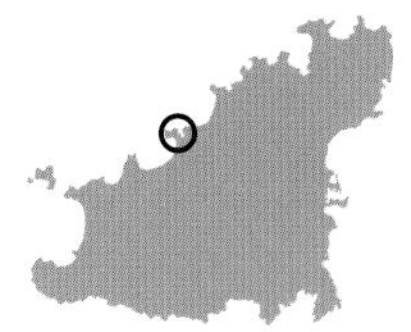

especially in the sun, the beholder is struck by the stunning imagery.

The outcrops of pinky-red granite are no less colourful than their counterparts across the bay stretching out at Grandes Rocques, but the elevation that the Albecq headland provides to the viewer is something extra special, with Grosse Rocque standing proud a mile or so away at the entrance to Cobo Bay and masses of pink granite stretching out to it, not to mention the equally rugged rocks down the coastal edge towards the white sands of Cobo.

It's an awe-inspiring sight – whether under the brightest blue skies of summer or the wildest, gale-beaten days of autumn or winter – and has been in my mind from the very first day mother dragged me out to surely one of the most beautifully situated doctor's surgeries in the world, Dr Heard's.

It's 30 years or more since the surgery shut its doors, to be replaced by the modern Cobo Health Centre in Route de Carteret.

Inland, Cobo has changed almost beyond recognition in 40 years but out on the point at Albecq few things alter, apart from the modernising of property.

The rocks have lost nothing of their rugged beauty and the pounding of them on a daily basis has led to some strangely shaped ones, the most impressive of all being the Lion Rock.

That lies on the Vazon side of the headland, while to the Cobo side are rocks which, if you look much more closely than required to see a lion around the corner, resemble a baboon and a camel.

Of the three, the Lion Rock bears the most uncanny look and there is arguably no better place to view it than from the lounge of Giffarderie residents John and Marlene Lihou.

Their renovated property, Bergen, was built by the Shaws in 1910 and was specifically situated to maximise the view of the lion's head and mane.

And lying back in John's reclining chiropractic chair, patients can admire the lion in its full glory.

The owner has a photograph on a wall of

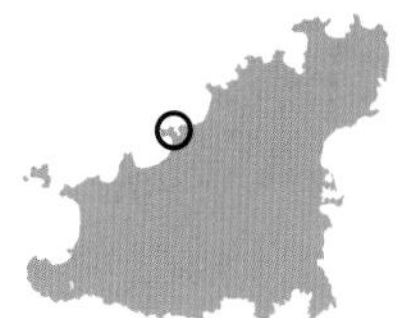

the midsummer's day sunset setting precisely over the lion's head.

Then there's the chateau that was on Lion's Rock.

Hundreds of years of erosion have only added to the issues of access, but it is hard to imagine it being anything remotely grandiose given the sheer unevenness of its base.

But clamber among the giant rocks which separate Albecq and Portelet bays and the odd remaining granite walls give lasting proof of some fashion of a building.

Then there is Albecq Bay itself, perfectly horseshoed but so sadly short in sand and swimming opportunity.

In past centuries, small fishing fleets operated from it and old plans of the bay clearly indicate a pier of sorts in the bay's centre, but nowadays you will see just one boat moored there in the summer months, owned by John.

His central mooring enables him to use his old wooden vessel from half-tide up to half-tide down, but as a regular user he is oblivious to any remnants of a pier, probably long worn away by the sea.

What is clear at low water is a beach passage cut through the granite, no doubt to enable carts to be pulled down to the centre of the bay.

To my mind, Albecq is a 'what-if?' bay, one which, if it had long stretches of sand across its innermost parts, would be a recreational delight to match the similarly-shaped Port Soif a couple of miles up the coast.

Opposite
Local youngsters splash around in the 'Randall' in 1938. the House of Mirrors is on the right.
Below
What is left of Chateaux Albecq

ROOMS WITH A VIEW

THE structure may not be to everyone's liking, but the situation is outstanding.

The sale of Manora, the early 20th-century house sitting on top of the Albecq peninsula, was one of the prize offerings on the local market in 2008.

Sarnia Estates was in number one position to sell the property – surely a seven-figure one – from the moment its boss, Noel Le Tissier, was born and raised there.

It may possess just about the most awkward front garden to mow in Guernsey, but Manora was a jewel in the island property crown when it went on the market following the death of Dorothy Le Tissier earlier this year.

Dorothy and her late husband Clarence bought it in around 1950 and raised six children, including Noel, the former star of the Guernsey hillclimb and motor sprint scene.

'It was fantastic to be brought up there as kids,' said Noel, who will always have a fondness for the property, even now it has slipped from the family's hands.

'The reason my parents bought it was that it had a lot of bedrooms,' he added.

Six to be precise.

Noel said it was a privilege to live there and sample the extraordinary views.

Right
A panoramic view of the Albecq headland

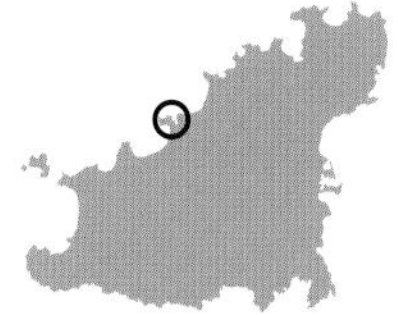

'The nicest time was in the winter when the elements were throwing everything at you.

It was absolutely amazing.' What few know is that when you own Manora, you own a stretch of land the other side of the road immediately above what old islanders know as the Randall.

The picnic area is in the deeds and it will be interesting to know whether the still-anonymous new owners plan to strip that part of their land of its scrub and return it to a more appealing grassy patch.

As children, the Le Tissiers would swim in the big, deep gully below, which takes its name from the brewing family who built the house in 1909.

When the Randalls moved in, they would have had relatively few neighbours, but one of them would have been Amos Chick, who operated the first Cobo Hotel, at the bottom of the Banquette hill.

Chick had owned a large slice of the Albecq headland, which attracted many an artist to its shoreline, not to mention iconic author, Victor Hugo.

The author had Albecq in his mind when he referred to its golden rocks as 'assassins of the night' in Toilers of the Sea.

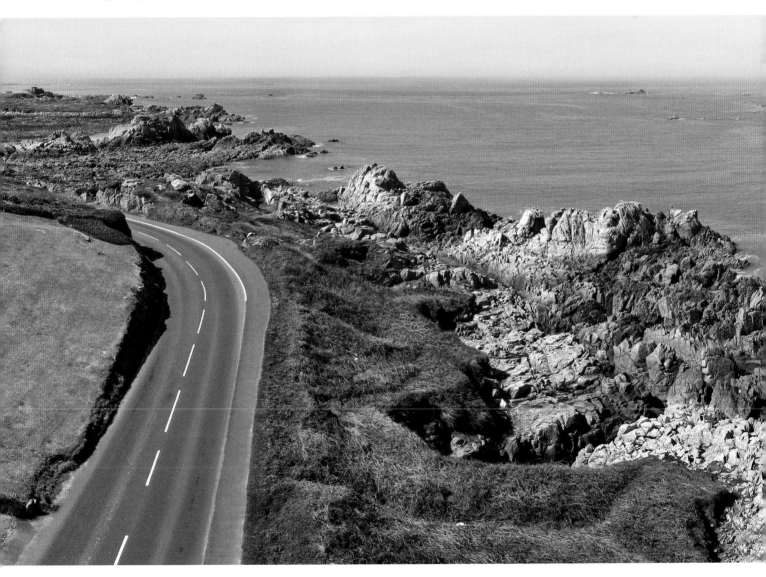

THE END OF THE ROAD

UP TO the late 19th century, a walk or ride from Cobo to Vazon necessitated a diversion up the Banquette Road and down the other side along La Giffarderie.

Then, in 1872 and for the less-than-princely-sum of £785, the States voted to buy the necessary land to make James Duquemin's coastal road plans a reality.

The detailed drawings – available to see at the Island Archives – reveal a few surprises, though, back in the day when Amos Chick's hotel at the foot of La Banquette was a popular stopping-off point for parties from Town seeking refreshments.

As a road, there is nothing special about it at all, being nothing more than a winding 20ft dust track running parallel with the coastline.

But more interesting is the route which the States engineer initially proposed but, for a reason undisclosed, was not followed up.

The plans clearly show that the road we all know was an alternative proposition to the one which the States engineer put forward, which would have taken a slightly more northerly route around the headland itself.

The Press of the time offered no discussion on the matter of plan choice, but it is reasonable to assume that the States opted for plan B due to costs.

Plan A would have necessitated more infill and, perhaps crucially, blasting apart more of the granite headland.

It also, with the benefit of more than a century of hindsight, saved many a speeding driver losing control and heading into Portelet bay on the Vazon side of the corner.

Had Duquemin's first plan been adopted, the angle might have been fine for horses and traps, but not for our modern-day cars and buses.

The logic in the decision is there for all to see, but what is mystifying is just why the engineer's 1872 plans highlight the need for a tunnel under the road into Portelet Bay.

The archway tunnel is drawn as 6ft in height, 5ft in width and opened into the freshwater abreuvoir at the central point of Portelet.

Such abreuvoirs – places for cattle to drink – may be a characteristic feature of the Guernsey landscape, with more than 140 granite ones built between about 1870 and 1920, but why would one be required at a place where today nobody but the very occasional out-of-control and speeding car driver venture?

The tunnel to the fresh-water drinking

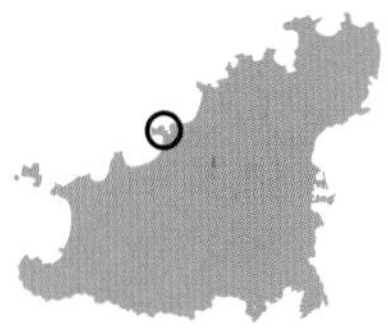

Left
Albecq Bay from the skies
Overleaf
Turning the corner in the early part of the 20th century

troughs is perhaps simple proof of Guernsey's early 19th-century love and dedication to the cow and that this subterranean access was required to allow the Albecq herds to wander down there to quench their thirst and feel the splash of salt on their faces.

After all, refreshing seawater beats flies.

It could be that the tunnel into the abreuvoir was situated on a natural stream into Portelet, but whatever is the truth, the hole under the road has long disappeared, probably hidden by the reinforcing concrete wall laid by the occupying forces as they laid a railway line along this stretch.

The other possibility, but unlikely need for a tunnel down to Portelet, was an exit for horsepulled stonecarts.

The same 1872 plans indicate headland quarries and it just might have been the best way to take away the blasted pink stone from the lower reaches of the quarries there.

Sadly we will never know and, indeed, there is no proof that Duquemin's tunnel was ever completed.

It's sentimentally warming to think that it was, though, and Albecq resident and landowner

119 GUERNSEY. — Cobo. — The Roadway. —

La Route. — LL.

Above
Rough weather day

John Lihou is aware that there is some sort of well and spring buried under a swathe of gorse on the slope close to the coast road.

Three landowners benefited from the Albecq road plan, but it hardly made them rich.

The largest proportions of the headland were owned by Edward Carre, William D. Girard and Cobo Hotel owner Amos Chick, while a P. Falla also sold off a small section, which years later became known as the site for Steve Duquemin's infamous bungalow, known as both the Glasshouse and the House of Mirrors.

It was razed by fire shortly before the Occupation and – like the idyllic, white seaside cottage, La Digue, destroyed by the Germans in 1942 – was never rebuilt: permission was refused by the States.

Dig deep among the bracken and weeds and telltale signs of Duquemin's coastal house – he also owned Bergen, another Albecq property in the Giffarderie – remain.

They also stay fairly vividly in the memory of Herbert Nichols, one of neighbouring Cobo's lingering and most respected links with old Guernsey.

He knew the property as the House of Mirrors for its unusual hallway, which, from its roadside entrance, had mirrors from top to bottom.

'I think he did it to light up the place,' recalls Herbert who, along with his Castel schoolmates at the start of the Occupation, found good use for the mirrors as they played among the charred ruins of the building.

'We used to hold them up like big picture frames and shine them at the Coquelin at Grandes Rocques,' he said.

'I'm not sure if they reached the Coquelin, but they'd shine a beam a long way. But then the Germans came around and told us we were not to do it any more.'

Herbert was 10 at the start of the Second World War and recalls other encounters with Germans at Albecq.

'At the beginning of the Occupation we'd put some crab pots off the rocks. There were loads of them [spider crabs] then and they would just walk up the side of the rocks.

'One day, we were coming up with some crabs in a sack and an officer stopped me and asked, 'What have you got there?'.

He was amazed.

'He could speak a bit of English and I gave him one and told him to try it. Anyway, a few days later I went down to the rocks again and he was there, lifting my pots.

I said, "Eh, what are you doing?".

He said that the crab was so good he wanted to get another one. An armed German against a 10-year-old is hardly a fair contest.

Sensibly, young Herbert told him he did not mind him taking them as long as he re-baited them afterwards.

'I showed him how to bait it with limpets. But in the end there was more and more barbed wire put down and they stopped us going onto the rocks.'

ALBECQ AXE MURDER

FIFTY years ago, the story of the year was centred on the quiet headland and the killing of Florence Murdoch by her insane daughter, Isabelle.

For quiet Guernsey, it was a chilling tale to match any before or since.

On 19 March 1958, the 88-year-old widow of 36 years was killed by a knife and axe attack.

Her daughter, Isabelle, 63, was charged with murder but at a court hearing two months later she was found not guilty on the grounds of her insanity and spent the rest of her days locked away at the Castel Hospital.

At the end of a three-day trial, the Royal Court confirmed she had killed her mother, but had been absent of her senses at the time.

The Bailiff, Ambrose Sherwill, described it as the most tragic case he had encountered.

Both women had shared the house, Dalbeattie, built by the family just before the Second World War.

Like many houses in the area, the Germans used it during the Occupation and, after extensive repairs to the eight-room house, the Murdochs had returned there after the war.

The ladies were described as charming people, members of the Ebenezer Church and always together.

But something went terribly wrong to the extent that, on that fateful day, the old lady was discovered battered to death in a ground-floor front room.

Her daughter was discovered unconscious outside a locked front door.

At the trial, it was heard that Isabelle had been devoted to looking after her ailing mother and had become very depressed in the months leading up to the tragic day.

Trial evidence painted the picture of her muddled mind.

'You mean to tell me, doctor, that I am accused of killing my mother?' she is reported to have asked her family doctor, Dr Heard, while in custody.

But she was more informative in front of a UK psychiatrist, saying that it was while chopping wood earlier in the day that she had decided to kill her mother, who was fretful of their financial situation.

'I used brute force,' she admitted.

'I hit her on the head with the mallet and she fell, saying, "Bella, Bella". I made sure she was dead by knocking the knife into her throat. It's all so hazy I can't remember a quarter of it.'

But she was also able to recall her own suicide attempt.

'I walked into the kitchen to put my head into the gas oven. I wanted to end it for the both of us.'

Below
Albecq murderer
Isabelle Murdoch

hear about the tragedy.

The two-storey house is of eight rooms. It stands back from the road and is in its own grounds. A gravel drive leads up to the front porch.

It was built before the last war and has been up for sale for some time. Some windows look out over the wide sweep of Vazon Bay.

On the wooden gate at the drive entrance is the name of the house and a brass plaque bearing the words "W. D. Murdoch."

Nearest neighbours of the Murdochs live at Keswick Lodge, which is owned by Mrs. Murdoch and occupied by Mr. and Mrs. Leslie Brassel, their daughter and young son.

MISS I. MURDOCH

WOMAN CHARGED WITH MURDER

IN THE MAGISTRATE'S COURT ON MARCH 22, BEFORE MR. FRANK GAHAN, Q.C., MISS ISABELLE MURDOCH, AGED 63, WAS CHARGED WITH THE MURDER OF HER MOTHER, 88-YEAR-OLD MRS. FLORENCE MURDOCH, OF DALBEATTIE, ALBECQ, CASTEL.

The charge was read by the Deputy Greffier, Mr. R. A. Mallett, and was as follows:

RECHARGING THE BATTERY

THE benefits of being among the island's old militia were probably not much more than a warm sense of doing your bit for the safety of the island and keeping that nasty Napoleon at bay.

But at least those posted on the various batteries down the west coast were able to enjoy priceless views – and none more so than at the Burton Battery at Albecq.

For many years, though, and up until this summer, the 18th-century battery was looking very sorry for itself.

But in July the combination of the National Children's Home, the Guernsey Museum Service and Ernst & Young came together to put sparkle back into the Napoleonic and Second World War fortification.

And it was a job very well done, albeit not much more than a much-needed tarting-up exercise.

While Mont Chinchon, along the way at Perelle, has benefited from a full renovation, it seems Museums and Monuments have no immediate plans to emulate that at Albecq, merely to prevent further deterioration.

A full restoration cannot come a day too soon – in the meantime, just go up there and enjoy the spectacular views.

Right and far right
Not gone for a Burton yet: the old Burton Battery provided fantastic views for the old Militia

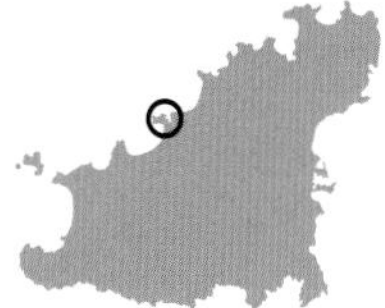

Fortification facts...

THE battery is one of more than 60 coastal batteries built towards the end of the 18th century due to the increased threat of invasion from France during the French Revolution and Napoleonic Wars (1793-1815).

The 1801 records call it the Two Gun Battery, as it had two 20-pounder cannons served by the 3rd Regiment of the Guernsey Militia.

By 1816, it was known as Fort Burton and had two more 20-pounders placed to defend the flanks of the position.

During the Occupation, the fort was utilised as a resistance nest and the armament included a mortar, three flamethrowers and several machine guns.

A reinforced personnel shelter and a small machine post are still visible.

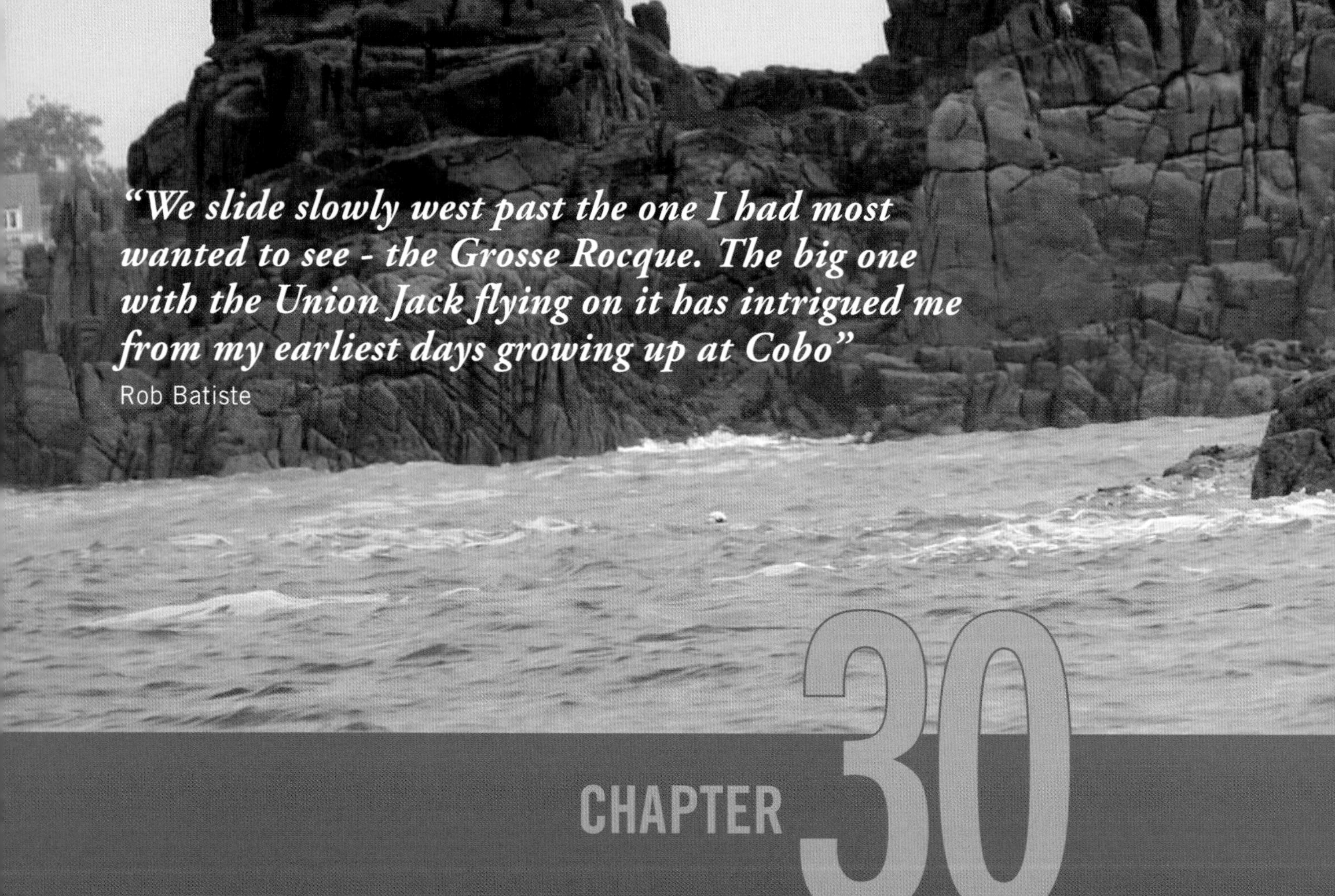

"We slide slowly west past the one I had most wanted to see - the Grosse Rocque. The big one with the Union Jack flying on it has intrigued me from my earliest days growing up at Cobo"

Rob Batiste

CHAPTER 30

THREE MEN
IN A BOAT

A spring low tide in late summer 2008 and Barry Paint, one of Guernsey's most knowledgeable men of local waters, gave the author and renowned Press photographer Brian Green a close up view of the island coastline from a boat.

ON THE ROCKS

SEAFARING is not a word you could readily use to describe me.

Come to think of it, I'm not clever in the air, either.

Like many, I feel comfortable only when the floor below me does not wobble like jelly and the horizon remains straight and doesn't veer up and down.

But an around-Guernsey boat trip, particularly one with an expert guide, has long been a personal ambition as has to see, at close quarters, the most iconic lump of granite I can think of – the Grosse Rocque.

So Barry Paint's offer of a circumnavigation of our waters was readily accepted and it was only a question of when the weather would be fair enough to set a backdrop for pretty pictures on a spring low.

Photographer Brian Green was also along for the ride on the St Sampson's pilot boat – once of the Falkland waters – but for the best part of two decades the vehicle used by Barry and his fellow pilots at the island's northern port to safely accompany the many ships down the Russel and into the harbour.

The sea would have to be flat, too, otherwise poor old Brian's expensive camera equipment could be lost overboard, along with the man himself.

So after several postponements and with the sun threatening to poke through for a sustained period, off we set through the pierheads rounding the north east coast to travel southwards eventually, once we reached the island's west coast.

Below
La Roche House peers down a south coast valley
Opposite
The Platte Fougere

THREE MEN IN A BOAT

OUR guide reckons there are 1,800 named rocks in Bailiwick waters.

Few people – if anyone – know more about them than Captain Paint, the newly elected Castel deputy.

Many rocks, of course, never get exposed to the sun and this trip was to highlight just how many lurk menacingly as the tide drops away to either create eddys, barely break the surface or lie in wait just beneath.

And while my eyes had seldom seen so much natural beauty for the first time, they were also opened to a new level of close-quarters danger.

Time and again Barry pointed to barely visible dark granite, intermittently exposed and quickly camouflaged again by a dark-blue and, as the clouds gathered, greying sea.

There was comfort at hand, though.

As well as the captain's local knowledge, accumulated over a lifetime, there was the mariners' version of sat-nav.

All we needed was the sea to behave itself and the next five-and-a-half hours would, in the words of our man with the lens, be 'wonderful' – an adjective he employed many times throughout our journey.

First stop was a visit via the mouth of the Beaucette Marina to La Platte Fougere light – 82ft of concrete tower that has stood for 98 years.

From Fort Doyle it looks barely more than a quarter-of-a-mile away when in fact it is more like a mile.

Up close – 50 metres or so away – you can clearly see the metal ladder which will take any visitor to a narrow landing which, with the aid of a grip rail, leads to a door 46ft up from the base rock.

It got its most recent facelift in the summer of 1968 when a mantle of concrete, 20ft high, was built around the existing tower, which had cost £8,500 when built to steer clear

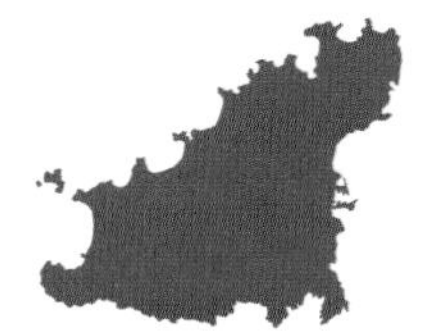

ships coming down the Russel bound for St Sampson's or St Peter Port.

When built, portland cement was used to form the base of the tower. The cement was placed in moulds, with iron bars driven into the solid rock to anchor the concrete.

On the northern side, on which the tower gets the greater pounding from the heaviest seas, massive beams of rolled steel were driven into the rock to give additional strength.

Back in 1909, when work got under way to replace the original wooden structure, the Platte became the first unmanned lighthouse in the British Isles.

For a century it has been sending out flashes, white or red, depending on direction, every 10 seconds, not to mention loudly belting out a fog warning.

Not far away to the north are the Brayes, a large group of rocks which, with their white-painted tops, dominate the view from Pembroke beach on spring lows.

In fact, they are two groups of rocks: Les Petites Brayes and slightly to the north, Les Grandes Brayes.

Between them and looking directly out from Fontenelle Bay is the first of the many Fourquies we were to come across during the afternoon.

Basically, they are everywhere off Guernsey.

Barry said there are 15 of the things – the same number as Perrons and Moulieres, the latter more associated with headlands.

A basic translation of fourquie is 'forked jagged-topped rock' and they connive to appear in the central entrance of most bays down the west coast.

'It's like the central rock of the bay,' is the captain's simple description of them.

I might have added the word 'ugly' to that.

Down through the 'Knife', a narrow stretch of water between dangerous slivers of rocks outside Creve Coeur, we soon arrive in Grand Havre, with Chouet beach blending into Ladies' Bay and then into Grand Havre itself.

The brief visit unearths another Paint fact: 'Chouet is the most sheltered bay in the Channel Islands.'

That, he explains, is due to the fact that only northerlies blow directly into it.

Back into the tidal flow down the coast, Lihou is already clear in the distance as the pilot boat moves down the Knife passage.

Next stop is Cobo, but before arriving we get a close-up view of the huge rocks outside Port Soif and ones that protect Grandes Rocques to the north.

Then we slide slowly west past the one I had most wanted to see – the Grosse Rocque.

The big one with the Union Jack flying on it has intrigued me from my earliest days growing up at Cobo.

Once, as a youth, I walked as far as I thought was possible down the reef that divides La Saline and Long Port bays.

It took me to within 100m or so of the mass and I had long wondered what it looked like from the channel side as opposed to the beach.

In truth, nothing special. Only very imposing and splattered in gull poo.

It remains a far more impressive scene from the beach. But onwards.

With a tidal time to be met at the site of the Prosperity tragedy, we could not hang about.

A quick dart into inner Cobo and close to the always-impressive Albecq headland was followed by a slow investigation of the Fort Hommet headland, which reveals the full majesty of the Fairy Cave.

We slid inside Petit Etat, in and out of Vazon and towards Barry's favourite haunt, Perelle.

It was there that he grew up and he was able to take us almost within touching distance of the beacon, also known as La Mare de la Grive [thrush].

Top left
The white-topped Brayes off L'Ancresse
Bottom left
Cormorants rest up off Creve Coeur

The sea there was still and shallow, but a couple of hundred metres back out into the bay, the swell was developing under the increasingly leaden sky to provide an extra chill to the stopping-off point at the head of La Conchee reef.

A few yards away lies the rusty remains of the doomed Prosperity's engines and generator.

All these years later it remains an eerie sight, stuck among ugly, sharpedged rocks that must have put the living fear into the Prosperity crew as they were pounded by heavy seas under darkness.

If only they had stayed on the bridge.

My mood had darkened.

It was not so much the Prosperity story but the slopping around at the entrance to the bay.

Three hours into our journey and my lunch was not nearly so secure.

Barry had been keen to retell his golden moment of a pilot's long and hugely successful career, the Vermontborg's escape off La Capelle reef and into the channel and safety.

It's a fascinating tale, but best heard a second time in the dry of the office than when feeling decidedly queasy at sea.

It really is a remarkable tale of one seaman's knowledge in horrendous weather on a dark, winter's night, with rocks to the left, right and centre to catch straying tugs or the big, empty hull which had been stranded for two weeks.

Barry directed operations in the knowledge that he had to keep the two tugs, Boxer and Lady Laura, off the bottom themselves as they sought to extricate the stricken ship.

Each had a draught of 21ft and out in the bay was the dangerous, submerged, Flabet rock.

In darkness and with no transits [visual marks], there was no way of knowing where Flabet was.

Not unless, of course, you parked the Guernsey lifeboat on top of it, which is what

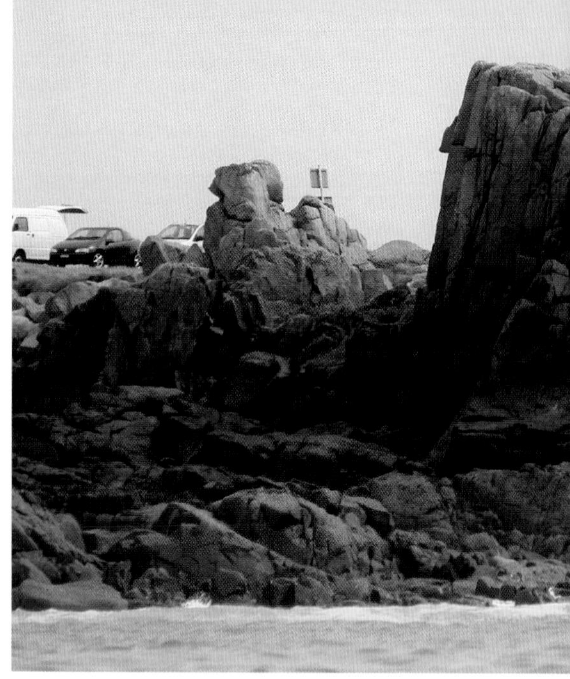

Top right
The signature rock at the mouth of Port Soif
Middle right
Lihoumel, just off Lihou Island
Bottom right
The rusty remains of the ill-fated Prosperity
Far right
Thrush Rock at Perelle

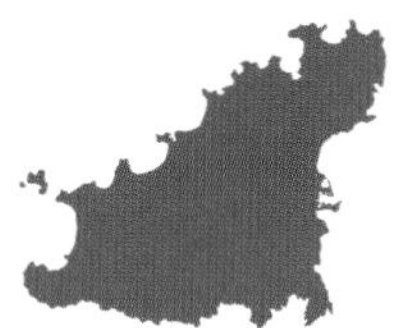

the illustrious captain did.

He said he had no choice.

'All we had was electronics and they only tell you where you have been, not where you are going. The tugs couldn't go over it. But by asking the lifeboat to sit on it, I had something to relate to.'

With 54 knots of wind blowing, it was always going to be a desperately tricky exercise, but the Vermontborg came off and Barry's plan worked a treat.

Meanwhile, the trip behind Lihou was doing nothing for my well-being.

Even with barely a breath of wind, the swells from the north Atlantic were making it very much an up-and-down experience.

A 10-minute break for a cuppa in Portelet was not nearly long enough to exact a full recovery and then it was full steam ahead for the Hanois.

With the spring tide at its lowest, the rocks on which the lighthouse has sat since 1862 were almost fully exposed.

On a sunny summer's afternoon with no wind to speak of, La Grande Boue Bissets rocks, on which the tower stands, La Mauve a short way to the north and Les Hanois reef, which sits in front of the lighthouse, must be a sight to behold at sea level.

On this occasion, the rocks were dark and ugly and as we parked in slack water 20m from the tower itself to have a picture taken,

le coq sportif

my mind was very much on matters other than the grandeur of the lighthouse.

'Let's get out of here quickly, please, Barry.' And our good old captain duly obliged, promising to take this green-gilled reporter into the lee of the south coast and calmer waters.

The half-hour stretch beneath the cliffs needed a cloudless sky to fully appreciate their splendour, but on that afternoon we clearly were not going to get it.

Gull Rock, or Les Tas de Pois d'Aval, or even Lower Peastacks, is an impressive enough site as we pass within the distance it takes Usain Bolt 9.69 seconds to run, and down from Les Tielles an abandoned vehicle reminds us of just how manageable it is to run a car off the cliffs.

We pass Creux Mahie, La Corbiere and La Roche House, white and snug in a dip of land between the big German watchtower on the west and La Prevote to the east, then into the pretty southern bays of Petit Bot, Portelet, Le Jaonnet, Saint's, Moulin Huet and Petit Port before reaching a second lot of Peastacks off Jerbourg, where our guide steered us through the narrowest of channels to save time.

The journey was all but complete, the stomach had settled and having stood virtually five hours non-stop – no wide leather seats in this boat – it was time to put the feet up, shut the eyes and try to relive the Hanois moment.

KNOW your rocks, respect the weather and you are halfway to reaching your destination. They are Barry Paint's simple rules of the sea.

'I'm not concerned about anywhere – only the weather,' he said.

'Your big dangers are with the weather, without question.' Asked if there is any stretch of Guernsey's coastline more dangerous than the rest, he replies: 'No, all of it. The nastiest piece of water is all the way within two to three miles of the coast. But any navigation is easy if you do it sensibly.'

Only one area was out of bounds on this trip and that was the renowned NW Grunes, which caught out the big bulk carrier, Elwood Mead.

'It was too dangerous to go around the NW Grunes – they are very dangerous with so many rocks around.'

Opposite
In safe hands with Barry Paint off the Hanois
Left and below
Gull Rock, aka the Lower Peastacks

"The Guardian of this sanctuary of bird and marine life is Le Petit Bon Homme d'Andriou, who stands on a grassy plateau"
Carel Toms

CHAPTER 31

ROCKS OF AGES

Thousands of rocks long protected 'old Guernsey' from sail-ship invaders. Many of them have become part of island folklore and, thankfully, there have been those who cared enough to put down on paper why they were named so and where exactly they are.

HEAVENLY FATHER OF ROCKS AND BAYS
STACKING PEAS

HEAVENLY FATHER OF ROCKS AND BAYS

THERE once was a local Reverend who had a passion for the sea.

Tourtel was his name and when he was not penning Sunday sermons at Torteval he was working on a little-known book with a title hardly like to appear at home in a Sunday Times Best Sellers List if it ever gets re-published.

Entitled 'Ancient Names of the Bays etc.' it lurks deep on the shelves of the Priaulx Library where it has no doubt slid into a small corner with all the alacrity of a Guernsey conger.

At little more than three dozen pages long and first aired in La Société Guernesiase Transactions it will certainly help you get to sleep at night, but what it also does in spades is provide a detailed and descriptive look at why the Bailiwick's many bays and both exposed and hidden rocky dangers, are called what they are today.

Remarkably, if Tourtel was right and 100% definitive in his findings Guernsey's coastline draws on names that have their beginnings in half of Europe and as far as Arabia.

From as close as Brittany, to further afield as Denmark, Norway, Sweden, Germany, Iceland, Greece and the Mediterranean as far as Syria.

The book lists more than 11 hundred named rocks and bays as, parish by parish, he circumnavigates the coastline and then moves further afield as Sark, Little Sark and, I did not know that it existed, Great Sark.

This was a Bailiwick of Victorian times, the work being published in 1898 and no doubt over the intervening generations names may have been given a modern or more local twist by fishermen and seamen in general, but it nevertheless is a fascinating insight to why the rocks were christened such.

It all starts in St Peter Port where early on Vermiere, the rock used to join the South Esplanade with the Castle all those years ago, is thought to get its name from 'Verm' a word

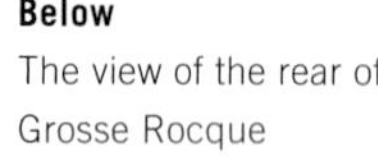

Below
The view of the rear of Grosse Rocque

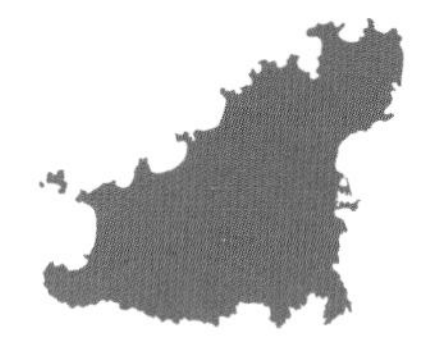

used for bait, or on the other hand may be of Celtic origin and signifying 'pointed'.

Havelet can be traced to a Scandinavian origin, and Tourtel puts his money on it to mean a very small bay or arm of the sea.

With Havelet out of the way he switched to dead women, or one anonymous one in particular,

Listed at No.12 is 'La Boue a la Morte Femme' but which poor soul inspired it is unknown.

It is, in fact, a cove where the men's pool at La Valette stands and legend has it that it was named as such because a woman's body was found floating in the area.

Anfre stems from the latin 'anfractus' - bent or broken round, winding, or as Tourtel suggests, it would stem from the Welsh word 'anfri' meaning disrespect.

The list of rocks is far too long to examine in detail here, but here are a few of my favourites.

Moving into St Martin's Bec du Nez is thought to mean either the point of the nest or the point of the coot.

Aiguillon, which can be prefixed by le petit version or le gros one, is a name given to many rocks tapering into a point.

Le Bateau a la Garce is a rock near Moulin Huet which was entitled such after a party of young ladies became surrounded by the tide.

Close by is an old spot known as 'Sous Les Cotils Dan de Mouilpied' so called from a former proprietor of a furze brake above the cliff.

Etacre is a name which crops up at various points around the island and may signify a strong stack or heap which, thankfully, most of which is forever submerged.

Off The Forest you might be unlucky enough to hit 'Le Manage au Vee', which emanates from the rock of refuge of the fairy.

Not so far away you come across La Boue au Logger, which has nothing to do with felling trees, and before we swap Forest for St Peter's and then Torteval there is La Corbiere, supposed to mean the haunt of the sea raven.

Pierre Guille, the old Guernsey discoverer, also gets his own rock, entitled La Boue de Pierre Guille.

In Torteval, Le Creux Mahie is named such due to its flattened cavern at the foot of the cliffs, or the cavern of the chief.

Les Tielles, equally foreboding when looking down from the cliff paths, may get its title from the phrase respect to the cliff.

Le Devaloir aux Vaches is the point where old horses and cows were thrown into the creek below, and not far west is Pleinmont itself, the name coming from the description 'bluff headland'.

Torteval also possesses Les Boues Arse, which these days would have an altogether more coarse meaning than the official 'rocks of defence'.

And talking of defence, few Guernsey reefs stand between a mariner and the safety of the shore, like the Hanois group.

Tourtel had names for them all, Hanois itself probably stemming from the Celtic word for agony. Apt, given the numbers that perished out there before a lighthouse was finally built.

The lighthouse itself is situated on the Bise rock, the word seeming to signify two united rocks.

What is hard to imagine is the story that in the year 709 the west coast was hit by a tsunami of sorts.

Les Hanois comprised a number of grass-topped small islets, but such was the power of the wave it was stripped of much of its soil and grass.

For the rest of the journey up the west coast veteran mariner Barry Paint contributed his vast knowledge gained by his years as a sea pilot.

Barry is well aware of Tourtel's works and is slowly working away on his own record of the Bailiwick rocks.

And as he regularly refers to his charts to show this novice the exact positioning of the distant reefs, it quickly becomes clear that many of the rocks Tourtel named have become anglicized in name almost out of recognition over a century and more.

The alterations are understandable and inevitable as different generations begin to introduce subtle variations to the rock titles, but what bothers Barry is that so many rocks are on the verge of becoming anonymous to future generations as their names become unused and forgotten.

Looking down on wider Rocquaine from our perch in the Pleinmont car park he points out a rock that Tourtel named Les Boues de la Genouinne.

Nowadays it is simply known as Nipple Rock due to its point always being above water.

Elsewhere in the bay is the most south-west of 14 Moulieres dotted around our coast, while across the bay at the Lihou headland side he points to Gourban which within in its possesses a hot-spot for ormers, if there is still such thing as a place.

It's at this point that Barry points out that Pleinmont is the only place on the island where you can see the three major lighthouses in the region - the Casquets, Les Hanois and Roches Douvres – all within 40-odd miles.

Before moving on up the coast we go back on ourselves a short distance to view the Gull Rock in Gull Bay or, as it was called in Tourtel's time, La Baie de Mauve.

Gull Rock's French name is La Tas de Pois d'Aval (lower Peastacks) and Barry then points south-east to the highly dangerous and always covered reef of Les Kaines d'Amant sitting off Long Avaleur or Long Avaleux which has long become left unnamed by modern mapping and charts.

Back on the west side Barry stops our trek at Perelle where he identifies La Conchee and Echeval which takes its name from its cone shape, Rousse on the end of La Capelle and within that reef which dries out the Le Haut Mare pond, another good site for ormering.

Perelle Bay also houses a submerged rock referred to by Tourtel as Le Richer Charles Le Cras who, as it happens, was Barry's grandfather and a Vazon fisherman, and at the bay's northern point he refers to an error in the modern sea charts which has La Jaune Pont and La Grand Pont wrongly positioned. They should be named the other way around.

Look closely and it is easy to see which is which as La Jaune Pont has a yellow tinge to it, hence the name.

Onto the Richmond headland my guide names three of the five slips as La Maladerie [meaning the burial ground], La Marette or La Ponture, as Barry refers to it, and Le Crocq.

'La Ponture' is another bay to lose its name over time and it even may be spelt differently as it has proved beyond me to find any official record of such a bay, but for the record it is the 100m or so stretch immediately north of La Jaune Pont.

The next stopping off point is at Fort Hommet where we look down on Le Grand and Le Petit Etacqs and, straight in front of us, some way off Le Grosse Rocque is the Black Mouliere, referred such due its dark colour.

A couple of miles north we stop off at Port Soif and from the elevated car park we look out at rocks such as Le Grand Sauf Rocher, L'Etacre, Le Boue Corneille and Black Rock which all seem to stretch north in a line.

Black Rock is where the Channel Queen

Opposite
An old Carel Toms' picture of Le Petit Bon Homme d'Andriou on the Peastacks

perished all those years ago and you have to both sympathise with and admire even more so, how in those days of sail a skipper could possibly navigate his way around this coastline littered with so many submerged, semi-submerged and, in many cases, openly potentially horrific hazards of nature.

If one rock did not get you, there were many others waiting to do so and the maritime records show that they did.

Our next stopping off point on this review of the west coast 'armoury' is Les Dicqs and the low tide highlights the full extent of Le Col du Point and the narrow small boat passage which joins Grand Havre with Port Grat.

At the end of it is La Naif or, to give its anglicized title, The Knife, ready and waiting to split open the most hardened hull.

As Tourtel noted all those years back, many rocks have the daftest of names.

Guillaume, for instance, was in Tourtel's mind named after 'hard, solid rock'. Well, which rocks don't fit that bill is a point I'd argue until the tide comes up and goes down again.

The further you travel up the coast the rocks become so obviously hazardous, but as you round Chouet and cross L'Ancresse we come to the always impressive 'Brayes' their tops coated in white paint to alert those yachts and motorboats of an extensive reef below.

Before the first stone was laid at Platte Fougere there were strong arguments put forward for the Brayes as the most ideal place to build the Russel's lighthouse.

They sit beyond the gun sights of the Fort Le Marchant shooters and on rifle competition days any craft venturing inside the Brayes will lead to a halt in the shooting, such is the range of the ammunition used by the Guernsey Rifle Club.

Right
Formidable rocks including the Peastacks and the Brayes

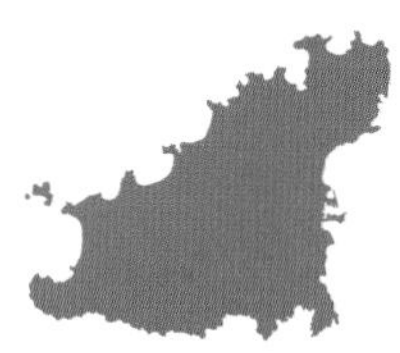

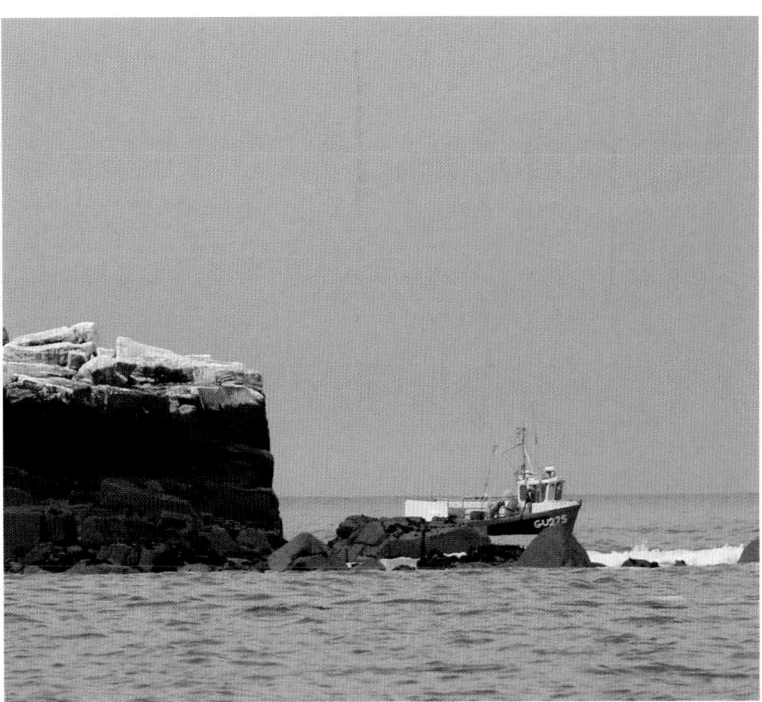

Our final stop is Noirmont, badly eroded Noirmont, with the glorious Houmet Paradis standing a six-hit away from shore.

It cannot be missed but just beyond is a an unnamed and dangerously submerged rock which Barry Paint was asked to research many years ago.

'Someone came to me because they had heard that their grandfather had drowned there in 1942 after his boat hit it. He was supposedly picked up dead, hanging onto a fish box.

'His name was George Bowditch and thereafter the old fishermen would refer to it as Bowditch's Rock.'

This is a journey which could be never ending such is the extent of the rock and reefs littered off the island.

We have just highlighted a small number and Barry Paint knows his task of naming and officially locating every rocks in our Bailiwick, is going to be a long one.

Tourtel stuck to names only. Barry's job is to position them and do his own little bit to prevent the long list of losses being added to in future.

STACKING PEAS

THE paths of Carel Toms and yours truly crossed all too briefly.

When I started out at the Press in the summer of 1977, Carel, then features editor, was quietly tucked away at one end of our first-floor Smith Street editorial office, this cub sports reporter at the other. I had not the slightest interest in what this master re-teller of Guernsey's heritage was renowned for and still is, eight years, after his passing.

Thirty-three years on, if by some miracle of nature we were colleagues once again, I would have pestered the old man into submission with enquiries as to all aspects of old Guernsey.

No man, arguably, knew more about the island than Carel.

All we are left with are his accounts in a collection of books and archived articles from the Guernsey Press, such as the one which I discovered and bring back to life in this chapter of the story that is Guernsey's COAST.

Our island nature makes for many candidates in the quest to unearth Guernsey's most famous rock or rocks.

I happen to have the softest spot for the Grosse Rocque, a magnificent sight when viewed a mile away from Cobo and no less impressive when seen from the crest of Albecq.

But, when I finally got to see it from the rear while bobbing away on Barry Paint's pilot boat, my disappointment was palpable.

The Cliff Rock at the Pecqueries, the Lion Rock at Albecq, Rocque du Poisson buried into the L'Eree coast road and a group of rocks that extend out from the Jerbourg headland complete my favourite five, and one has to admit that it is the latter which are arguably most synonymous with the Guernsey coastline. We are talking, of course, the Pea Stacks or to give them their traditional Guernsey name 'Le Tas de Pois d'Amont' to distinguish itself from its mate at the opposite end of the south coast cliffs, 'Le Tas de Pois d'Aval.'

Now far from me to encourage the dangerous practice of clambering over cliffs, but this is a story that needs to be told.

The urge to explore cliff edges has always appeared daft in the extreme to myself and there are a catalogue of fatalities or serious injuries to prove the point.

But discovering what is on the end of the Pea Stacks, arguably one of Guernsey's most renowned set of rocks, and how you might get there is not such a silly idea.

I know not a man alive who has experienced the route from the mainland cliff path and, one-by-one, pick off the four peaks that make the Pea Stacks.

But it has been done many a time and in 1949 Carel Toms wrote a piece for the Guernsey Evening Press which offered a fascinating insight in not only how to reach the distant Tas de Pois d'Amont but what he found on the way there.

My imagination captured, I instantly wondered what it would be like to follow in Carel's footsteps and do it myself.

But, as yet, the courage to do so has not been found within and, more importantly, a reliable and trusting guide needs to be found.

Instead, I prefer to re-read Carel's account, then shut my eyes and let the imagination do the rest.

Even with a guide surely this is a trek which necessitates a good level of fitness, agility, a good set of reliable knees and a head for heights.

So instead of trying yourself, read on and let Carel tell how it was done and what is out there on those peaked granite protectors of the Moulin Huet coastline.

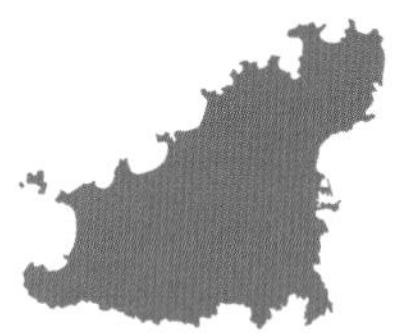

EVERYBODY knows the familiar group of rocks off Jerbourg Point known as the Pea Stacks. Islanders and visitors never fail to admire these picturesque piles as they are seen from the 'tunnel' of trees bordering Le Vallon estate across the blue waters of Moulin Huet Bay.

These lonely islets are a regular breeding ground of a variety of gulls; a nesting place for shags and oystercatchers; an occasional retreat of sparrow hawks; and on one rare occasion, that robber of the skies, the peregrine falcon, had an eyrie there.

In the surrounding sea, congers lurk and multi-coloured rockfish disport.

Among the rocks, crabs and lobsters abound. But most interesting of all the denizens of the sea found there were baby ormers no larger than the head of a six-inch nail.

The Guardian of this sanctuary of bird and marine life is Le Petit Bon Homme d'Andriou, who stands on a grassy plateau on L'Aiguillou d'Andriou, and is much like the statue-menhirs in St Martin's and the Castel, except that he is fashioned by nature alone.

Less than half-a-century ago this 12-foot tall 'good little man' was a 'sacred' stone and fishermen used to make offerings of food, wine or cider at the beginning of the fishing

Above
Peastacks explorer
Carel Toms

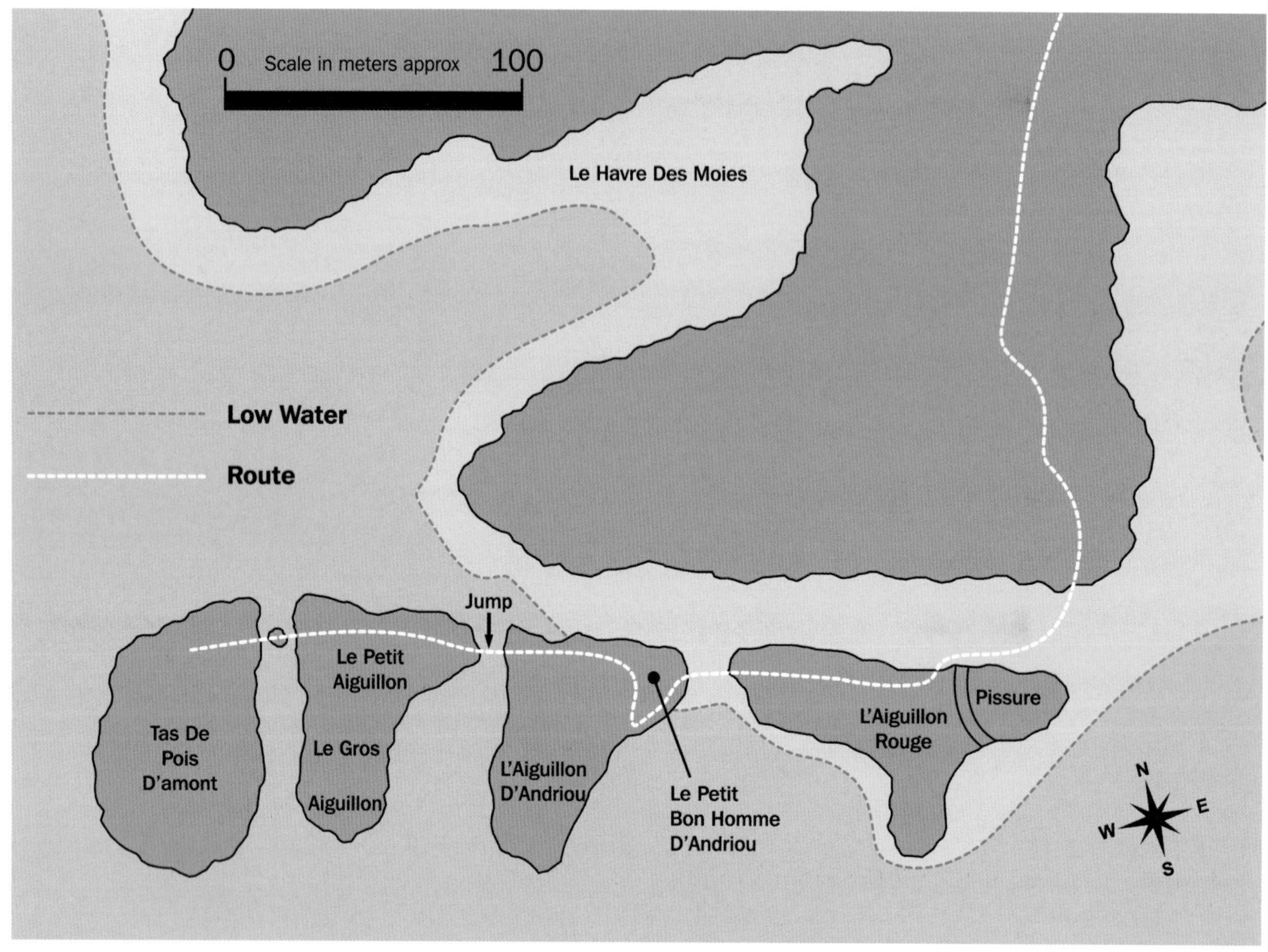

Above
Toms' route across the Peastacks

season. Perhaps an old garment, which may have been aboard the boat, was cast into the sea to bring good luck to them.

Artists and cameramen have often brought the Pea Stacks into their pictures, and the late Mr Caparne, whose studio was at Bon Port (between Moulin Huet and Saints Bay) painted many a brilliant watercolour of these rocks; and he certainly observed them in all moods of weather. One sketch depicted the Tas de Pois amid a boiling sea, with the spume lashing right over its 100ft steep cliff.

Possessed with an inherited spirit of discovery, I found the group many years ago and since those boyhood days I have climbed over them, fished from their rocky ledges, ormered among the boulders at their feet, passed between one pair in a motor boat and sailed through the channel dividing another pair in my own craft.

To reach the Pea Stacks one takes the cliff path, which is easily followed from where the rough road ends beyond Jerbourg Barracks, and eventually leads on to a 'neck' above the Havre des Mois. The path is not so apparent here but can be traced to the left, where it descends steeply over red rocks to the eastern end of a gorge, which separates all five Pea Stacks from the mainland and makes them islands at high water.

Linger awhile before descending, and ahead is a miniature canyon around which stand rocky outgrowths worn by wind and weather into fantastic shapes, covered with long grey

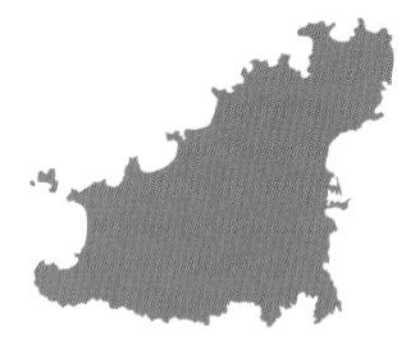

lichen. The springtime scene here is beautiful; with gorse, broom, foxgloves and ox-eye daisies, which appear to grow in scarcely any soil.

Once the explorer reaches the head of the gorge the climbing starts and if the way is not known it is easy to come to a 'dead end'; or a pool, which cannot be negotiated. The first of the group, Aiguillon Rouge, is skirted on the left by a tricky bit of rockwork, and there is an interesting fissure there running off at right angles.

On the seaward side of the Red Needle is a favourite spot for rockfish, but woe-betide the man who lingers too long and forgets the rising tide in his piscatorial enthusiasm. He would have to retreat on to the red granite ledges and wait for the half ebb again before getting back to the mainland; or he might perhaps attempt to swim back.

The main reasons for many of my early expeditions was for the sheer joy of climbing over the rocks and discovering the gulls' nests and eggs in the late spring; then returning later in the season to see the youngsters.

In March 1936, I went there with a Dutch friend for the purpose of identifying some of the islets' flora, and on L'Aiguillon d'Andriou we found the legs and a bundle of feathers of some unknown bird, and evidence of other aerial battles, which had resulted in the death of the weaker creatures.

This 'find' quickened our interest and on our next visit a few weeks later we decided to explore all the rocks in turn. Crossing from the Red Needle to Andriou's Needle – which is connected by rocks and dry gullies – we rested awhile on the grass at the feet of Le Petit Bon Homme before proceeding.

To cross from there to Le Petit Aiguillon is not so easy. There is a steep climb down the west face and a deep gully is confronted, which never dries out at low water. It is about six feet wide at the narrowest part and for the agile and long-legged the way over is to jump, which we duly did.

This jump might easily end in disaster, as not only is there water beneath, but there are only two ledges from which to spring and land. Added to this, the landing ledge on the outward journey is some five feet below the take-off; therefore, on the return, one has to jump across and upwards at the same time. On previous occasions, I have crossed this gully on a bridge made from three thick bamboos lashed together.

It was on this Little Needle that we found our first peregrine falcon's nest and also the answer to the birds' legs and feathers discovered previously.

This incident was mentioned at the time in the 'Press', but the locality was not disclosed. The eyrie was a bare ledge near the top of Le Petit Aiguillon, with an over-hanging rock sheltering it. It contained three downy young falcons and one rich, orange-brown egg.

It was a difficult and dangerous climb to this pinnacle but worth every breathtaking moment.

Both falcon and tiercel – but more especially the former – screamed out their war cry of 'kak-kak-kak; kak-kak-kak; kak-kak-kak' – swooping at us with closed wings while we were near their home. Their high-pitched cries echoed among the surrounding crags above the yelling gulls, and had we remained there much longer I feel sure they would have attacked us. We left the eyrie with a feeling of exultation that day, and from the mainland watched the falcons' movements through a pair of binoculars.

Our next visit proved without a doubt that the falcon family were very partial to fresh meat in the form of pigeons, and a closer inspection of the edge revealed the skulls and wings of many birds. One leg was obviously that of a homing pigeon, for it still had an aluminium ring attached to it, with a number. Alongside was a bunch of feathers and one was clearly stamped with a Staffordshire address.

By this time the egg was hatched and the family was growing rapidly. To watch these birds was a great joy, even though the toll of racing pigeons may have been alarming to their owners; but to have disclosed the whereabouts of the eyrie would have meant its instant destruction, I felt sure, and the idea of this I could not face, having had the birds' home under observation for many weeks.

The fourth rock of this group is known as Le Gros Aiguillon, and between it and the Pea Stack itself is a wide gully with a large boulder near the north-east end, which makes the crossing easy when the tide serves. Le Tas de Pois d'Amont, as the outer rock is labelled (Pea Stack of the east; as there is also a Tas de Pois d'Aval, or Pea Stack of the west) receives the frontal attack of all the southerly storms, and 'when the sea rolls around the Pea Stacks it is a sure sign of rain' used to be a popular saying.

Around the feet of this gullery and haunt of shags I used to go ormering at the very low spring tides, but found by experience that the catches here were small compared with other localities. No only that, the individual ormers were small as well. Then, on another ormering tide at the same place, I happened to be wading

Right
Ship ahoy off the Peastacks

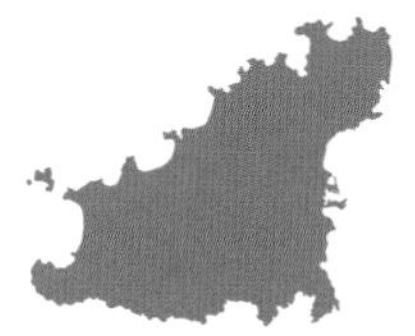

about (up to my thighs) and I saw attached to the broad fronds of tangled seaweed surrounding me, some tiny blue coloured objects about a quarter of an inch in diameter. On closer inspection they were seen to be baby ormers and even at that age they appeared to have been enjoying a feed of seaweed, for it was nibbled around the edges.

This experience, and other folks' information, about small ormers being found in this locality indicates that it is a breeding ground for the mollusc, and as the shell-fish appears to have greatly diminished in numbers of late years, plus the possibility of its complete eclipse in the near future, is it asking too much for legislation to ban ormering in this area so as to perpetuate a long-cherished gem of the sea?

My last visit was in February of this year when I climbed over alone to photograph the Good Little Man, and as I sat on the grass waiting for the sun to peep through the casement of clouds, it occurred to me that these four needle-like rocks, their outer bastion and their Guardian Angel 'who watches over all,' stand for all to see, for all to admire and for all to climb. They stand for more; they are lonely outposts of Guernsey's southern shores where the seeker of solitude can commune with nature, observing the birds, the sea-shore creatures, or just 'stand and stare.'

May Le Petit Bon Homme d'Andriou long guard this little bit of wild Guernsey.

ARTICLE PUBLICATION DATES

The articles in this book were all published in The Guernsey Press and Star

CHAPTER 1
COBO
14 March 2007

CHAPTER 2
LONG PORT
30 April 2009

CHAPTER 3
GRANDES ROCQUES
10 July 2008

CHAPTER 4
PORT SOIF
1 October 2009

CHAPTER 5
PORTINFER, PECQUERIES & PULIAS
8 April 2010

CHAPTER 6
GRAND HAVRE, LES AMARREURS & LADIES BAY
8 July 2010

CHAPTER 7
CHOUET
9 October 2008

CHAPTER 8
PEMBROKE & LA JAONNEUSE
30 April 2009

CHAPTER 9
L'ANCRESSE & LA FONTENELLE
16 January 2008

CHAPTER 10
MIELLETTE BAY & NOIRMONT
9 July 2009

CHAPTER 11
BORDEAUX
12 June 2008

CHAPTER 12
ST SAMPSON'S, NORTH & SOUTH SIDES
11 and 26 October 2007

CHAPTER 13
LONGUE HOUGUE TO SPUR POINT
15 November 2007

CHAPTER 14
BELLE GREVE
15 May 2008

CHAPTER 15
LA SALERIE
3 June 2010

CHAPTER 16
ST PETER PORT
18 September 2008,
13 November 2008
and 12 August 2010

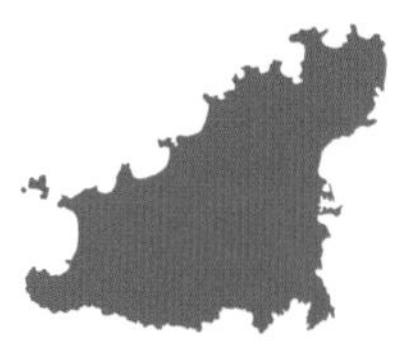

CHAPTER 17
LITTLE RUSSEL & BREHON TOWER
28 May 2009 and 26 August 2009

CHAPTER 18
HAVELET
31 July 2008

CHAPTER 19
FERMAIN BAY
6 December 2007

CHAPTER 20
MOULIN HUET, BEC DU NEZ
& ST MARTIN'S POINT
21 February 2008

CHAPTER 21
PETIT PORT
14 June 2007

CHAPTER 22
SAINTS BAY
12 April 2007

CHAPTER 23
ICART, PETIT BOT & LA MOYE
12 March 2009

CHAPTER 24
LE GOUFFRE, CREUX MAHIE
& PLEINMONT POINT
5 February 2009

CHAPTER 25
HANOIS & ROCQUAINE BAY
27 March 2008

CHAPTER 26
L'EREE & LIHOU ISLAND
7 February 2008

CHAPTER 27
PERELLE
10 January 2008

CHAPTER 28
VAZON
30 August 2007
and 10 September 2010

CHAPTER 29
ALBECQ
11 December 2008

CHAPTER 30
THREE MEN IN A BOAT
18 September 2008

CHAPTER 31
ROCKS OF AGES
7 October 2010

ACKNOWLEDGMENTS

They may not be aware of their influence but so many people of past and present have played a key role in the publication of the story of 'Guernsey's Coast'.

It is a story beyond the knowledge of one man and the author would have been sunk had he not been able to tap into the wealth of information, which came in books and old newspaper features, by the likes of Victor Coysh, Eric Sharp, James Marr and C.P. Le Huray, men long gone but with an influence on island history that will linger as long as Guernsey exists.

Their collective knowledge gave me the confidence to pursue an extended COAST series in the Guernsey Press, as did the comfort of knowing that if I ever should hit a brickwall there was always our brilliantly helpful Priaulx Library and Island Archives to fall back on.

In both establishments of history a succession of men and women have always been unfailing in their assistance, but several stand out, notably Nathan Coyde at the Archives and, at the Priaulx, the never-to-be-beaten Ricky Allen, his head librarian, Amanda Bennett and Margaret Edwards.

But the biggest contributor and huge debt of thanks to colleagues at the Guernsey Press and, in particular, to editor Richard Digard, features editor Di Digard and, managing director Mark Lewis, who have all encouraged myself to take this route and allow me to maximise the remarkable archive resources of the Press.

Then there are all the many GP photographers, past and present.

I want to give particular thanks to the always supportive Brian Green who has provided many a fine photograph and accompanied yours truly and Barry Paint on our circumnavigation of the island by boat, today's head of photographics John O'Neill and all those many men who have snapped away in the GP cause over a century.

Then there is, of course, Andrew Le Poidevin, who so believed in the COAST project and this remarkable story of our coastline heritage, that he offered his remarkable collection of unique semi-aerial views of the island to lead into most of the 31 chapters.

He did as a proud Guernseyman, wishing to play his own not insignificant part in showing Guernsey for what it is – beautiful and crammed full of so many remarkable characters.

Finally, but most importantly, there is Darren Duquemin, the fellow 'Cobo boy' who has so believed in the project he set up Guernsey Books to ensure it happened.

Additional pictures:

Courtesy of Alex Wallace, the Priaulx Library and its Carel Toms Collection.

FROOME
KATO
BOB FROOME

Guernsey Books
PO Box 635
Guernsey GY1 3DS
www.guernseybooks.com

First published 2010

A CIP catalogue record for this book is available from the British Library

ISBN: 978-0-9567644-0-9